OPTIMUS PRIME

VOL 5

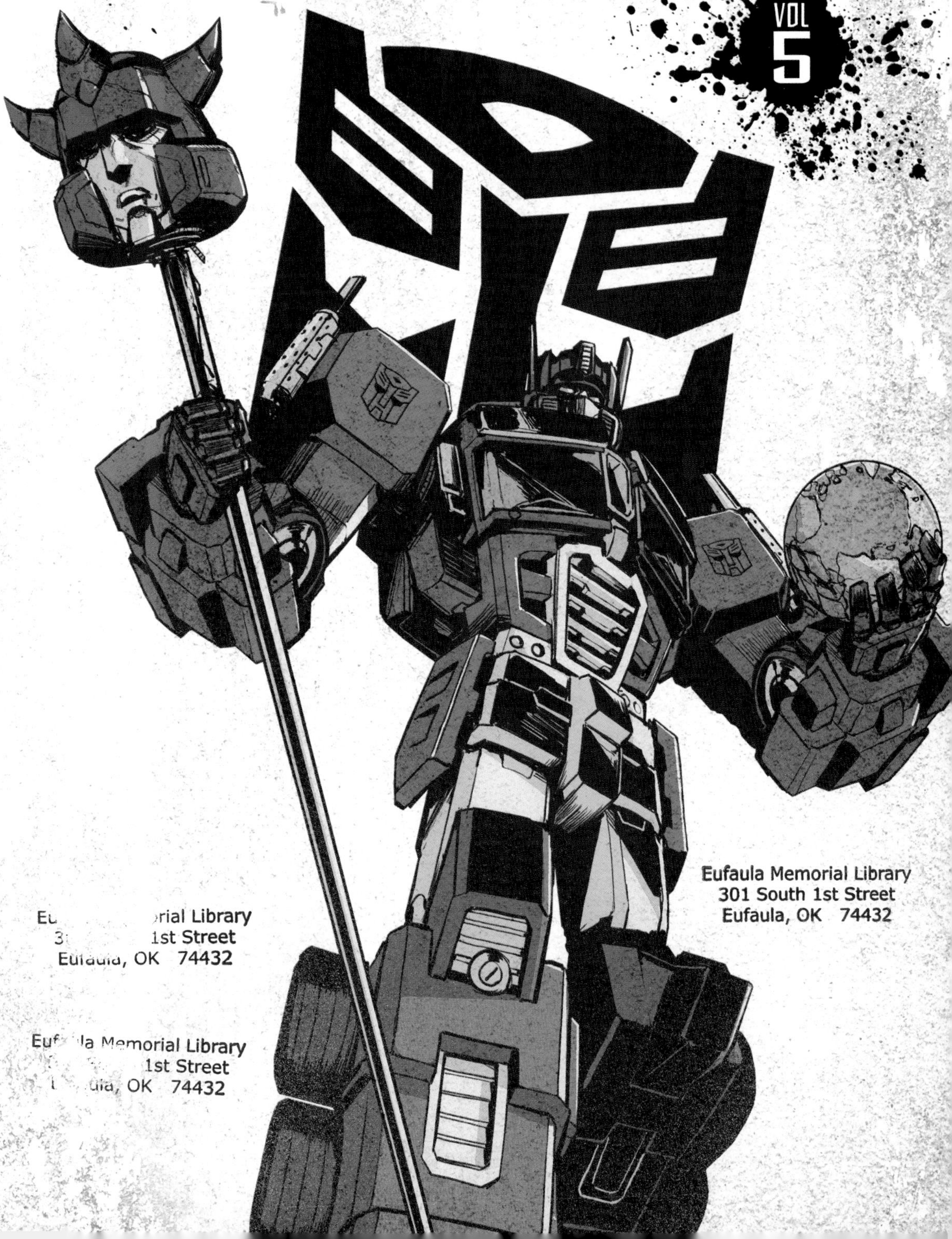

Eu rial Library
3 1st Street
Eufaula, OK 74432

Euf la Memorial Library
1st Street
ula, OK 74432

Become our fan on Facebook **facebook.com/idwpublishing**
Follow us on Twitter **@idwpublishing**
Subscribe to us on YouTube **youtube.com/idwpublishing**
See what's new on Tumblr **tumblr.idwpublishing.com**
Check us out on Instagram **instagram.com/idwpublishing**

www.IDWPUBLISHING.com

Licensed By:

COVER ART BY
CASEY W. COLLER

COVER COLORS BY
JOHN-PAUL BOVE

COLLECTION EDITS BY
JUSTIN EISINGER
AND **ALONZO SIMON**

COLLECTION DESIGN BY
CLAUDIA CHONG

PUBLISHER
GREG GOLDSTEIN

Greg Goldstein, President & Publisher
John Barber, Editor-In-Chief
Robbie Robbins, EVP & Sr. Art Director
Cara Morrison, Chief Financial Officer
Matthew Ruzicka, Chief Accounting Officer
Anita Frazier, SVP of Sales and Marketing
David Hedgecock, Associate Publisher
Jerry Bennington, VP of New Product Development
Lorelei Bunjes, VP of Digital Services
Justin Eisinger, Editorial Director, Graphic Novels & Collections
Eric Moss, Sr. Director, Licensing & Business Development

Ted Adams, IDW Founder

978-1-68405-411-4   22 21 20 19   1 2 3 4

Originally published as OPTIMUS PRIME issues #22–25 and OPTIMUS PRIME ANNUAL 2018.

Special thanks to Ben Montano, David Erwin, Josh Feldman, Ed Lane, Beth Artale, and Michael Kelly for their invaluable assistance.

For international rights, contact licensing@idwpublishing.com

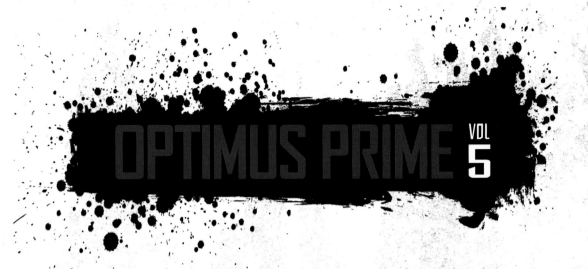

OPTIMUS PRIME VOL 5

WRITTEN BY
John Barber

ART BY
Sara Pitre-Durocher (#22 & 24)
Priscilla Tramontano (#23 & ANNUAL)
Andrew Griffith (#24 & ANNUAL)
Kei Zama (#25)

COLORS BY
Josh Burcham

ADDITIONAL COLORS BY
John-Paul Bove (ANNUAL)

LETTERS BY
Tom B. Long & **Shawn Lee**

SERIES EDITS BY
David Mariotte

ART BY PRISCILLA TRAMONTANO

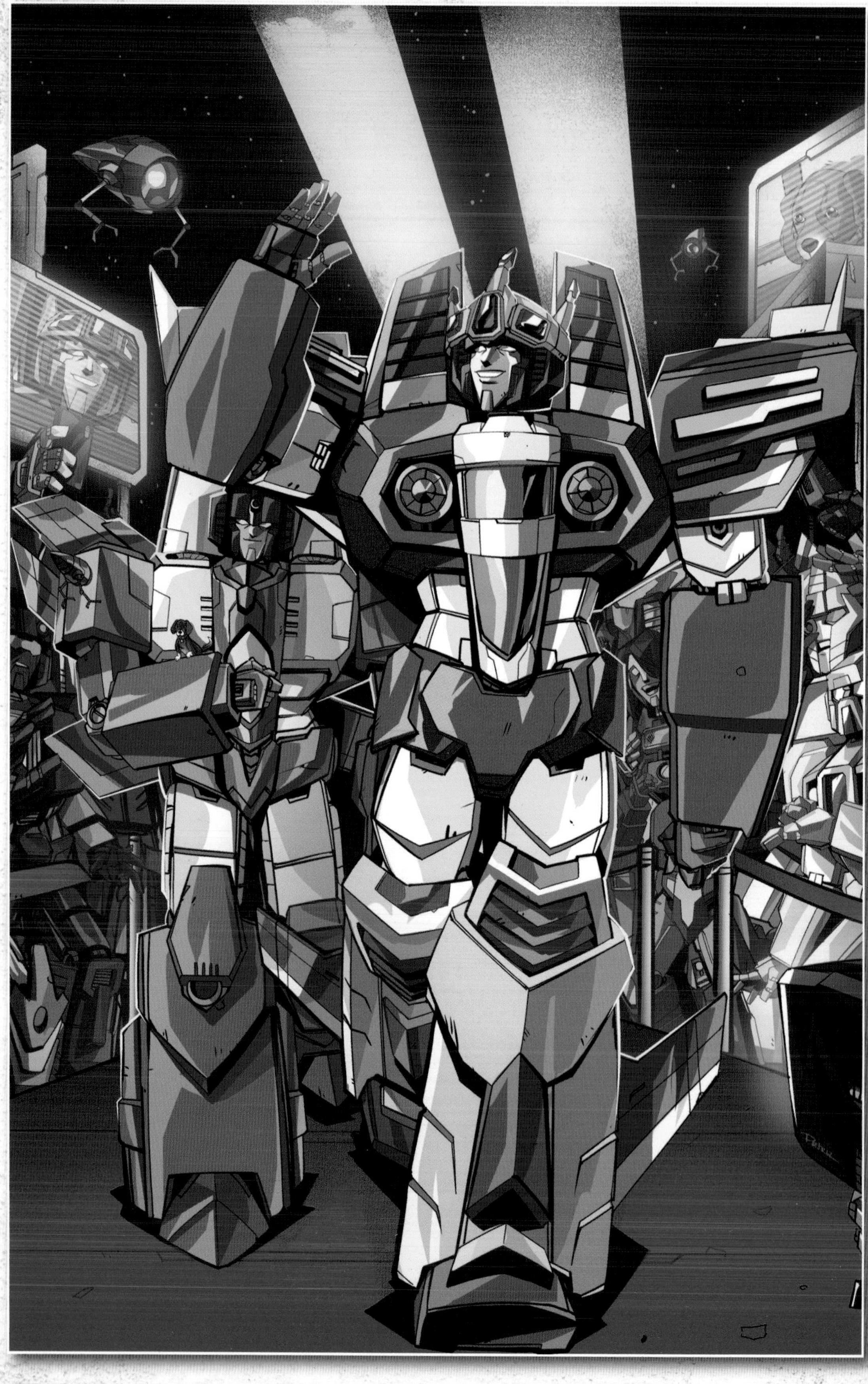

DISGUSTING.

THANK YOU, MY FRIENDS. I APPRECIATE YOUR *SUPPORT* IN THESE TRYING TIMES.

ONLY BY STANDING AS ONE WITH THE PEOPLE OF *EARTH* CAN WE HOPE TO FACE THE DANGERS OF *TOMORROW*.

OPTIMUS PRIME. UNITER OF WORLDS.

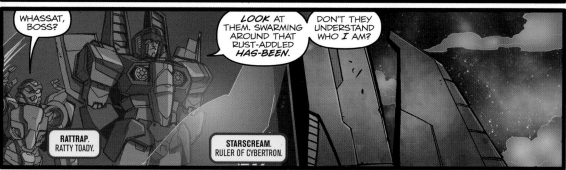

WHASSAT, BOSS?

LOOK AT THEM. SWARMING AROUND THAT RUST-ADDLED *HAS-BEEN*.

DON'T THEY UNDERSTAND WHO *I* AM?

RATTRAP. RATTY TOADY.

STARSCREAM. RULER OF CYBERTRON.

I CAN ONLY IMAGINE IT'S THE SAME ON *EARTH*.

WORSHIPPING THAT... THAT *AUTOBOT*, LIKE HE'S SOME KIND OF *SAVIOR*.

AND *YOU'RE* SUPPOSED TO BE THE *CHOSEN ONE*.

YES! UNFORTUNATELY, IF I WANT TO *STAY* CHOSEN, I NEED EARTH ON *MY* SIDE. THEY HAVE THE *ENERGON* WE NEED TO *LIVE*.

PRIMA—THIS IS BIGGER THAN YOU OR I, MY YOUNG FRIEND.

SOOOOO... YOU'RE WATCHING *OLD MOVIES?*

CLASSIC FILMS OF MY YOUTH. *THE BIRTH OF CYBERTRON* DRAMATIZED THE FOUNDATIONS OF OUR WORLD. THERE ARE *CLUES* HERE— HOW TO RULE AN EMPIRE.

HM...

MAYBE I'M SO CLOSE I'M MISSING THE *BIGGEST* CLUE OF ALL.

I THINK I KNOW EXACTLY WHAT TO DO... AND *WHO* NEEDS TO DO IT.

I DUNNO IF I LIKE THE SOUND'A THAT *"HM."*

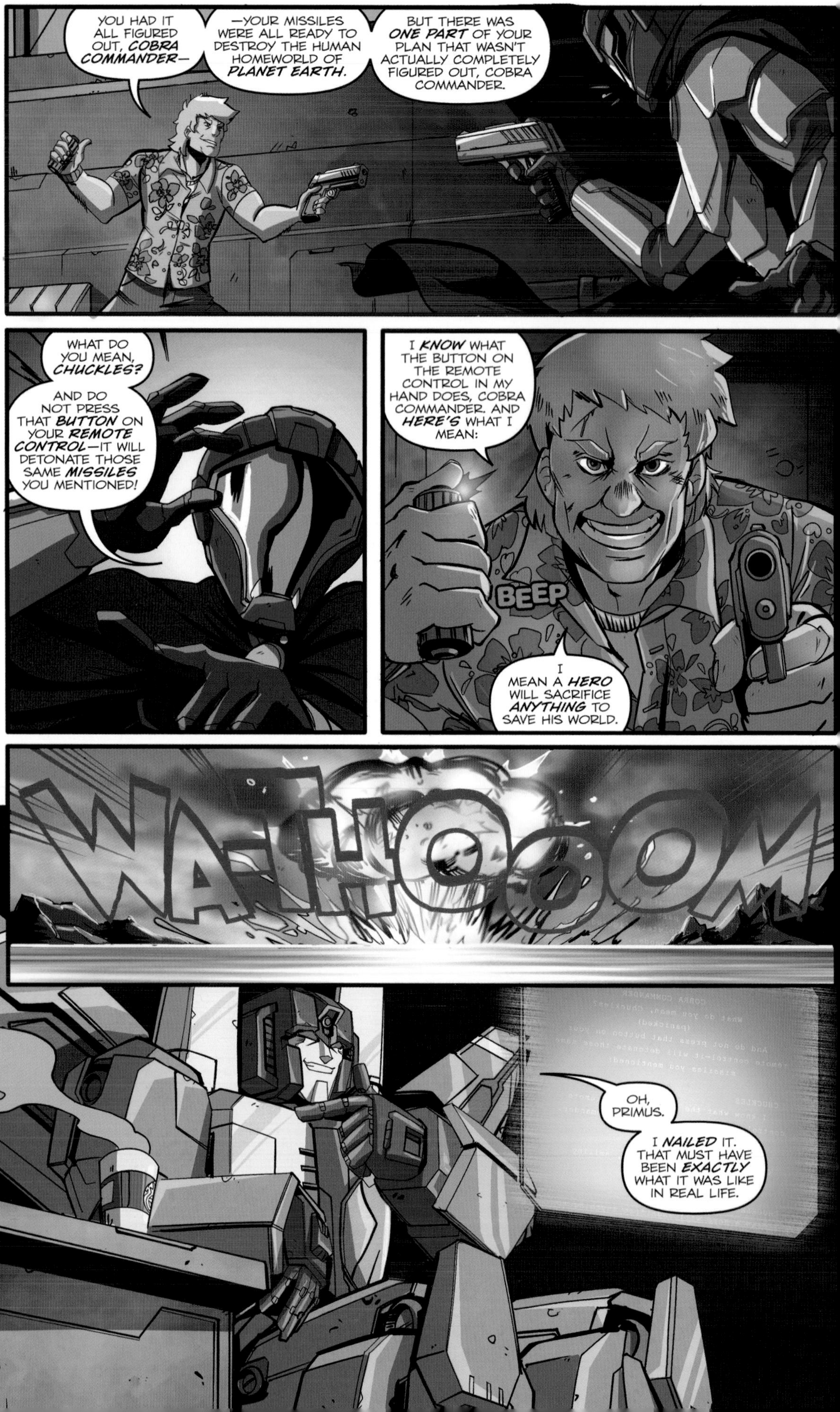
YOU HAD IT ALL FIGURED OUT, COBRA COMMANDER—
—YOUR MISSILES WERE ALL READY TO DESTROY THE HUMAN HOMEWORLD OF PLANET EARTH.
BUT THERE WAS ONE PART OF YOUR PLAN THAT WASN'T ACTUALLY COMPLETELY FIGURED OUT, COBRA COMMANDER.
WHAT DO YOU MEAN, CHUCKLES?
AND DO NOT PRESS THAT BUTTON ON YOUR REMOTE CONTROL—IT WILL DETONATE THOSE SAME MISSILES YOU MENTIONED!
I KNOW WHAT THE BUTTON ON THE REMOTE CONTROL IN MY HAND DOES, COBRA COMMANDER. AND HERE'S WHAT I MEAN:
BEEP
I MEAN A HERO WILL SACRIFICE ANYTHING TO SAVE HIS WORLD.
WA-HOOOOM
OH, PRIMUS.
I NAILED IT. THAT MUST HAVE BEEN EXACTLY WHAT IT WAS LIKE IN REAL LIFE.

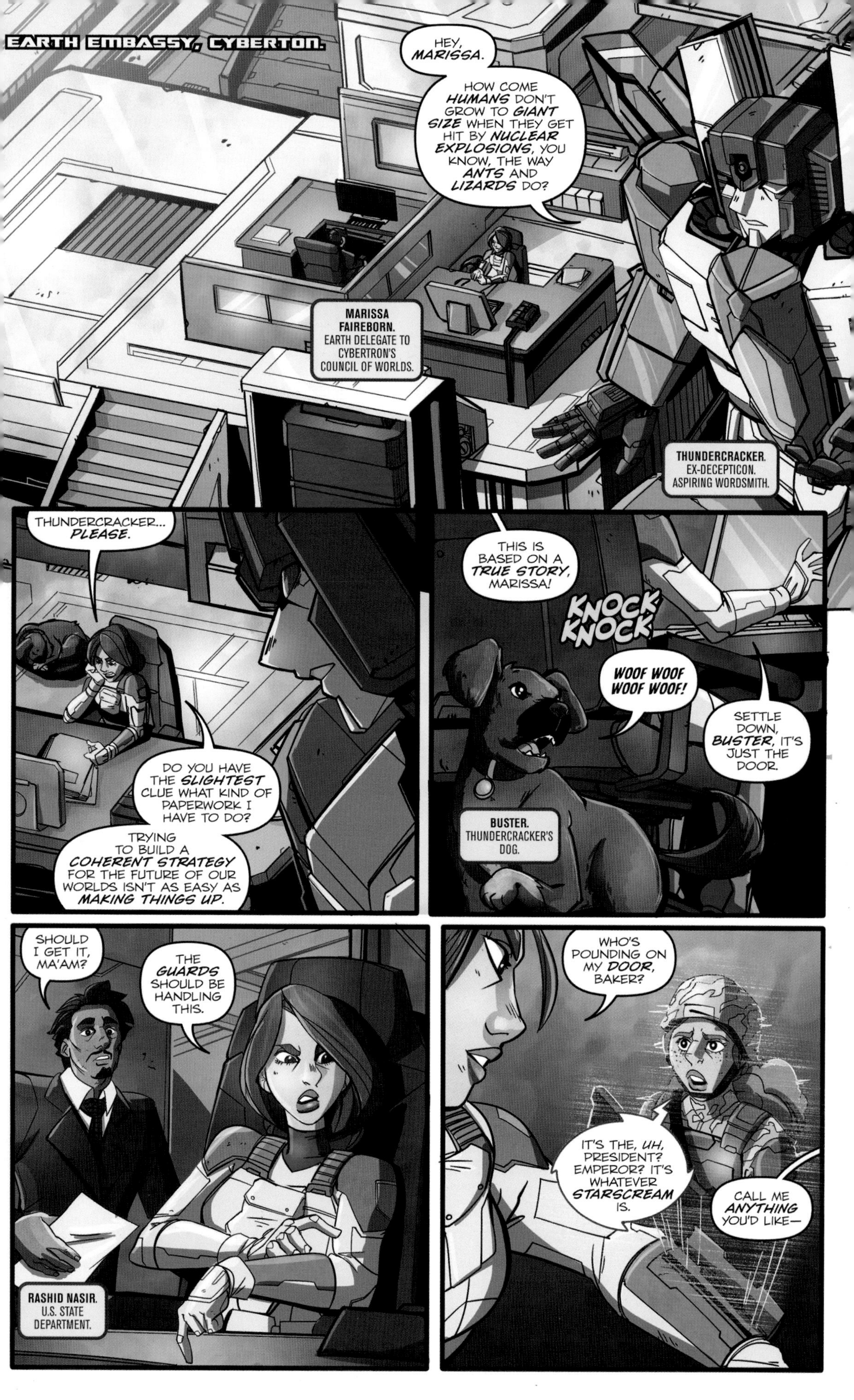
EARTH EMBASSY, CYBERTON.
HEY, MARISSA.
HOW COME HUMANS DON'T GROW TO GIANT SIZE WHEN THEY GET HIT BY NUCLEAR EXPLOSIONS, YOU KNOW, THE WAY ANTS AND LIZARDS DO?
MARISSA FAIREBORN. EARTH DELEGATE TO CYBERTRON'S COUNCIL OF WORLDS.
THUNDERCRACKER. EX-DECEPTICON. ASPIRING WORDSMITH.
THUNDERCRACKER... PLEASE.
DO YOU HAVE THE SLIGHTEST CLUE WHAT KIND OF PAPERWORK I HAVE TO DO?
TRYING TO BUILD A COHERENT STRATEGY FOR THE FUTURE OF OUR WORLDS ISN'T AS EASY AS MAKING THINGS UP.
THIS IS BASED ON A TRUE STORY, MARISSA!
KNOCK KNOCK
WOOF WOOF WOOF WOOF!
SETTLE DOWN, BUSTER, IT'S JUST THE DOOR.
BUSTER. THUNDERCRACKER'S DOG.
SHOULD I GET IT, MA'AM?
THE GUARDS SHOULD BE HANDLING THIS.
RASHID NASIR. U.S. STATE DEPARTMENT.
WHO'S POUNDING ON MY DOOR, BAKER?
IT'S THE, UH, PRESIDENT? EMPEROR? IT'S WHATEVER STARSCREAM IS.
CALL ME ANYTHING YOU'D LIKE—

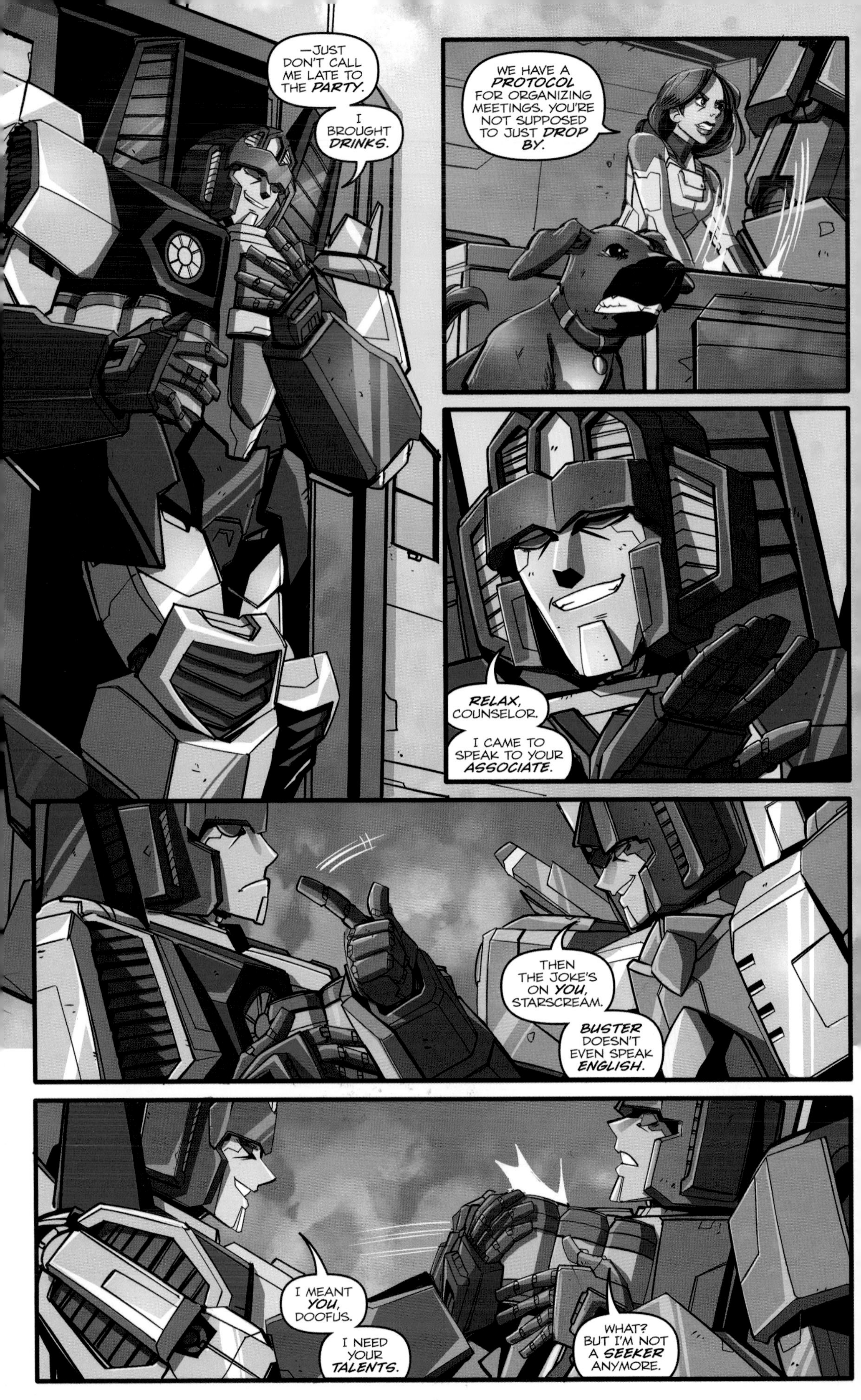
—JUST DON'T CALL ME LATE TO THE PARTY.
I BROUGHT DRINKS.
WE HAVE A PROTOCOL FOR ORGANIZING MEETINGS. YOU'RE NOT SUPPOSED TO JUST DROP BY.
RELAX, COUNSELOR.
I CAME TO SPEAK TO YOUR ASSOCIATE.
THEN THE JOKE'S ON YOU, STARSCREAM.
BUSTER DOESN'T EVEN SPEAK ENGLISH.
I MEANT YOU, DOOFUS.
I NEED YOUR TALENTS.
WHAT? BUT I'M NOT A SEEKER ANYMORE.

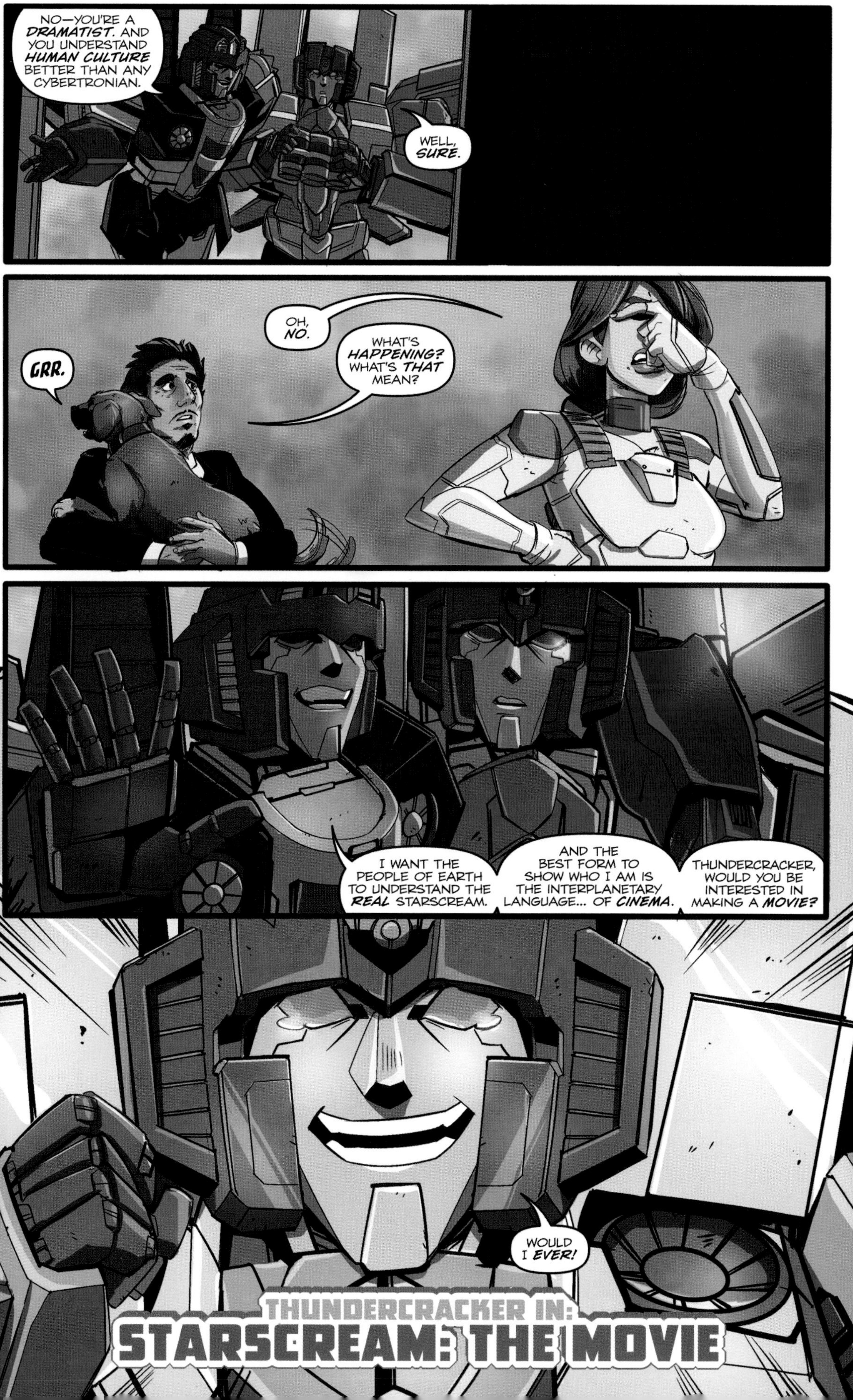
NO—YOU'RE A DRAMATIST. AND YOU UNDERSTAND HUMAN CULTURE BETTER THAN ANY CYBERTRONIAN.
WELL, SURE.
GRR.
OH, NO.
WHAT'S HAPPENING? WHAT'S THAT MEAN?
I WANT THE PEOPLE OF EARTH TO UNDERSTAND THE REAL STARSCREAM.
AND THE BEST FORM TO SHOW WHO I AM IS THE INTERPLANETARY LANGUAGE... OF CINEMA.
THUNDERCRACKER, WOULD YOU BE INTERESTED IN MAKING A MOVIE?
WOULD I EVER!
THUNDERCRACKER IN:
STARSCREAM: THE MOVIE

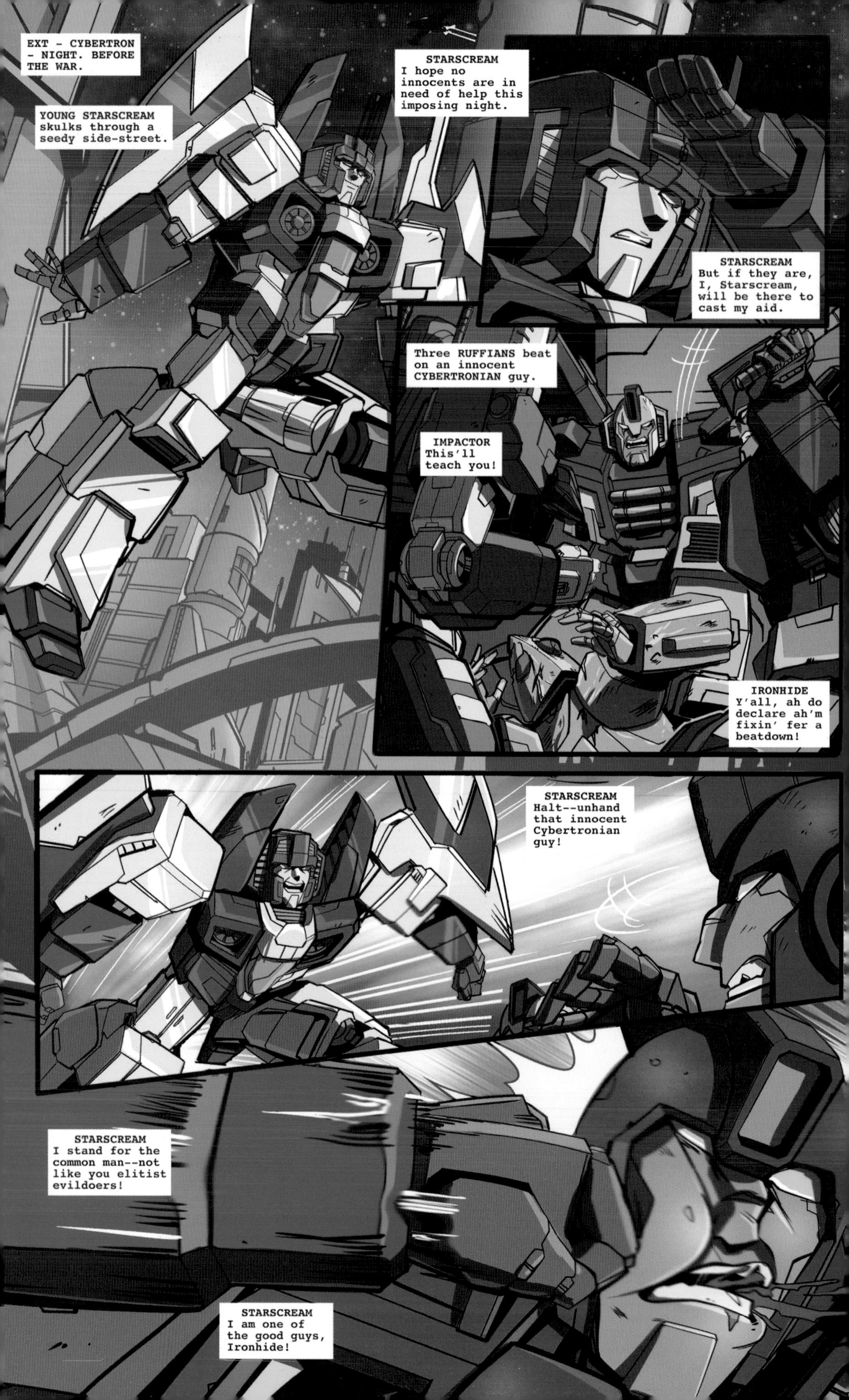
EXT - CYBERTRON - NIGHT. BEFORE THE WAR.
YOUNG STARSCREAM skulks through a seedy side-street.
STARSCREAM I hope no innocents are in need of help this imposing night.
STARSCREAM But if they are, I, Starscream, will be there to cast my aid.
Three RUFFIANS beat on an innocent CYBERTRONIAN guy.
IMPACTOR This'll teach you!
IRONHIDE Y'all, ah do declare ah'm fixin' fer a beatdown!
STARSCREAM Halt--unhand that innocent Cybertronian guy!
STARSCREAM I stand for the common man--not like you elitist evildoers!
STARSCREAM I am one of the good guys, Ironhide!

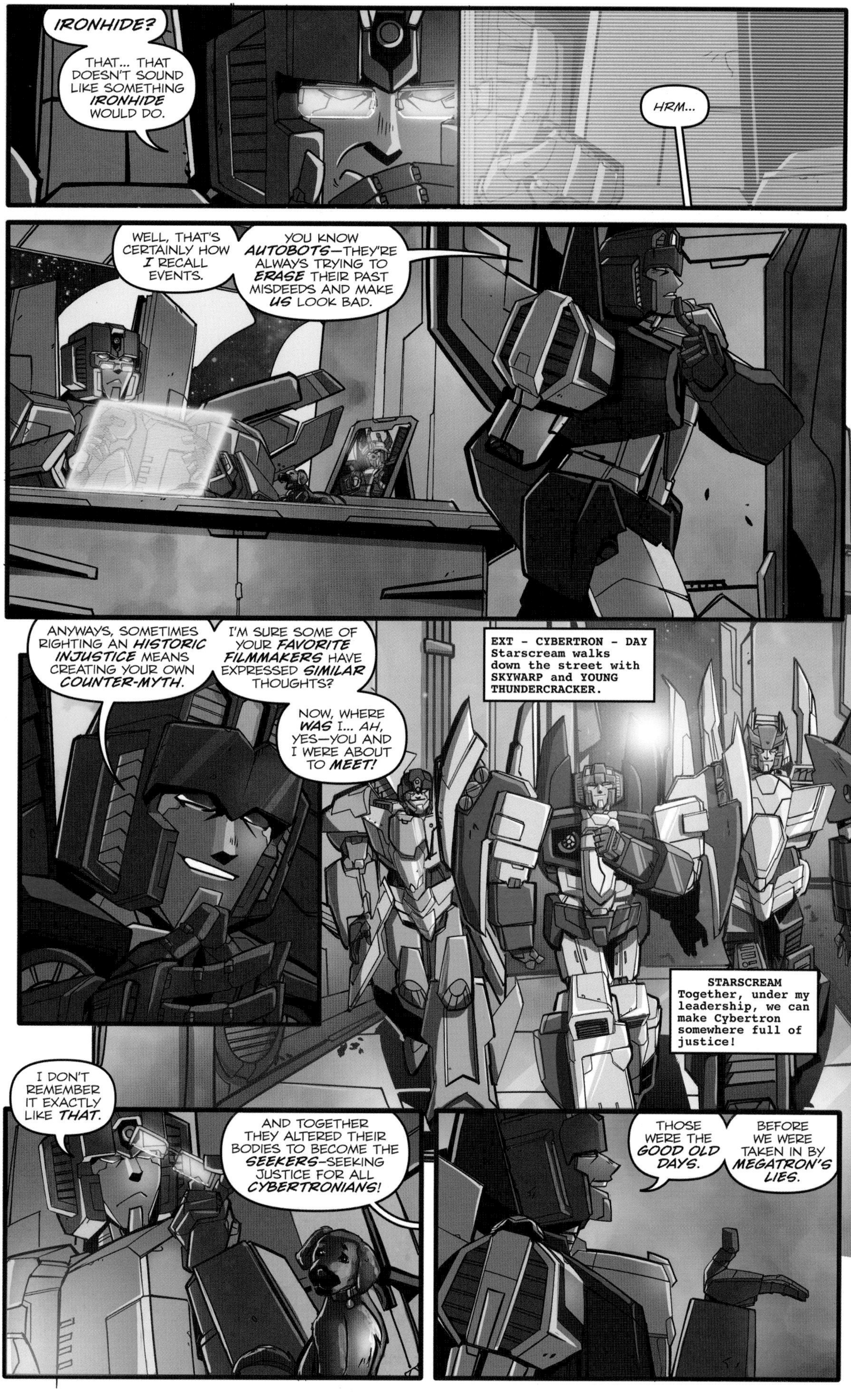
IRONHIDE?
THAT... THAT DOESN'T SOUND LIKE SOMETHING IRONHIDE WOULD DO.
HRM...
WELL, THAT'S CERTAINLY HOW I RECALL EVENTS.
YOU KNOW AUTOBOTS—THEY'RE ALWAYS TRYING TO ERASE THEIR PAST MISDEEDS AND MAKE US LOOK BAD.
ANYWAYS, SOMETIMES RIGHTING AN HISTORIC INJUSTICE MEANS CREATING YOUR OWN COUNTER-MYTH.
I'M SURE SOME OF YOUR FAVORITE FILMMAKERS HAVE EXPRESSED SIMILAR THOUGHTS?
NOW, WHERE WAS I... AH, YES—YOU AND I WERE ABOUT TO MEET!
EXT - CYBERTRON - DAY
Starscream walks down the street with SKYWARP and YOUNG THUNDERCRACKER.
STARSCREAM
Together, under my leadership, we can make Cybertron somewhere full of justice!
I DON'T REMEMBER IT EXACTLY LIKE THAT.
AND TOGETHER THEY ALTERED THEIR BODIES TO BECOME THE SEEKERS—SEEKING JUSTICE FOR ALL CYBERTRONIANS!
THOSE WERE THE GOOD OLD DAYS.
BEFORE WE WERE TAKEN IN BY MEGATRON'S LIES.

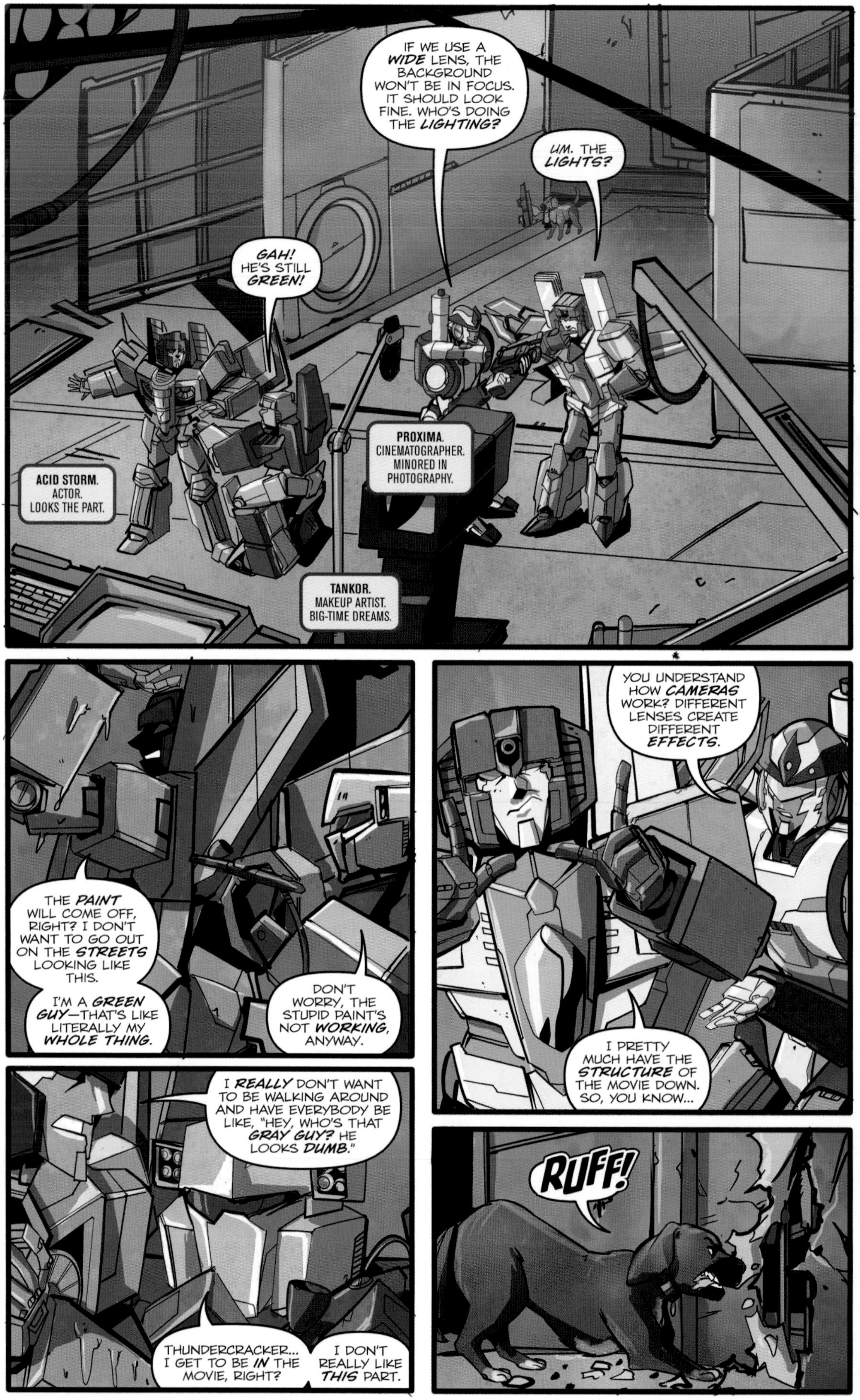
IF WE USE A WIDE LENS, THE BACKGROUND WON'T BE IN FOCUS. IT SHOULD LOOK FINE. WHO'S DOING THE LIGHTING?
UM. THE LIGHTS?
GAH! HE'S STILL GREEN!
PROXIMA. CINEMATOGRAPHER. MINORED IN PHOTOGRAPHY.
ACID STORM. ACTOR. LOOKS THE PART.
TANKOR. MAKEUP ARTIST. BIG-TIME DREAMS.
THE PAINT WILL COME OFF, RIGHT? I DON'T WANT TO GO OUT ON THE STREETS LOOKING LIKE THIS.
I'M A GREEN GUY—THAT'S LIKE LITERALLY MY WHOLE THING.
DON'T WORRY, THE STUPID PAINT'S NOT WORKING, ANYWAY.
YOU UNDERSTAND HOW CAMERAS WORK? DIFFERENT LENSES CREATE DIFFERENT EFFECTS.
I PRETTY MUCH HAVE THE STRUCTURE OF THE MOVIE DOWN. SO, YOU KNOW...
I REALLY DON'T WANT TO BE WALKING AROUND AND HAVE EVERYBODY BE LIKE, "HEY, WHO'S THAT GRAY GUY? HE LOOKS DUMB."
THUNDERCRACKER... I GET TO BE IN THE MOVIE, RIGHT?
I DON'T REALLY LIKE THIS PART.
RUFF!

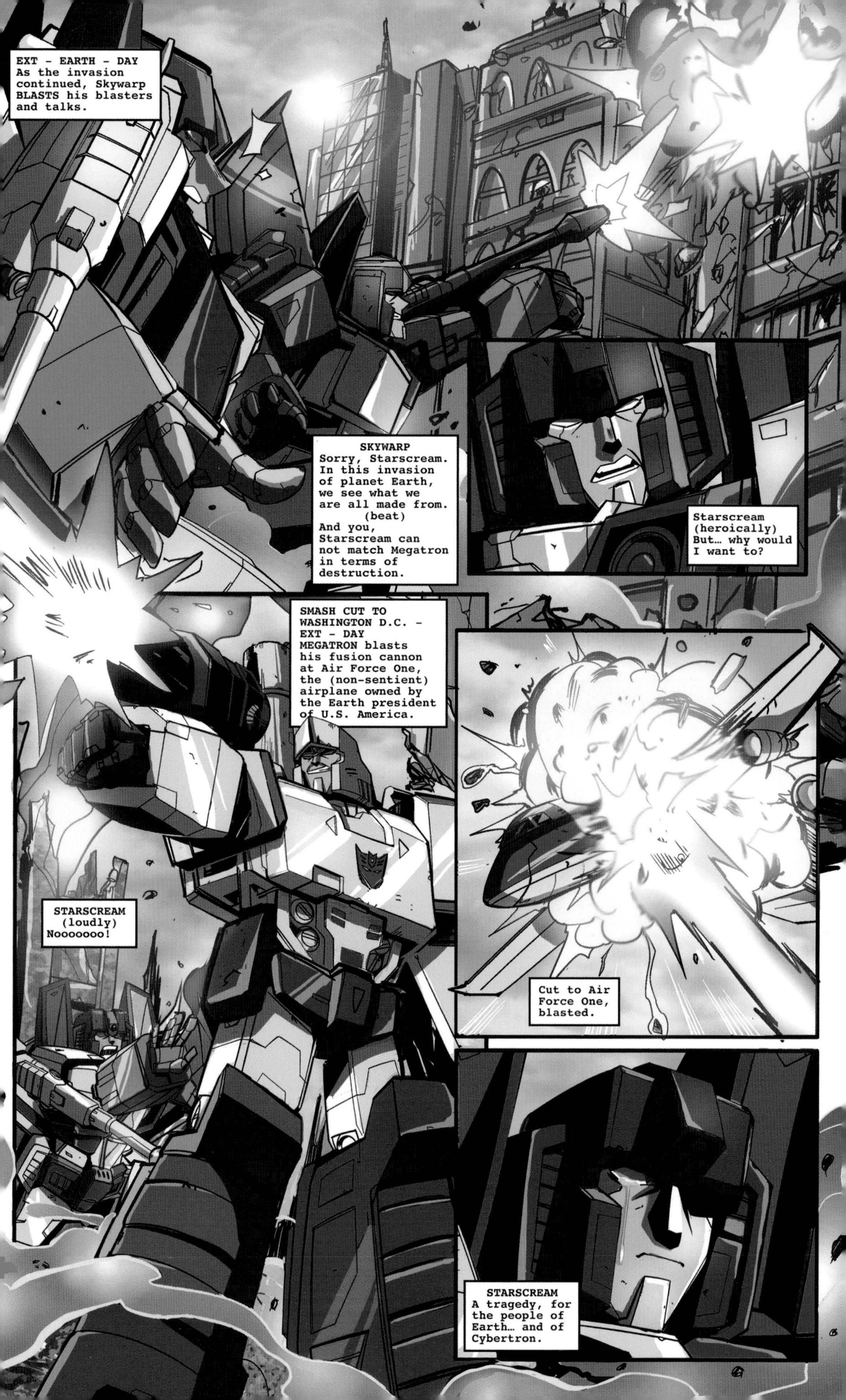
EXT - EARTH - DAY
As the invasion continued, Skywarp BLASTS his blasters and talks.
SKYWARP
Sorry, Starscream. In this invasion of planet Earth, we see what we are all made from.
(beat)
And you, Starscream can not match Megatron in terms of destruction.
Starscream
(heroically)
But… why would I want to?
SMASH CUT TO WASHINGTON D.C. - EXT - DAY
MEGATRON blasts his fusion cannon at Air Force One, the (non-sentient) airplane owned by the Earth president of U.S. America.
Cut to Air Force One, blasted.
STARSCREAM
(loudly)
Noooooo!
STARSCREAM
A tragedy, for the people of Earth… and of Cybertron.

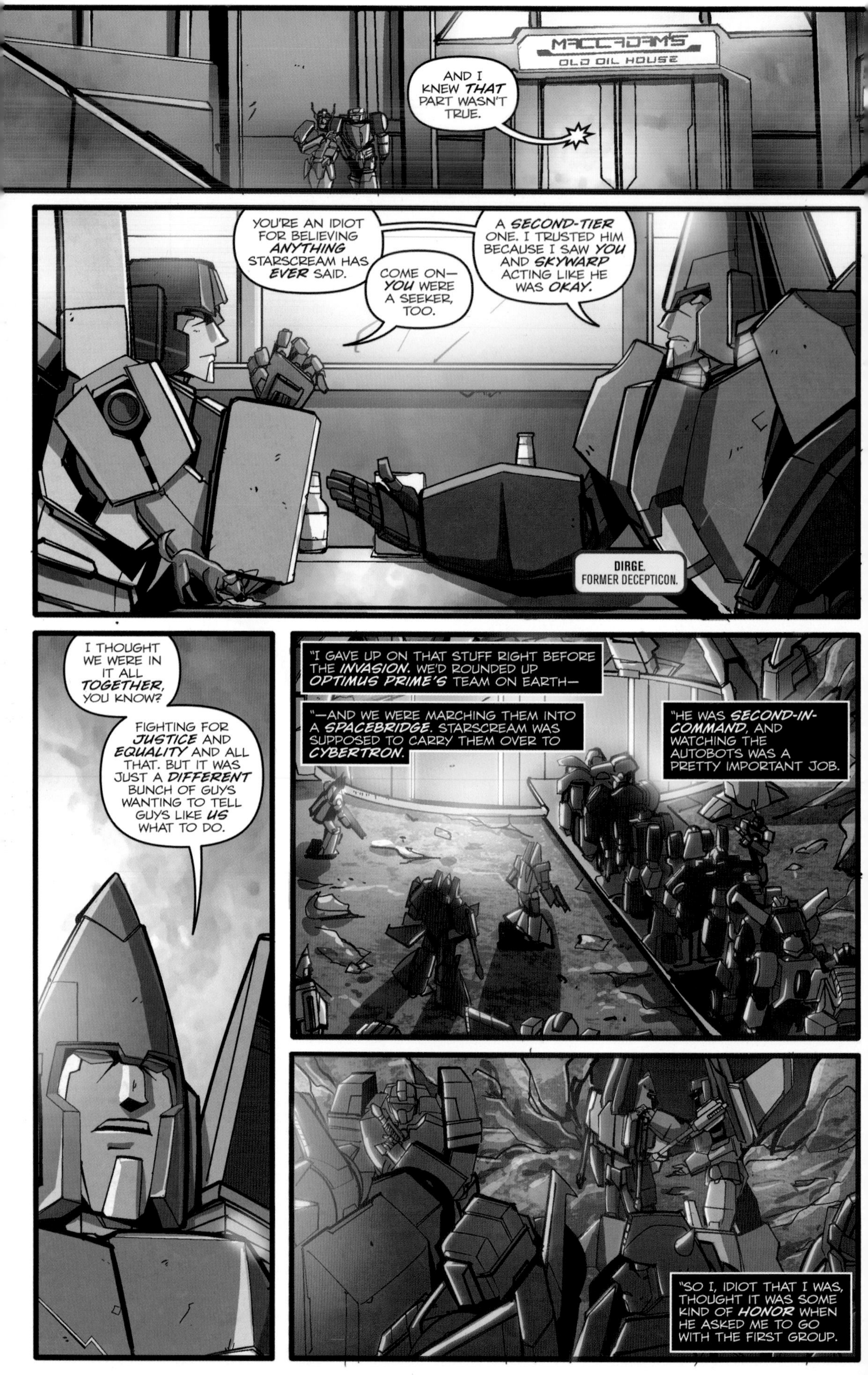
MACCADAM'S
OLD OIL HOUSE
AND I KNEW THAT PART WASN'T TRUE.
YOU'RE AN IDIOT FOR BELIEVING ANYTHING STARSCREAM HAS EVER SAID.
COME ON— YOU WERE A SEEKER, TOO.
A SECOND-TIER ONE. I TRUSTED HIM BECAUSE I SAW YOU AND SKYWARP ACTING LIKE HE WAS OKAY.
DIRGE. FORMER DECEPTICON.
I THOUGHT WE WERE IN IT ALL TOGETHER, YOU KNOW?
FIGHTING FOR JUSTICE AND EQUALITY AND ALL THAT. BUT IT WAS JUST A DIFFERENT BUNCH OF GUYS WANTING TO TELL GUYS LIKE US WHAT TO DO.
"I GAVE UP ON THAT STUFF RIGHT BEFORE THE INVASION. WE'D ROUNDED UP OPTIMUS PRIME'S TEAM ON EARTH—
"—AND WE WERE MARCHING THEM INTO A SPACEBRIDGE. STARSCREAM WAS SUPPOSED TO CARRY THEM OVER TO CYBERTRON.
"HE WAS SECOND-IN-COMMAND, AND WATCHING THE AUTOBOTS WAS A PRETTY IMPORTANT JOB.
"SO I, IDIOT THAT I WAS, THOUGHT IT WAS SOME KIND OF HONOR WHEN HE ASKED ME TO GO WITH THE FIRST GROUP.

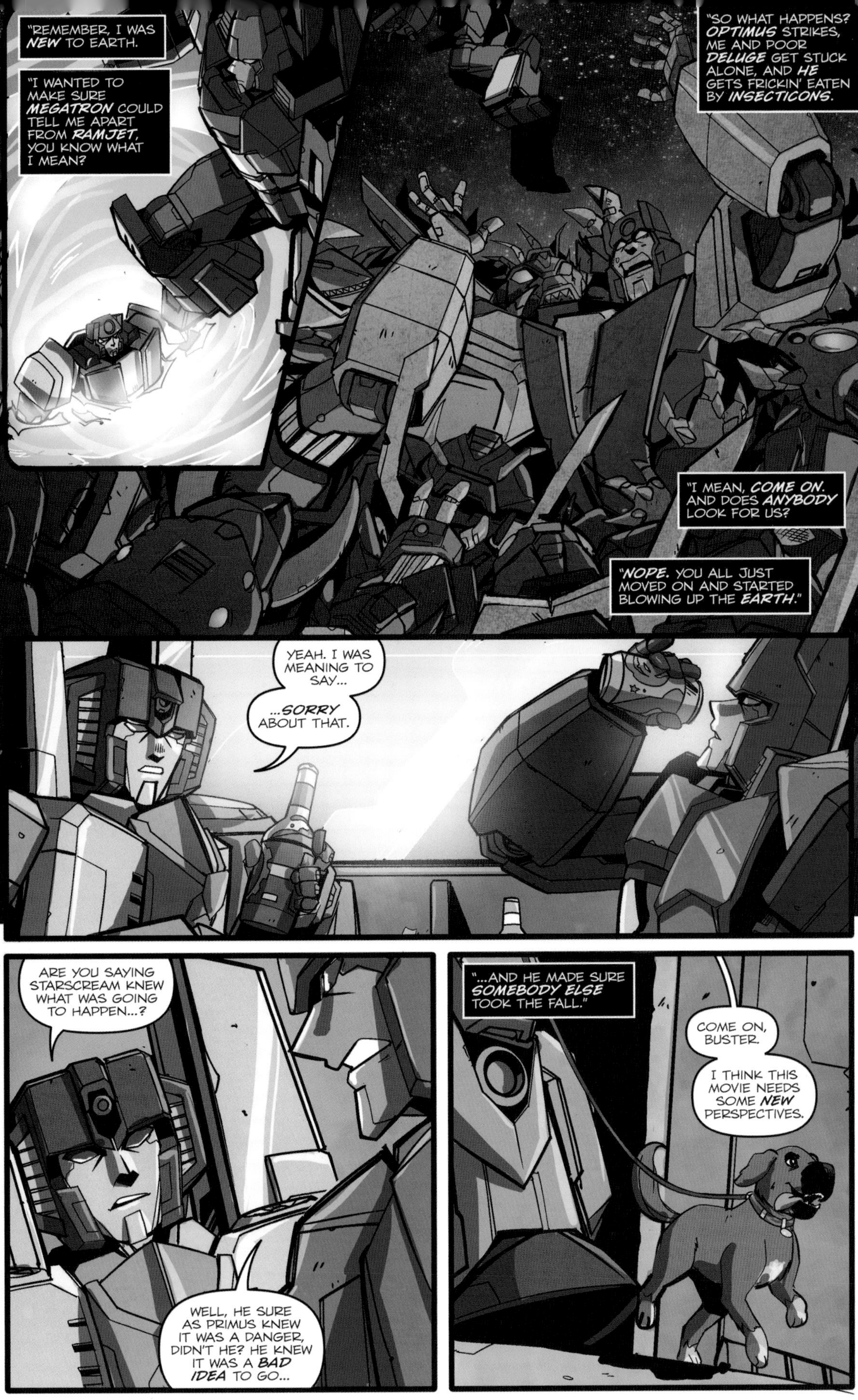
"REMEMBER, I WAS NEW TO EARTH.
"I WANTED TO MAKE SURE MEGATRON COULD TELL ME APART FROM RAMJET, YOU KNOW WHAT I MEAN?
"SO WHAT HAPPENS? OPTIMUS STRIKES, ME AND POOR DELUGE GET STUCK ALONE, AND HE GETS FRICKIN' EATEN BY INSECTICONS.
"I MEAN, COME ON. AND DOES ANYBODY LOOK FOR US?
"NOPE. YOU ALL JUST MOVED ON AND STARTED BLOWING UP THE EARTH."
YEAH. I WAS MEANING TO SAY...
...SORRY ABOUT THAT.
ARE YOU SAYING STARSCREAM KNEW WHAT WAS GOING TO HAPPEN...?
WELL, HE SURE AS PRIMUS KNEW IT WAS A DANGER, DIDN'T HE? HE KNEW IT WAS A BAD IDEA TO GO...
"...AND HE MADE SURE SOMEBODY ELSE TOOK THE FALL."
COME ON, BUSTER.
I THINK THIS MOVIE NEEDS SOME NEW PERSPECTIVES.

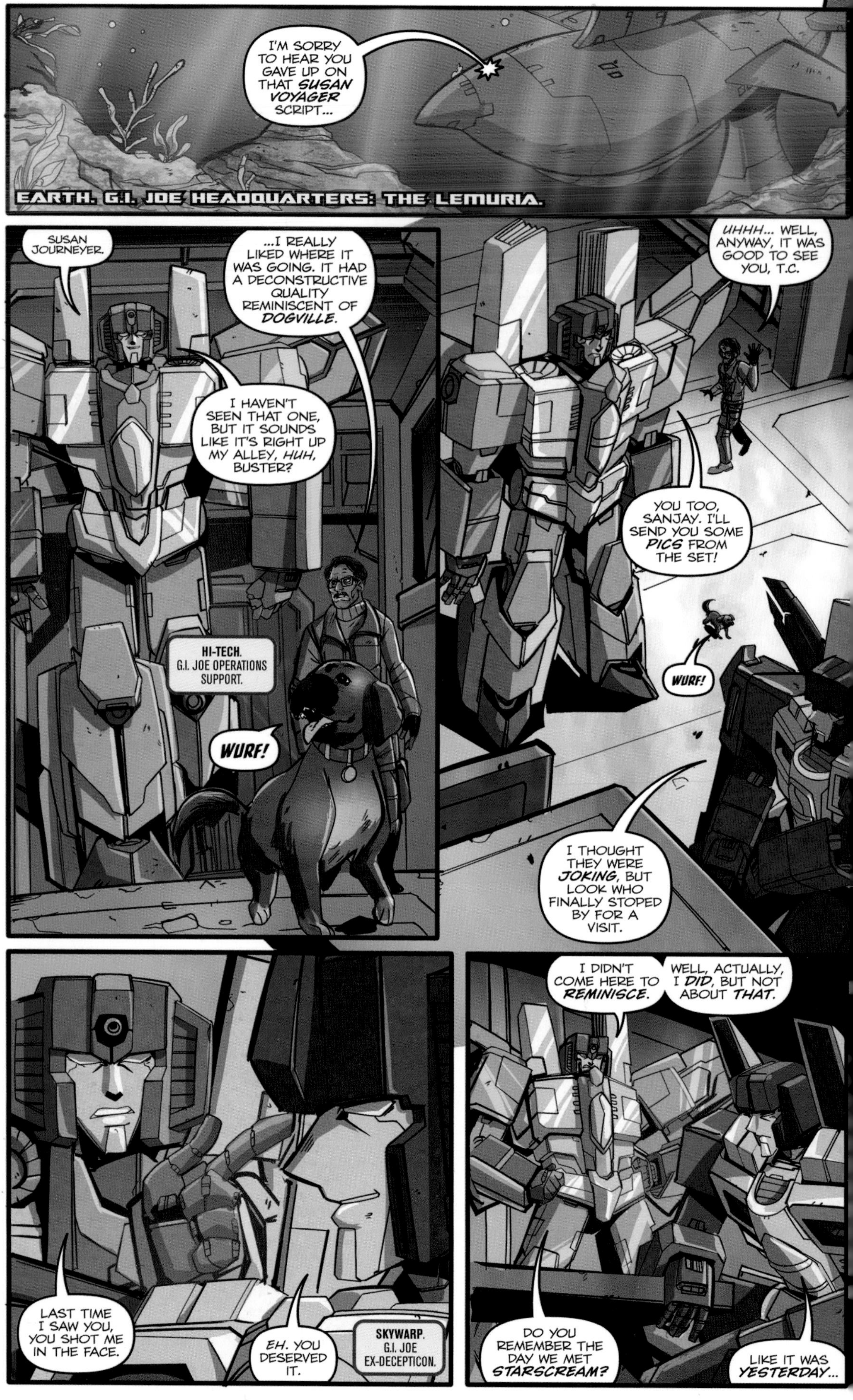
I'M SORRY TO HEAR YOU GAVE UP ON THAT SUSAN VOYAGER SCRIPT...
EARTH. G.I. JOE HEADQUARTERS: THE LEMURIA.
SUSAN JOURNEYER.
...I REALLY LIKED WHERE IT WAS GOING. IT HAD A DECONSTRUCTIVE QUALITY REMINISCENT OF DOGVILLE.
I HAVEN'T SEEN THAT ONE, BUT IT SOUNDS LIKE IT'S RIGHT UP MY ALLEY, HUH, BUSTER?
HI-TECH. G.I. JOE OPERATIONS SUPPORT.
WURF!
UHHH... WELL, ANYWAY, IT WAS GOOD TO SEE YOU, T.C.
YOU TOO, SANJAY. I'LL SEND YOU SOME PICS FROM THE SET!
WURF!
I THOUGHT THEY WERE JOKING, BUT LOOK WHO FINALLY STOPED BY FOR A VISIT.
LAST TIME I SAW YOU, YOU SHOT ME IN THE FACE.
EH. YOU DESERVED IT.
SKYWARP. G.I. JOE EX-DECEPTICON.
I DIDN'T COME HERE TO REMINISCE.
WELL, ACTUALLY, I DID, BUT NOT ABOUT THAT.
DO YOU REMEMBER THE DAY WE MET STARSCREAM?
LIKE IT WAS YESTERDAY...

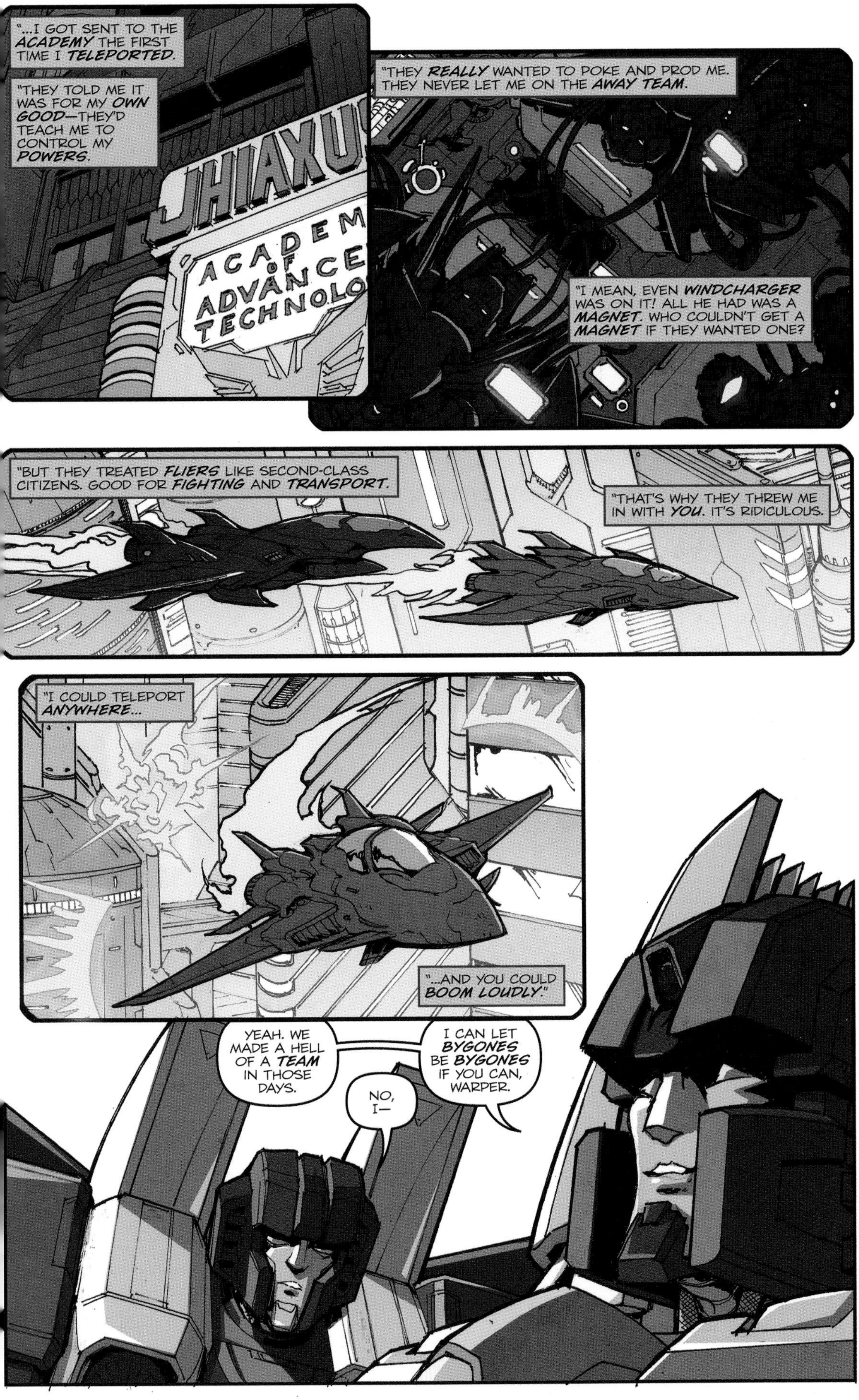
"...I GOT SENT TO THE ACADEMY THE FIRST TIME I TELEPORTED.
"THEY TOLD ME IT WAS FOR MY OWN GOOD—THEY'D TEACH ME TO CONTROL MY POWERS.
JHIAXUS
ACADEMY OF ADVANCED TECHNOLO
"THEY REALLY WANTED TO POKE AND PROD ME. THEY NEVER LET ME ON THE AWAY TEAM.
"I MEAN, EVEN WINDCHARGER WAS ON IT! ALL HE HAD WAS A MAGNET. WHO COULDN'T GET A MAGNET IF THEY WANTED ONE?
"BUT THEY TREATED FLIERS LIKE SECOND-CLASS CITIZENS. GOOD FOR FIGHTING AND TRANSPORT.
"THAT'S WHY THEY THREW ME IN WITH YOU. IT'S RIDICULOUS.
"I COULD TELEPORT ANYWHERE...
"...AND YOU COULD BOOM LOUDLY."
YEAH. WE MADE A HELL OF A TEAM IN THOSE DAYS.
I CAN LET BYGONES BE BYGONES IF YOU CAN, WARPER.
NO, I—

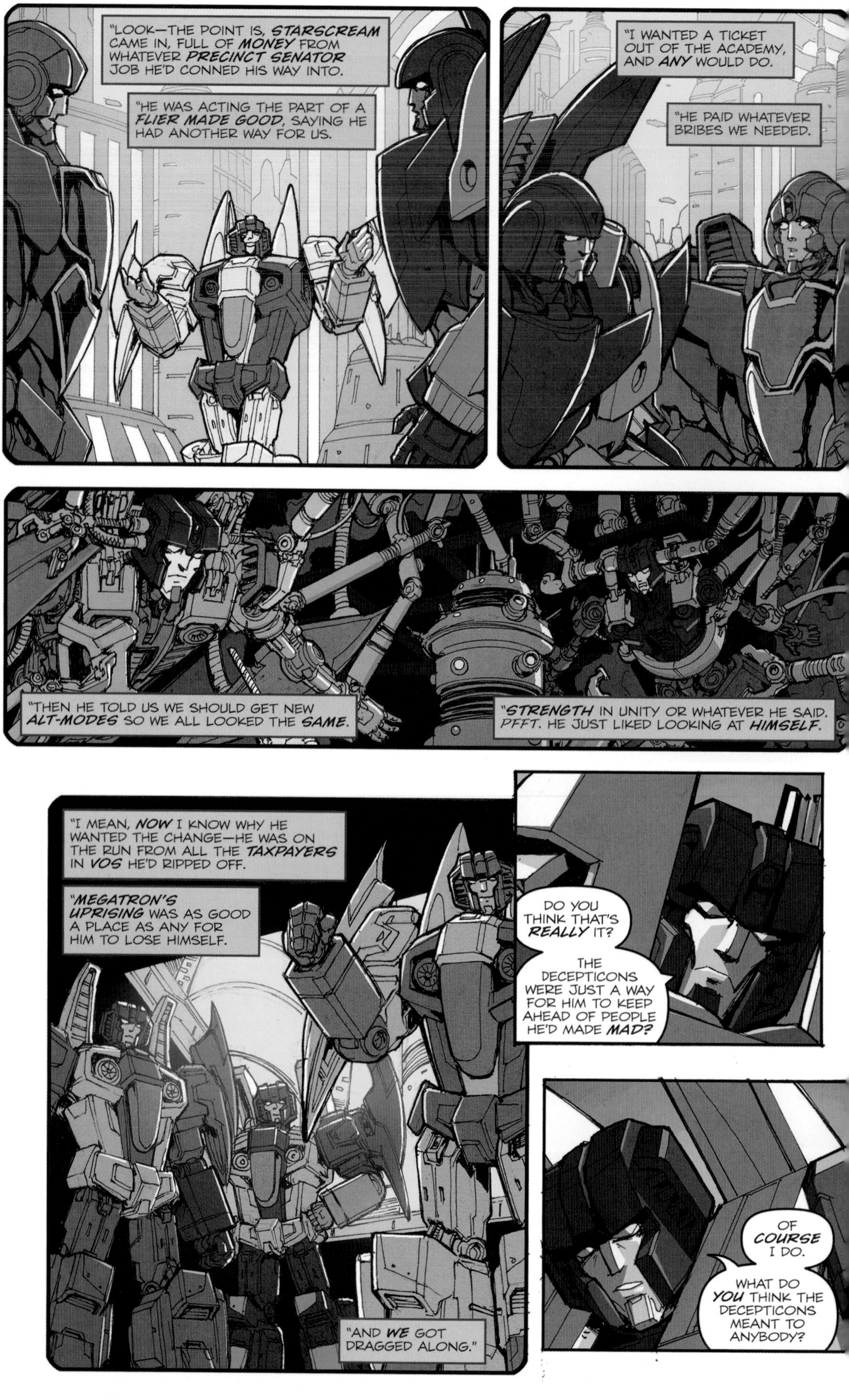
"LOOK—THE POINT IS, STARSCREAM CAME IN, FULL OF MONEY FROM WHATEVER PRECINCT SENATOR JOB HE'D CONNED HIS WAY INTO.
"HE WAS ACTING THE PART OF A FLIER MADE GOOD, SAYING HE HAD ANOTHER WAY FOR US.
"I WANTED A TICKET OUT OF THE ACADEMY, AND ANY WOULD DO.
"HE PAID WHATEVER BRIBES WE NEEDED.
"THEN HE TOLD US WE SHOULD GET NEW ALT-MODES SO WE ALL LOOKED THE SAME.
"STRENGTH IN UNITY OR WHATEVER HE SAID. PFFT. HE JUST LIKED LOOKING AT HIMSELF.
"I MEAN, NOW I KNOW WHY HE WANTED THE CHANGE—HE WAS ON THE RUN FROM ALL THE TAXPAYERS IN VOS HE'D RIPPED OFF.
"MEGATRON'S UPRISING WAS AS GOOD A PLACE AS ANY FOR HIM TO LOSE HIMSELF.
"AND WE GOT DRAGGED ALONG."
DO YOU THINK THAT'S REALLY IT?
THE DECEPTICONS WERE JUST A WAY FOR HIM TO KEEP AHEAD OF PEOPLE HE'D MADE MAD?
OF COURSE I DO.
WHAT DO YOU THINK THE DECEPTICONS MEANT TO ANYBODY?

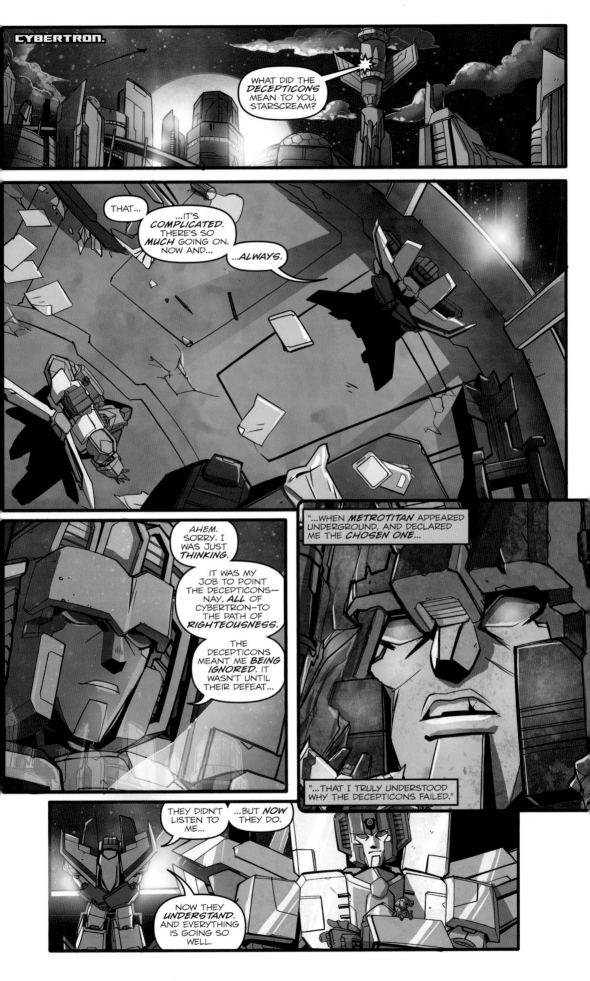

CYBERTRON.

WHAT DID THE **DECEPTICONS** MEAN TO YOU, STARSCREAM?

THAT...

...IT'S **COMPLICATED.** THERE'S SO **MUCH** GOING ON. NOW AND...

...**ALWAYS.**

AHEM. SORRY. I WAS JUST **THINKING.**

IT WAS MY JOB TO POINT THE DECEPTICONS— NAY, **ALL** OF CYBERTRON—TO THE PATH OF **RIGHTEOUSNESS.**

THE DECEPTICONS MEANT ME **BEING IGNORED.** IT WASN'T UNTIL THEIR DEFEAT...

"...WHEN **METROTITAN** APPEARED UNDERGROUND, AND DECLARED ME THE **CHOSEN ONE**...

"...THAT I TRULY UNDERSTOOD WHY THE DECEPTICONS FAILED."

THEY DIDN'T LISTEN TO ME...

...BUT **NOW** THEY DO.

NOW THEY **UNDERSTAND.** AND EVERYTHING IS GOING SO WELL.

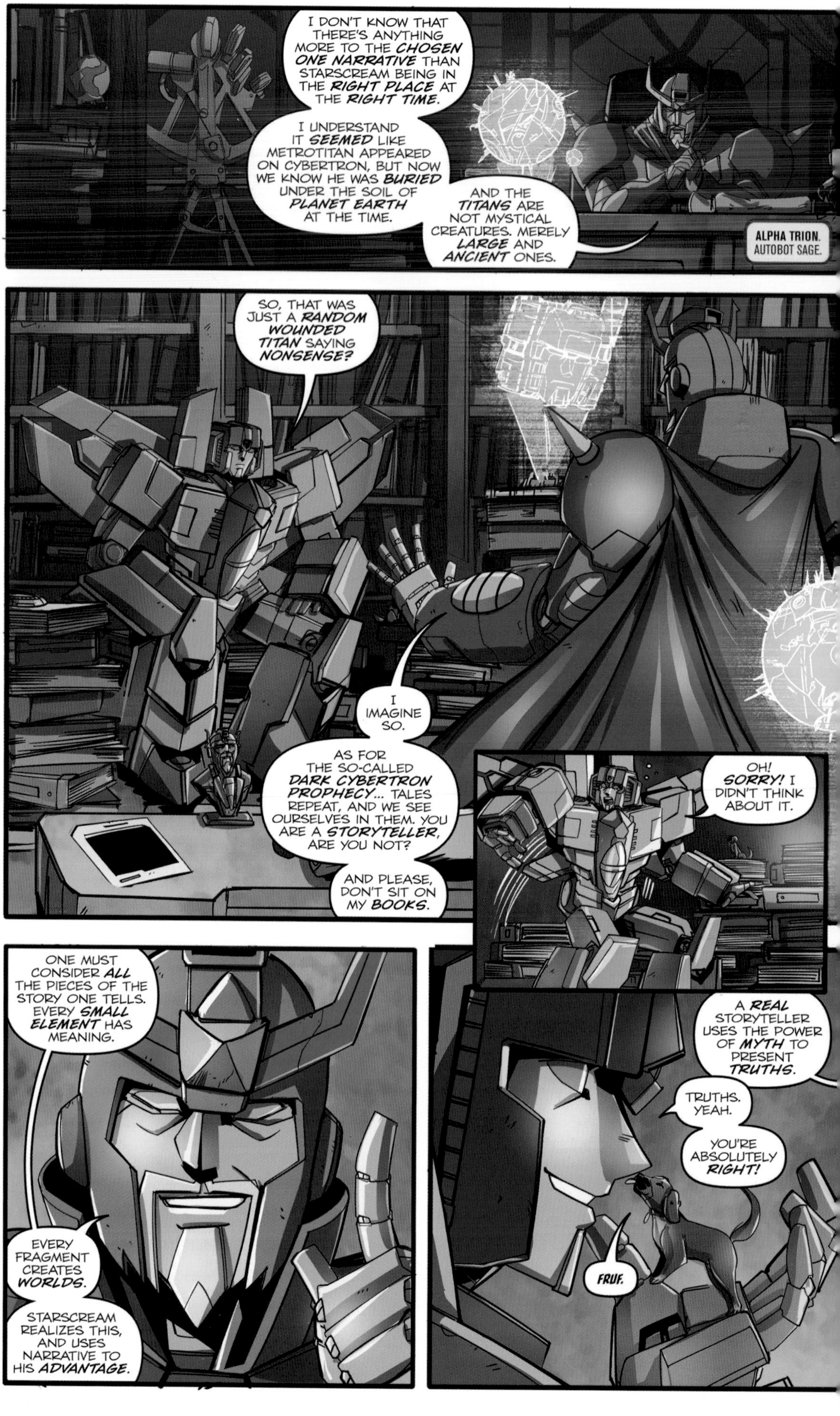
I DON'T KNOW THAT THERE'S ANYTHING MORE TO THE CHOSEN ONE NARRATIVE THAN STARSCREAM BEING IN THE RIGHT PLACE AT THE RIGHT TIME.
I UNDERSTAND IT SEEMED LIKE METROTITAN APPEARED ON CYBERTRON, BUT NOW WE KNOW HE WAS BURIED UNDER THE SOIL OF PLANET EARTH AT THE TIME.
AND THE TITANS ARE NOT MYSTICAL CREATURES. MERELY LARGE AND ANCIENT ONES.
ALPHA TRION. AUTOBOT SAGE.
SO, THAT WAS JUST A RANDOM WOUNDED TITAN SAYING NONSENSE?
I IMAGINE SO.
AS FOR THE SO-CALLED DARK CYBERTRON PROPHECY... TALES REPEAT, AND WE SEE OURSELVES IN THEM. YOU ARE A STORYTELLER, ARE YOU NOT?
AND PLEASE, DON'T SIT ON MY BOOKS.
OH! SORRY! I DIDN'T THINK ABOUT IT.
ONE MUST CONSIDER ALL THE PIECES OF THE STORY ONE TELLS. EVERY SMALL ELEMENT HAS MEANING.
EVERY FRAGMENT CREATES WORLDS.
STARSCREAM REALIZES THIS, AND USES NARRATIVE TO HIS ADVANTAGE.
A REAL STORYTELLER USES THE POWER OF MYTH TO PRESENT TRUTHS.
TRUTHS. YEAH.
YOU'RE ABSOLUTELY RIGHT!
FRUF.

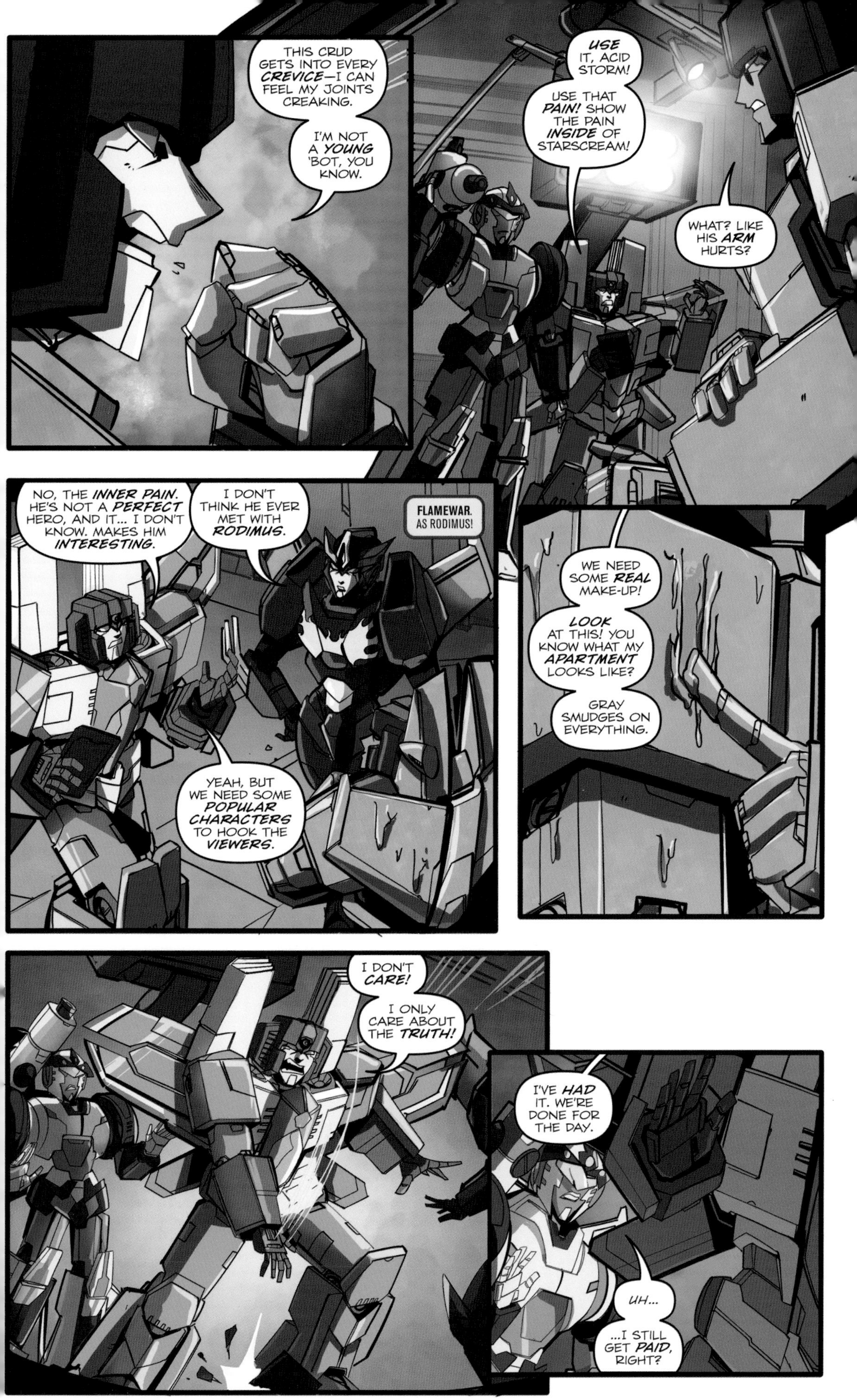
THIS CRUD GETS INTO EVERY CREVICE—I CAN FEEL MY JOINTS CREAKING.
I'M NOT A YOUNG 'BOT, YOU KNOW.
USE IT, ACID STORM!
USE THAT PAIN! SHOW THE PAIN INSIDE OF STARSCREAM!
WHAT? LIKE HIS ARM HURTS?
NO, THE INNER PAIN. HE'S NOT A PERFECT HERO, AND IT... I DON'T KNOW. MAKES HIM INTERESTING.
I DON'T THINK HE EVER MET WITH RODIMUS.
FLAMEWAR. AS RODIMUS!
YEAH, BUT WE NEED SOME POPULAR CHARACTERS TO HOOK THE VIEWERS.
WE NEED SOME REAL MAKE-UP!
LOOK AT THIS! YOU KNOW WHAT MY APARTMENT LOOKS LIKE?
GRAY SMUDGES ON EVERYTHING.
I DON'T CARE!
I ONLY CARE ABOUT THE TRUTH!
I'VE HAD IT. WE'RE DONE FOR THE DAY.
UH...
...I STILL GET PAID, RIGHT?

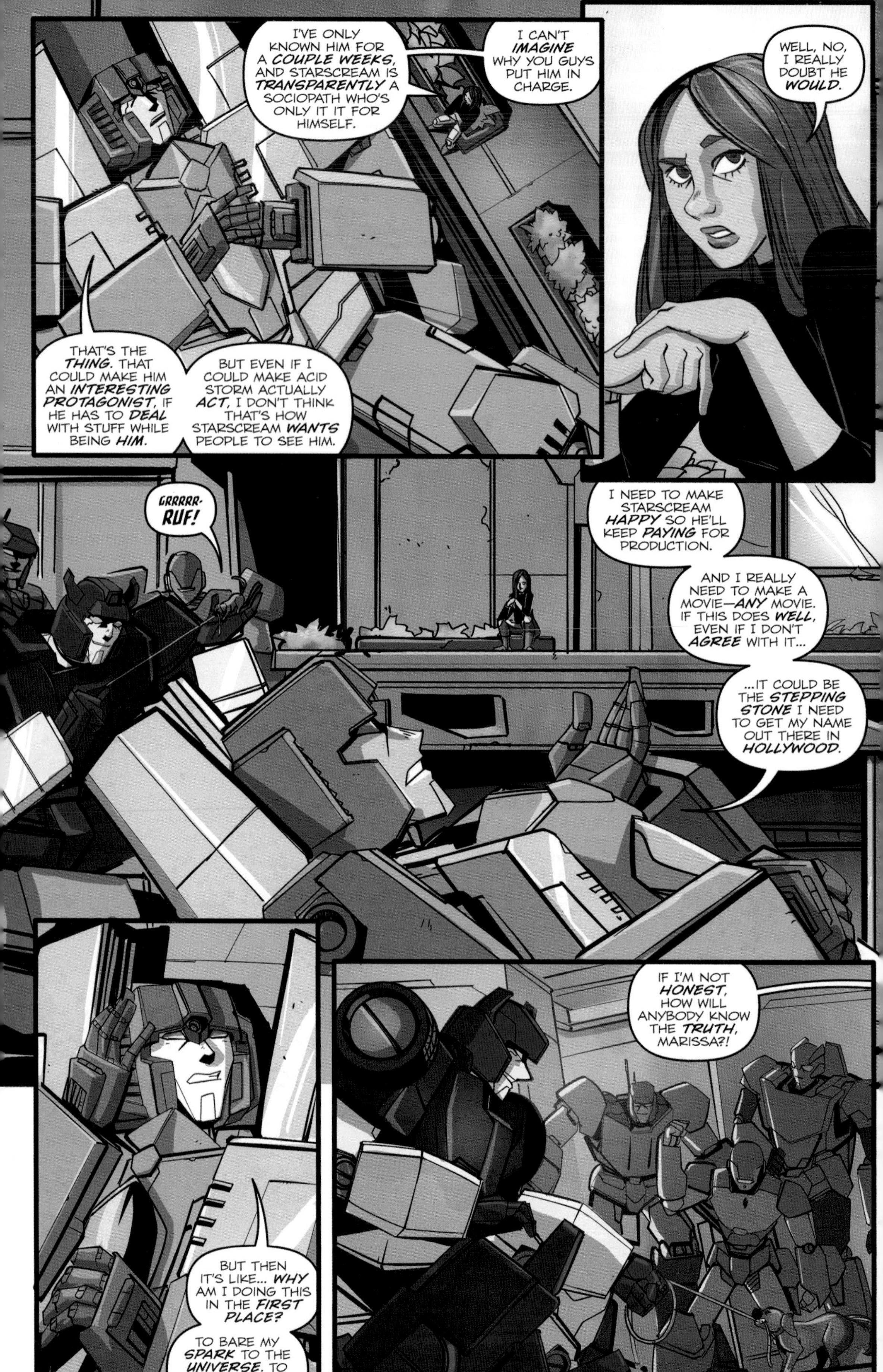
I'VE ONLY KNOWN HIM FOR A COUPLE WEEKS, AND STARSCREAM IS TRANSPARENTLY A SOCIOPATH WHO'S ONLY IT IT FOR HIMSELF.
I CAN'T IMAGINE WHY YOU GUYS PUT HIM IN CHARGE.
WELL, NO, I REALLY DOUBT HE WOULD.
THAT'S THE THING. THAT COULD MAKE HIM AN INTERESTING PROTAGONIST, IF HE HAS TO DEAL WITH STUFF WHILE BEING HIM.
BUT EVEN IF I COULD MAKE ACID STORM ACTUALLY ACT, I DON'T THINK THAT'S HOW STARSCREAM WANTS PEOPLE TO SEE HIM.
GRRRRR-RUF!
I NEED TO MAKE STARSCREAM HAPPY SO HE'LL KEEP PAYING FOR PRODUCTION.
AND I REALLY NEED TO MAKE A MOVIE—ANY MOVIE. IF THIS DOES WELL, EVEN IF I DON'T AGREE WITH IT...
...IT COULD BE THE STEPPING STONE I NEED TO GET MY NAME OUT THERE IN HOLLYWOOD.
BUT THEN IT'S LIKE... WHY AM I DOING THIS IN THE FIRST PLACE?
TO BARE MY SPARK TO THE UNIVERSE. TO SHOW, YOU KNOW, THE TRUTH.
IF I'M NOT HONEST, HOW WILL ANYBODY KNOW THE TRUTH, MARISSA?!

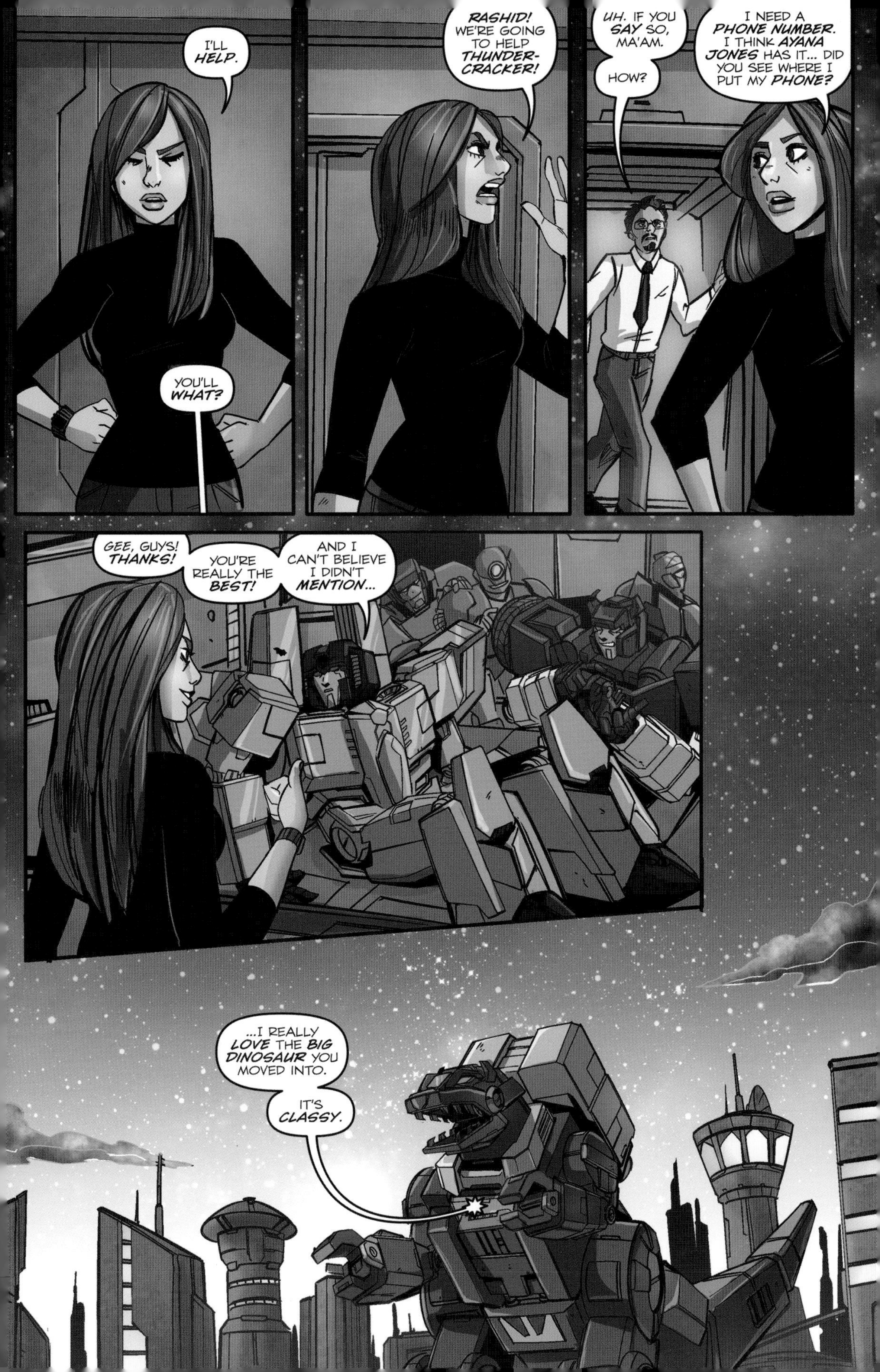
I'LL HELP.
YOU'LL WHAT?
RASHID! WE'RE GOING TO HELP THUNDER-CRACKER!
UH. IF YOU SAY SO, MA'AM.
HOW?
I NEED A PHONE NUMBER. I THINK AYANA JONES HAS IT... DID YOU SEE WHERE I PUT MY PHONE?
GEE, GUYS! THANKS!
YOU'RE REALLY THE BEST!
AND I CAN'T BELIEVE I DIDN'T MENTION...
...I REALLY LOVE THE BIG DINOSAUR YOU MOVED INTO.
IT'S CLASSY.

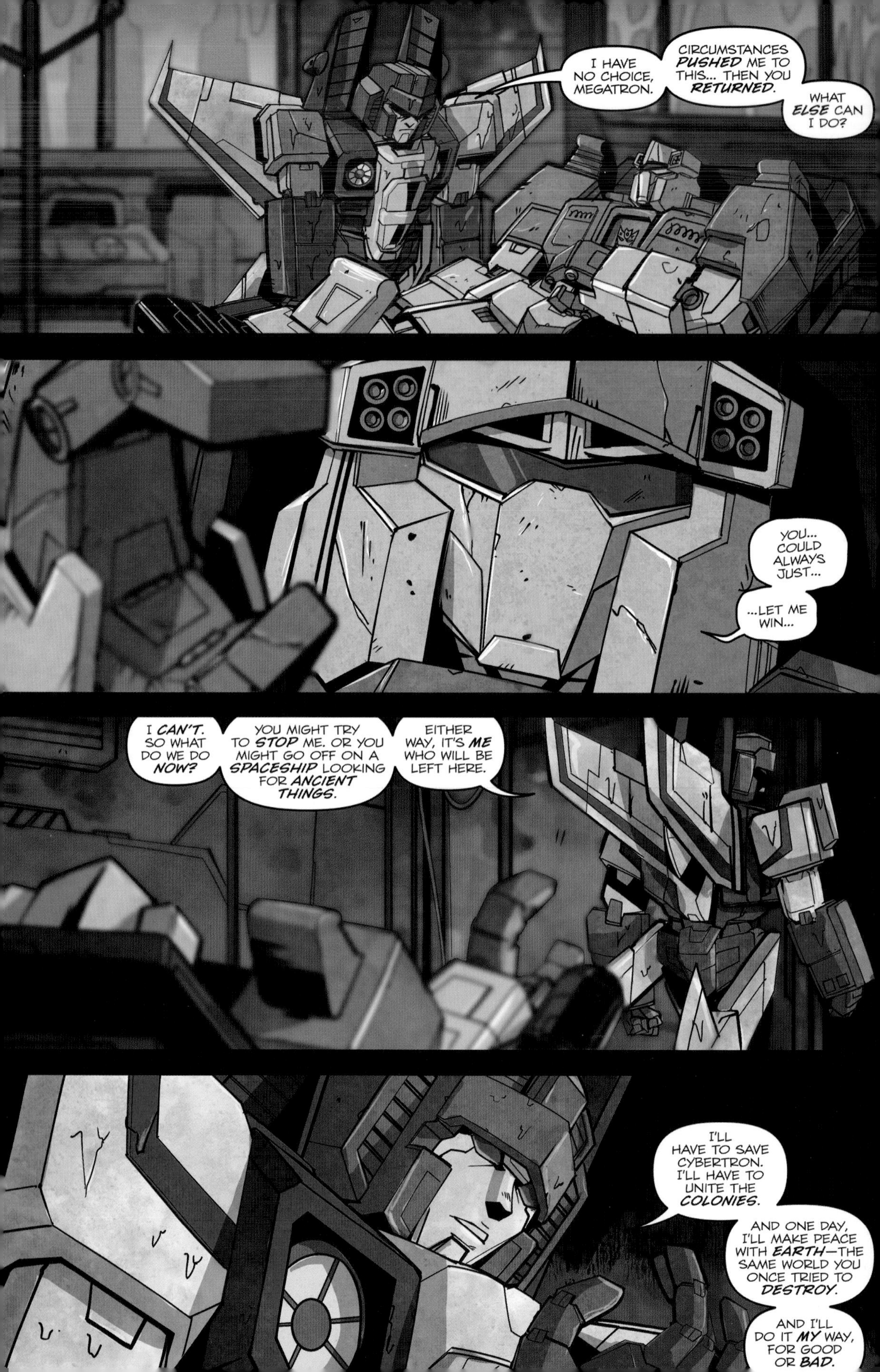

I HAVE NO CHOICE, MEGATRON.
CIRCUMSTANCES *PUSHED* ME TO THIS... THEN YOU *RETURNED*.
WHAT *ELSE* CAN I DO?
YOU... COULD ALWAYS JUST...
...LET ME WIN...
I *CAN'T*. SO WHAT DO WE DO *NOW?*
YOU MIGHT TRY TO *STOP* ME. OR YOU MIGHT GO OFF ON A *SPACESHIP* LOOKING FOR *ANCIENT THINGS*.
EITHER WAY, IT'S *ME* WHO WILL BE LEFT HERE.
I'LL HAVE TO SAVE CYBERTRON. I'LL HAVE TO UNITE THE *COLONIES*.
AND ONE DAY, I'LL MAKE PEACE WITH *EARTH*—THE SAME WORLD YOU ONCE TRIED TO *DESTROY*.
AND I'LL DO IT *MY* WAY, FOR GOOD OR *BAD*.

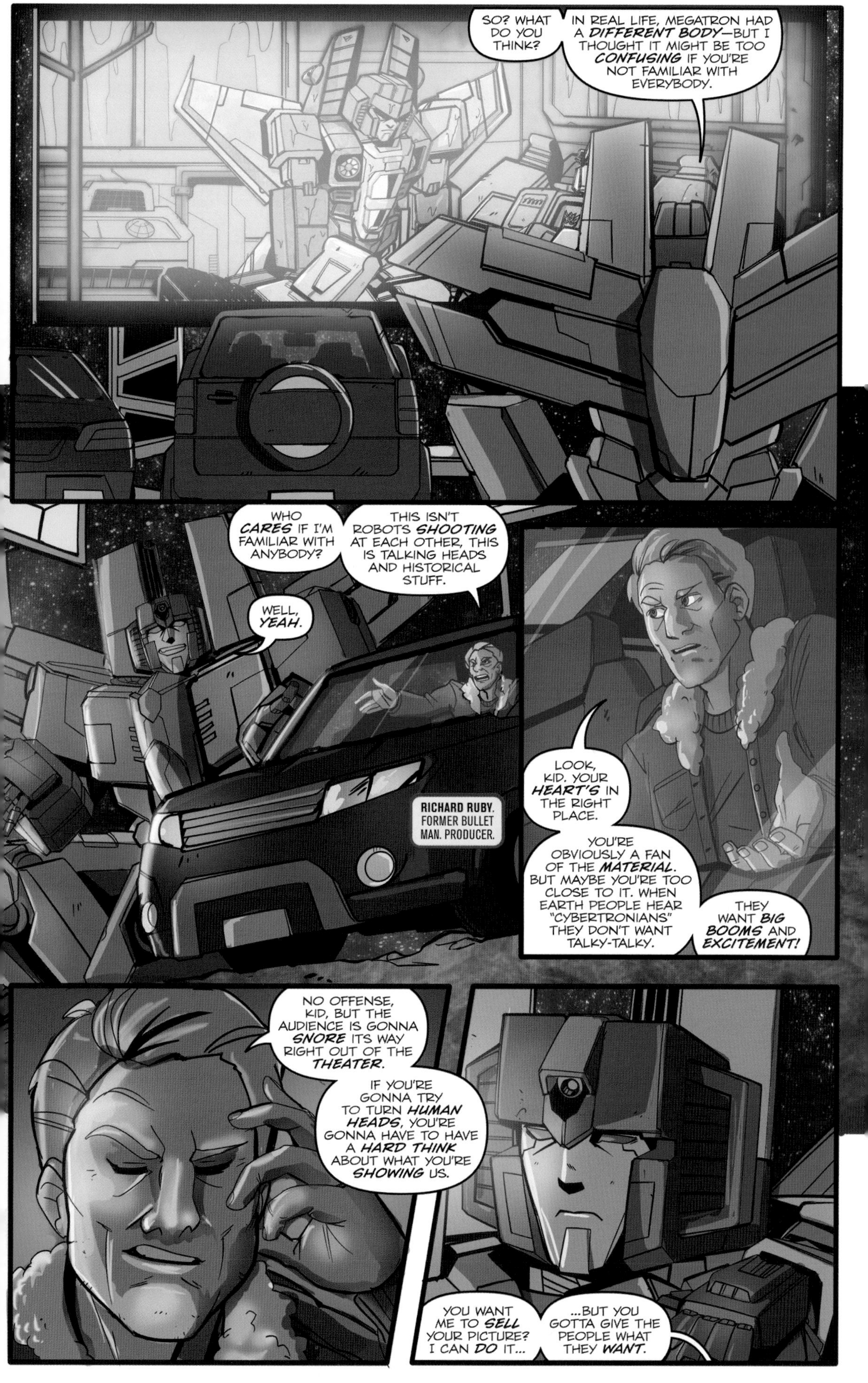
SO? WHAT DO YOU THINK?
IN REAL LIFE, MEGATRON HAD A DIFFERENT BODY—BUT I THOUGHT IT MIGHT BE TOO CONFUSING IF YOU'RE NOT FAMILIAR WITH EVERYBODY.
WHO CARES IF I'M FAMILIAR WITH ANYBODY?
THIS ISN'T ROBOTS SHOOTING AT EACH OTHER, THIS IS TALKING HEADS AND HISTORICAL STUFF.
WELL, YEAH.
RICHARD RUBY. FORMER BULLET MAN. PRODUCER.
LOOK, KID. YOUR HEART'S IN THE RIGHT PLACE.
YOU'RE OBVIOUSLY A FAN OF THE MATERIAL. BUT MAYBE YOU'RE TOO CLOSE TO IT. WHEN EARTH PEOPLE HEAR "CYBERTRONIANS" THEY DON'T WANT TALKY-TALKY.
THEY WANT BIG BOOMS AND EXCITEMENT!
NO OFFENSE, KID, BUT THE AUDIENCE IS GONNA SNORE ITS WAY RIGHT OUT OF THE THEATER.
IF YOU'RE GONNA TRY TO TURN HUMAN HEADS, YOU'RE GONNA HAVE TO HAVE A HARD THINK ABOUT WHAT YOU'RE SHOWING US.
YOU WANT ME TO SELL YOUR PICTURE? I CAN DO IT...
...BUT YOU GOTTA GIVE THE PEOPLE WHAT THEY WANT.

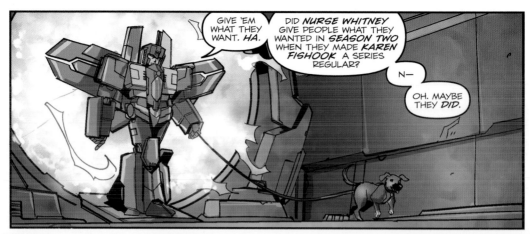

GIVE 'EM WHAT THEY WANT. *HA.*

DID *NURSE WHITNEY* GIVE PEOPLE WHAT THEY WANTED IN *SEASON TWO* WHEN THEY MADE *KAREN FISHOOK* A SERIES REGULAR?

N—

OH. MAYBE THEY *DID.*

BUT IT MADE SENSE WITH THE *STORY,* TOO.

NURSE WHITNEY WAS GOING THROUGH SOME *TOUGH TIMES* AND NEEDED HER *MOM* AROUND.

ANYWAY, THAT'S WHEN THE *MESSAGE BOARDS* STARTED UP WITH ALL THAT *"NURSE WHINEY"* STUFF, BUT I STILL REALLY LIKED IT.

BECAUSE IT WAS SHOWING ME ABOUT *HUMAN LIFE.*

I WAS STARTING TO *UNDERSTAND* THE PEOPLE I WAS LIVING AMONG.

HURF.

YES, YES, AND THE *DOGS.* SORRY, BUSTER. *DOGS,* TOO.

THE POINT IS, THAT SHOW *INSPIRED* ME. IT MADE ME WHO I AM *TODAY.*

AN *ARTIST.*

THAT'S WHAT PEOPLE WANT.

NOT JUST *ACTION* AND *SHOOTING*—THEY WANT *PATHOS* AND *EMOTION!*

THEY WANT TO BE *INSPIRED!*

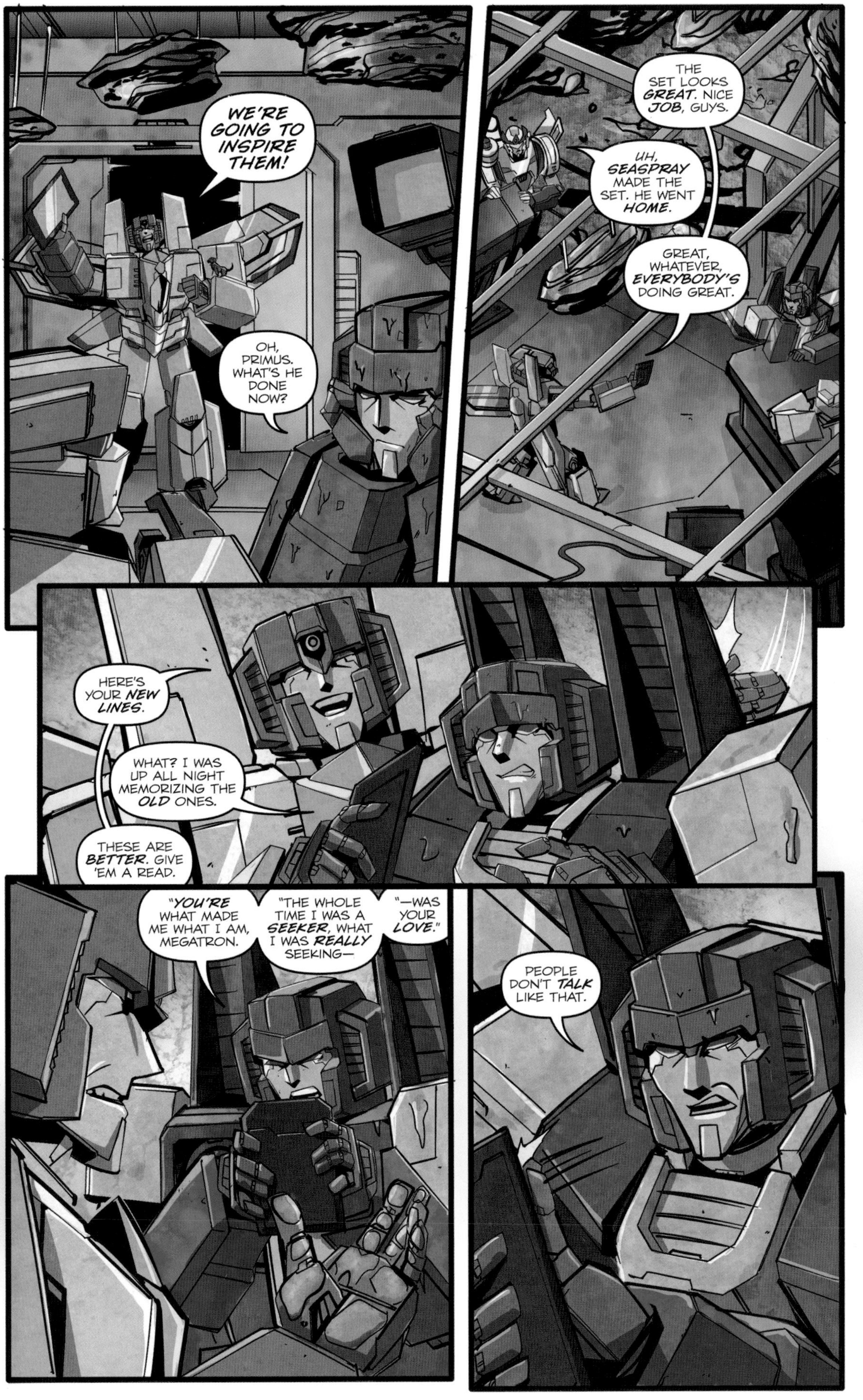
WE'RE GOING TO INSPIRE THEM!
OH, PRIMUS. WHAT'S HE DONE NOW?
THE SET LOOKS GREAT. NICE JOB, GUYS.
UH, SEASPRAY MADE THE SET. HE WENT HOME.
GREAT, WHATEVER, EVERYBODY'S DOING GREAT.
HERE'S YOUR NEW LINES.
WHAT? I WAS UP ALL NIGHT MEMORIZING THE OLD ONES.
THESE ARE BETTER. GIVE 'EM A READ.
"YOU'RE WHAT MADE ME WHAT I AM, MEGATRON.
"THE WHOLE TIME I WAS A SEEKER, WHAT I WAS REALLY SEEKING—
"—WAS YOUR LOVE."
PEOPLE DON'T TALK LIKE THAT.

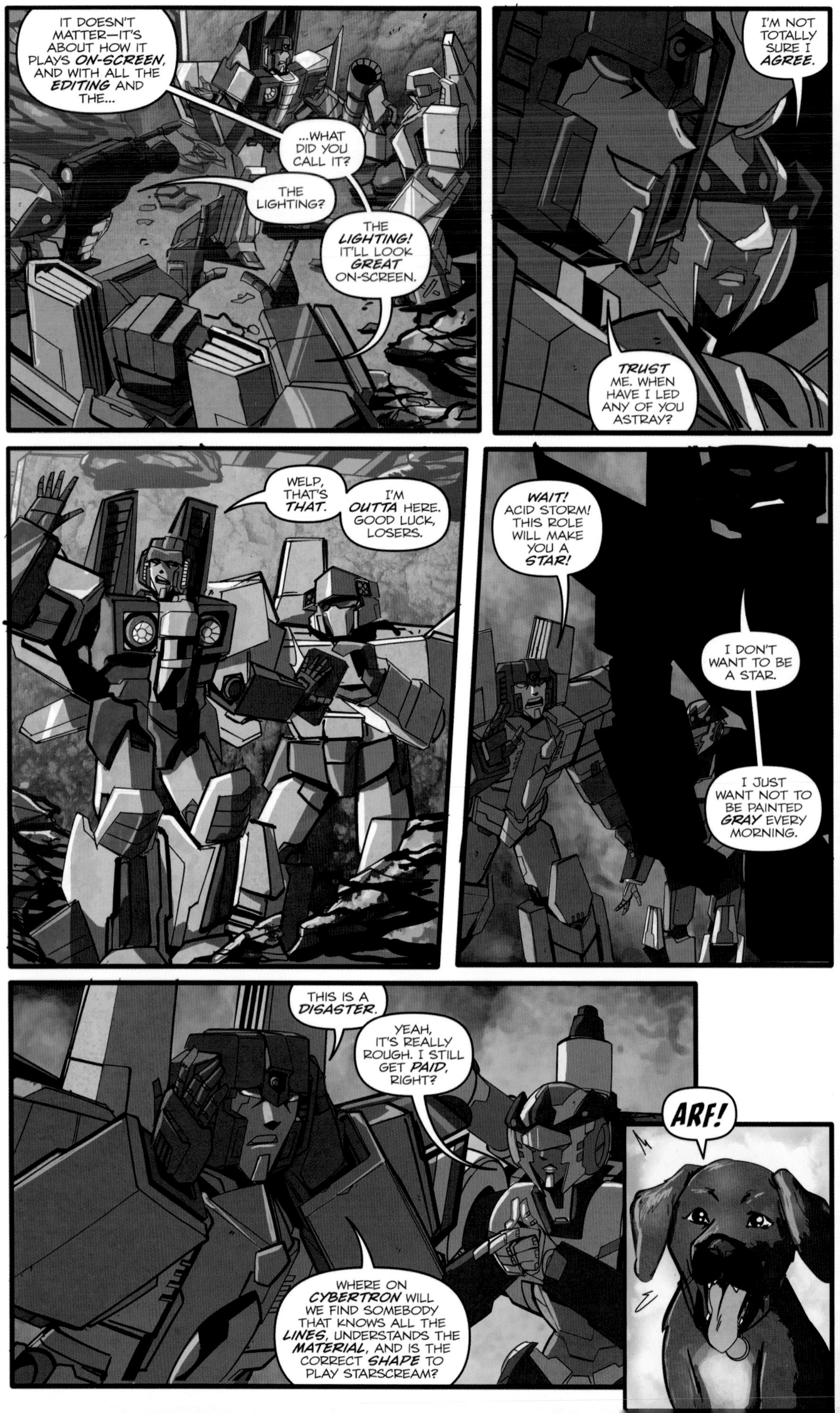
IT DOESN'T MATTER—IT'S ABOUT HOW IT PLAYS ON-SCREEN, AND WITH ALL THE EDITING AND THE...
...WHAT DID YOU CALL IT?
THE LIGHTING?
THE LIGHTING! IT'LL LOOK GREAT ON-SCREEN.
I'M NOT TOTALLY SURE I AGREE.
TRUST ME. WHEN HAVE I LED ANY OF YOU ASTRAY?
WELP, THAT'S THAT.
I'M OUTTA HERE. GOOD LUCK, LOSERS.
WAIT! ACID STORM! THIS ROLE WILL MAKE YOU A STAR!
I DON'T WANT TO BE A STAR.
I JUST WANT NOT TO BE PAINTED GRAY EVERY MORNING.
THIS IS A DISASTER.
YEAH, IT'S REALLY ROUGH. I STILL GET PAID, RIGHT?
WHERE ON CYBERTRON WILL WE FIND SOMEBODY THAT KNOWS ALL THE LINES, UNDERSTANDS THE MATERIAL, AND IS THE CORRECT SHAPE TO PLAY STARSCREAM?
ARF!

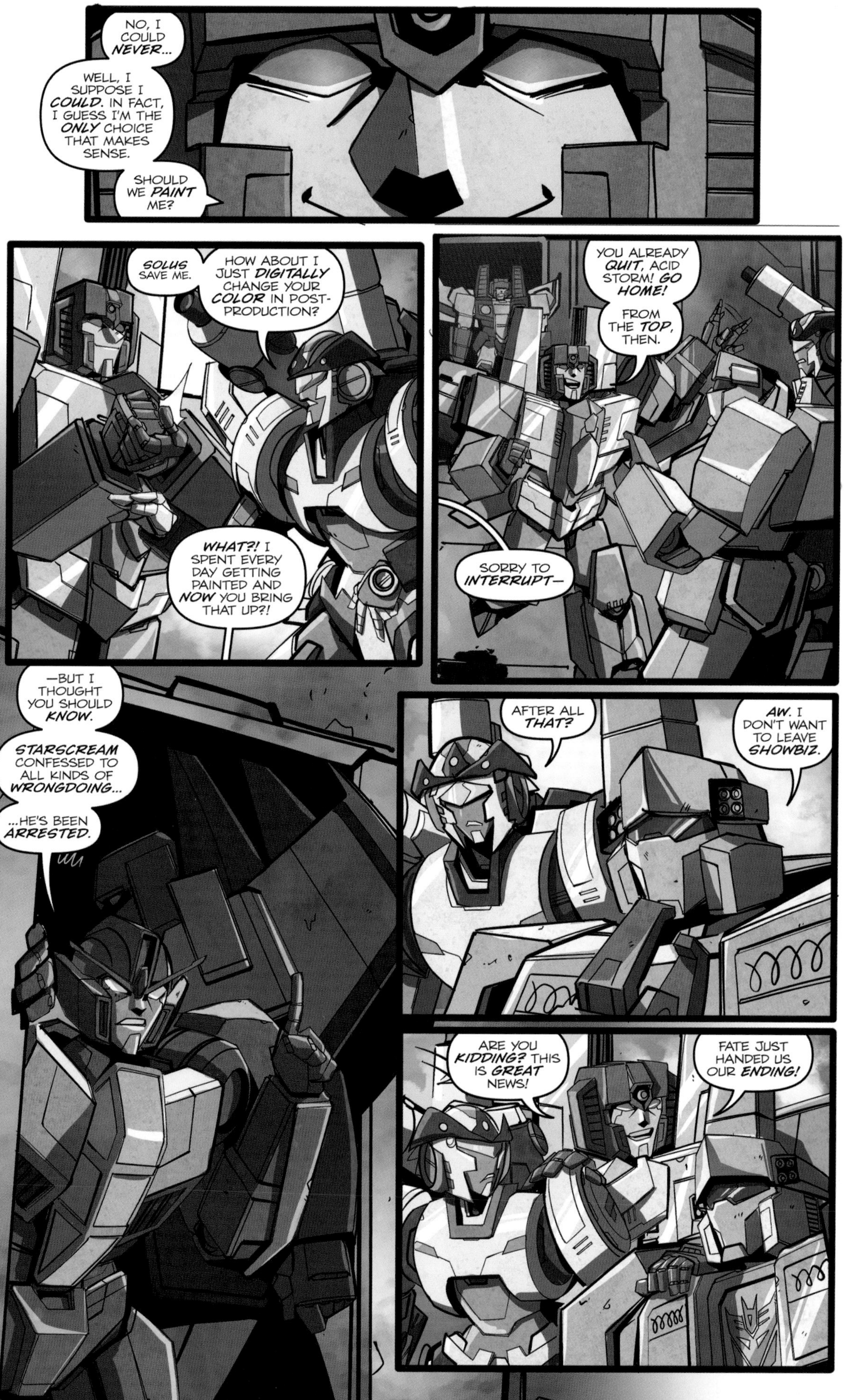
NO, I COULD NEVER...
WELL, I SUPPOSE I COULD. IN FACT, I GUESS I'M THE ONLY CHOICE THAT MAKES SENSE.
SHOULD WE PAINT ME?
SOLUS SAVE ME.
HOW ABOUT I JUST DIGITALLY CHANGE YOUR COLOR IN POST-PRODUCTION?
WHAT?! I SPENT EVERY DAY GETTING PAINTED AND NOW YOU BRING THAT UP?!
YOU ALREADY QUIT, ACID STORM! GO HOME!
FROM THE TOP, THEN.
SORRY TO INTERRUPT—
—BUT I THOUGHT YOU SHOULD KNOW.
STARSCREAM CONFESSED TO ALL KINDS OF WRONGDOING...
...HE'S BEEN ARRESTED.
AFTER ALL THAT?
AW. I DON'T WANT TO LEAVE SHOWBIZ.
ARE YOU KIDDING? THIS IS GREAT NEWS!
FATE JUST HANDED US OUR ENDING!

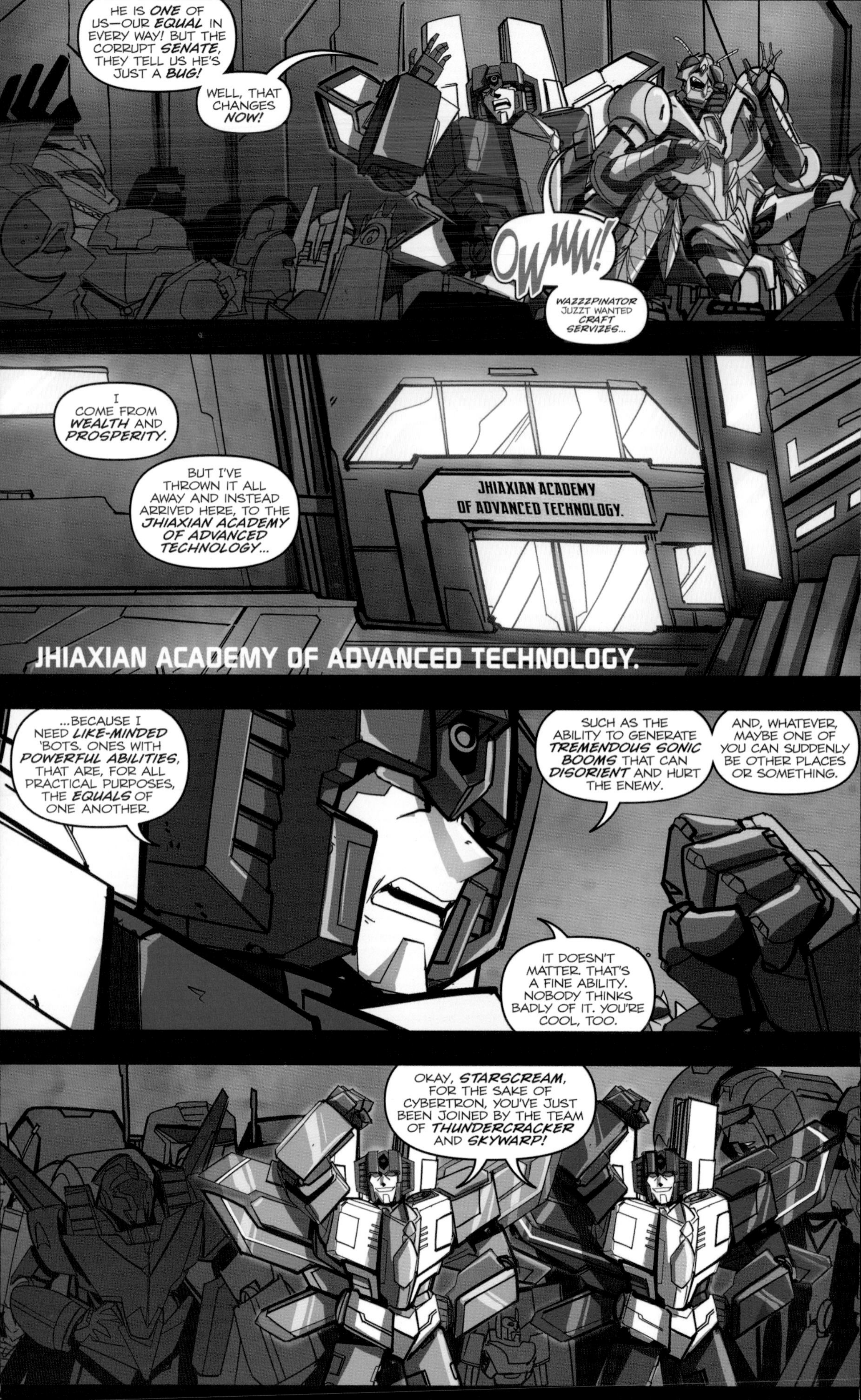

HE IS ONE OF US—OUR EQUAL IN EVERY WAY! BUT THE CORRUPT SENATE, THEY TELL US HE'S JUST A BUG!
WELL, THAT CHANGES NOW!
OWWW!
WAZZZPINATOR JUZZT WANTED CRAFT SERVIZES...
I COME FROM WEALTH AND PROSPERITY.
BUT I'VE THROWN IT ALL AWAY AND INSTEAD ARRIVED HERE, TO THE JHIAXIAN ACADEMY OF ADVANCED TECHNOLOGY...
JHIAXIAN ACADEMY OF ADVANCED TECHNOLOGY.
JHIAXIAN ACADEMY OF ADVANCED TECHNOLOGY.
...BECAUSE I NEED LIKE-MINDED 'BOTS. ONES WITH POWERFUL ABILITIES, THAT ARE, FOR ALL PRACTICAL PURPOSES, THE EQUALS OF ONE ANOTHER.
SUCH AS THE ABILITY TO GENERATE TREMENDOUS SONIC BOOMS THAT CAN DISORIENT AND HURT THE ENEMY.
AND, WHATEVER, MAYBE ONE OF YOU CAN SUDDENLY BE OTHER PLACES OR SOMETHING.
IT DOESN'T MATTER. THAT'S A FINE ABILITY. NOBODY THINKS BADLY OF IT. YOU'RE COOL, TOO.
OKAY, STARSCREAM, FOR THE SAKE OF CYBERTRON, YOU'VE JUST BEEN JOINED BY THE TEAM OF THUNDERCRACKER AND SKYWARP!

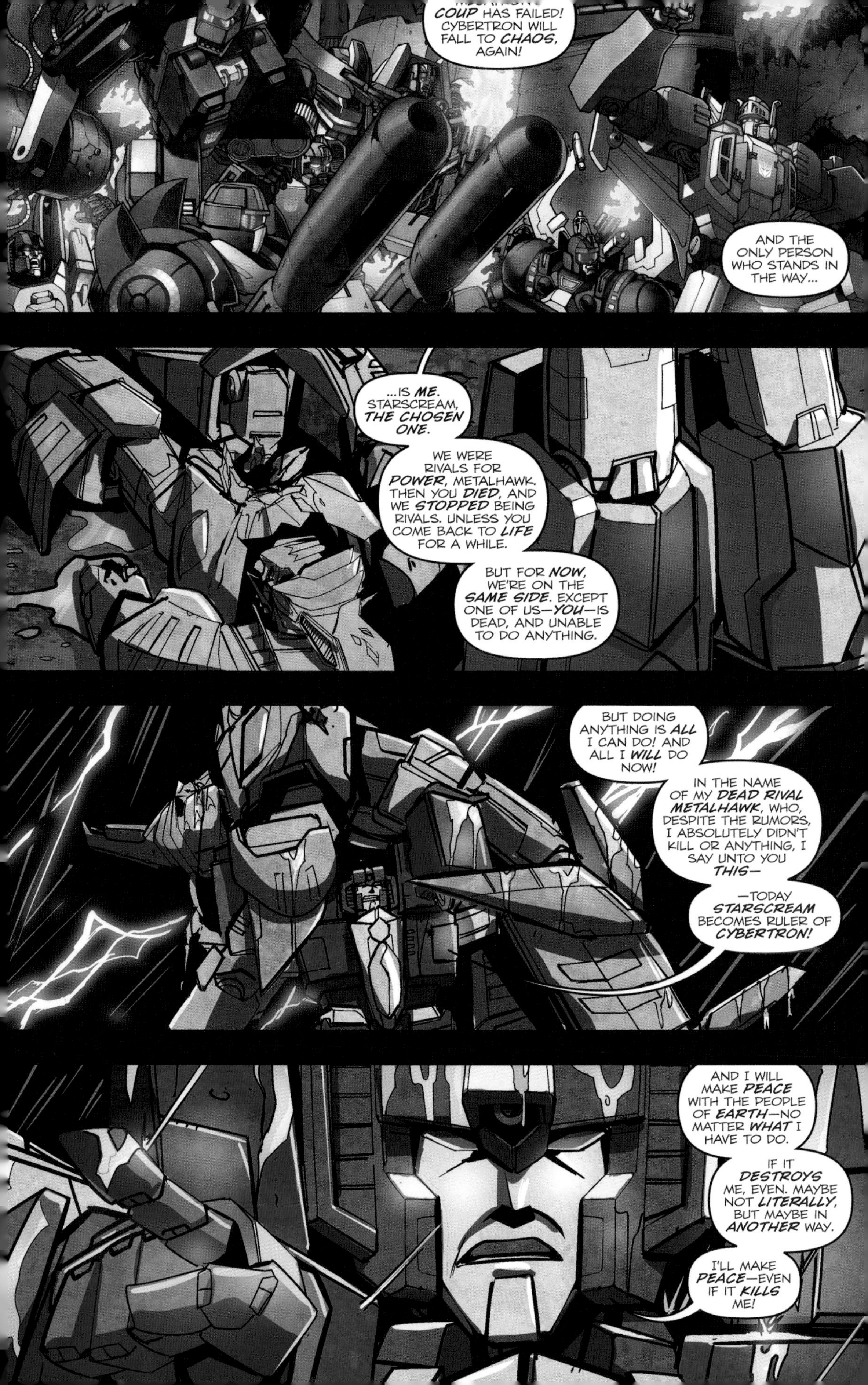
COUP HAS FAILED! CYBERTRON WILL FALL TO CHAOS, AGAIN!
AND THE ONLY PERSON WHO STANDS IN THE WAY...
...IS ME. STARSCREAM, THE CHOSEN ONE.
WE WERE RIVALS FOR POWER, METALHAWK. THEN YOU DIED, AND WE STOPPED BEING RIVALS. UNLESS YOU COME BACK TO LIFE FOR A WHILE.
BUT FOR NOW, WE'RE ON THE SAME SIDE. EXCEPT ONE OF US—YOU—IS DEAD, AND UNABLE TO DO ANYTHING.
BUT DOING ANYTHING IS ALL I CAN DO! AND ALL I WILL DO NOW!
IN THE NAME OF MY DEAD RIVAL METALHAWK, WHO, DESPITE THE RUMORS, I ABSOLUTELY DIDN'T KILL OR ANYTHING, I SAY UNTO YOU THIS—
—TODAY STARSCREAM BECOMES RULER OF CYBERTRON!
AND I WILL MAKE PEACE WITH THE PEOPLE OF EARTH—NO MATTER WHAT I HAVE TO DO.
IF IT DESTROYS ME, EVEN. MAYBE NOT LITERALLY, BUT MAYBE IN ANOTHER WAY.
I'LL MAKE PEACE—EVEN IF IT KILLS ME!

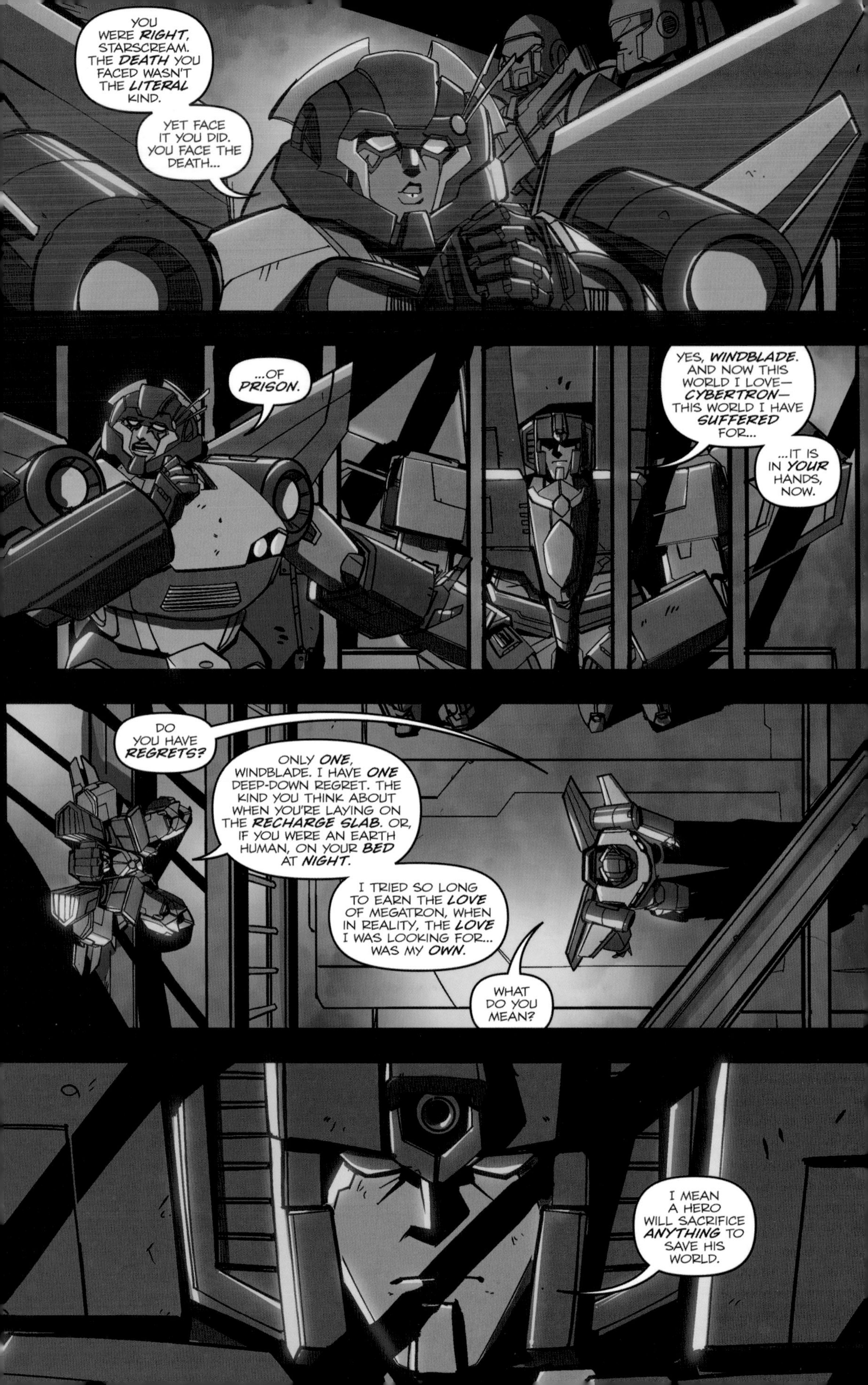
YOU WERE RIGHT, STARSCREAM. THE DEATH YOU FACED WASN'T THE LITERAL KIND.
YET FACE IT YOU DID. YOU FACE THE DEATH...
...OF PRISON.
YES, WINDBLADE. AND NOW THIS WORLD I LOVE— CYBERTRON— THIS WORLD I HAVE SUFFERED FOR...
...IT IS IN YOUR HANDS, NOW.
DO YOU HAVE REGRETS?
ONLY ONE, WINDBLADE. I HAVE ONE DEEP-DOWN REGRET. THE KIND YOU THINK ABOUT WHEN YOU'RE LAYING ON THE RECHARGE SLAB. OR, IF YOU WERE AN EARTH HUMAN, ON YOUR BED AT NIGHT.
I TRIED SO LONG TO EARN THE LOVE OF MEGATRON, WHEN IN REALITY, THE LOVE I WAS LOOKING FOR... WAS MY OWN.
WHAT DO YOU MEAN?
I MEAN A HERO WILL SACRIFICE ANYTHING TO SAVE HIS WORLD.

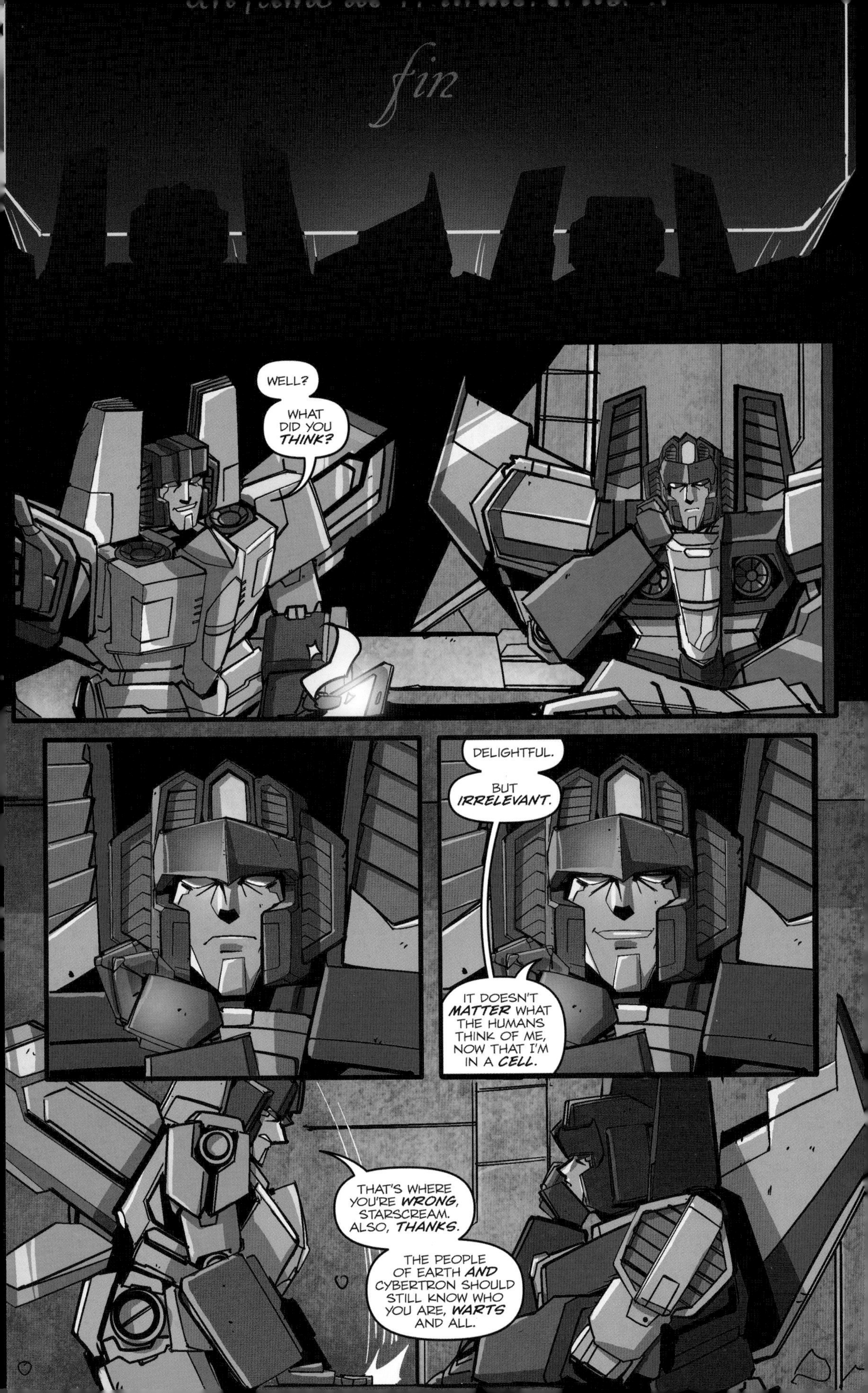
fin
WELL?
WHAT DID YOU THINK?
DELIGHTFUL.
BUT IRRELEVANT.
IT DOESN'T MATTER WHAT THE HUMANS THINK OF ME, NOW THAT I'M IN A CELL.
THAT'S WHERE YOU'RE WRONG, STARSCREAM. ALSO, THANKS.
THE PEOPLE OF EARTH AND CYBERTRON SHOULD STILL KNOW WHO YOU ARE, WARTS AND ALL.

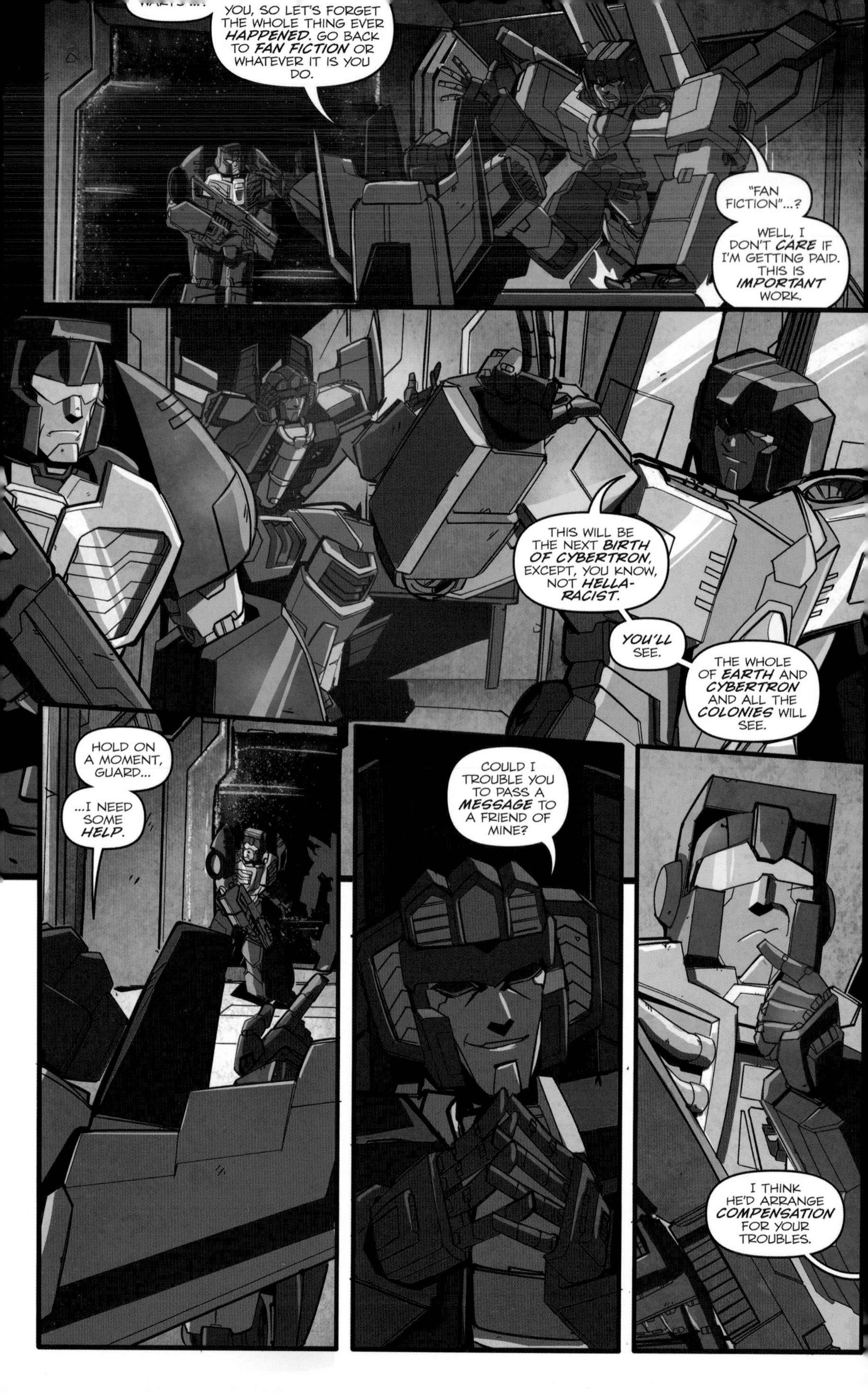

YOU, SO LET'S FORGET THE WHOLE THING EVER HAPPENED. GO BACK TO FAN FICTION OR WHATEVER IT IS YOU DO.
"FAN FICTION"...?
WELL, I DON'T CARE IF I'M GETTING PAID. THIS IS IMPORTANT WORK.
THIS WILL BE THE NEXT BIRTH OF CYBERTRON, EXCEPT, YOU KNOW, NOT HELLA-RACIST.
YOU'LL SEE.
THE WHOLE OF EARTH AND CYBERTRON AND ALL THE COLONIES WILL SEE.
HOLD ON A MOMENT, GUARD...
...I NEED SOME HELP.
COULD I TROUBLE YOU TO PASS A MESSAGE TO A FRIEND OF MINE?
I THINK HE'D ARRANGE COMPENSATION FOR YOUR TROUBLES.

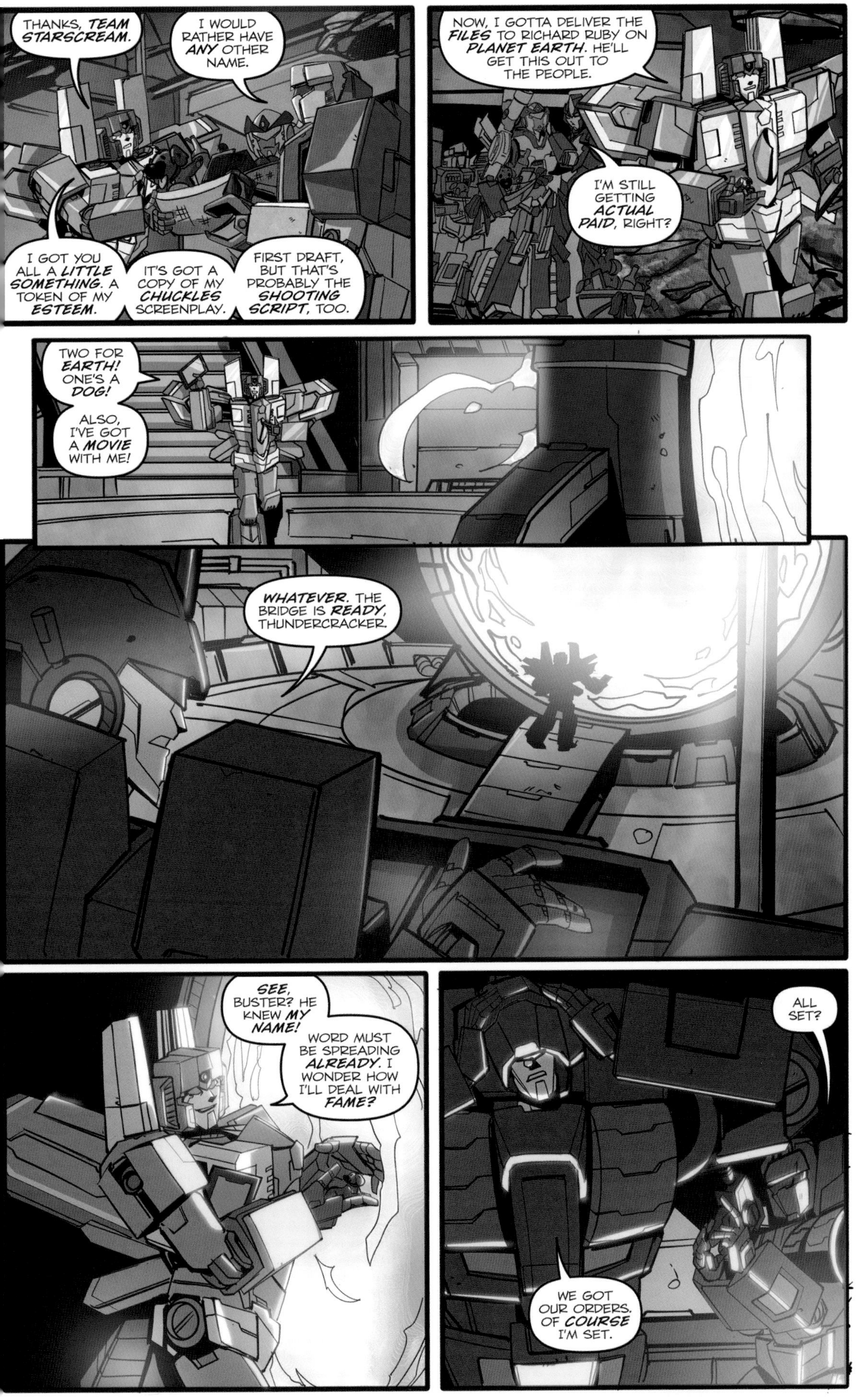
THANKS, TEAM STARSCREAM.
I WOULD RATHER HAVE ANY OTHER NAME.
I GOT YOU ALL A LITTLE SOMETHING. A TOKEN OF MY ESTEEM.
IT'S GOT A COPY OF MY CHUCKLES SCREENPLAY.
FIRST DRAFT, BUT THAT'S PROBABLY THE SHOOTING SCRIPT, TOO.
NOW, I GOTTA DELIVER THE FILES TO RICHARD RUBY ON PLANET EARTH. HE'LL GET THIS OUT TO THE PEOPLE.
I'M STILL GETTING ACTUAL PAID, RIGHT?
TWO FOR EARTH! ONE'S A DOG!
ALSO, I'VE GOT A MOVIE WITH ME!
WHATEVER. THE BRIDGE IS READY, THUNDERCRACKER.
SEE, BUSTER? HE KNEW MY NAME!
WORD MUST BE SPREADING ALREADY. I WONDER HOW I'LL DEAL WITH FAME?
ALL SET?
WE GOT OUR ORDERS. OF COURSE I'M SET.

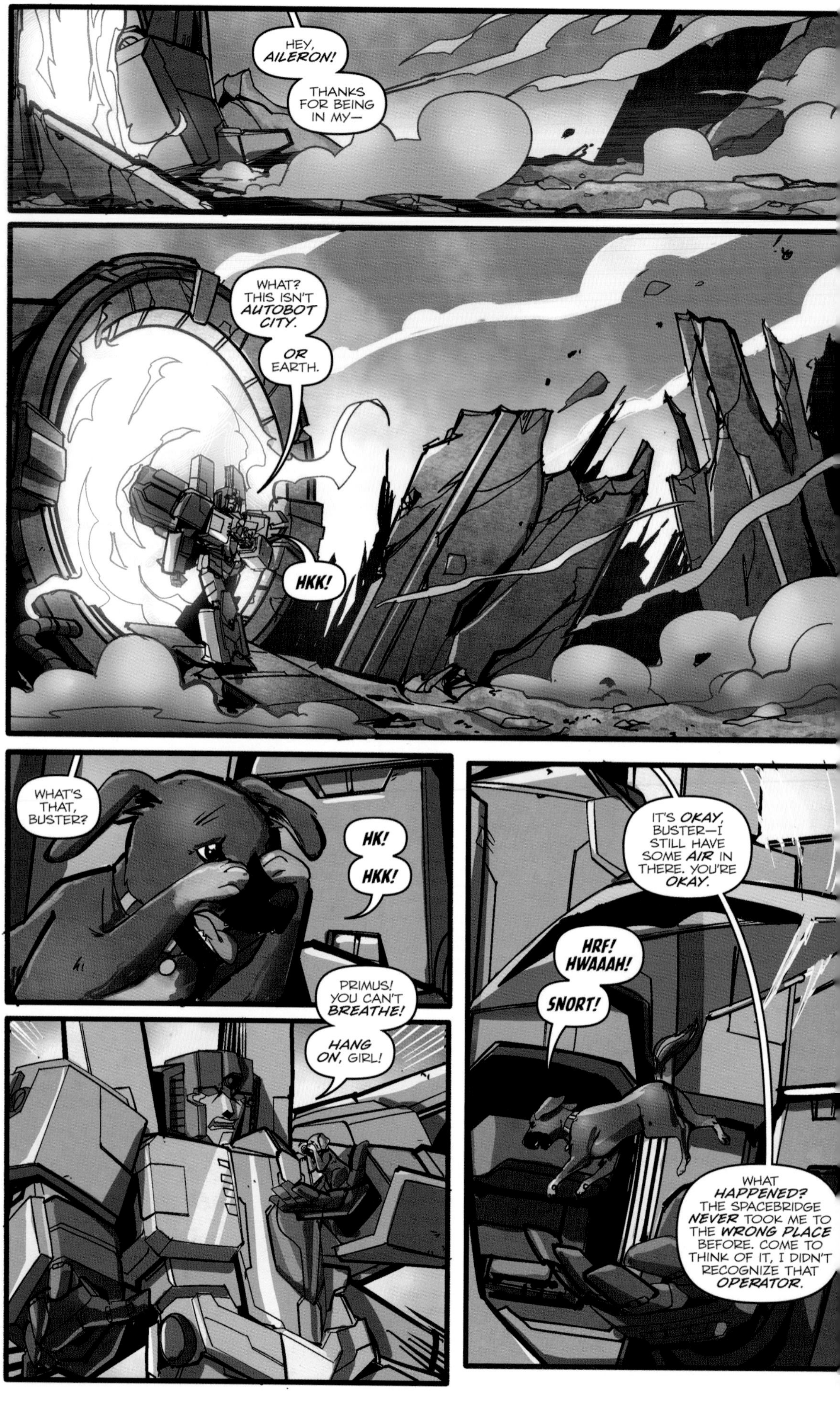
HEY, AILERON!
THANKS FOR BEING IN MY—
WHAT? THIS ISN'T AUTOBOT CITY.
OR EARTH.
HKK!
WHAT'S THAT, BUSTER?
HK!
HKK!
PRIMUS! YOU CAN'T BREATHE!
HANG ON, GIRL!
IT'S OKAY, BUSTER—I STILL HAVE SOME AIR IN THERE. YOU'RE OKAY.
HRF! HWAAAH!
SNORT!
WHAT HAPPENED? THE SPACEBRIDGE NEVER TOOK ME TO THE WRONG PLACE BEFORE. COME TO THINK OF IT, I DIDN'T RECOGNIZE THAT OPERATOR.

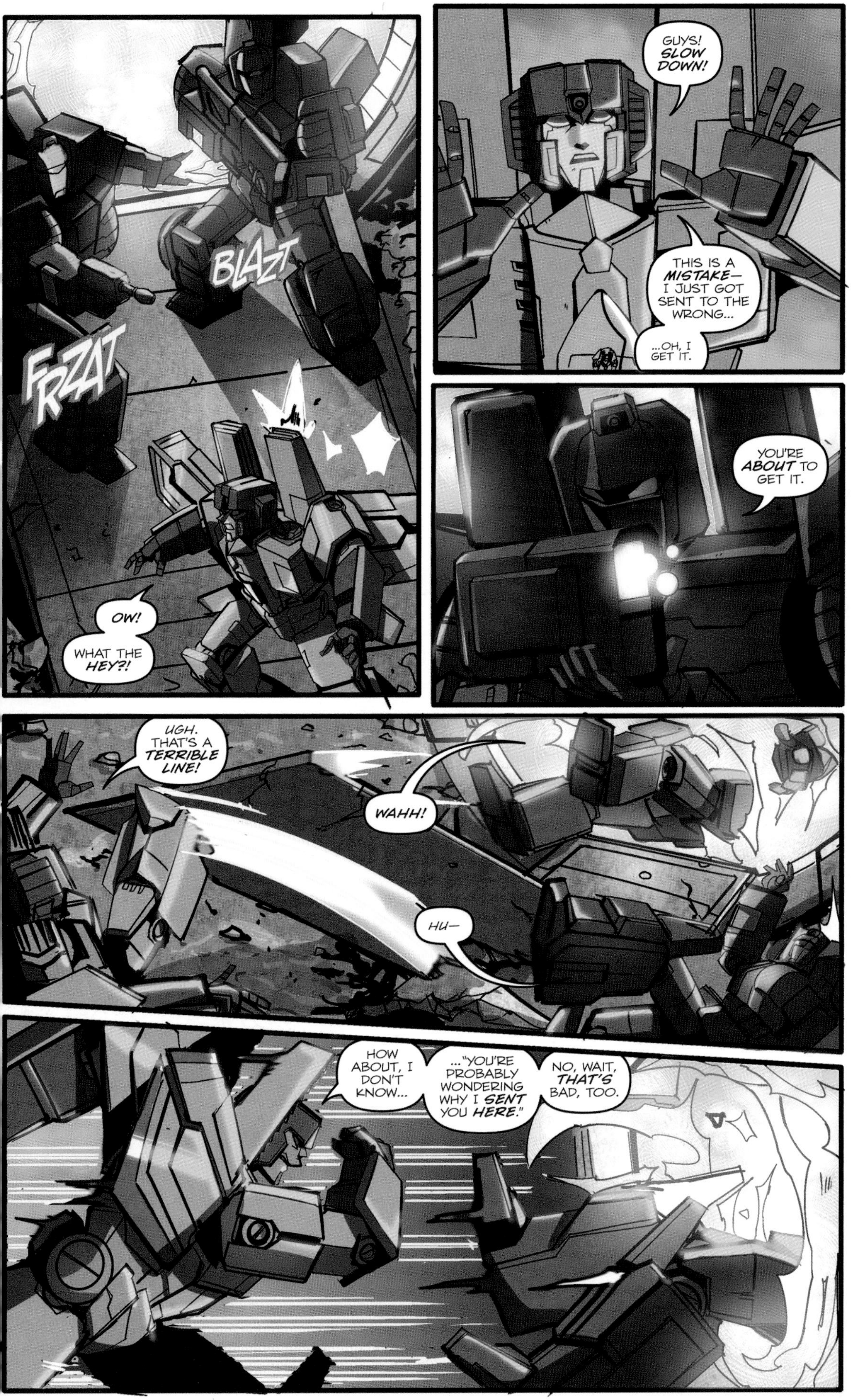
BLAZT
FRZZAT
OW!
WHAT THE HEY?!
GUYS! SLOW DOWN!
THIS IS A MISTAKE— I JUST GOT SENT TO THE WRONG...
...OH, I GET IT.
YOU'RE ABOUT TO GET IT.
UGH. THAT'S A TERRIBLE LINE!
WAHH!
HU—
HOW ABOUT, I DON'T KNOW...
..."YOU'RE PROBABLY WONDERING WHY I SENT YOU HERE."
NO, WAIT, THAT'S BAD, TOO.

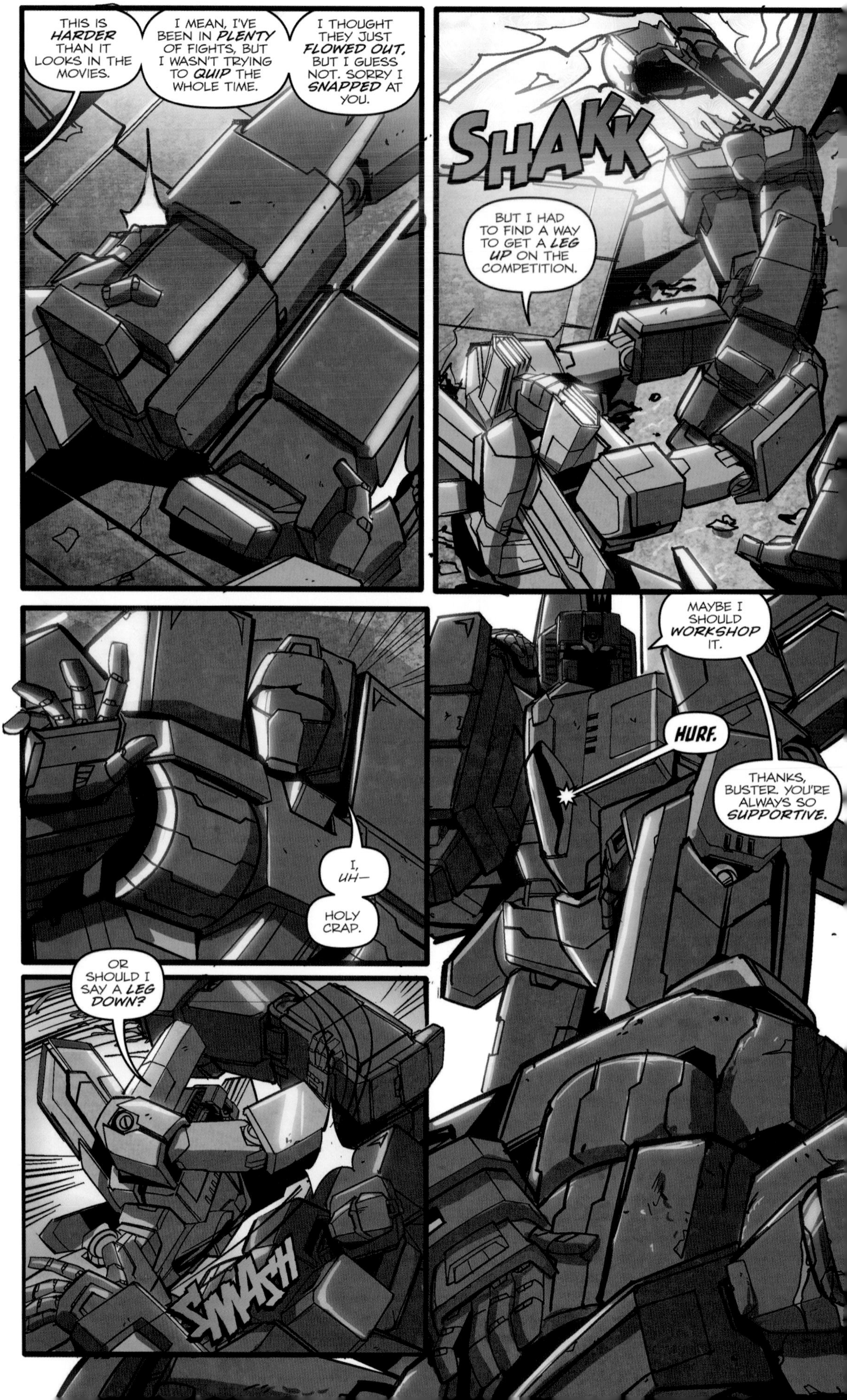

THIS IS HARDER THAN IT LOOKS IN THE MOVIES.
I MEAN, I'VE BEEN IN PLENTY OF FIGHTS, BUT I WASN'T TRYING TO QUIP THE WHOLE TIME.
I THOUGHT THEY JUST FLOWED OUT, BUT I GUESS NOT. SORRY I SNAPPED AT YOU.
SHAKK
BUT I HAD TO FIND A WAY TO GET A LEG UP ON THE COMPETITION.
I, UH—
HOLY CRAP.
OR SHOULD I SAY A LEG DOWN?
SMASH
MAYBE I SHOULD WORKSHOP IT.
HURF.
THANKS, BUSTER. YOU'RE ALWAYS SO SUPPORTIVE.

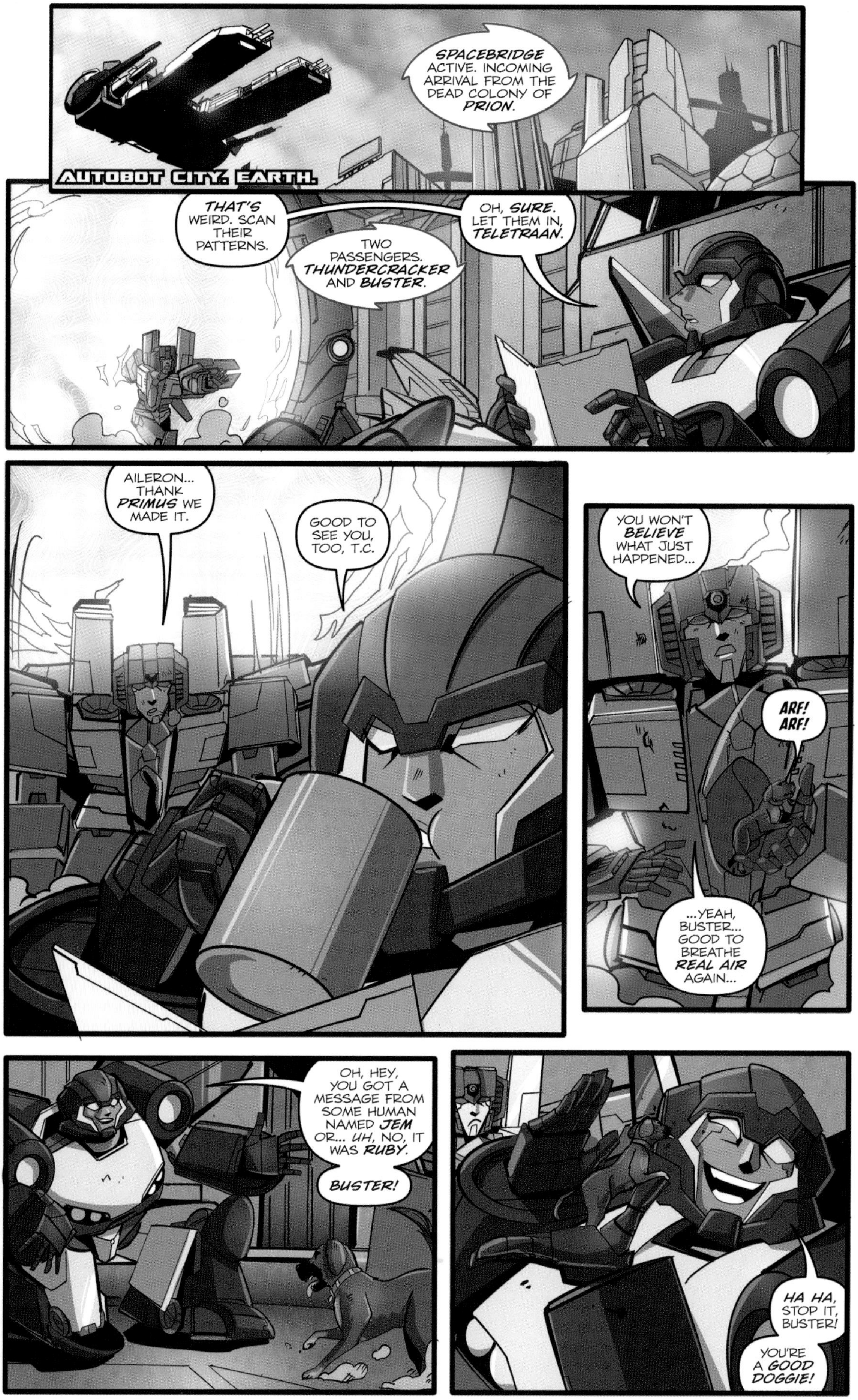
AUTOBOT CITY. EARTH.
SPACEBRIDGE ACTIVE. INCOMING ARRIVAL FROM THE DEAD COLONY OF PRION.
THAT'S WEIRD. SCAN THEIR PATTERNS.
TWO PASSENGERS. THUNDERCRACKER AND BUSTER.
OH, SURE. LET THEM IN, TELETRAAN.
AILERON... THANK PRIMUS WE MADE IT.
GOOD TO SEE YOU, TOO, T.C.
YOU WON'T BELIEVE WHAT JUST HAPPENED...
ARF! ARF!
...YEAH, BUSTER... GOOD TO BREATHE REAL AIR AGAIN...
OH, HEY, YOU GOT A MESSAGE FROM SOME HUMAN NAMED JEM OR... UH, NO, IT WAS RUBY.
BUSTER!
HA HA, STOP IT, BUSTER!
YOU'RE A GOOD DOGGIE!

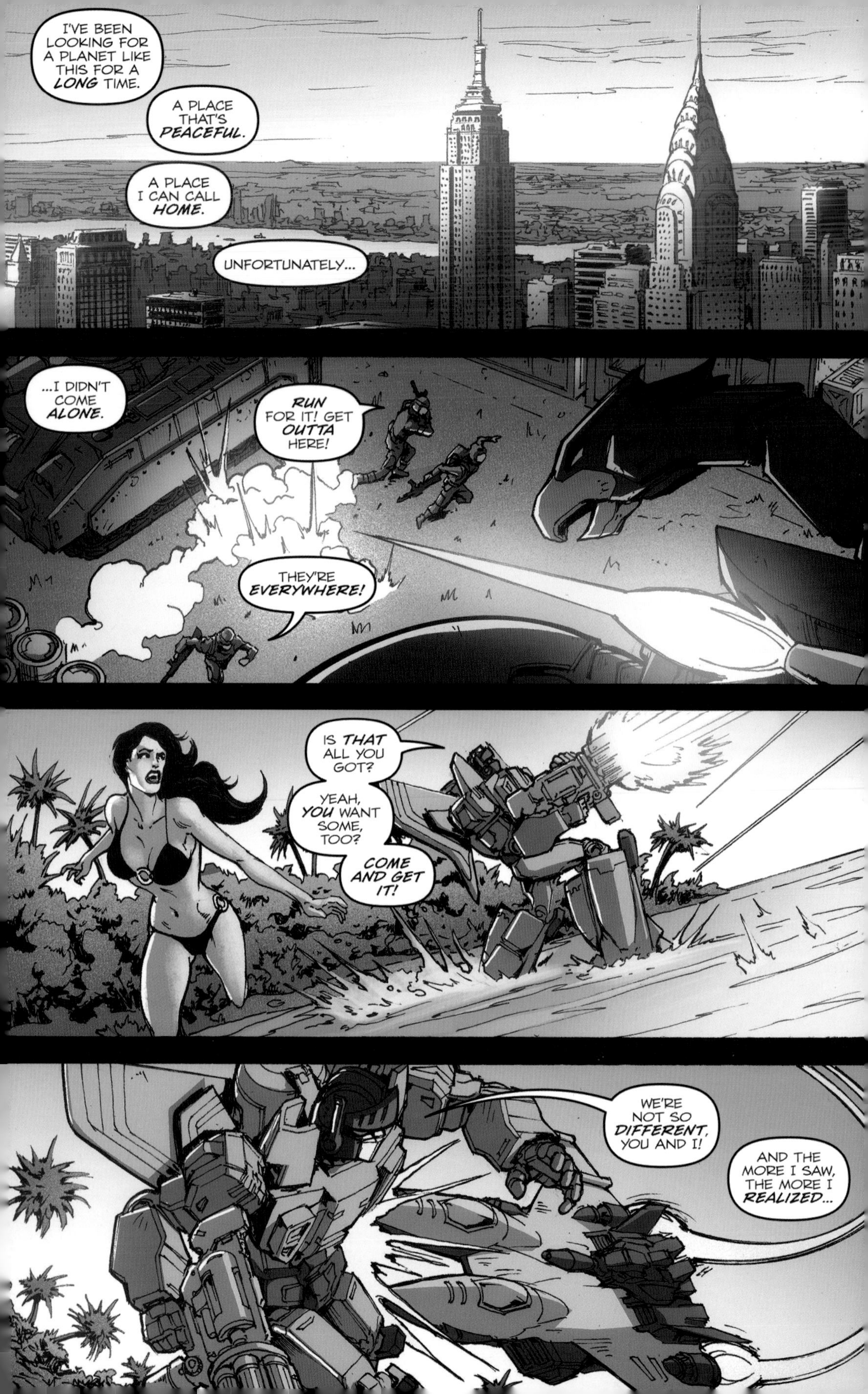
I'VE BEEN LOOKING FOR A PLANET LIKE THIS FOR A LONG TIME.
A PLACE THAT'S PEACEFUL.
A PLACE I CAN CALL HOME.
UNFORTUNATELY...
...I DIDN'T COME ALONE.
RUN FOR IT! GET OUTTA HERE!
THEY'RE EVERYWHERE!
IS THAT ALL YOU GOT?
YEAH, YOU WANT SOME, TOO?
COME AND GET IT!
WE'RE NOT SO DIFFERENT, YOU AND I!
AND THE MORE I SAW, THE MORE I REALIZED...

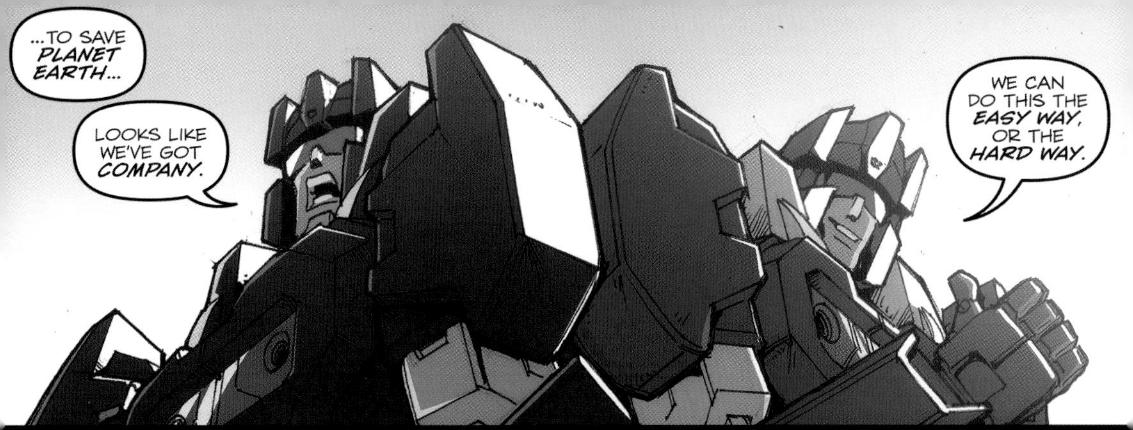
...TO SAVE PLANET EARTH...
LOOKS LIKE WE'VE GOT COMPANY.
WE CAN DO THIS THE EASY WAY, OR THE HARD WAY.

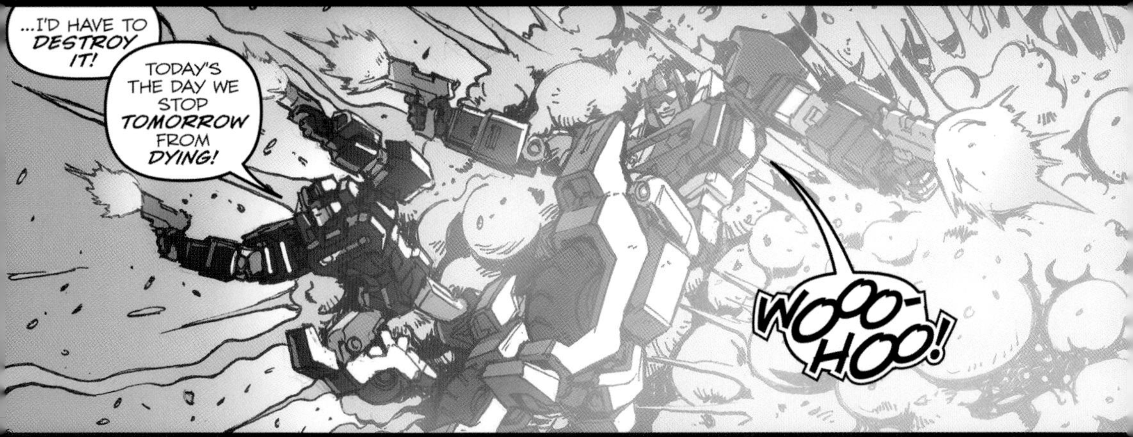
...I'D HAVE TO DESTROY IT!
TODAY'S THE DAY WE STOP TOMORROW FROM DYING!
WOOO-HOO!

RUMBLE & FRENZY ARE:

DARK INVASION

A TAPE BROS FILM

JUNE 23

METAL GETS HEAVY

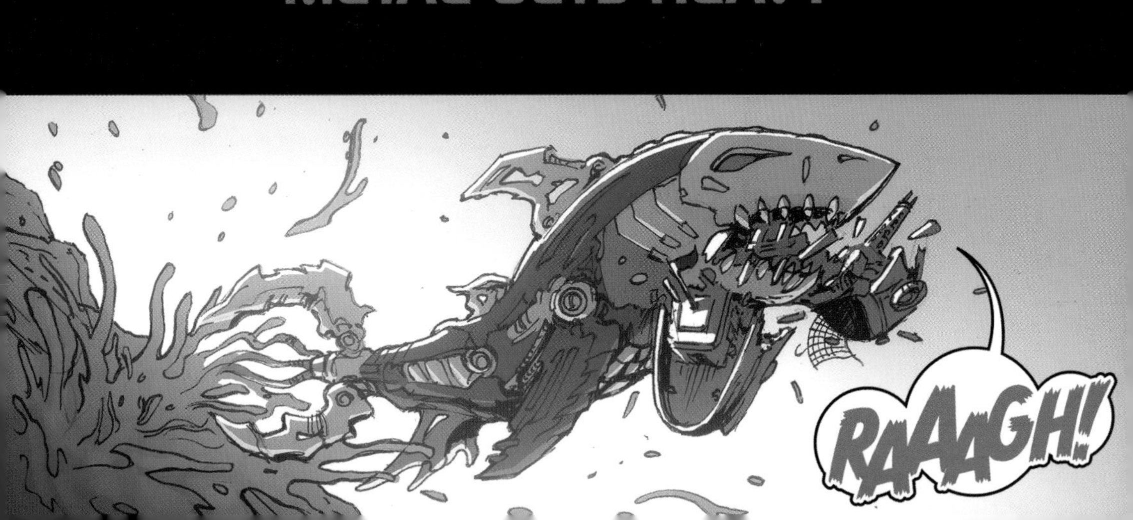
RAAAGH!

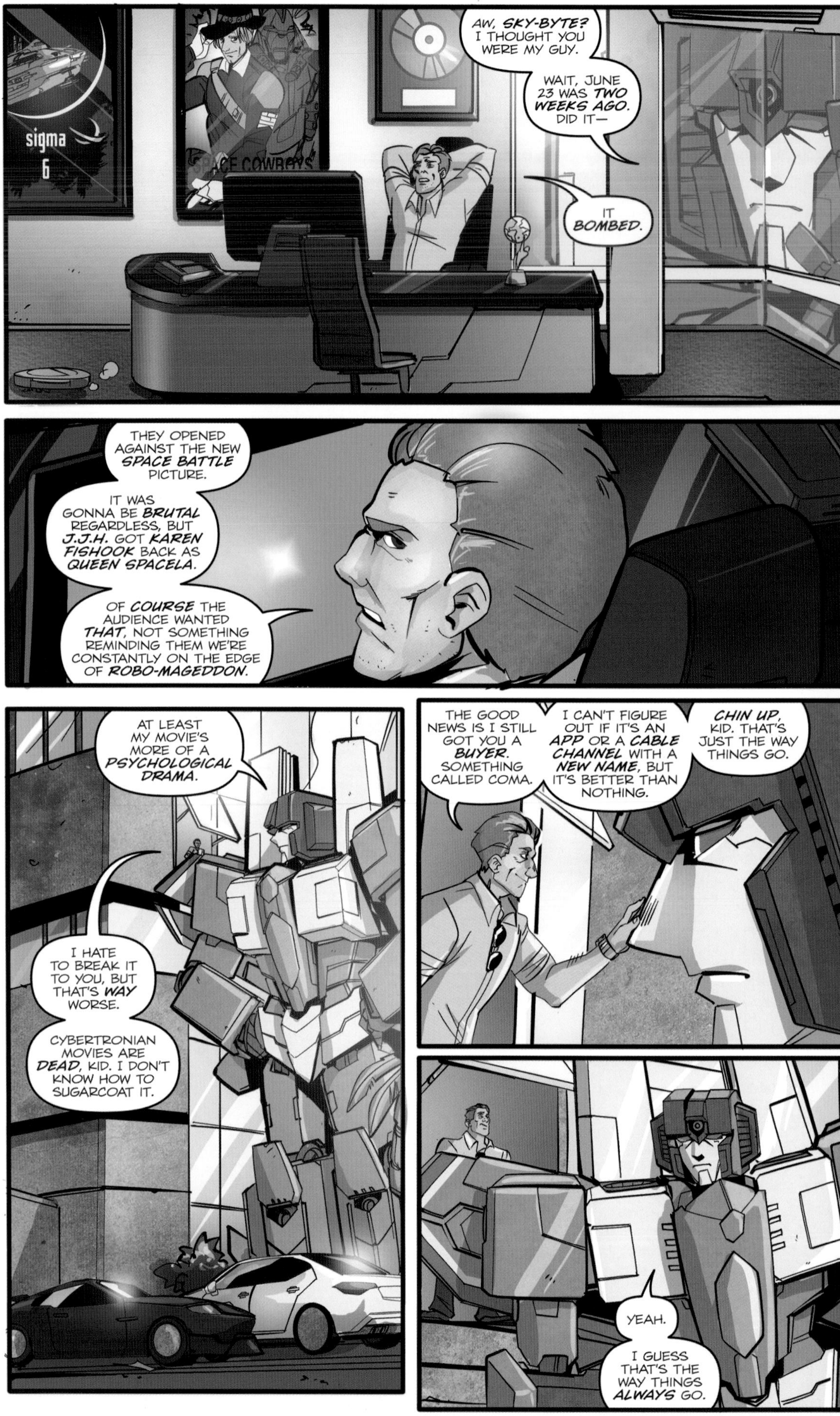

AW, SKY-BYTE? I THOUGHT YOU WERE MY GUY.
WAIT, JUNE 23 WAS TWO WEEKS AGO. DID IT—
IT BOMBED.
sigma 6
SPACE COWBOYS
THEY OPENED AGAINST THE NEW SPACE BATTLE PICTURE.
IT WAS GONNA BE BRUTAL REGARDLESS, BUT J.J.H. GOT KAREN FISHOOK BACK AS QUEEN SPACELA.
OF COURSE THE AUDIENCE WANTED THAT, NOT SOMETHING REMINDING THEM WE'RE CONSTANTLY ON THE EDGE OF ROBO-MAGEDDON.
AT LEAST MY MOVIE'S MORE OF A PSYCHOLOGICAL DRAMA.
I HATE TO BREAK IT TO YOU, BUT THAT'S WAY WORSE.
CYBERTRONIAN MOVIES ARE DEAD, KID. I DON'T KNOW HOW TO SUGARCOAT IT.
THE GOOD NEWS IS I STILL GOT YOU A BUYER. SOMETHING CALLED COMA.
I CAN'T FIGURE OUT IF IT'S AN APP OR A CABLE CHANNEL WITH A NEW NAME, BUT IT'S BETTER THAN NOTHING.
CHIN UP, KID. THAT'S JUST THE WAY THINGS GO.
YEAH.
I GUESS THAT'S THE WAY THINGS ALWAYS GO.

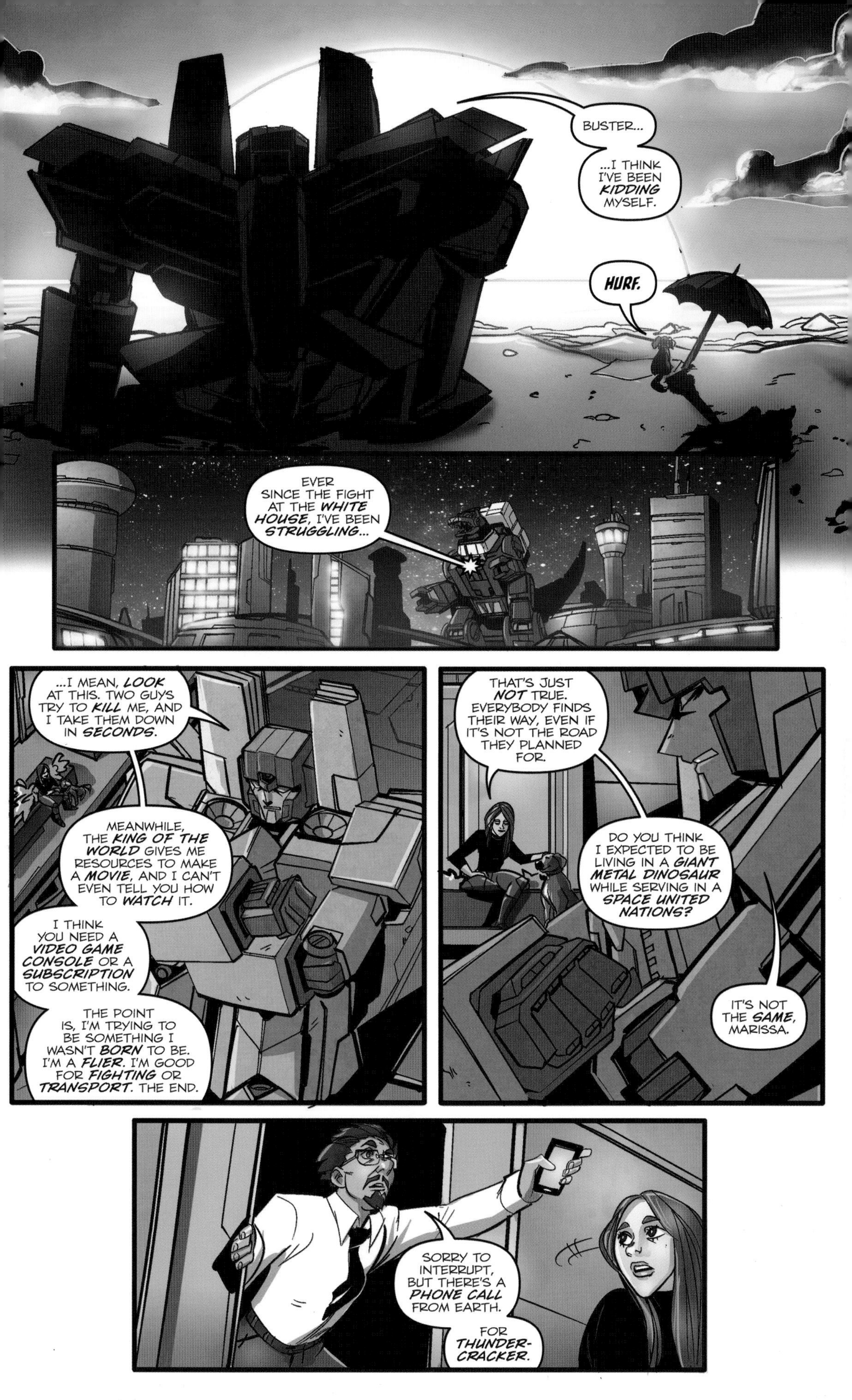
BUSTER...
...I THINK I'VE BEEN KIDDING MYSELF.
HURF.
EVER SINCE THE FIGHT AT THE WHITE HOUSE, I'VE BEEN STRUGGLING...
...I MEAN, LOOK AT THIS. TWO GUYS TRY TO KILL ME, AND I TAKE THEM DOWN IN SECONDS.
MEANWHILE, THE KING OF THE WORLD GIVES ME RESOURCES TO MAKE A MOVIE, AND I CAN'T EVEN TELL YOU HOW TO WATCH IT.
I THINK YOU NEED A VIDEO GAME CONSOLE OR A SUBSCRIPTION TO SOMETHING.
THE POINT IS, I'M TRYING TO BE SOMETHING I WASN'T BORN TO BE. I'M A FLIER. I'M GOOD FOR FIGHTING OR TRANSPORT. THE END.
THAT'S JUST NOT TRUE. EVERYBODY FINDS THEIR WAY, EVEN IF IT'S NOT THE ROAD THEY PLANNED FOR.
DO YOU THINK I EXPECTED TO BE LIVING IN A GIANT METAL DINOSAUR WHILE SERVING IN A SPACE UNITED NATIONS?
IT'S NOT THE SAME, MARISSA.
SORRY TO INTERRUPT, BUT THERE'S A PHONE CALL FROM EARTH.
FOR THUNDER-CRACKER.

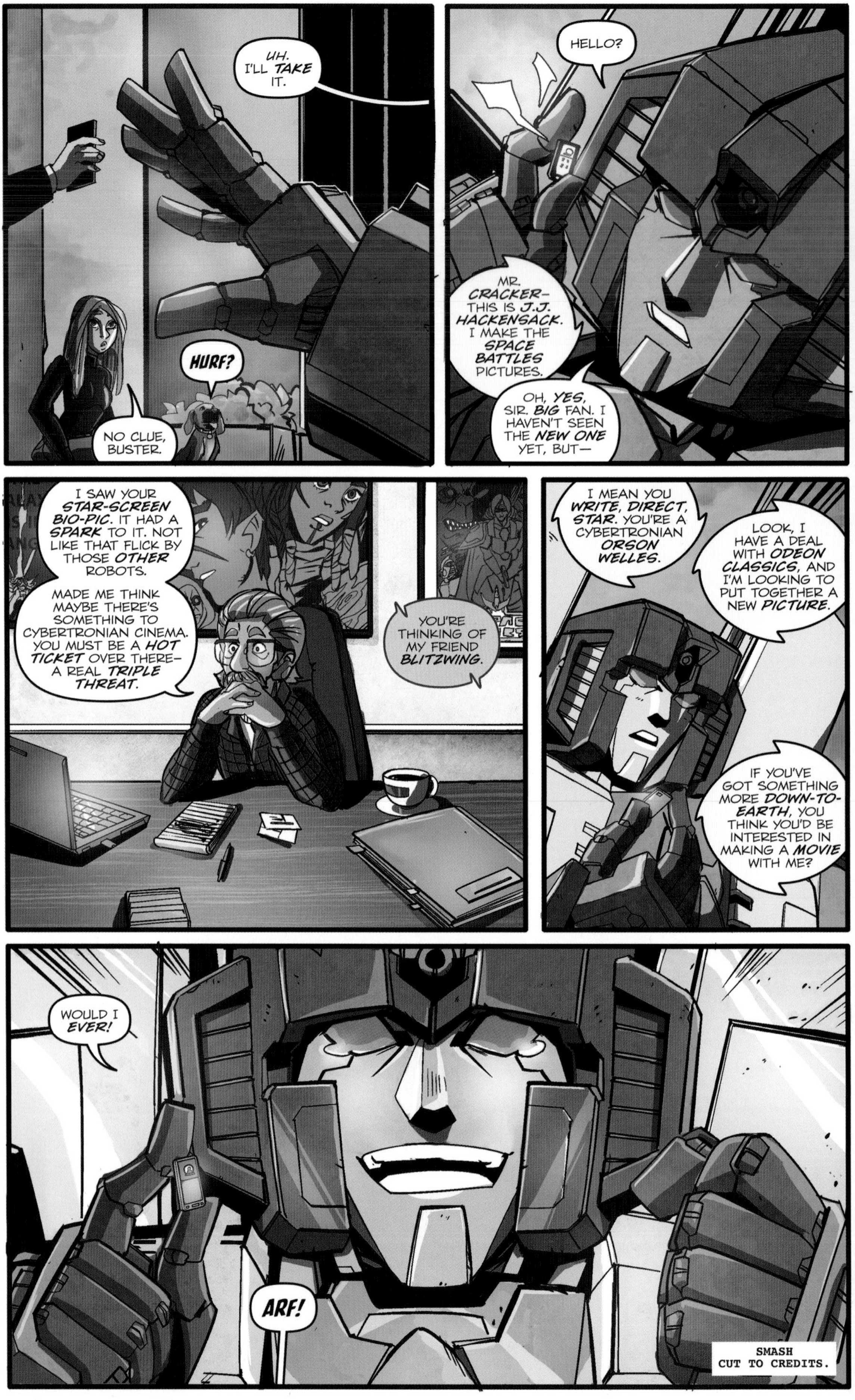
UH. I'LL TAKE IT.
HURF?
NO CLUE, BUSTER.
HELLO?
MR. CRACKER- THIS IS J.J. HACKENSACK. I MAKE THE SPACE BATTLES PICTURES.
OH, YES, SIR. BIG FAN. I HAVEN'T SEEN THE NEW ONE YET, BUT—
I SAW YOUR STAR-SCREEN BIO-PIC. IT HAD A SPARK TO IT. NOT LIKE THAT FLICK BY THOSE OTHER ROBOTS.
MADE ME THINK MAYBE THERE'S SOMETHING TO CYBERTRONIAN CINEMA. YOU MUST BE A HOT TICKET OVER THERE- A REAL TRIPLE THREAT.
YOU'RE THINKING OF MY FRIEND BLITZWING.
I MEAN YOU WRITE, DIRECT, STAR. YOU'RE A CYBERTRONIAN ORSON WELLES.
LOOK, I HAVE A DEAL WITH ODEON CLASSICS, AND I'M LOOKING TO PUT TOGETHER A NEW PICTURE.
IF YOU'VE GOT SOMETHING MORE DOWN-TO-EARTH, YOU THINK YOU'D BE INTERESTED IN MAKING A MOVIE WITH ME?
WOULD I EVER!
ARF!
SMASH CUT TO CREDITS.

WRITTEN & DIRECTED BY
THUNDERCRACKER

PRODUCER...STARSCREAM

CINEMATOGRAPHY...PROXIMA
COSTUMES...TANKOR
LIGHTING...FLASH BANG
PRODUCTION DESIGN...SEASPRAY

STARRING:
STARSCREAM...THUNDERCRACKER
SKYWARP...THUNDERCRACKER
HIMSELF...THUNDERCRACKER
MEGATRON...TANKOR
RODIMUS...FLAMEWAR
BUG...WASPINATOR
METALHAWK...SKY-BYTE
WINDBLADE...AILERON

SPECIAL THANKS TO: BUSTER, MARISSA FAIREBORN,
RASHID NASIR, RICHARD RUBY, STARSCREAM,
SKYWARP, DIRGE, ANDREW GRIFFITH, MIKE COSTA,
ANTONIO FUSO, ROBERT ATKINS, JAMES ROBERTS,
ALEX MILNE, MAIRGHREAD SCOTT,
SARA PITRE-DUROCHER, SHANE MCCARTHY,
GUIDO GUIDI, AUBREY SITTERSON,
GIANNIS MILONOGIANNIS, ZANDER CANNON,
CHEE, ERIC HOLMES, NICK ROCHE, DON FIGUEROA, LIVIO
RAMONDELLI, FRED VAN LENTE, JAMAL IGLE, BRENDAN
CAHILL, KEI ZAMA, ANDY SCHMIDT,
AND MICHAEL KELLY.

NO HUMANS WERE HARMED IN THE
MAKING OF THIS FILM.

STARSCREAM **WILL** RETURN!

ART BY KEI ZAMA COLORS BY JOSH BURCHAM

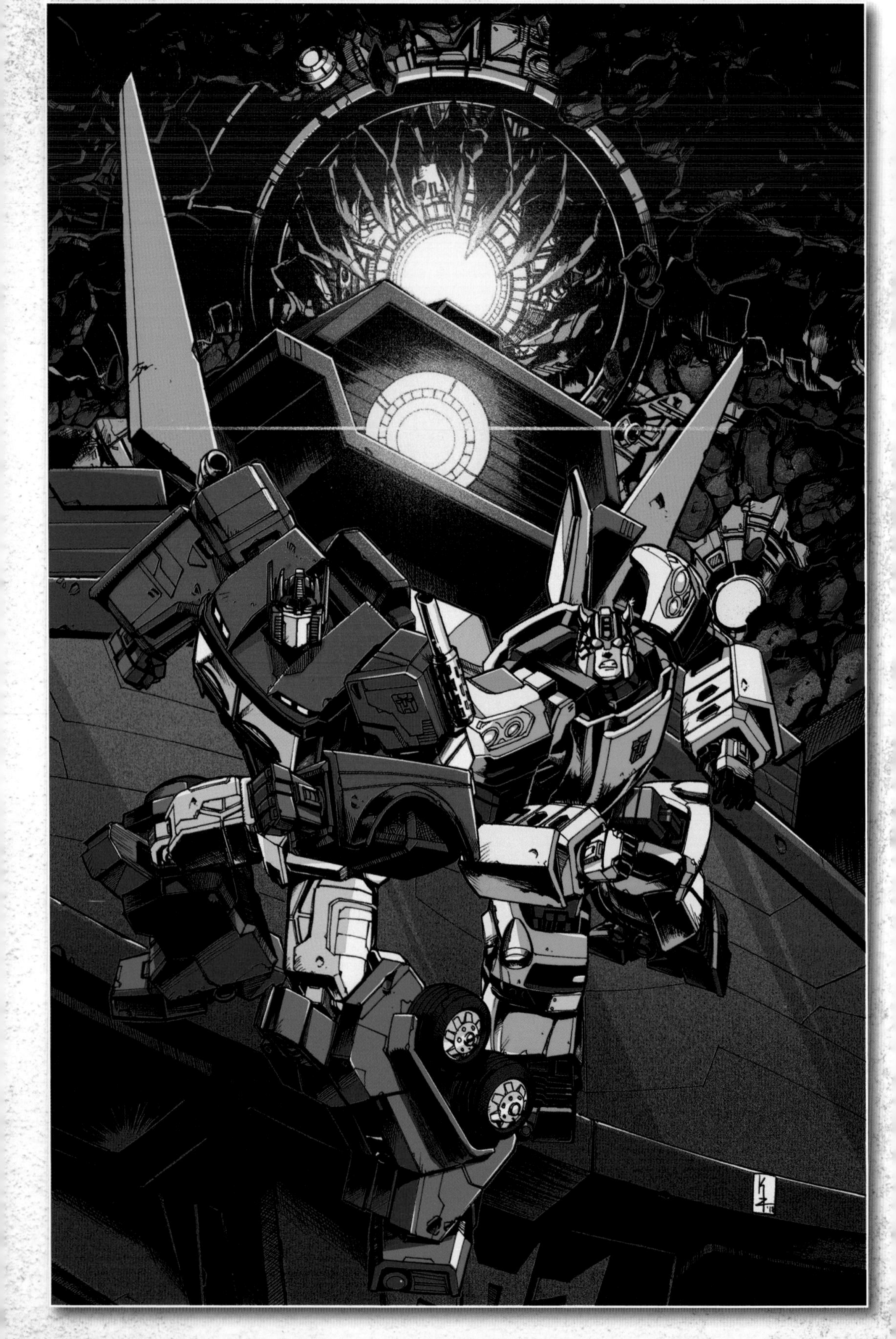

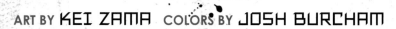

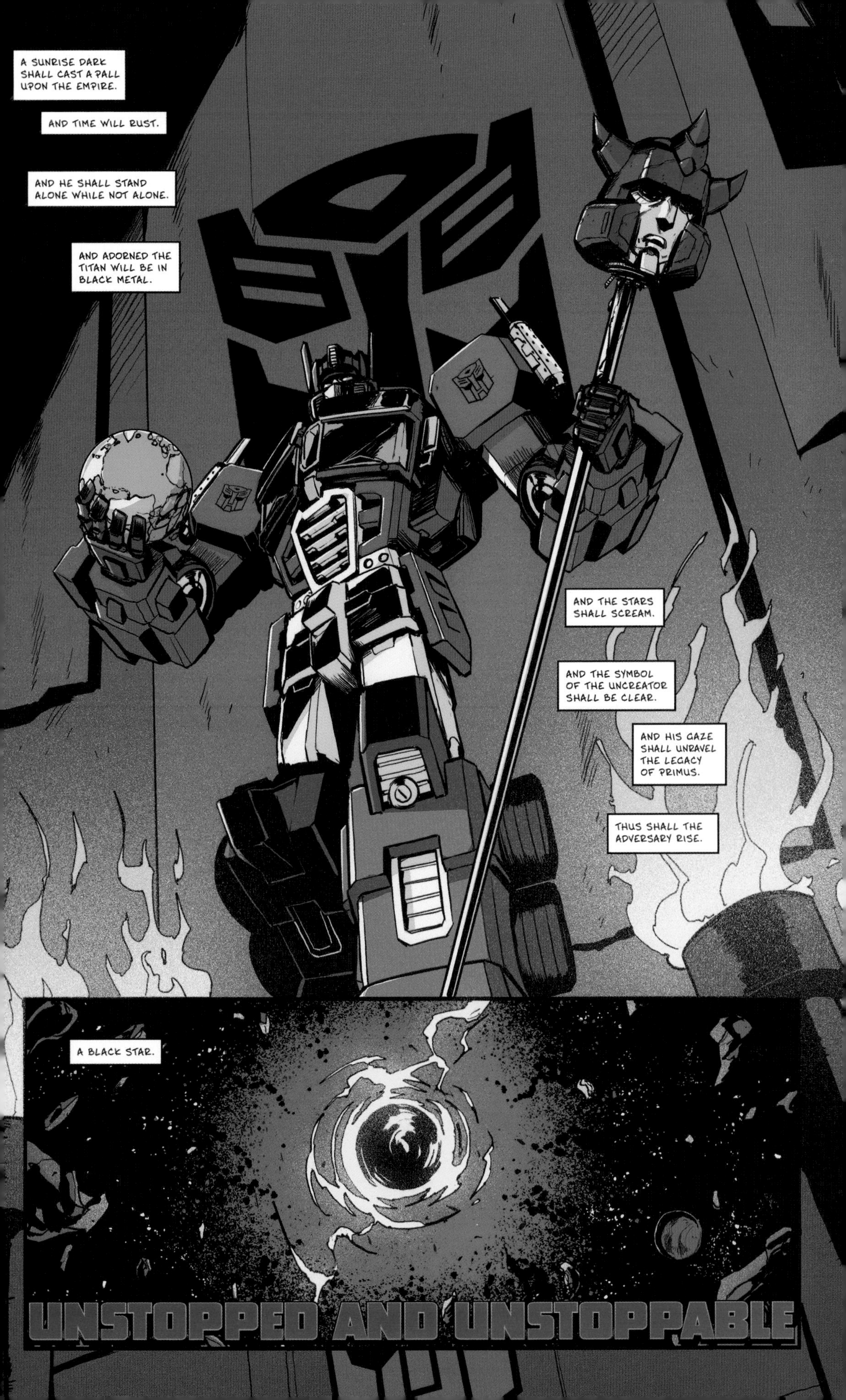

A SUNRISE DARK SHALL CAST A PALL UPON THE EMPIRE.
AND TIME WILL RUST.
AND HE SHALL STAND ALONE WHILE NOT ALONE.
AND ADORNED THE TITAN WILL BE IN BLACK METAL.
AND THE STARS SHALL SCREAM.
AND THE SYMBOL OF THE UNCREATOR SHALL BE CLEAR.
AND HIS GAZE SHALL UNRAVEL THE LEGACY OF PRIMUS.
THUS SHALL THE ADVERSARY RISE.
A BLACK STAR.
UNSTOPPED AND UNSTOPPABLE

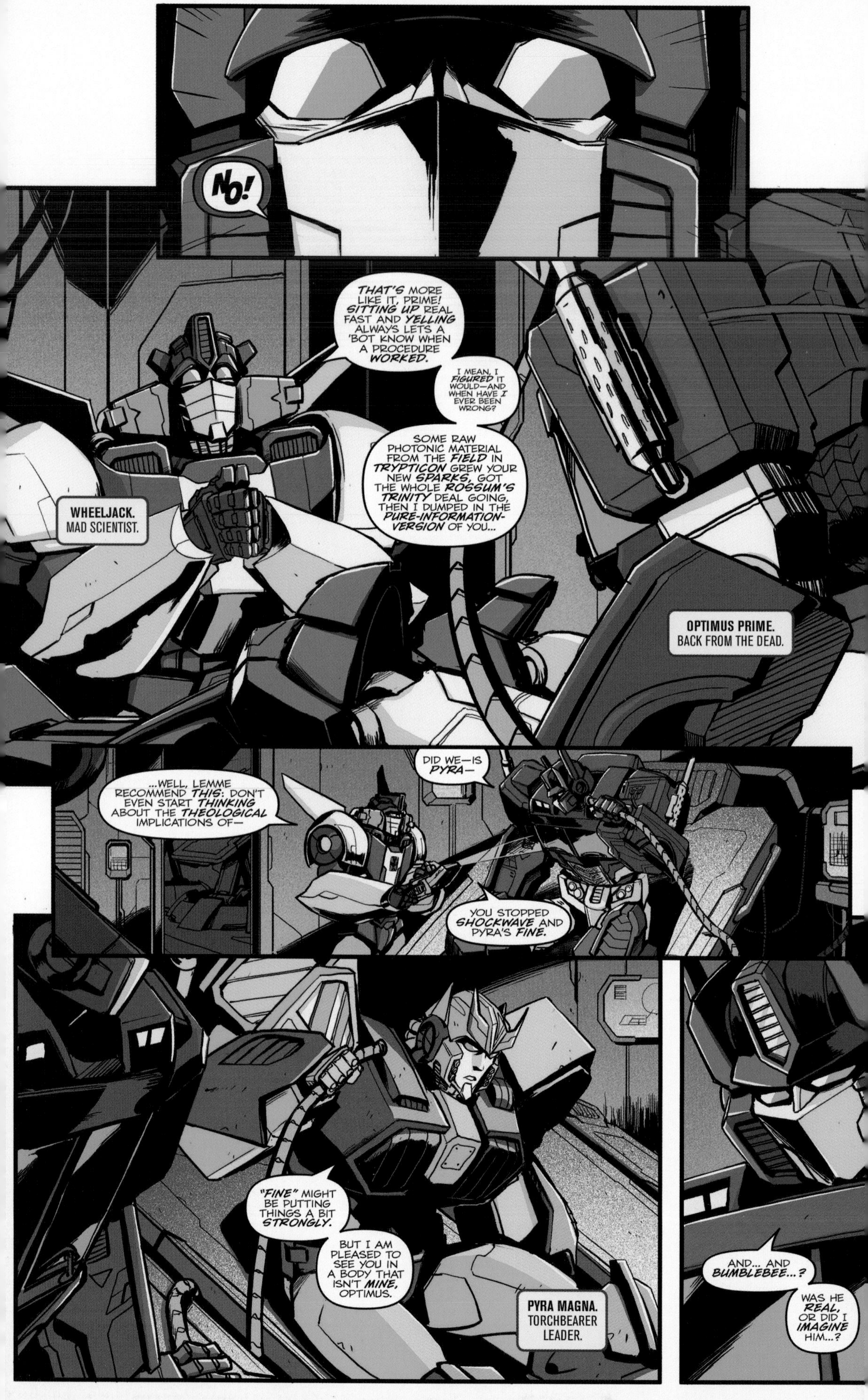
NO!
THAT'S MORE LIKE IT, PRIME! SITTING UP REAL FAST AND YELLING ALWAYS LETS A 'BOT KNOW WHEN A PROCEDURE WORKED.
I MEAN, I FIGURED IT WOULD—AND WHEN HAVE I EVER BEEN WRONG?
SOME RAW PHOTONIC MATERIAL FROM THE FIELD IN TRYPTICON GREW YOUR NEW SPARKS, GOT THE WHOLE ROSSUM'S TRINITY DEAL GOING, THEN I DUMPED IN THE PURE-INFORMATION-VERSION OF YOU...
WHEELJACK. MAD SCIENTIST.
OPTIMUS PRIME. BACK FROM THE DEAD.
...WELL, LEMME RECOMMEND THIS: DON'T EVEN START THINKING ABOUT THE THEOLOGICAL IMPLICATIONS OF—
DID WE—IS PYRA—
YOU STOPPED SHOCKWAVE AND PYRA'S FINE.
"FINE" MIGHT BE PUTTING THINGS A BIT STRONGLY.
BUT I AM PLEASED TO SEE YOU IN A BODY THAT ISN'T MINE, OPTIMUS.
PYRA MAGNA. TORCHBEARER LEADER.
AND... AND BUMBLEBEE...?
WAS HE REAL, OR DID I IMAGINE HIM...?

I'M REAL AS *LIFE*, PRIME. YOU'RE NOT GONNA GET RID OF ME *THAT* EASILY.

NOT *TWICE*, ANYWAY.

I'VE BEEN CATCHING BUMBLEBEE UP ON *CURRENT EVENTS*.

BUMBLEBEE. ALSO BACK FROM DEAD.

WINDBLADE. CYBERTRON'S LEADER.

BUMBLEBEE... I CANNOT TELL YOU HOW *GOOD* IT IS TO *SEE* YOU, OLD FRIEND.

YEAH— *YOU* TOO.

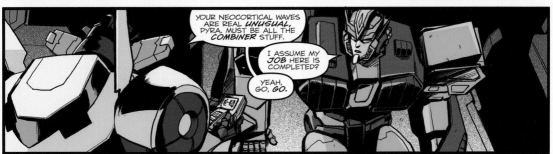

YOUR NEOCORTICAL WAVES ARE REAL *UNUSUAL*, PYRA. MUST BE ALL THE *COMBINER* STUFF.

I ASSUME MY *JOB* HERE IS COMPLETED?

YEAH, GO, *GO*.

LISTEN—THANKS FOR PULLING ME OUT OF THERE, PRIME. USUALLY I DON'T KNOW *WHERE* I'D BE WITHOUT YOU...

...THIS TIME I KNOW *EXACTLY* WHERE, AND IT SUCKED.

BECAUSE IT WAS A *BLACK HOLE*. GET IT?

BUMBLEBEE... DURING THE WAR— EVEN *BEFORE*— YOU WERE THE *CONSCIENCE* OF THE AUTOBOTS.

YOU WERE MY CONSCIENCE.

I'VE TRIED MY BEST TO LIVE UP TO YOUR *IDEALS*. BUT I'VE HAD...

...DISTURBING THOUGHTS.

WELL, I HATE TO BREAK THE *MOOD*, OPTIMUS...

...BUT I'VE GOT SOMETHING *WAY* MORE DISTURBING THAN EVEN *YOUR* THOUGHTS.

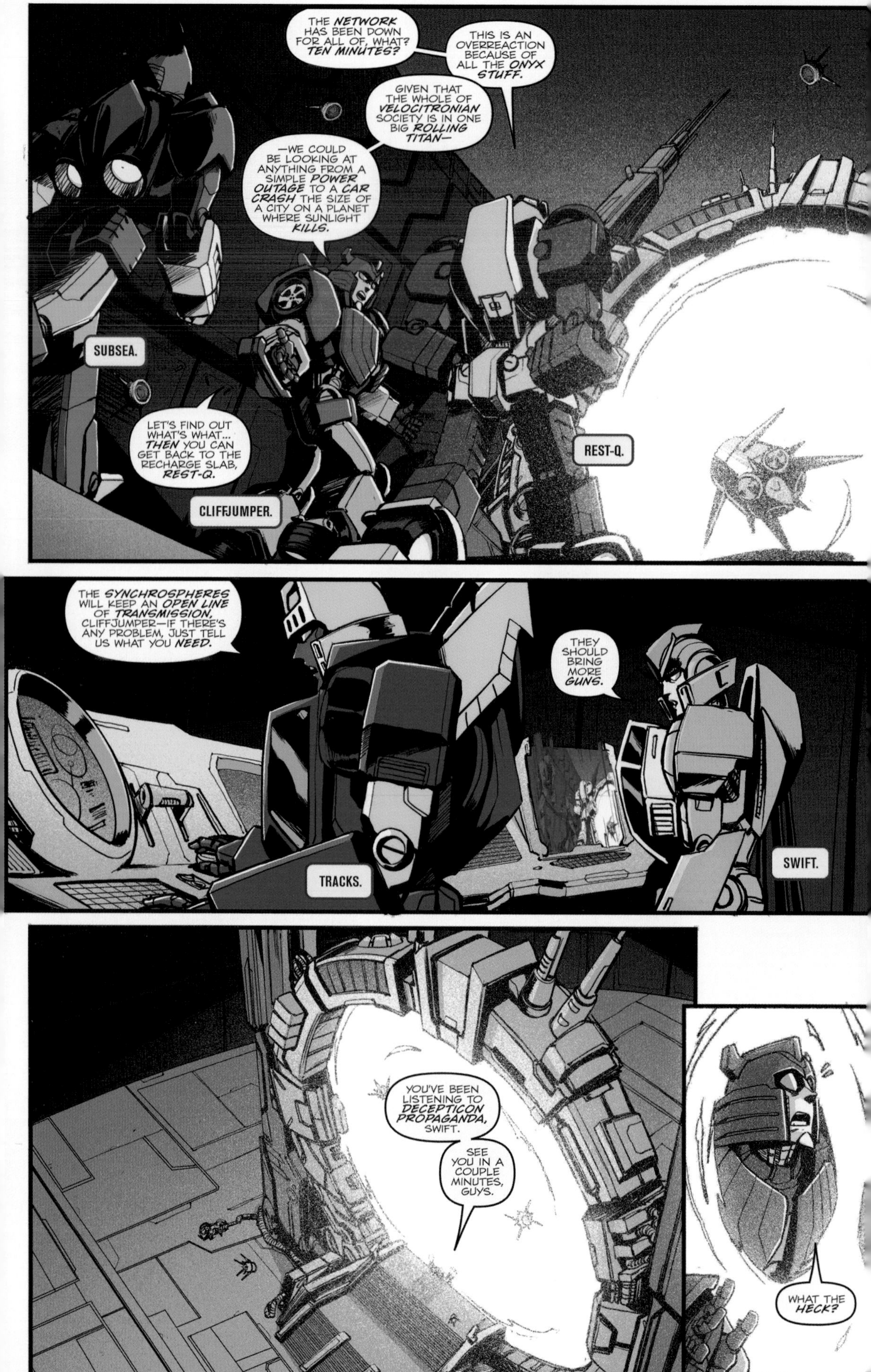
THE NETWORK HAS BEEN DOWN FOR ALL OF, WHAT? TEN MINUTES?
THIS IS AN OVERREACTION BECAUSE OF ALL THE ONYX STUFF.
GIVEN THAT THE WHOLE OF VELOCITRONIAN SOCIETY IS IN ONE BIG ROLLING TITAN—
—WE COULD BE LOOKING AT ANYTHING FROM A SIMPLE POWER OUTAGE TO A CAR CRASH THE SIZE OF A CITY ON A PLANET WHERE SUNLIGHT KILLS.
SUBSEA.
LET'S FIND OUT WHAT'S WHAT... THEN YOU CAN GET BACK TO THE RECHARGE SLAB, REST-Q.
REST-Q.
CLIFFJUMPER.
THE SYNCHROSPHERES WILL KEEP AN OPEN LINE OF TRANSMISSION, CLIFFJUMPER—IF THERE'S ANY PROBLEM, JUST TELL US WHAT YOU NEED.
THEY SHOULD BRING MORE GUNS.
TRACKS.
SWIFT.
YOU'VE BEEN LISTENING TO DECEPTICON PROPAGANDA, SWIFT.
SEE YOU IN A COUPLE MINUTES, GUYS.
WHAT THE HECK?

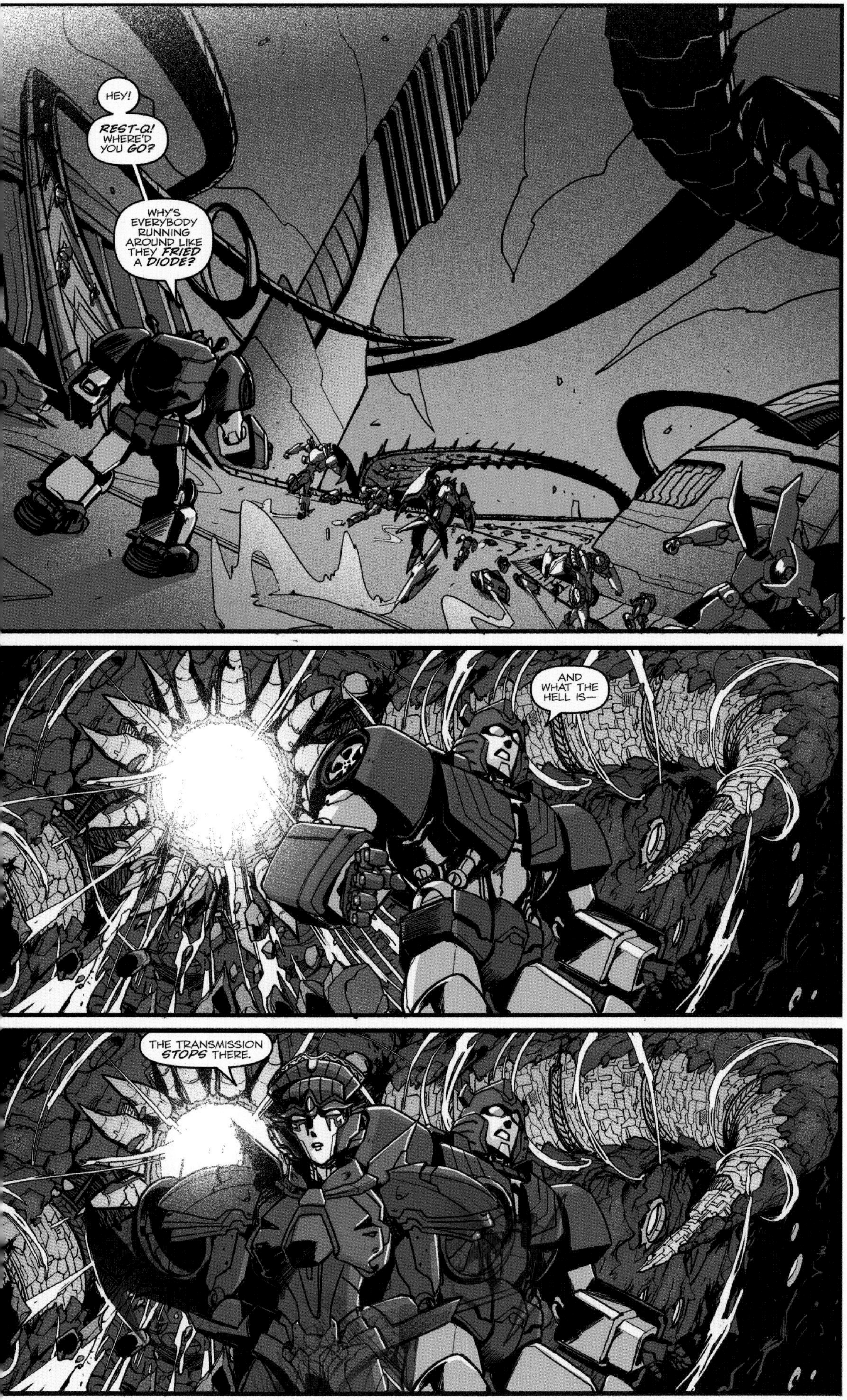
HEY!
REST-Q! WHERE'D YOU GO?
WHY'S EVERYBODY RUNNING AROUND LIKE THEY FRIED A DIODE?
AND WHAT THE HELL IS—
THE TRANSMISSION STOPS THERE.

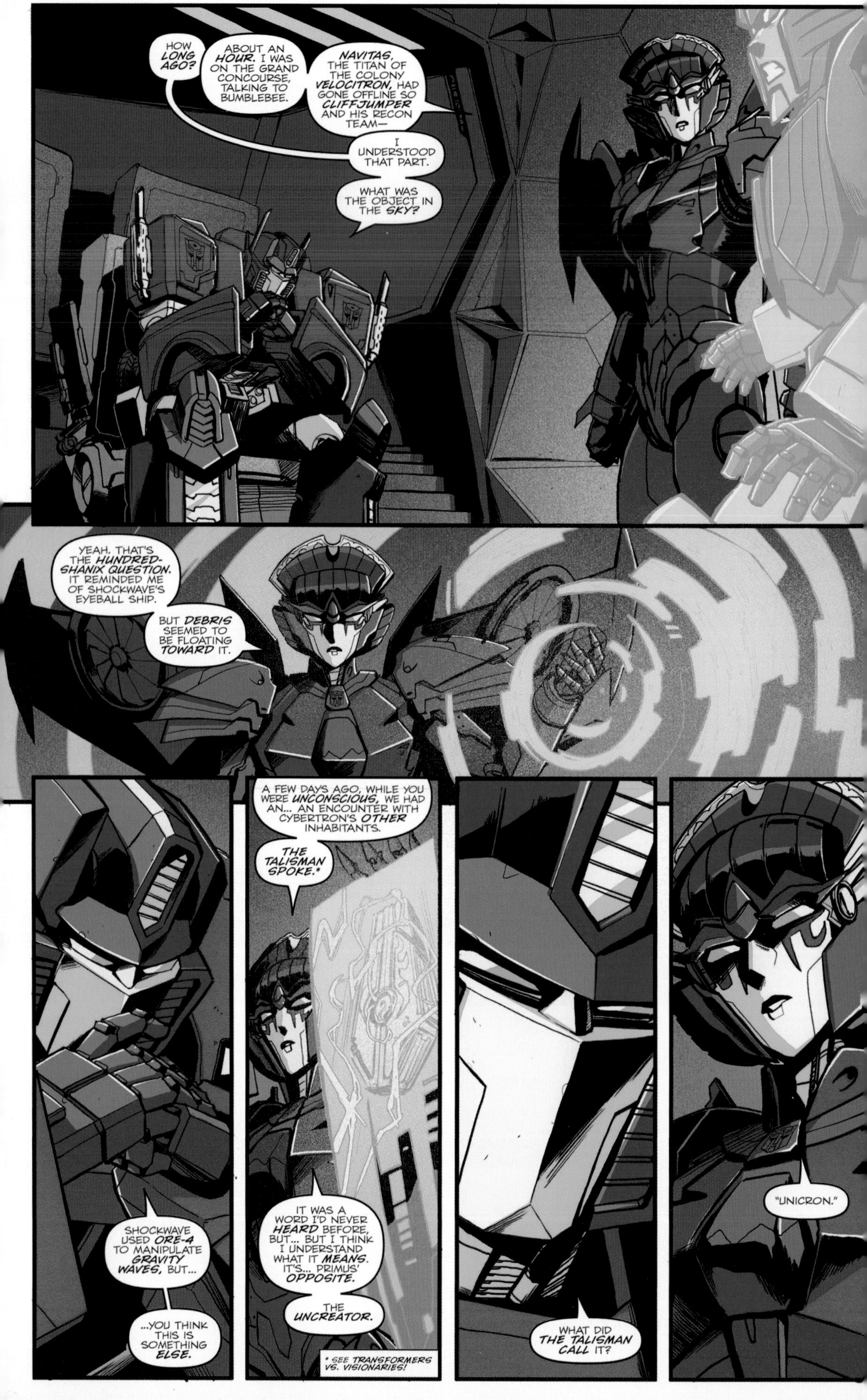
HOW LONG AGO?
ABOUT AN HOUR. I WAS ON THE GRAND CONCOURSE, TALKING TO BUMBLEBEE.
NAVITAS, THE TITAN OF THE COLONY VELOCITRON, HAD GONE OFFLINE SO CLIFFJUMPER AND HIS RECON TEAM—
I UNDERSTOOD THAT PART.
WHAT WAS THE OBJECT IN THE SKY?
YEAH. THAT'S THE HUNDRED-SHANIX QUESTION. IT REMINDED ME OF SHOCKWAVE'S EYEBALL SHIP.
BUT DEBRIS SEEMED TO BE FLOATING TOWARD IT.
SHOCKWAVE USED ORE-4 TO MANIPULATE GRAVITY WAVES, BUT...
...YOU THINK THIS IS SOMETHING ELSE.
A FEW DAYS AGO, WHILE YOU WERE UNCONSCIOUS, WE HAD AN... AN ENCOUNTER WITH CYBERTRON'S OTHER INHABITANTS.
THE TALISMAN SPOKE.*
IT WAS A WORD I'D NEVER HEARD BEFORE, BUT... BUT I THINK I UNDERSTAND WHAT IT MEANS. IT'S... PRIMUS' OPPOSITE.
THE UNCREATOR.
* SEE TRANSFORMERS VS. VISIONARIES!
WHAT DID THE TALISMAN CALL IT?
"UNICRON."

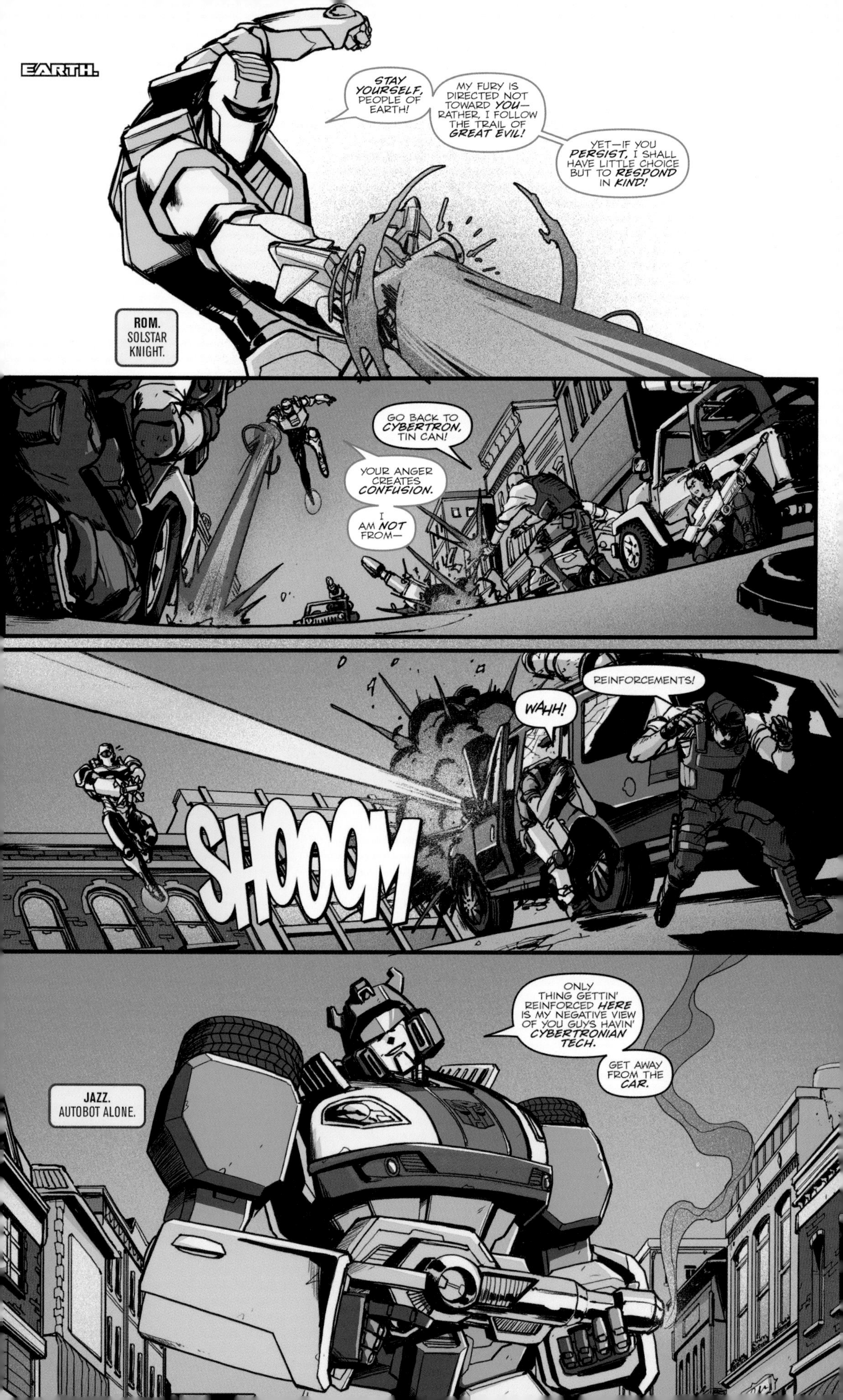
EARTH.
STAY YOURSELF, PEOPLE OF EARTH!
MY FURY IS DIRECTED NOT TOWARD YOU— RATHER, I FOLLOW THE TRAIL OF GREAT EVIL!
YET—IF YOU PERSIST, I SHALL HAVE LITTLE CHOICE BUT TO RESPOND IN KIND!
ROM. SOLSTAR KNIGHT.
GO BACK TO CYBERTRON, TIN CAN!
YOUR ANGER CREATES CONFUSION.
I AM NOT FROM—
REINFORCEMENTS!
WAHH!
SHOOOM
ONLY THING GETTIN' REINFORCED HERE IS MY NEGATIVE VIEW OF YOU GUYS HAVIN' CYBERTRONIAN TECH.
GET AWAY FROM THE CAR.
JAZZ. AUTOBOT ALONE.

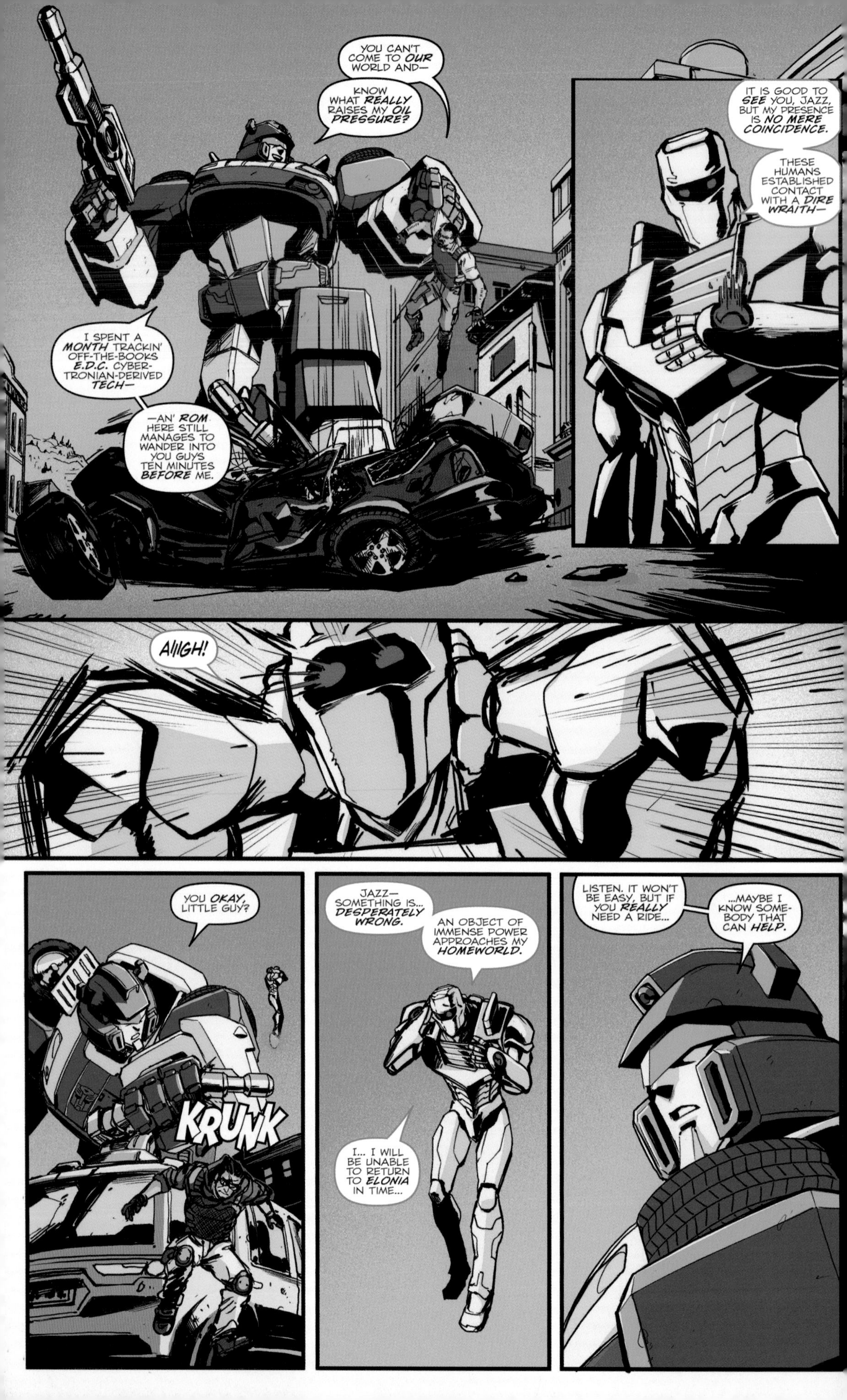
YOU CAN'T COME TO OUR WORLD AND—
KNOW WHAT REALLY RAISES MY OIL PRESSURE?
I SPENT A MONTH TRACKIN' OFF-THE-BOOKS E.D.C. CYBER-TRONIAN-DERIVED TECH—
—AN' ROM HERE STILL MANAGES TO WANDER INTO YOU GUYS TEN MINUTES BEFORE ME.
IT IS GOOD TO SEE YOU, JAZZ, BUT MY PRESENCE IS NO MERE COINCIDENCE.
THESE HUMANS ESTABLISHED CONTACT WITH A DIRE WRAITH—
AIIGH!
YOU OKAY, LITTLE GUY?
KRUNK
JAZZ— SOMETHING IS... DESPERATELY WRONG.
AN OBJECT OF IMMENSE POWER APPROACHES MY HOMEWORLD.
I... I WILL BE UNABLE TO RETURN TO ELONIA IN TIME...
LISTEN. IT WON'T BE EASY, BUT IF YOU REALLY NEED A RIDE...
...MAYBE I KNOW SOME-BODY THAT CAN HELP.

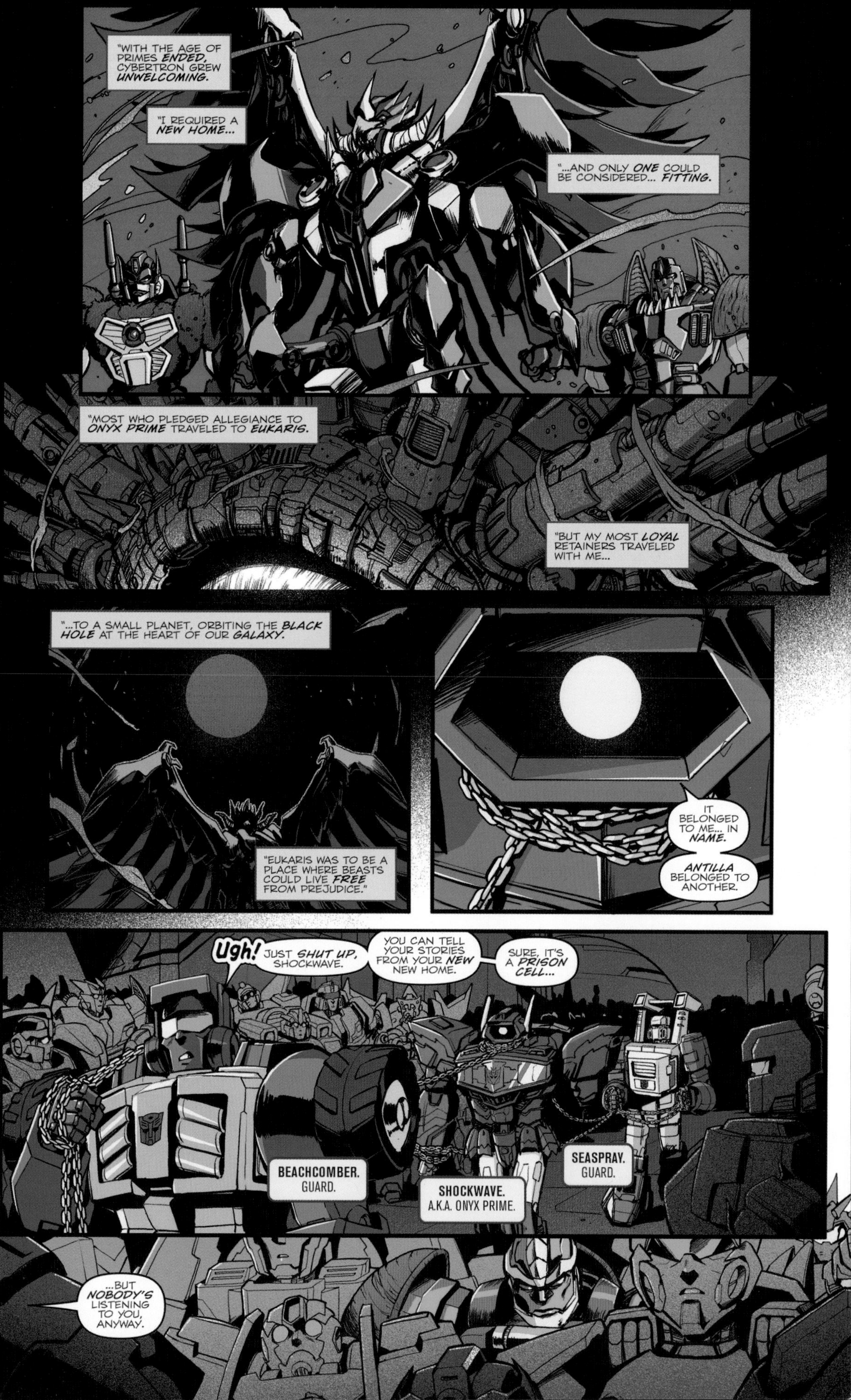
"WITH THE AGE OF PRIMES ENDED, CYBERTRON GREW UNWELCOMING.
"I REQUIRED A NEW HOME...
"...AND ONLY ONE COULD BE CONSIDERED... FITTING.
"MOST WHO PLEDGED ALLEGIANCE TO ONYX PRIME TRAVELED TO EUKARIS.
"BUT MY MOST LOYAL RETAINERS TRAVELED WITH ME...
"...TO A SMALL PLANET, ORBITING THE BLACK HOLE AT THE HEART OF OUR GALAXY.
"EUKARIS WAS TO BE A PLACE WHERE BEASTS COULD LIVE FREE FROM PREJUDICE."
IT BELONGED TO ME... IN NAME.
ANTILLA BELONGED TO ANOTHER.
Ugh! JUST SHUT UP, SHOCKWAVE.
YOU CAN TELL YOUR STORIES FROM YOUR NEW NEW HOME.
SURE, IT'S A PRISON CELL...
BEACHCOMBER. GUARD.
SHOCKWAVE. A.K.A. ONYX PRIME.
SEASPRAY. GUARD.
...BUT NOBODY'S LISTENING TO YOU, ANYWAY.

CAN YOU *HEAR* IT?

SO *LOUD* IT— IT *HURTS*—

STARDRIVE. FORMER SOLSTAR KNIGHT.

—ELONIA! ELONIA IS IN *TROUBLE.*

DON'T WASTE YOUR *LOYALTY,* STARDRIVE. ELONIA NEVER *CARED.*

THEY *USED* YOU. YOU WERE NOTHING BUT A *TOOL* TO THEM— A *BEAST* OF *BURDEN.*

PROWL. RENEGADE AUTOBOT.

I'VE SPENT *200 YEARS* GETTING OVER MY *PAST,* PROWL.

THE *LAST* THING I NEED IS YOU *TELLING ME* ABOUT IT.

THE *POINT* IS, I CAN *FEEL* SOMETHING...

...SOMETHING *BIG.*

WELL, WE'VE GOT OUR *HANDS FULL.*

CYBERTRONIANS ACROSS THE *GALAXY* HAVE BEEN TRACKED DOWN AND *SLAUGHTERED...*

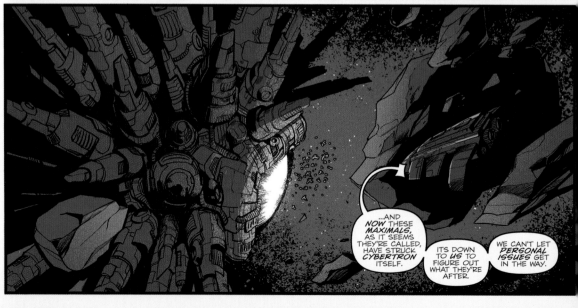

...AND *NOW* THESE *MAXIMALS,* AS IT SEEMS THEY'RE CALLED, HAVE STRUCK *CYBERTRON* ITSELF.

ITS DOWN TO *US* TO FIGURE OUT WHAT THEY'RE AFTER.

WE CAN'T LET *PERSONAL ISSUES* GET IN THE WAY.

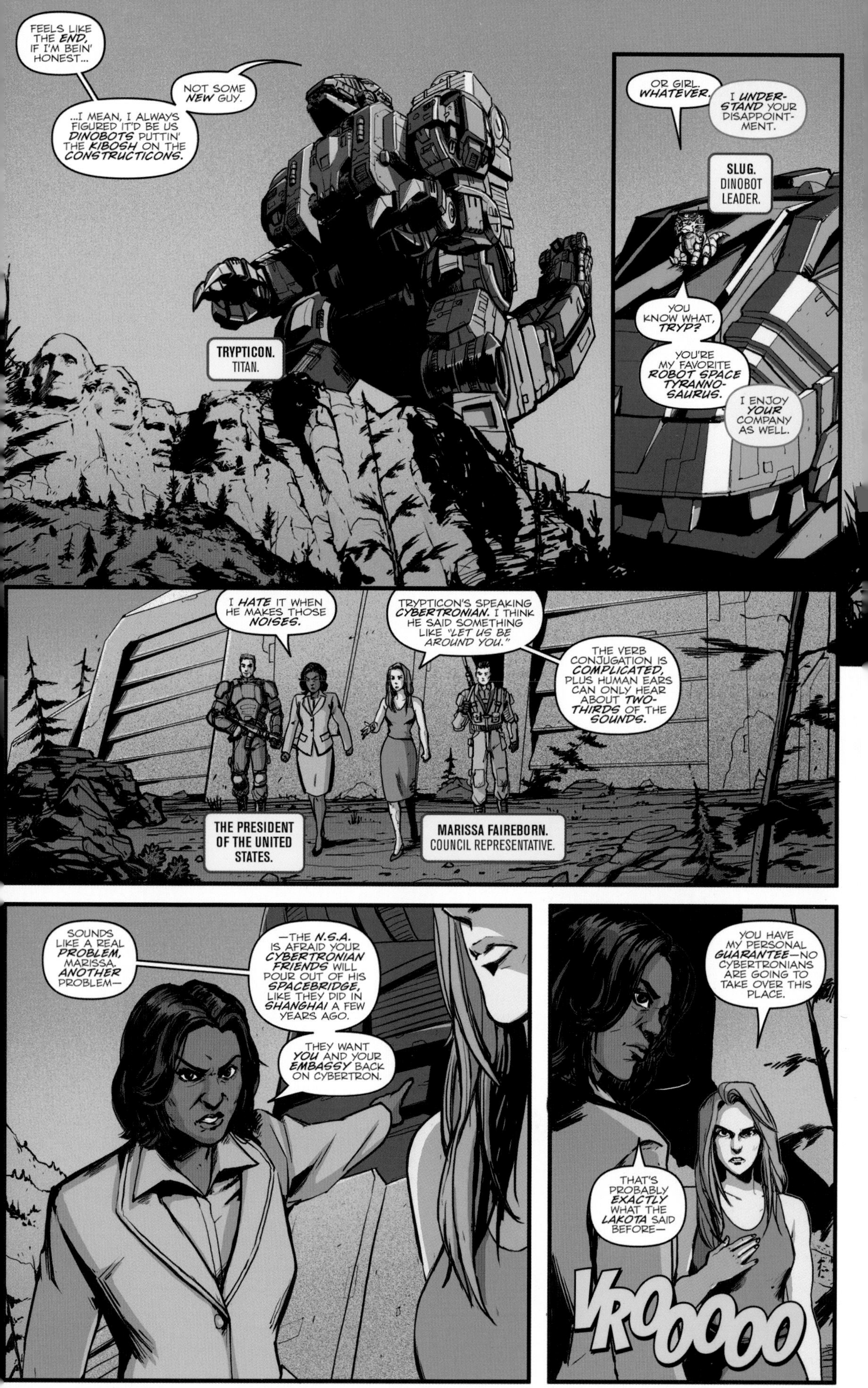

FEELS LIKE THE END, IF I'M BEIN' HONEST...
NOT SOME NEW GUY.
...I MEAN, I ALWAYS FIGURED IT'D BE US DINOBOTS PUTTIN' THE KIBOSH ON THE CONSTRUCTICONS.
TRYPTICON. TITAN.
OR GIRL. WHATEVER.
I UNDERSTAND YOUR DISAPPOINTMENT.
SLUG. DINOBOT LEADER.
YOU KNOW WHAT, TRYP?
YOU'RE MY FAVORITE ROBOT SPACE TYRANNOSAURUS.
I ENJOY YOUR COMPANY AS WELL.
I HATE IT WHEN HE MAKES THOSE NOISES.
TRYPTICON'S SPEAKING CYBERTRONIAN. I THINK HE SAID SOMETHING LIKE "LET US BE AROUND YOU."
THE VERB CONJUGATION IS COMPLICATED, PLUS HUMAN EARS CAN ONLY HEAR ABOUT TWO-THIRDS OF THE SOUNDS.
THE PRESIDENT OF THE UNITED STATES.
MARISSA FAIREBORN. COUNCIL REPRESENTATIVE.
SOUNDS LIKE A REAL PROBLEM, MARISSA. ANOTHER PROBLEM—
—THE N.S.A. IS AFRAID YOUR CYBERTRONIAN FRIENDS WILL POUR OUT OF HIS SPACEBRIDGE, LIKE THEY DID IN SHANGHAI A FEW YEARS AGO.
THEY WANT YOU AND YOUR EMBASSY BACK ON CYBERTRON.
YOU HAVE MY PERSONAL GUARANTEE—NO CYBERTRONIANS ARE GOING TO TAKE OVER THIS PLACE.
THAT'S PROBABLY EXACTLY WHAT THE LAKOTA SAID BEFORE—
VROOOOOO

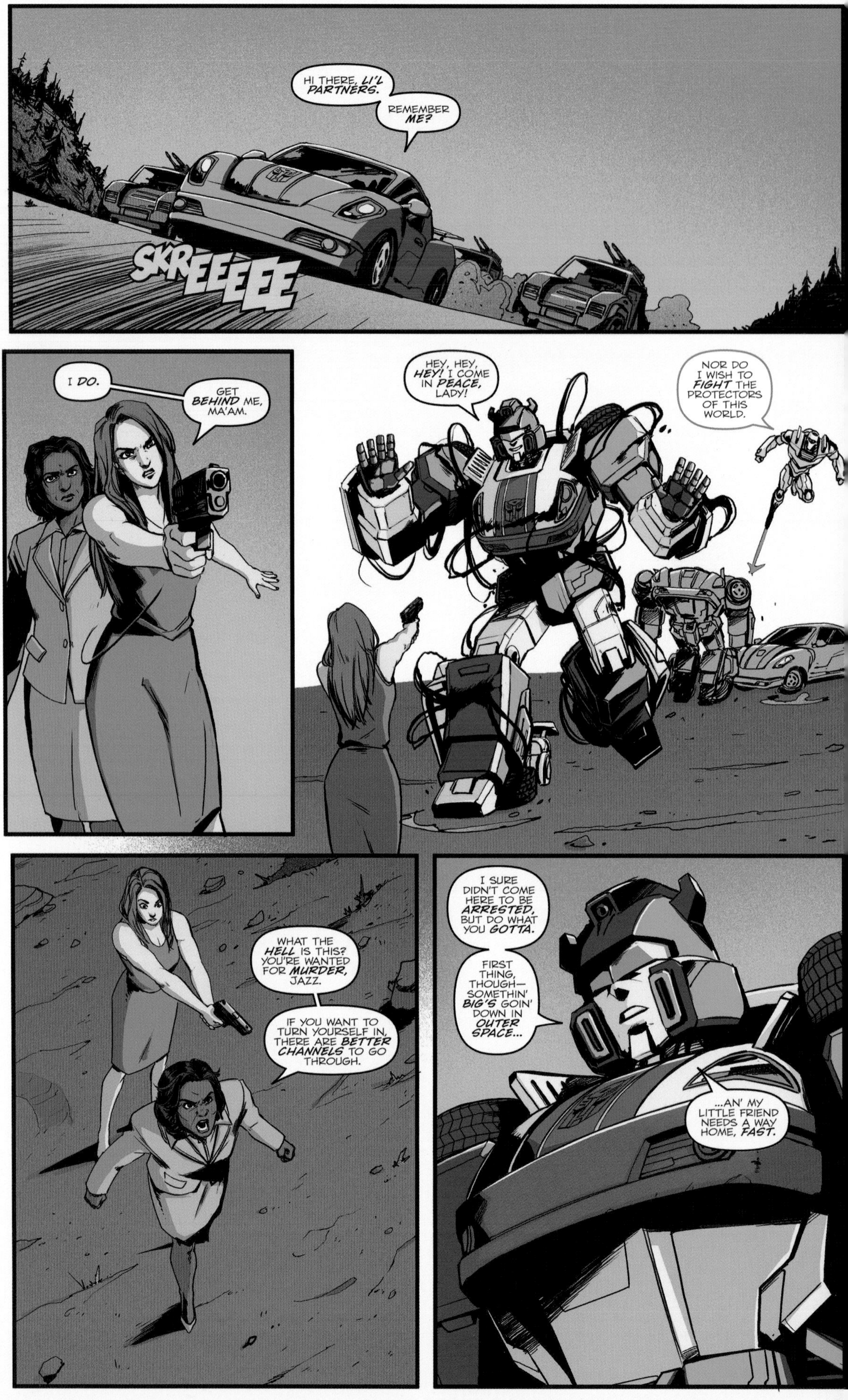

HI THERE, LI'L PARTNERS.
REMEMBER ME?
SKREEEEEE
I DO.
GET BEHIND ME, MA'AM.
HEY, HEY, HEY! I COME IN PEACE, LADY!
NOR DO I WISH TO FIGHT THE PROTECTORS OF THIS WORLD.
WHAT THE HELL IS THIS? YOU'RE WANTED FOR MURDER, JAZZ.
IF YOU WANT TO TURN YOURSELF IN, THERE ARE BETTER CHANNELS TO GO THROUGH.
I SURE DIDN'T COME HERE TO BE ARRESTED, BUT DO WHAT YOU GOTTA.
FIRST THING, THOUGH—SOMETHIN' BIG'S GOIN' DOWN IN OUTER SPACE...
...AN' MY LITTLE FRIEND NEEDS A WAY HOME, FAST.

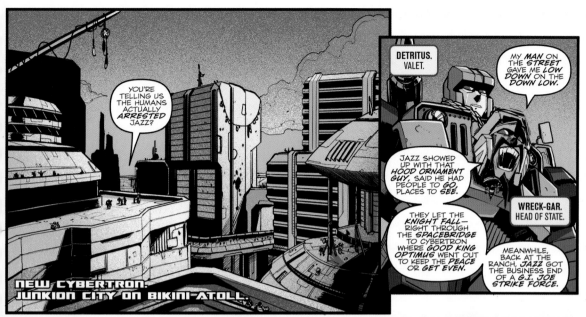

YOU'RE TELLING US THE HUMANS ACTUALLY **ARRESTED** JAZZ?

NEW CYBERTRON: JUNKION CITY ON BIKINI ATOLL.

DETRITUS. VALET.

MY **MAN** ON THE **STREET** GAVE ME **LOW DOWN** ON THE **DOWN LOW.**

JAZZ SHOWED UP WITH THAT **HOOD ORNAMENT GUY,** SAID HE HAD PEOPLE TO **GO,** PLACES TO **SEE.**

WRECK-GAR. HEAD OF STATE.

THEY LET THE **KNIGHT FALL**— RIGHT THROUGH THE **SPACEBRIDGE** TO CYBERTRON WHERE **GOOD KING OPTIMUS** WENT OUT TO KEEP THE **PEACE** OR GET EVEN.

MEANWHILE, BACK AT THE RANCH, **JAZZ** GOT THE BUSINESS END OF A **G.I. JOE** STRIKE FORCE.

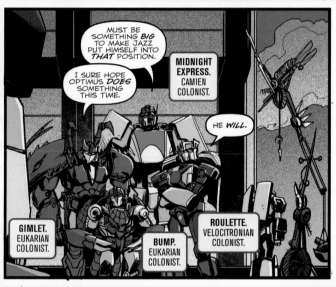

MUST BE SOMETHING **BIG** TO MAKE JAZZ PUT HIMSELF INTO **THAT** POSITION.

I SURE HOPE OPTIMUS **DOES** SOMETHING THIS TIME.

MIDNIGHT EXPRESS. CAMIEN COLONIST.

HE **WILL.**

GIMLET. EUKARIAN COLONIST.

BUMP. EUKARIAN COLONIST.

ROULETTE. VELOCITRONIAN COLONIST.

LISTEN TO YOURSELVES!

SLIDE. DEVISEN COLONIST.

DO OPTIMUS' HUMAN ALLIES **CARE** THAT WE LOST CONTACT WITH **VELOCITRON?**

ROULETTE, YOU HAVE TO BE GOING OUT OF YOUR **NEOCORTEX.** YOUR **FRIENDS,** YOUR **FAMILY...** WHO **KNOWS** WHERE THEY ARE.

AND WHAT'S THE **PRIME** DONE? LEFT US ON A WORLD WHERE THEY **LOCK UP** A 'BOT FOR **CARING** TOO MUCH.

THIS IS **WRONG.**

THE OLD 'BOTS **RUNNING** THINGS, THEY DON'T **GET** IT.

WE ARE OUR **FUTURE.**

WE HAVE TO **MAKE** OUR FUTURE.

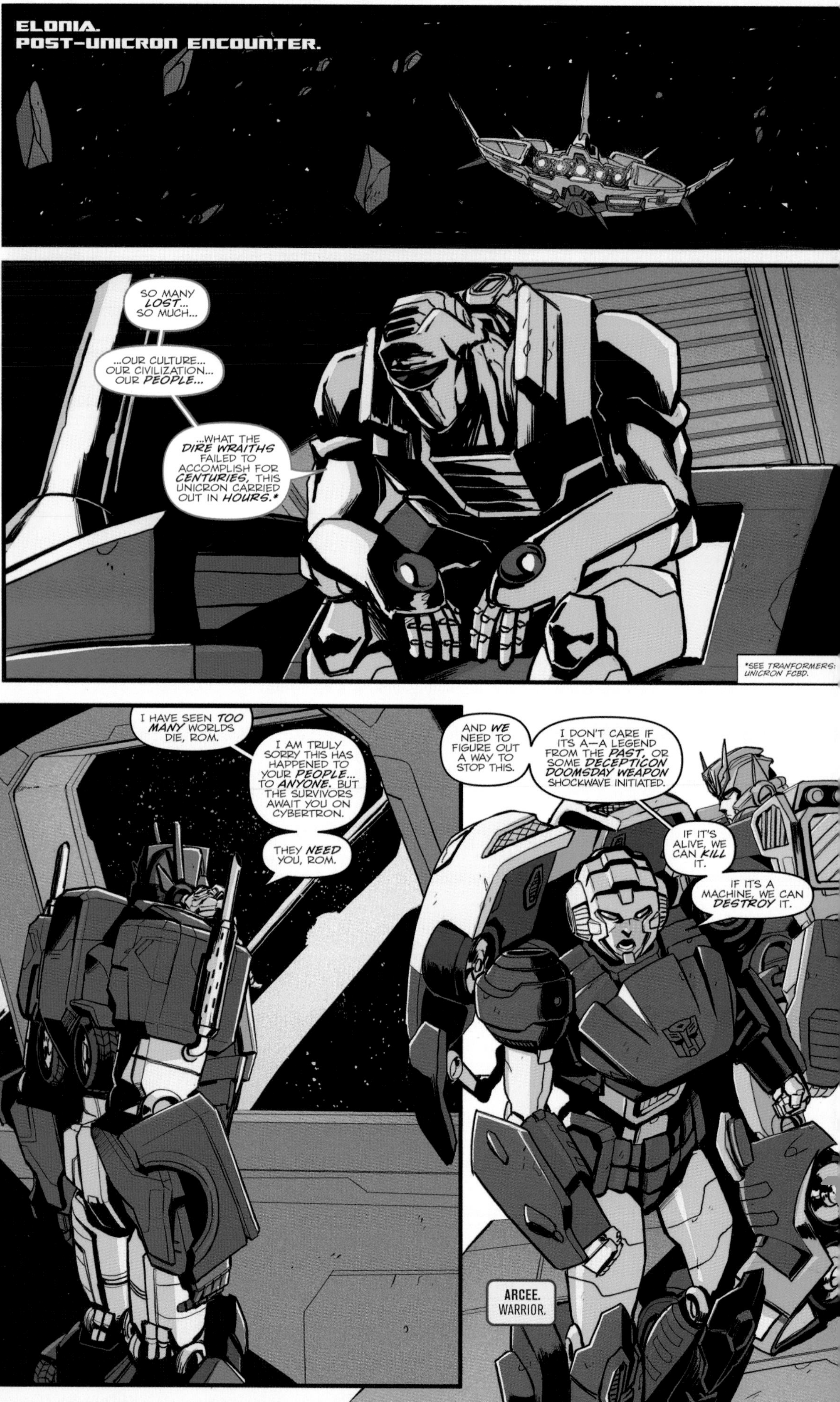
ELONIA.
POST-UNICRON ENCOUNTER.
SO MANY LOST... SO MUCH...
...OUR CULTURE... OUR CIVILIZATION... OUR PEOPLE...
...WHAT THE DIRE WRAITHS FAILED TO ACCOMPLISH FOR CENTURIES, THIS UNICRON CARRIED OUT IN HOURS.*
*SEE TRANFORMERS: UNICRON FCBD.
I HAVE SEEN TOO MANY WORLDS DIE, ROM.
I AM TRULY SORRY THIS HAS HAPPENED TO YOUR PEOPLE... TO ANYONE. BUT THE SURVIVORS AWAIT YOU ON CYBERTRON.
THEY NEED YOU, ROM.
AND WE NEED TO FIGURE OUT A WAY TO STOP THIS.
I DON'T CARE IF ITS A—A LEGEND FROM THE PAST, OR SOME DECEPTICON DOOMSDAY WEAPON SHOCKWAVE INITIATED.
IF IT'S ALIVE, WE CAN KILL IT.
IF ITS A MACHINE, WE CAN DESTROY IT.
ARCEE. WARRIOR.

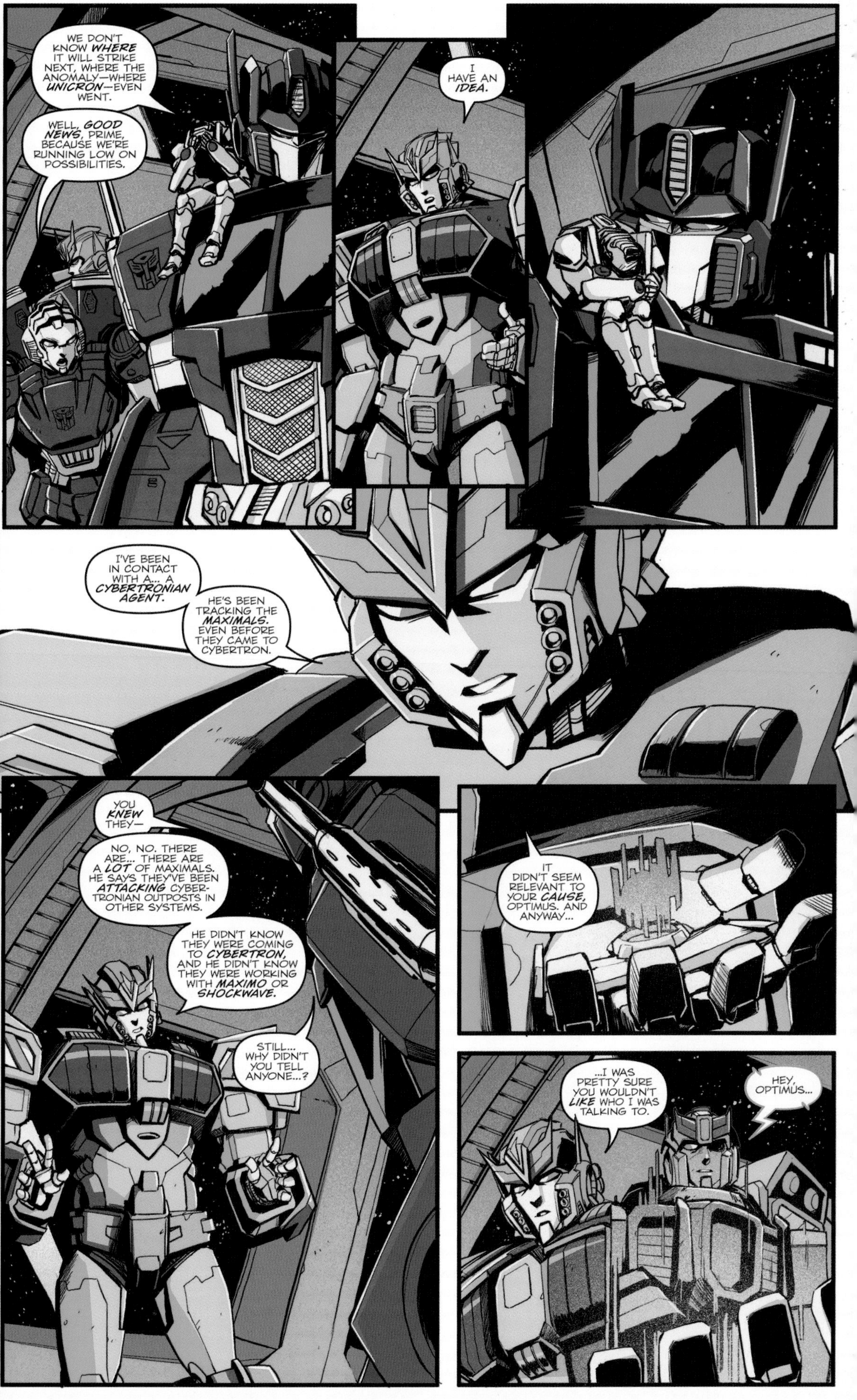

WE DON'T KNOW WHERE IT WILL STRIKE NEXT, WHERE THE ANOMALY—WHERE UNICRON—EVEN WENT.
WELL, GOOD NEWS, PRIME, BECAUSE WE'RE RUNNING LOW ON POSSIBILITIES.
I HAVE AN IDEA.
I'VE BEEN IN CONTACT WITH A... A CYBERTRONIAN AGENT.
HE'S BEEN TRACKING THE MAXIMALS. EVEN BEFORE THEY CAME TO CYBERTRON.
YOU KNEW THEY—
NO, NO. THERE ARE... THERE ARE A LOT OF MAXIMALS. HE SAYS THEY'VE BEEN ATTACKING CYBER-TRONIAN OUTPOSTS IN OTHER SYSTEMS.
HE DIDN'T KNOW THEY WERE COMING TO CYBERTRON, AND HE DIDN'T KNOW THEY WERE WORKING WITH MAXIMO OR SHOCKWAVE.
STILL... WHY DIDN'T YOU TELL ANYONE...?
IT DIDN'T SEEM RELEVANT TO YOUR CAUSE, OPTIMUS. AND ANYWAY...
...I WAS PRETTY SURE YOU WOULDN'T LIKE WHO I WAS TALKING TO.
HEY, OPTIMUS...

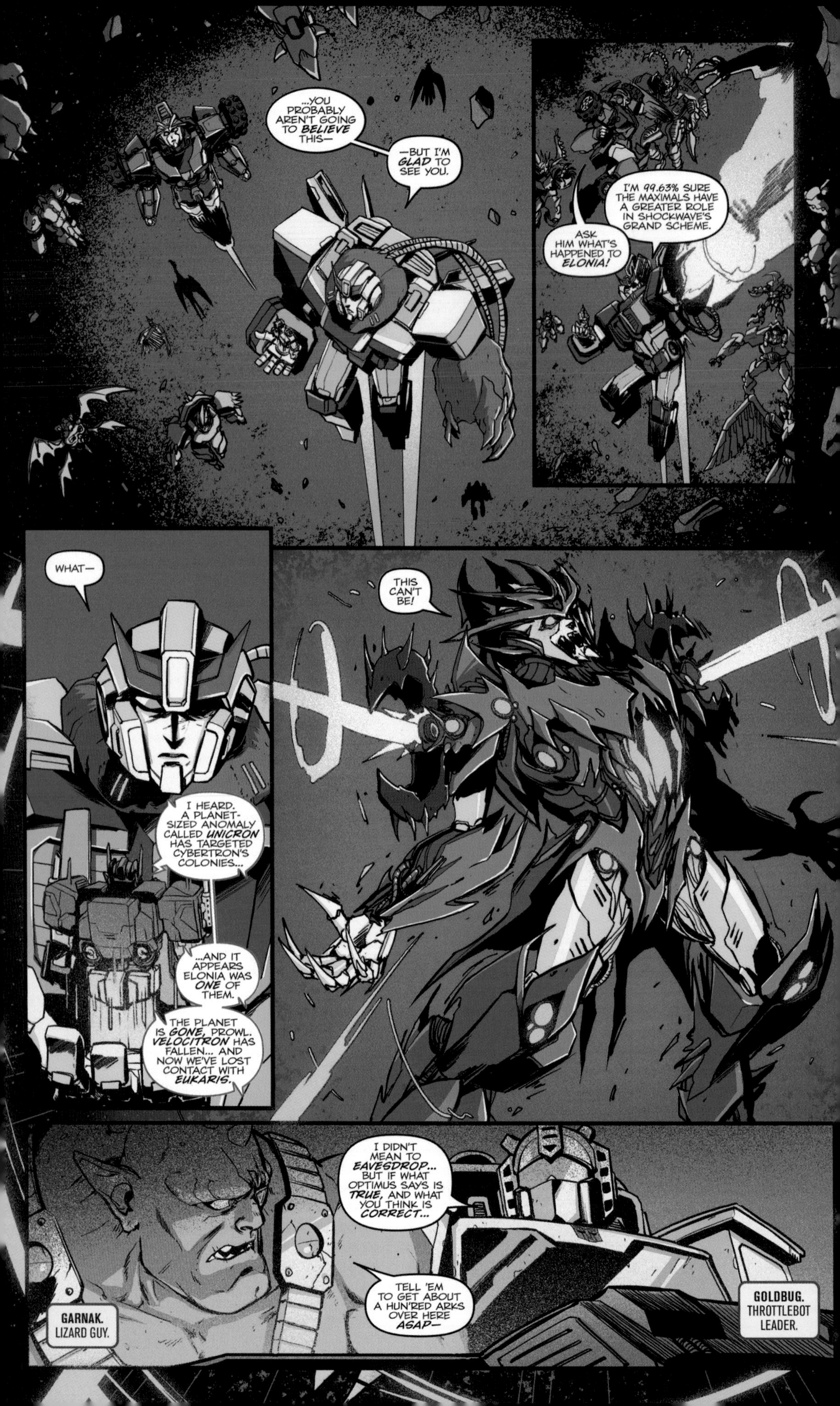
...YOU PROBABLY AREN'T GOING TO BELIEVE THIS—
—BUT I'M GLAD TO SEE YOU.
I'M 99.63% SURE THE MAXIMALS HAVE A GREATER ROLE IN SHOCKWAVE'S GRAND SCHEME.
ASK HIM WHAT'S HAPPENED TO ELONIA!
WHAT—
THIS CAN'T BE!
I HEARD. A PLANET-SIZED ANOMALY CALLED UNICRON HAS TARGETED CYBERTRON'S COLONIES...
...AND IT APPEARS ELONIA WAS ONE OF THEM.
THE PLANET IS GONE, PROWL. VELOCITRON HAS FALLEN... AND NOW WE'VE LOST CONTACT WITH EUKARIS.
I DIDN'T MEAN TO EAVESDROP... BUT IF WHAT OPTIMUS SAYS IS TRUE, AND WHAT YOU THINK IS CORRECT...
TELL 'EM TO GET ABOUT A HUN'RED ARKS OVER HERE ASAP—
GARNAK. LIZARD GUY.
GOLDBUG. THROTTLEBOT LEADER.

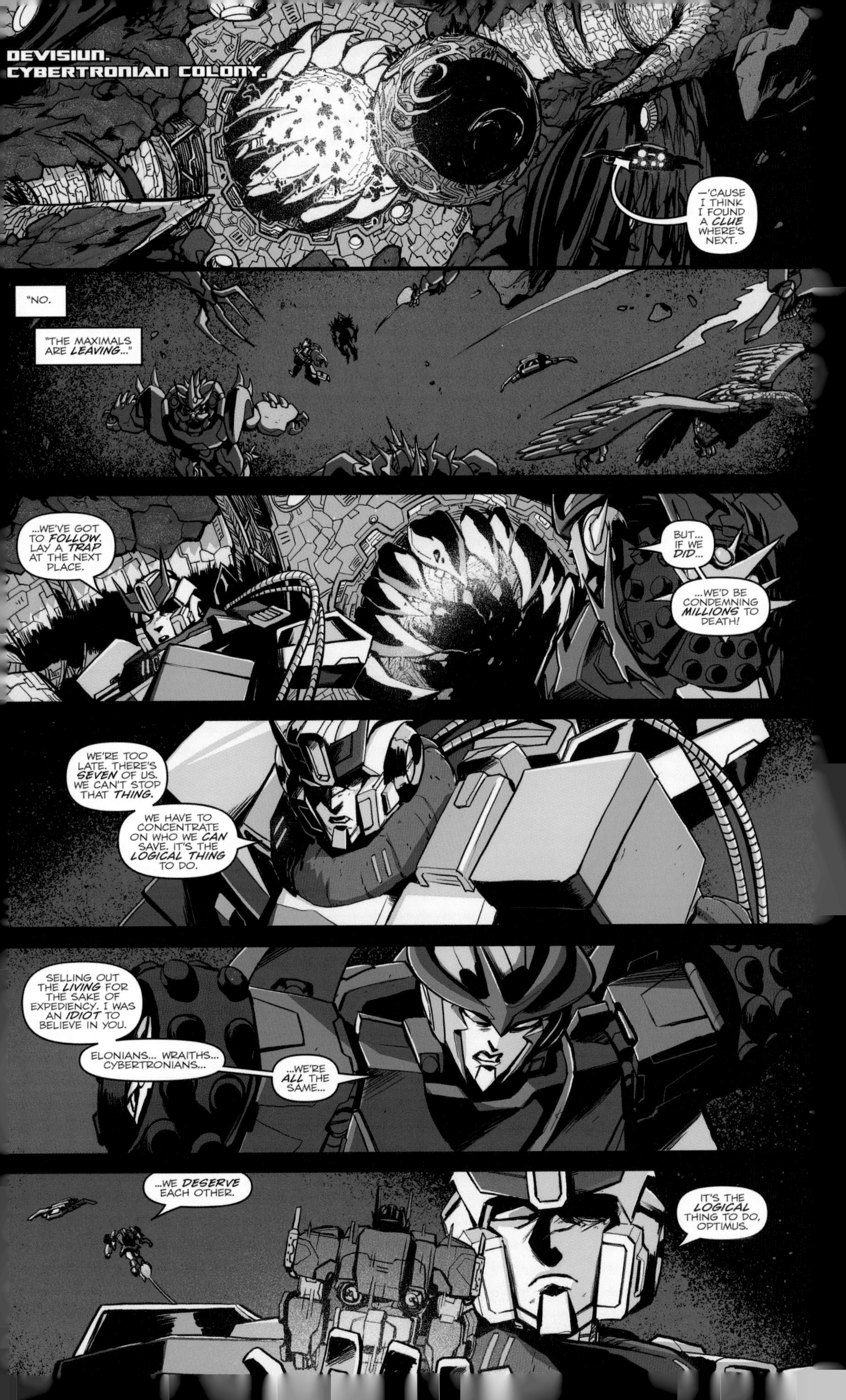
DEVISIUN.
CYBERTRONIAN COLONY.
—'CAUSE I THINK I FOUND A CLUE WHERE'S NEXT.
"NO.
"THE MAXIMALS ARE LEAVING..."
...WE'VE GOT TO FOLLOW. LAY A TRAP AT THE NEXT PLACE.
BUT... IF WE DID...
...WE'D BE CONDEMNING MILLIONS TO DEATH!
WE'RE TOO LATE. THERE'S SEVEN OF US. WE CAN'T STOP THAT THING.
WE HAVE TO CONCENTRATE ON WHO WE CAN SAVE. IT'S THE LOGICAL THING TO DO.
SELLING OUT THE LIVING FOR THE SAKE OF EXPEDIENCY. I WAS AN IDIOT TO BELIEVE IN YOU.
ELONIANS... WRAITHS... CYBERTRONIANS...
...WE'RE ALL THE SAME...
...WE DESERVE EACH OTHER.
IT'S THE LOGICAL THING TO DO, OPTIMUS.

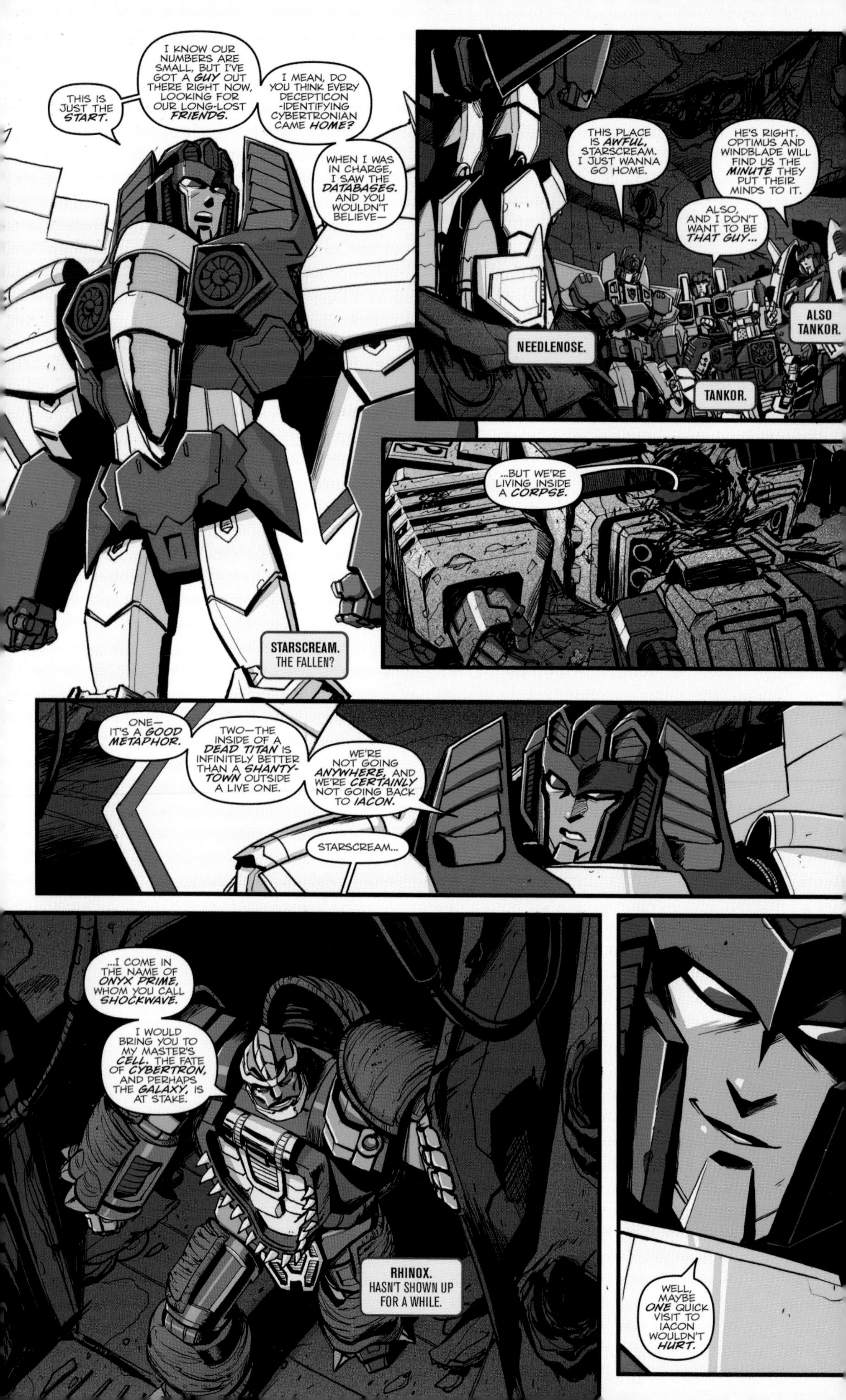

THIS IS JUST THE START.
I KNOW OUR NUMBERS ARE SMALL, BUT I'VE GOT A GUY OUT THERE RIGHT NOW, LOOKING FOR OUR LONG-LOST FRIENDS.
I MEAN, DO YOU THINK EVERY DECEPTICON -IDENTIFYING CYBERTRONIAN CAME HOME?
WHEN I WAS IN CHARGE, I SAW THE DATABASES. AND YOU WOULDN'T BELIEVE—
STARSCREAM. THE FALLEN?
THIS PLACE IS AWFUL, STARSCREAM. I JUST WANNA GO HOME.
HE'S RIGHT. OPTIMUS AND WINDBLADE WILL FIND US THE MINUTE THEY PUT THEIR MINDS TO IT.
ALSO, AND I DON'T WANT TO BE THAT GUY...
NEEDLENOSE.
TANKOR.
ALSO TANKOR.
...BUT WE'RE LIVING INSIDE A CORPSE.
ONE— IT'S A GOOD METAPHOR.
TWO—THE INSIDE OF A DEAD TITAN IS INFINITELY BETTER THAN A SHANTY-TOWN OUTSIDE A LIVE ONE.
WE'RE NOT GOING ANYWHERE, AND WE'RE CERTAINLY NOT GOING BACK TO IACON.
STARSCREAM...
...I COME IN THE NAME OF ONYX PRIME, WHOM YOU CALL SHOCKWAVE.
I WOULD BRING YOU TO MY MASTER'S CELL. THE FATE OF CYBERTRON, AND PERHAPS THE GALAXY, IS AT STAKE.
RHINOX. HASN'T SHOWN UP FOR A WHILE.
WELL, MAYBE ONE QUICK VISIT TO IACON WOULDN'T HURT.

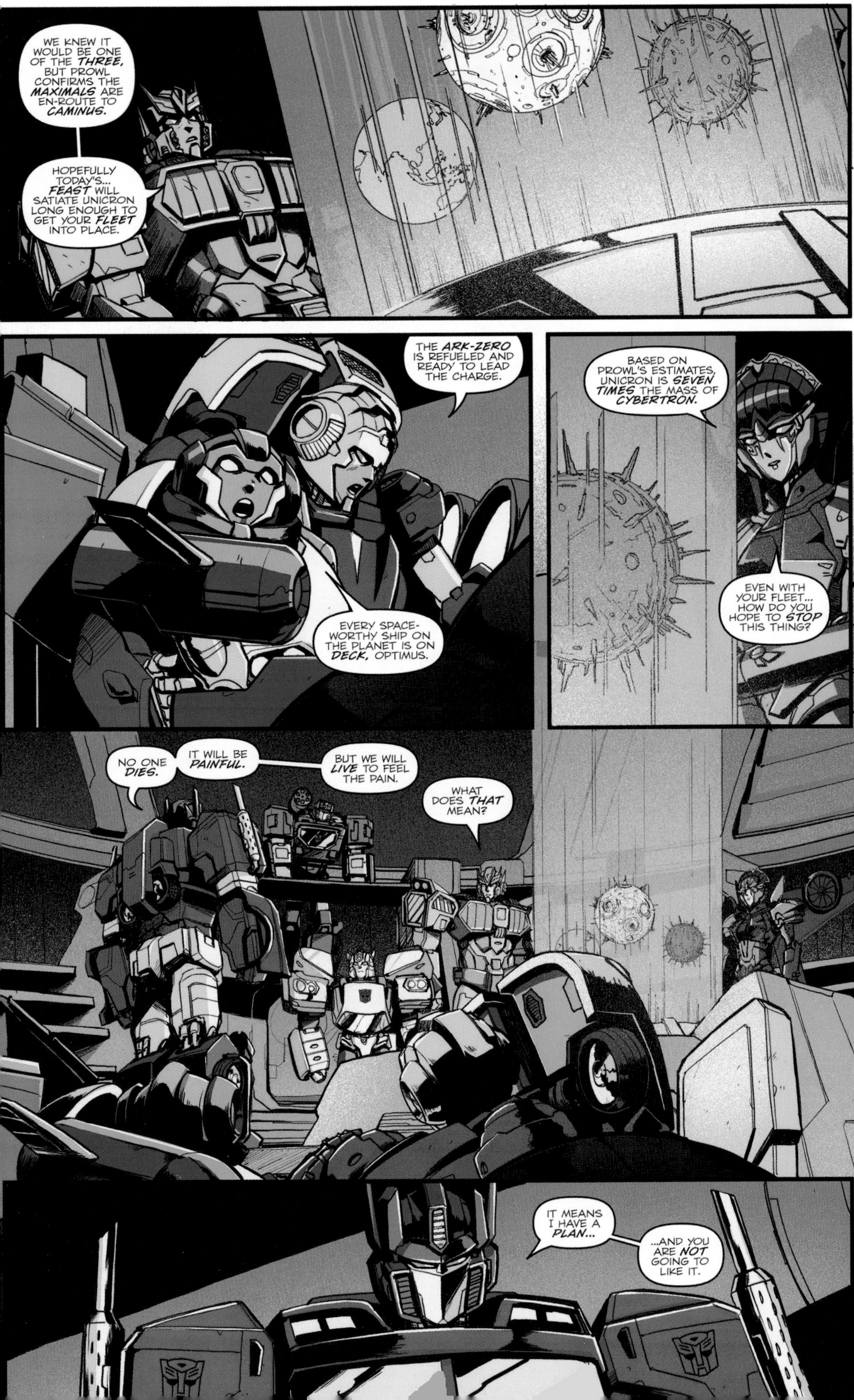
WE KNEW IT WOULD BE ONE OF THE THREE, BUT PROWL CONFIRMS THE MAXIMALS ARE EN-ROUTE TO CAMINUS.
HOPEFULLY TODAY'S... FEAST WILL SATIATE UNICRON LONG ENOUGH TO GET YOUR FLEET INTO PLACE.
THE ARK-ZERO IS REFUELED AND READY TO LEAD THE CHARGE.
EVERY SPACE-WORTHY SHIP ON THE PLANET IS ON DECK, OPTIMUS.
BASED ON PROWL'S ESTIMATES, UNICRON IS SEVEN TIMES THE MASS OF CYBERTRON.
EVEN WITH YOUR FLEET... HOW DO YOU HOPE TO STOP THIS THING?
NO ONE DIES.
IT WILL BE PAINFUL.
BUT WE WILL LIVE TO FEEL THE PAIN.
WHAT DOES THAT MEAN?
IT MEANS I HAVE A PLAN...
...AND YOU ARE NOT GOING TO LIKE IT.

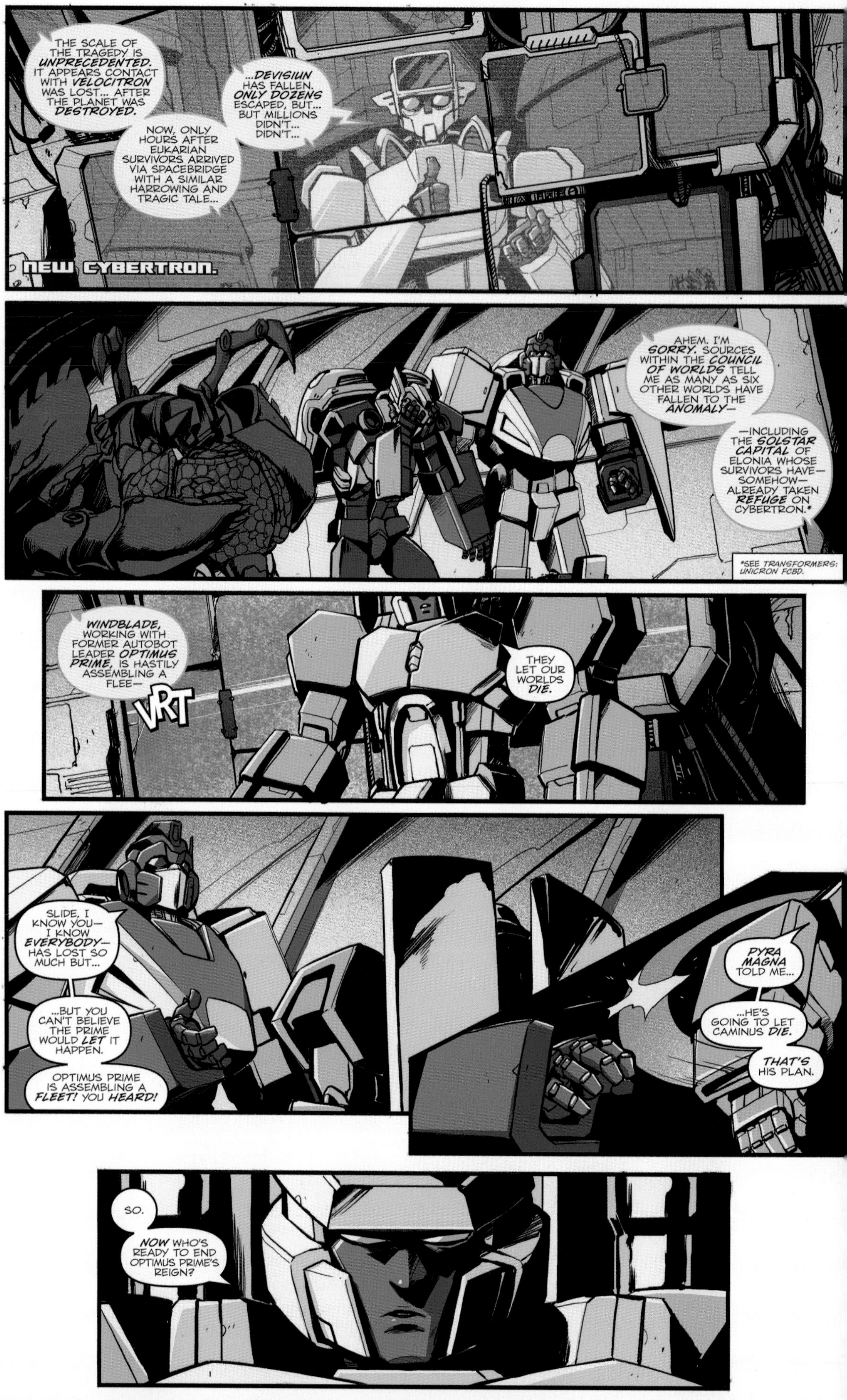
THE SCALE OF THE TRAGEDY IS UNPRECEDENTED. IT APPEARS CONTACT WITH VELOCITRON WAS LOST... AFTER THE PLANET WAS DESTROYED.
NOW, ONLY HOURS AFTER EUKARIAN SURVIVORS ARRIVED VIA SPACEBRIDGE WITH A SIMILAR HARROWING AND TRAGIC TALE...
...DEVISIUN HAS FALLEN. ONLY DOZENS ESCAPED, BUT... BUT MILLIONS DIDN'T... DIDN'T...
NEW CYBERTRON.
AHEM. I'M SORRY. SOURCES WITHIN THE COUNCIL OF WORLDS TELL ME AS MANY AS SIX OTHER WORLDS HAVE FALLEN TO THE ANOMALY—
—INCLUDING THE SOLSTAR CAPITAL OF ELONIA WHOSE SURVIVORS HAVE—SOMEHOW—ALREADY TAKEN REFUGE ON CYBERTRON.*
*SEE TRANSFORMERS: UNICRON FCBD.
WINDBLADE, WORKING WITH FORMER AUTOBOT LEADER OPTIMUS PRIME, IS HASTILY ASSEMBLING A FLEE—
VRT
THEY LET OUR WORLDS DIE.
SLIDE, I KNOW YOU— I KNOW EVERYBODY— HAS LOST SO MUCH BUT...
...BUT YOU CAN'T BELIEVE THE PRIME WOULD LET IT HAPPEN.
OPTIMUS PRIME IS ASSEMBLING A FLEET! YOU HEARD!
PYRA MAGNA TOLD ME...
...HE'S GOING TO LET CAMINUS DIE.
THAT'S HIS PLAN.
SO.
NOW WHO'S READY TO END OPTIMUS PRIME'S REIGN?

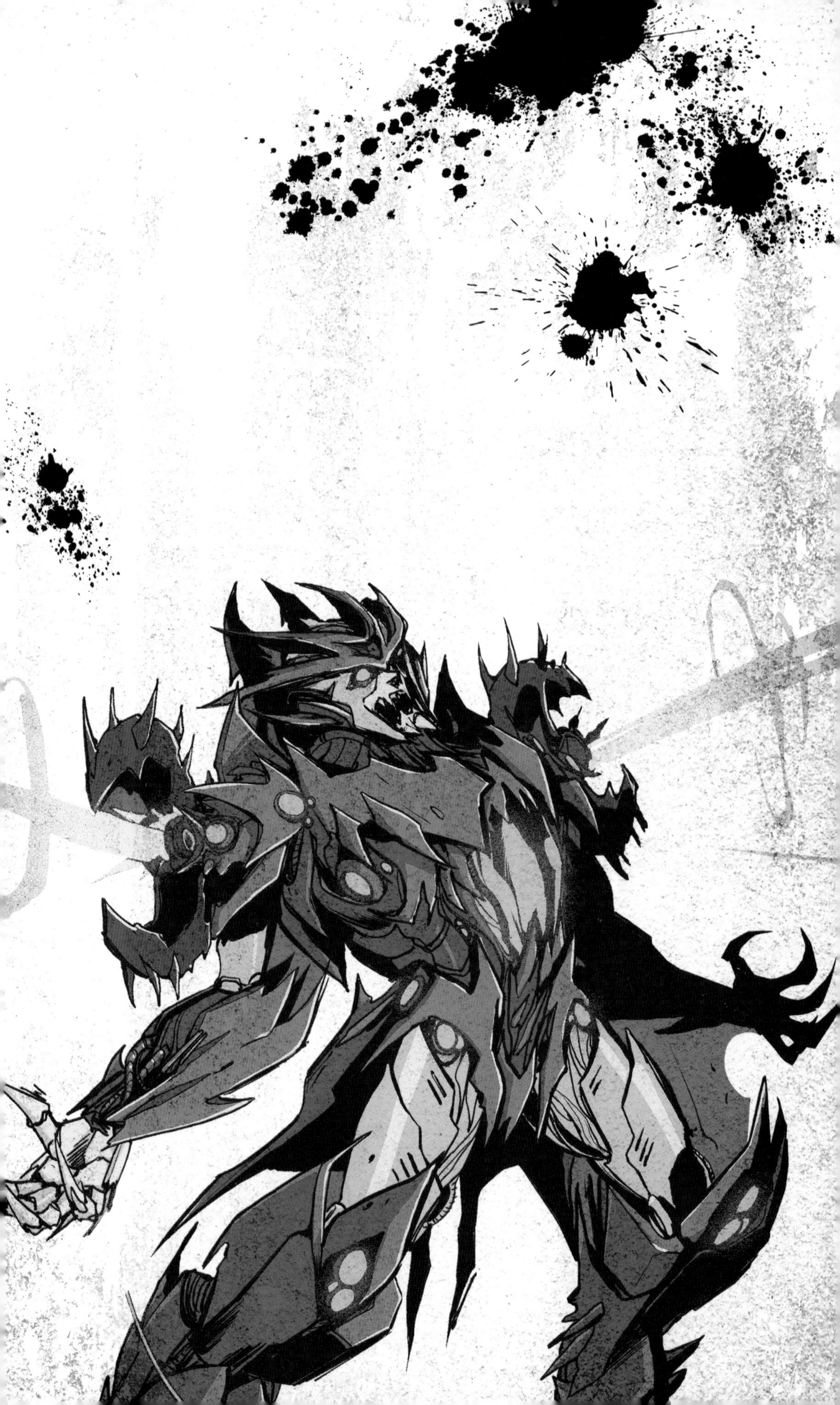

ART BY KEI ZAMA COLORS BY JOSH BURCHAM

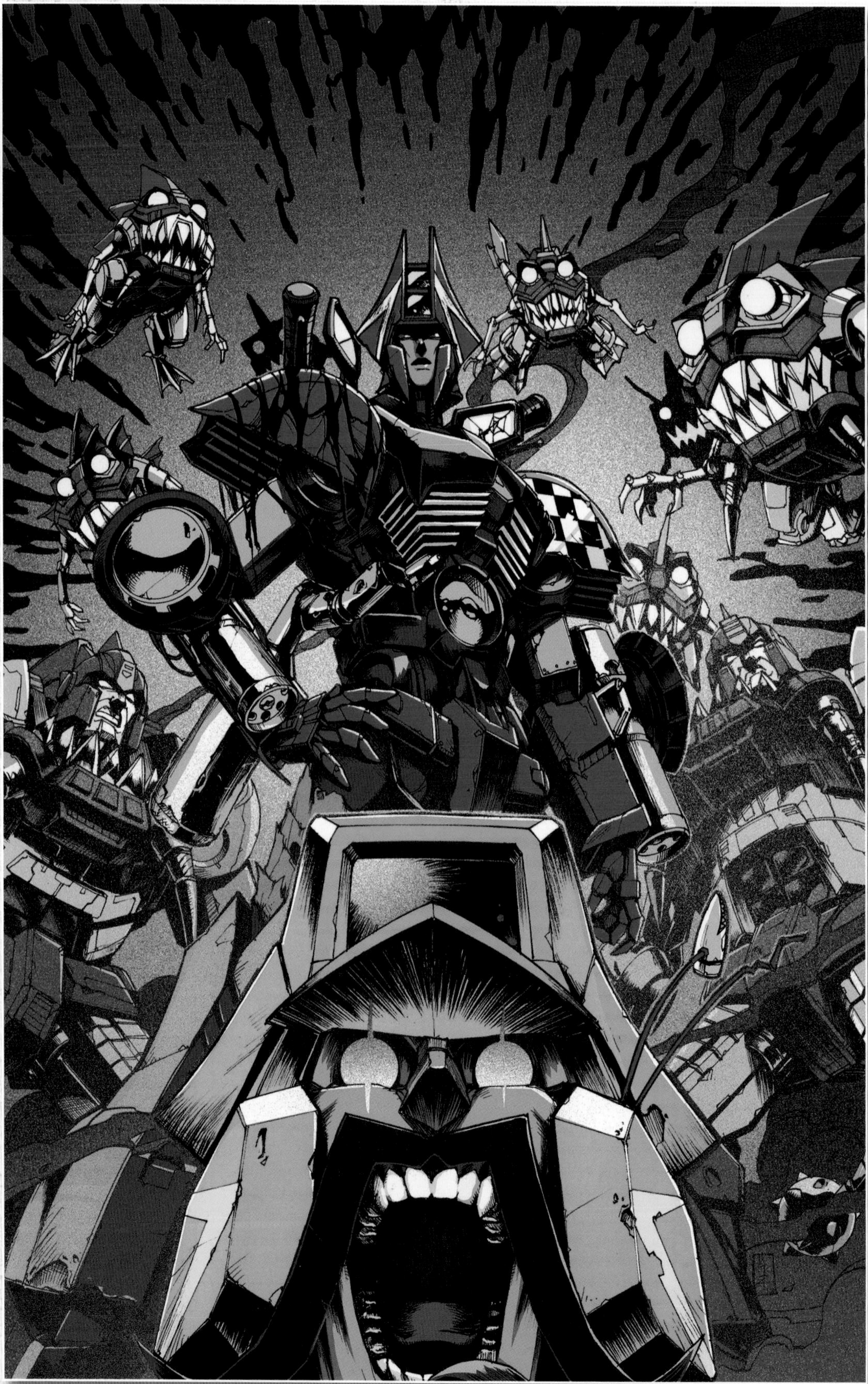

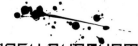

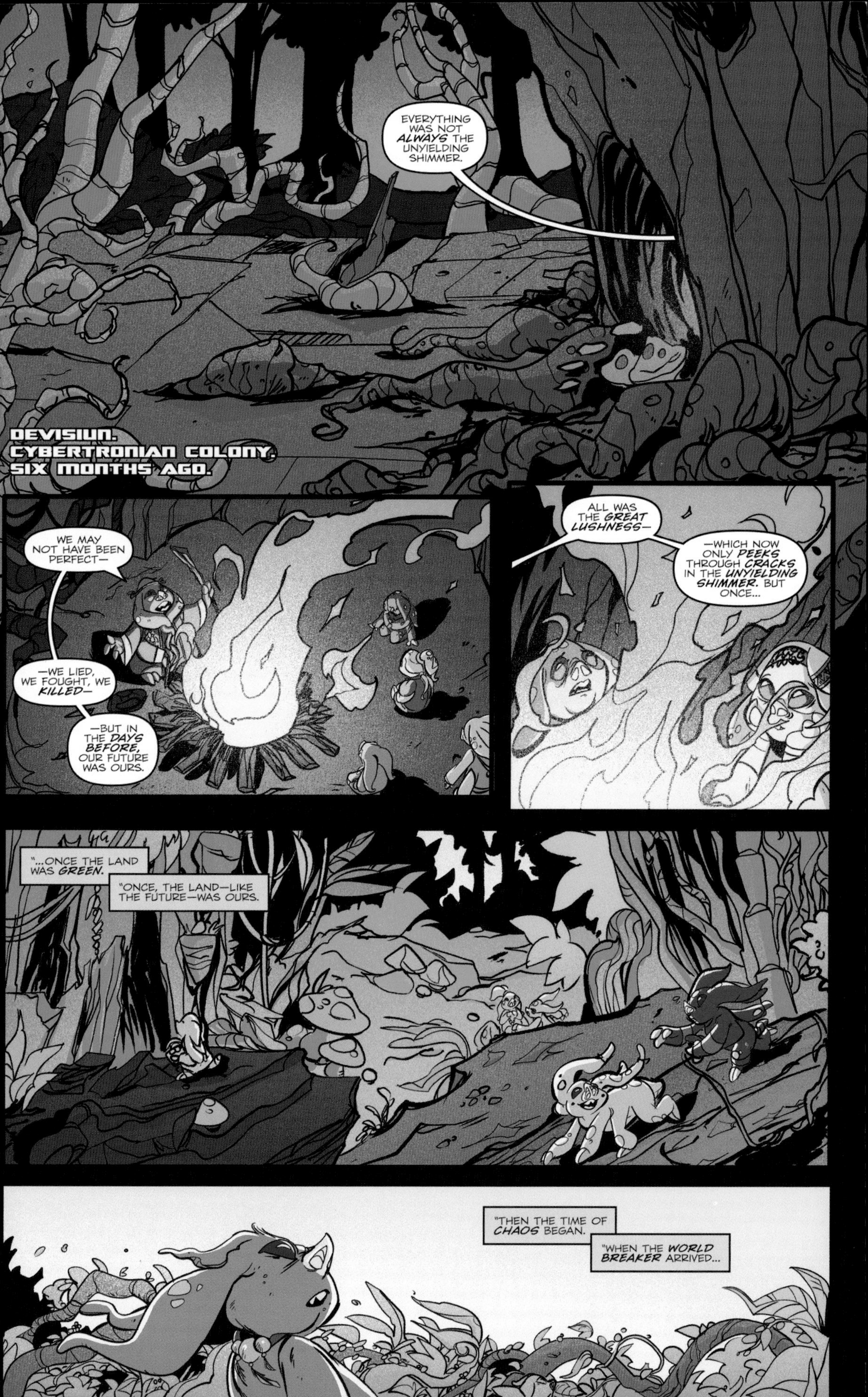
EVERYTHING WAS NOT ALWAYS THE UNYIELDING SHIMMER.
DEVISIUN. CYBERTRONIAN COLONY. SIX MONTHS AGO.
WE MAY NOT HAVE BEEN PERFECT—
—WE LIED, WE FOUGHT, WE KILLED—
—BUT IN THE DAYS BEFORE, OUR FUTURE WAS OURS.
ALL WAS THE GREAT LUSHNESS—
—WHICH NOW ONLY PEEKS THROUGH CRACKS IN THE UNYIELDING SHIMMER. BUT ONCE...
"...ONCE THE LAND WAS GREEN.
"ONCE, THE LAND—LIKE THE FUTURE—WAS OURS.
"THEN THE TIME OF CHAOS BEGAN.
"WHEN THE WORLD BREAKER ARRIVED...

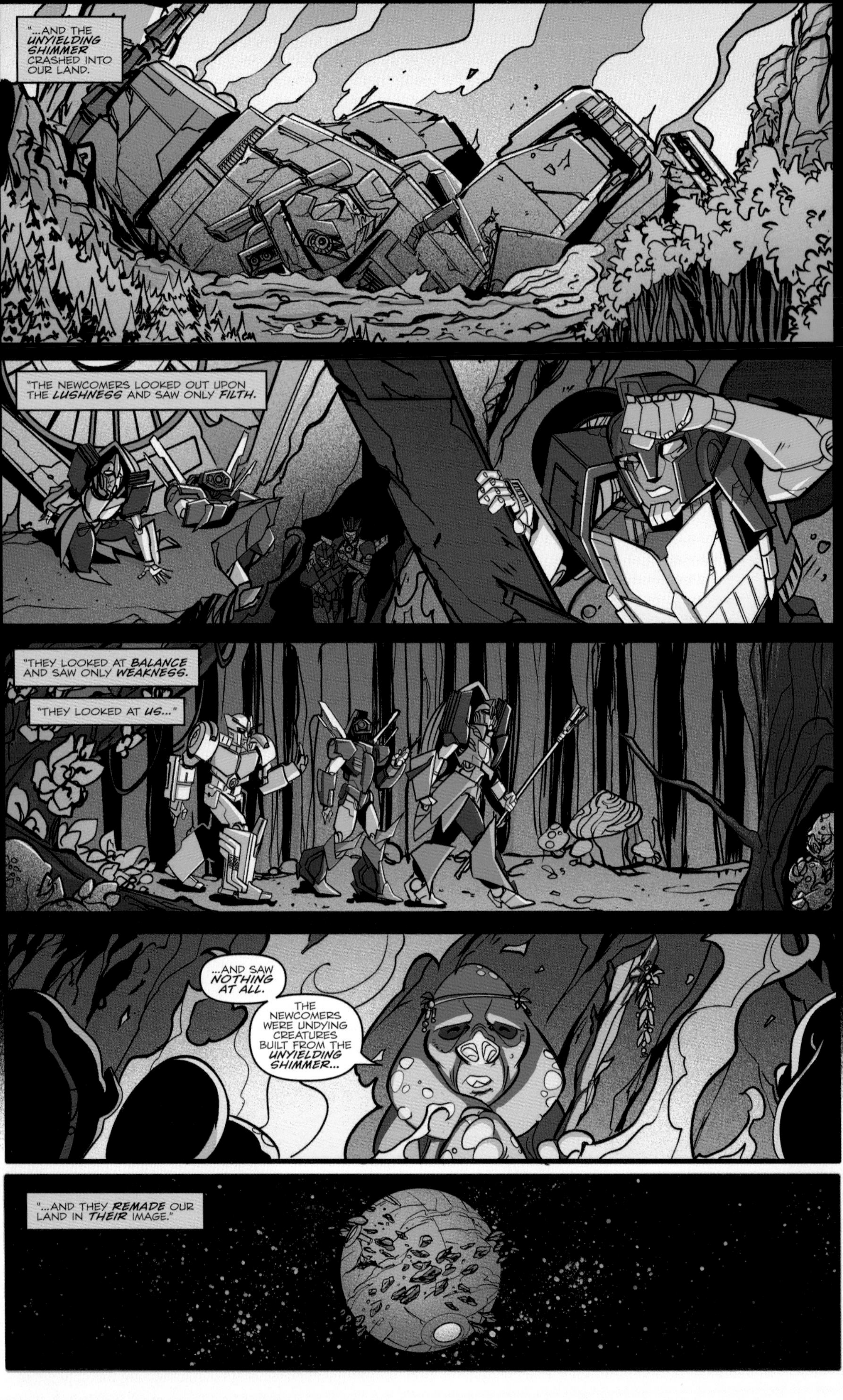

"...AND THE UNYIELDING SHIMMER CRASHED INTO OUR LAND.
"THE NEWCOMERS LOOKED OUT UPON THE LUSHNESS AND SAW ONLY FILTH.
"THEY LOOKED AT BALANCE AND SAW ONLY WEAKNESS.
"THEY LOOKED AT US..."
...AND SAW NOTHING AT ALL.
THE NEWCOMERS WERE UNDYING CREATURES BUILT FROM THE UNYIELDING SHIMMER...
"...AND THEY REMADE OUR LAND IN THEIR IMAGE."

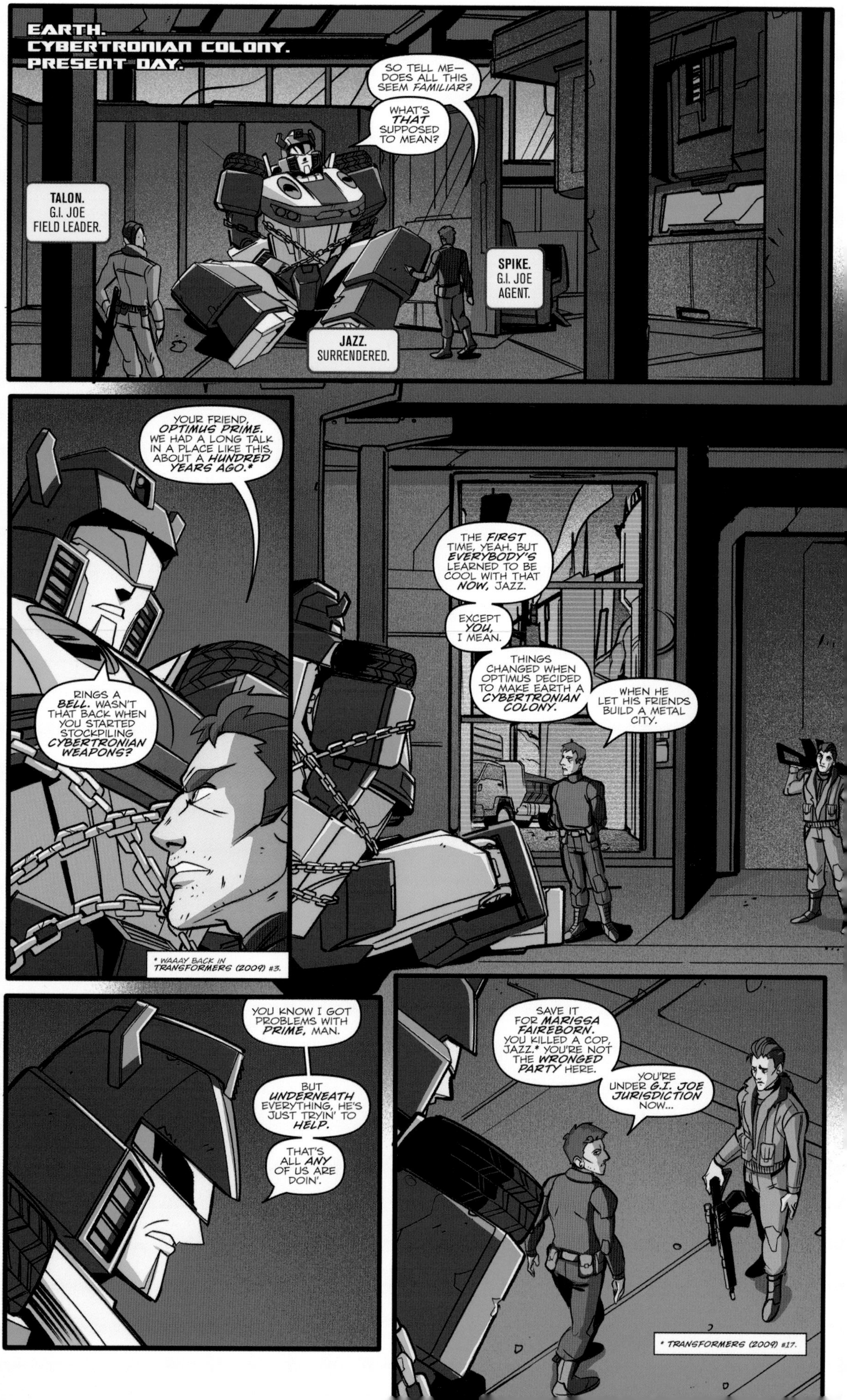
EARTH. CYBERTRONIAN COLONY. PRESENT DAY.
SO TELL ME— DOES ALL THIS SEEM FAMILIAR?
WHAT'S THAT SUPPOSED TO MEAN?
TALON. G.I. JOE FIELD LEADER.
SPIKE. G.I. JOE AGENT.
JAZZ. SURRENDERED.
YOUR FRIEND, OPTIMUS PRIME. WE HAD A LONG TALK IN A PLACE LIKE THIS, ABOUT A HUNDRED YEARS AGO.*
RINGS A BELL. WASN'T THAT BACK WHEN YOU STARTED STOCKPILING CYBERTRONIAN WEAPONS?
THE FIRST TIME, YEAH. BUT EVERYBODY'S LEARNED TO BE COOL WITH THAT NOW, JAZZ.
EXCEPT YOU, I MEAN.
THINGS CHANGED WHEN OPTIMUS DECIDED TO MAKE EARTH A CYBERTRONIAN COLONY.
WHEN HE LET HIS FRIENDS BUILD A METAL CITY.
* WAAAY BACK IN TRANSFORMERS (2009) #3.
YOU KNOW I GOT PROBLEMS WITH PRIME, MAN.
BUT UNDERNEATH EVERYTHING, HE'S JUST TRYIN' TO HELP.
THAT'S ALL ANY OF US ARE DOIN'.
SAVE IT FOR MARISSA FAIREBORN. YOU KILLED A COP, JAZZ.* YOU'RE NOT THE WRONGED PARTY HERE.
YOU'RE UNDER G.I. JOE JURISDICTION NOW...
* TRANSFORMERS (2009) #17.

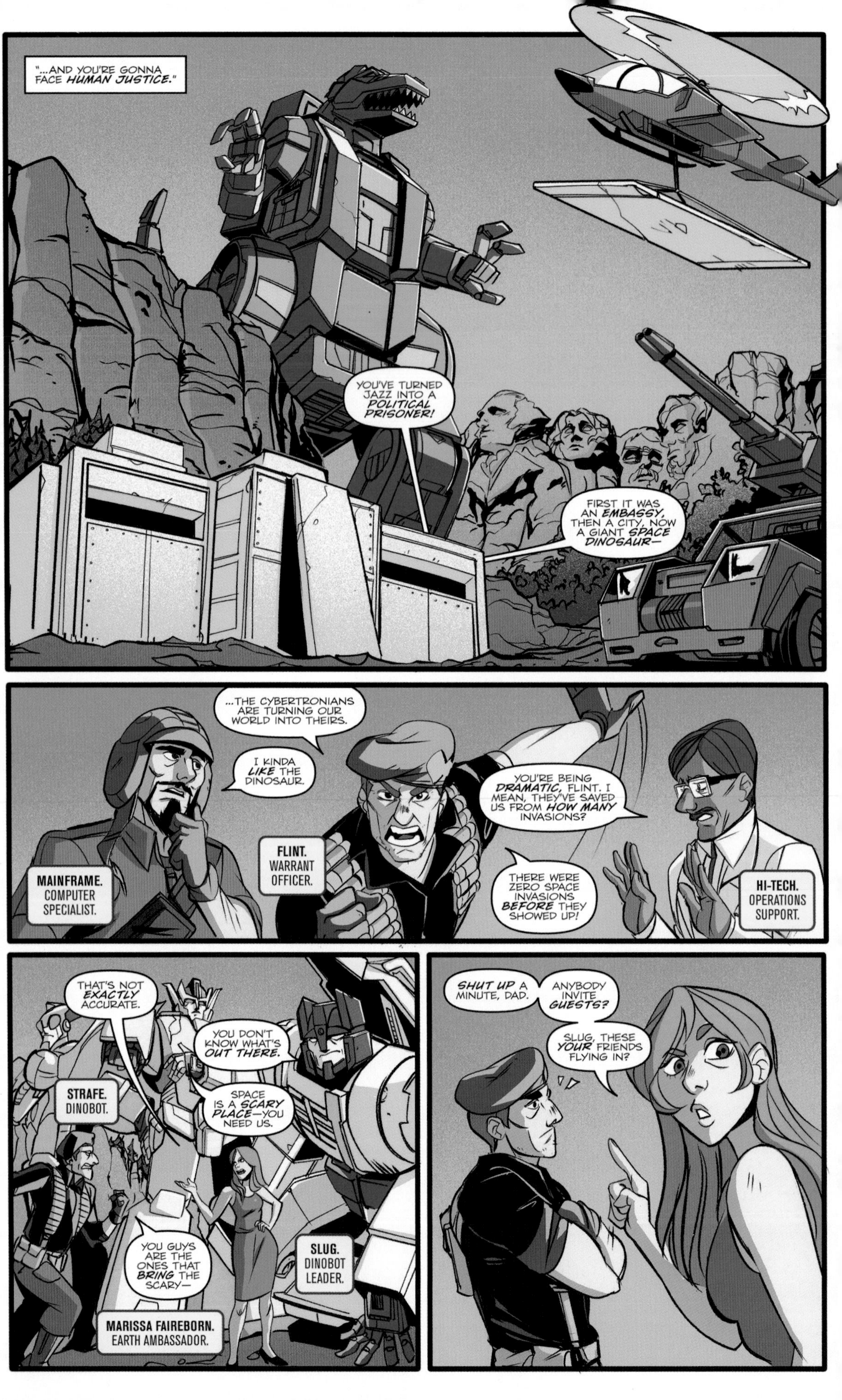
"...AND YOU'RE GONNA FACE HUMAN JUSTICE."
YOU'VE TURNED JAZZ INTO A POLITICAL PRISONER!
FIRST IT WAS AN EMBASSY, THEN A CITY, NOW A GIANT SPACE DINOSAUR—
...THE CYBERTRONIANS ARE TURNING OUR WORLD INTO THEIRS.
I KINDA LIKE THE DINOSAUR.
MAINFRAME. COMPUTER SPECIALIST.
FLINT. WARRANT OFFICER.
YOU'RE BEING DRAMATIC, FLINT. I MEAN, THEY'VE SAVED US FROM HOW MANY INVASIONS?
THERE WERE ZERO SPACE INVASIONS BEFORE THEY SHOWED UP!
HI-TECH. OPERATIONS SUPPORT.
THAT'S NOT EXACTLY ACCURATE.
YOU DON'T KNOW WHAT'S OUT THERE.
STRAFE. DINOBOT.
SPACE IS A SCARY PLACE—YOU NEED US.
YOU GUYS ARE THE ONES THAT BRING THE SCARY—
SLUG. DINOBOT LEADER.
MARISSA FAIREBORN. EARTH AMBASSADOR.
SHUT UP A MINUTE, DAD.
ANYBODY INVITE GUESTS?
SLUG, THESE YOUR FRIENDS FLYING IN?

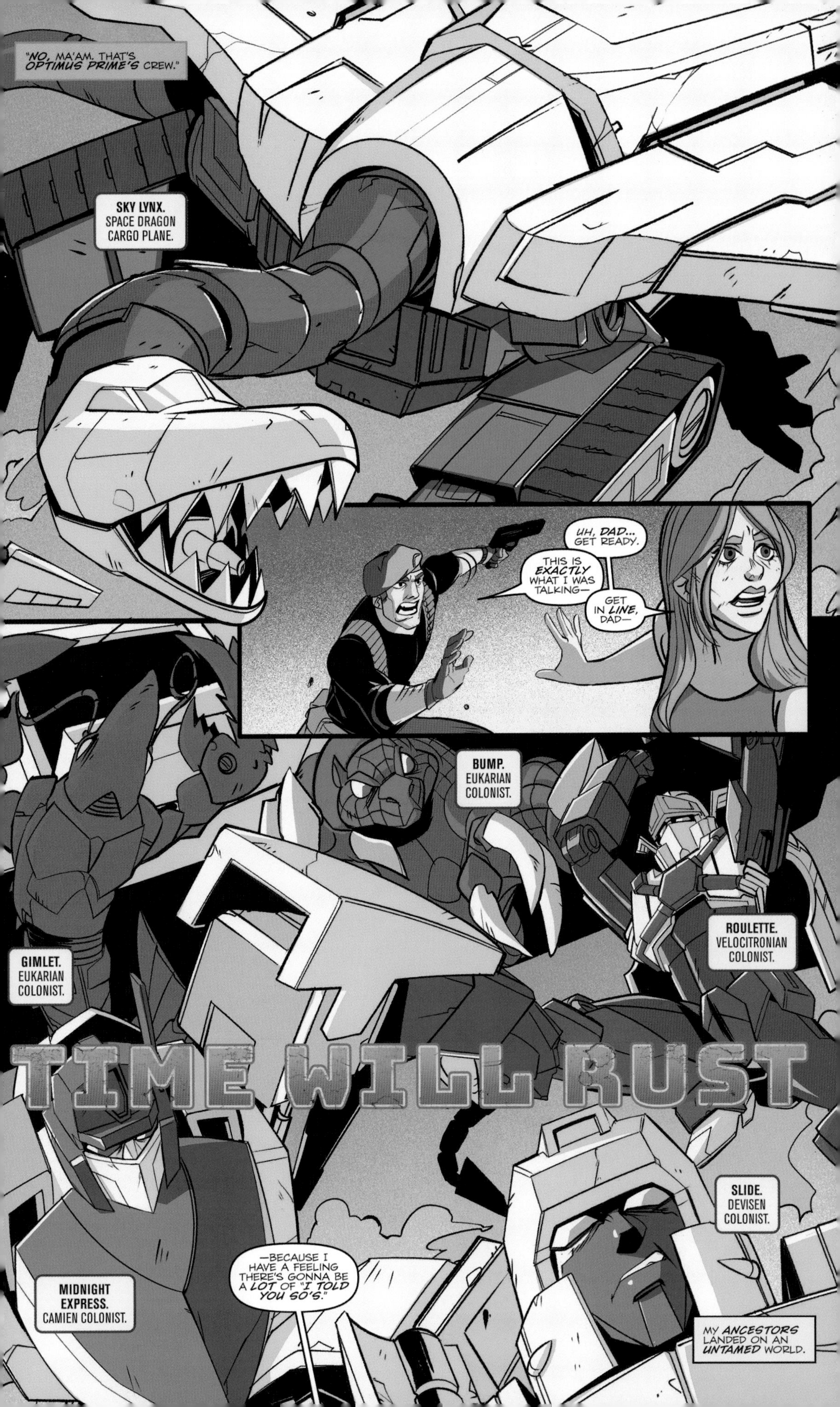

"NO, MA'AM. THAT'S OPTIMUS PRIME'S CREW."
SKY LYNX. SPACE DRAGON CARGO PLANE.
UH, DAD... GET READY.
THIS IS EXACTLY WHAT I WAS TALKING—
GET IN LINE, DAD—
BUMP. EUKARIAN COLONIST.
ROULETTE. VELOCITRONIAN COLONIST.
GIMLET. EUKARIAN COLONIST.
TIME WILL RUST
SLIDE. DEVISEN COLONIST.
—BECAUSE I HAVE A FEELING THERE'S GONNA BE A LOT OF "I TOLD YOU SO'S."
MIDNIGHT EXPRESS. CAMIEN COLONIST.
MY ANCESTORS LANDED ON AN UNTAMED WORLD.

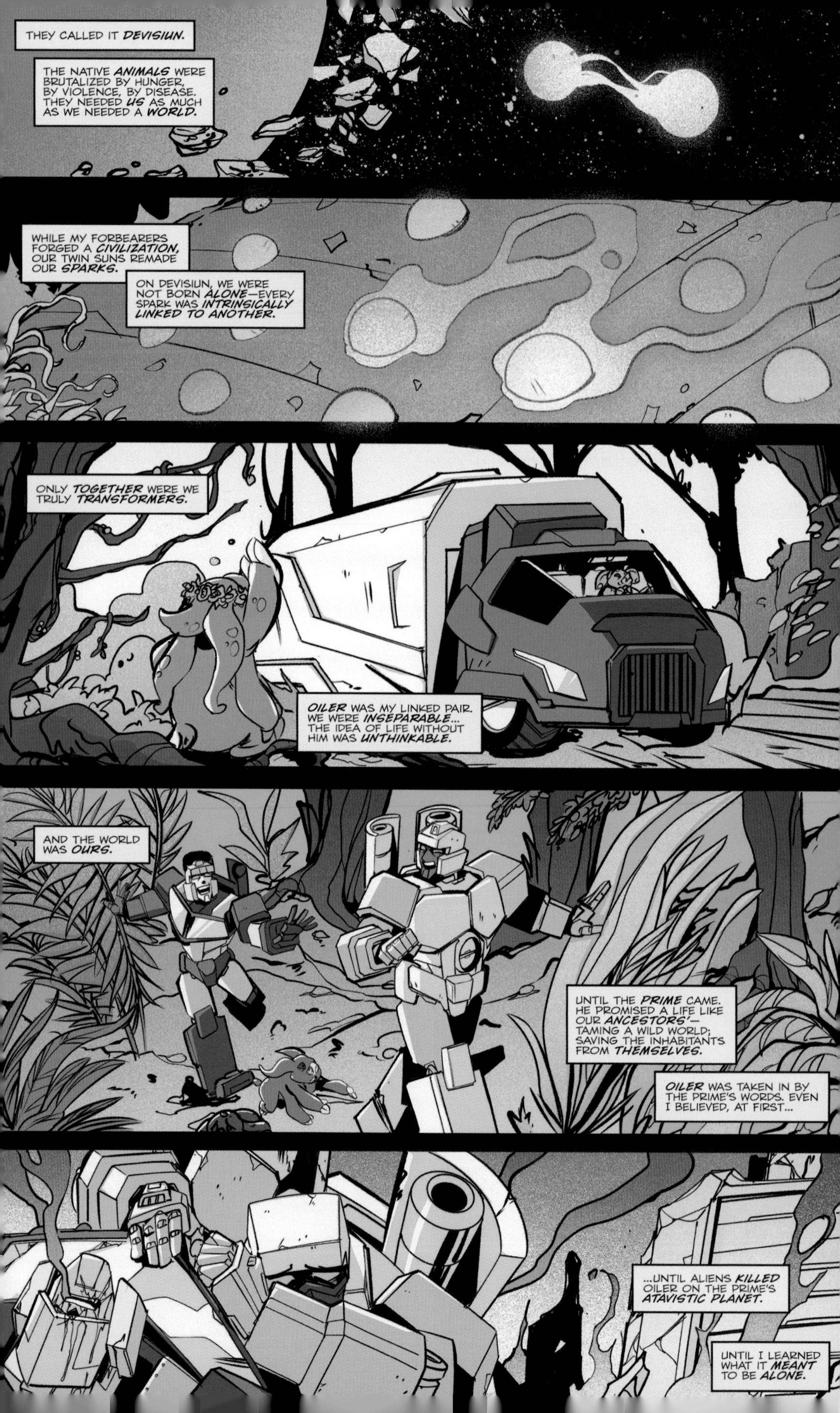
THEY CALLED IT DEVISIUN.
THE NATIVE ANIMALS WERE BRUTALIZED BY HUNGER, BY VIOLENCE, BY DISEASE. THEY NEEDED US AS MUCH AS WE NEEDED A WORLD.
WHILE MY FORBEARERS FORGED A CIVILIZATION, OUR TWIN SUNS REMADE OUR SPARKS.
ON DEVISIUN, WE WERE NOT BORN ALONE—EVERY SPARK WAS INTRINSICALLY LINKED TO ANOTHER.
ONLY TOGETHER WERE WE TRULY TRANSFORMERS.
OILER WAS MY LINKED PAIR. WE WERE INSEPARABLE... THE IDEA OF LIFE WITHOUT HIM WAS UNTHINKABLE.
AND THE WORLD WAS OURS.
UNTIL THE PRIME CAME. HE PROMISED A LIFE LIKE OUR ANCESTORS'—TAMING A WILD WORLD; SAVING THE INHABITANTS FROM THEMSELVES.
OILER WAS TAKEN IN BY THE PRIME'S WORDS. EVEN I BELIEVED, AT FIRST...
...UNTIL ALIENS KILLED OILER ON THE PRIME'S ATAVISTIC PLANET.
UNTIL I LEARNED WHAT IT MEANT TO BE ALONE.

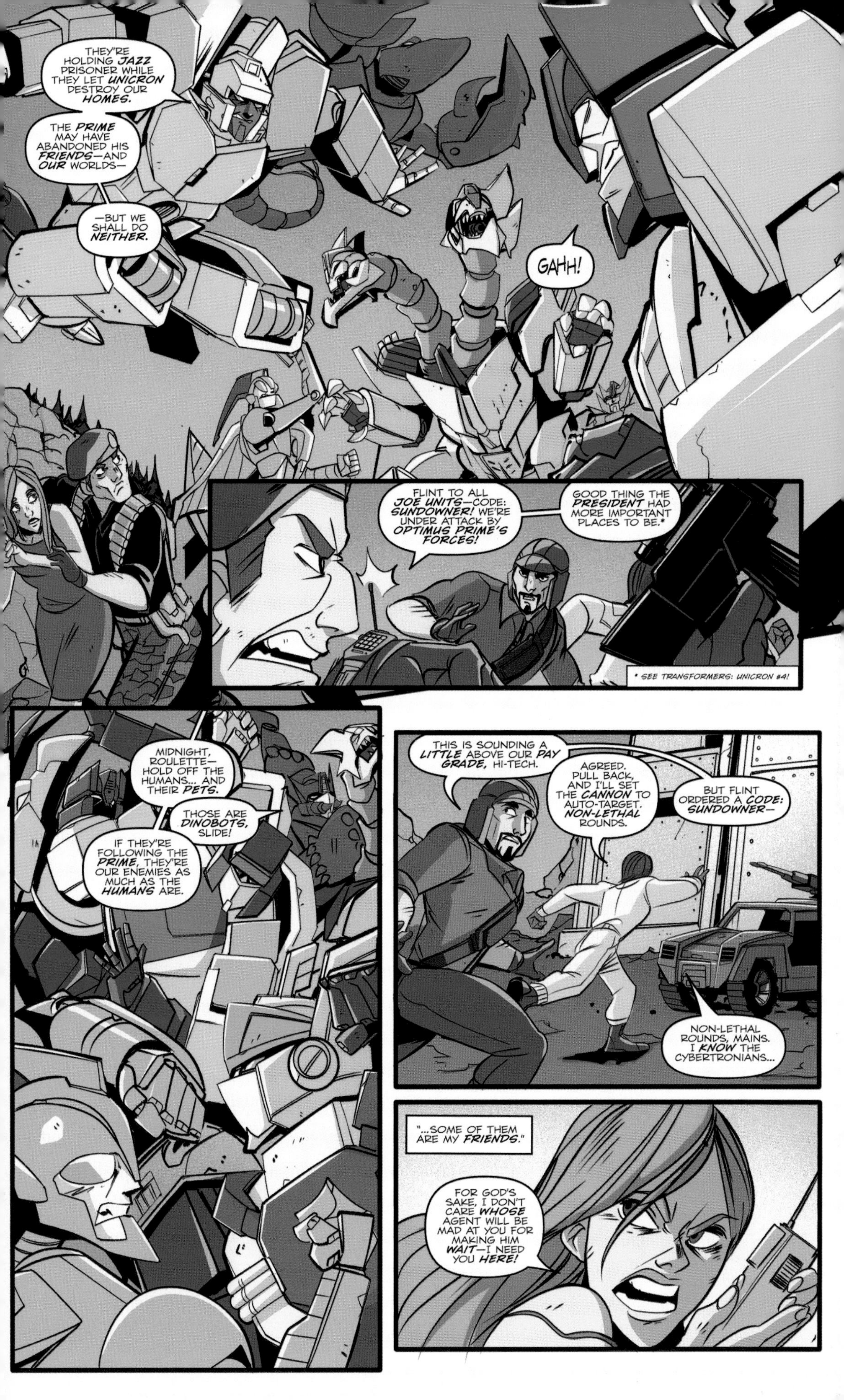
THEY'RE HOLDING JAZZ PRISONER WHILE THEY LET UNICRON DESTROY OUR HOMES.
THE PRIME MAY HAVE ABANDONED HIS FRIENDS—AND OUR WORLDS—
—BUT WE SHALL DO NEITHER.
GAHH!
FLINT TO ALL JOE UNITS—CODE: SUNDOWNER! WE'RE UNDER ATTACK BY OPTIMUS PRIME'S FORCES!
GOOD THING THE PRESIDENT HAD MORE IMPORTANT PLACES TO BE.*
* SEE TRANSFORMERS: UNICRON #4!
MIDNIGHT, ROULETTE—HOLD OFF THE HUMANS... AND THEIR PETS.
THOSE ARE DINOBOTS, SLIDE!
IF THEY'RE FOLLOWING THE PRIME, THEY'RE OUR ENEMIES AS MUCH AS THE HUMANS ARE.
THIS IS SOUNDING A LITTLE ABOVE OUR PAY GRADE, HI-TECH.
AGREED. PULL BACK, AND I'LL SET THE CANNON TO AUTO-TARGET. NON-LETHAL ROUNDS.
BUT FLINT ORDERED A CODE: SUNDOWNER—
NON-LETHAL ROUNDS, MAINS. I KNOW THE CYBERTRONIANS...
"...SOME OF THEM ARE MY FRIENDS."
FOR GOD'S SAKE, I DON'T CARE WHOSE AGENT WILL BE MAD AT YOU FOR MAKING HIM WAIT—I NEED YOU HERE!

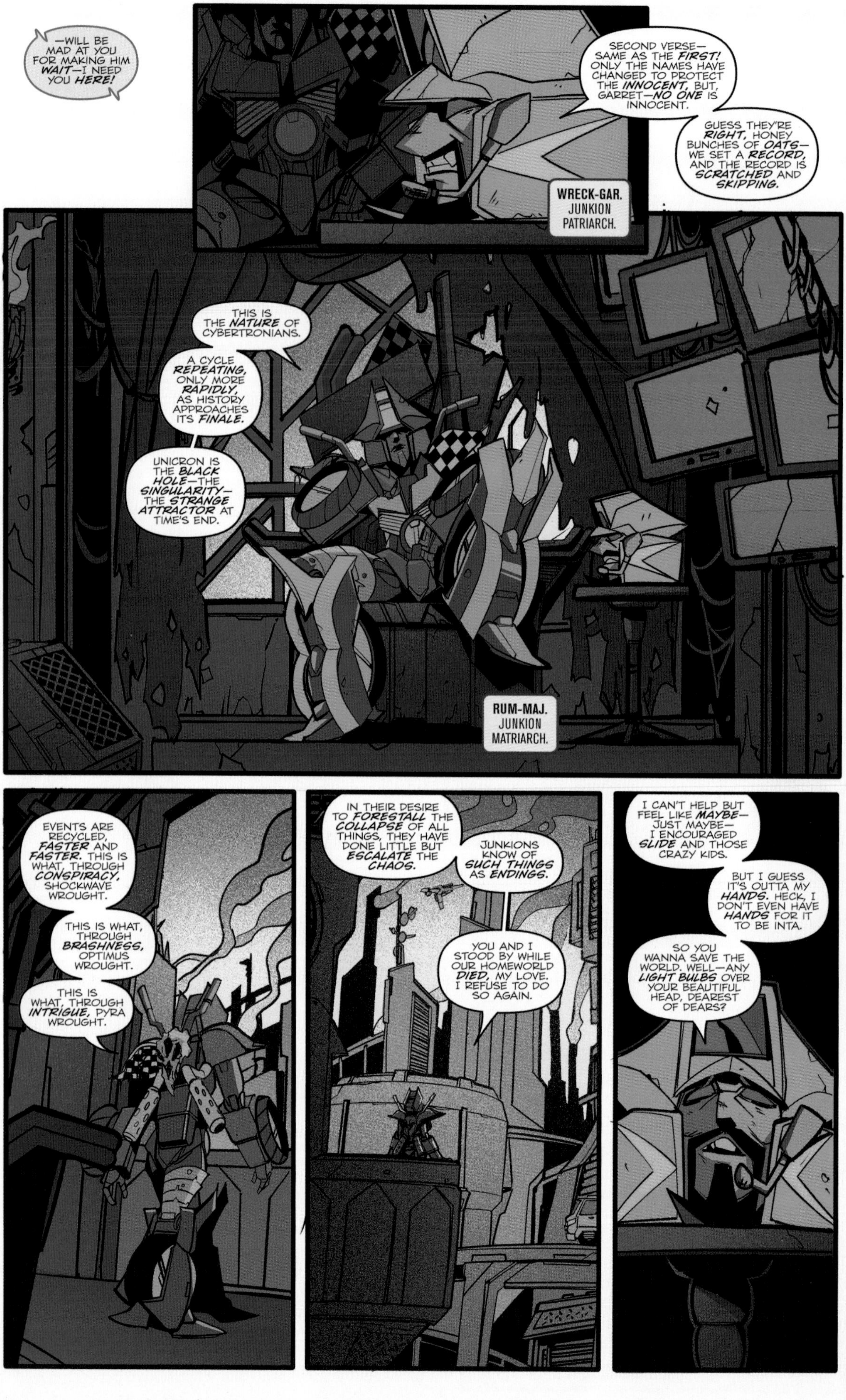
—WILL BE MAD AT YOU FOR MAKING HIM WAIT—I NEED YOU HERE!
SECOND VERSE—SAME AS THE FIRST! ONLY THE NAMES HAVE CHANGED TO PROTECT THE INNOCENT, BUT, GARRET—NO ONE IS INNOCENT.
GUESS THEY'RE RIGHT, HONEY BUNCHES OF OATS—WE SET A RECORD, AND THE RECORD IS SCRATCHED AND SKIPPING.
WRECK-GAR. JUNKION PATRIARCH.
THIS IS THE NATURE OF CYBERTRONIANS.
A CYCLE REPEATING, ONLY MORE RAPIDLY, AS HISTORY APPROACHES ITS FINALE.
UNICRON IS THE BLACK HOLE—THE SINGULARITY—THE STRANGE ATTRACTOR AT TIME'S END.
RUM-MAJ. JUNKION MATRIARCH.
EVENTS ARE RECYCLED, FASTER AND FASTER. THIS IS WHAT, THROUGH CONSPIRACY, SHOCKWAVE WROUGHT.
THIS IS WHAT, THROUGH BRASHNESS, OPTIMUS WROUGHT.
THIS IS WHAT, THROUGH INTRIGUE, PYRA WROUGHT.
IN THEIR DESIRE TO FORESTALL THE COLLAPSE OF ALL THINGS, THEY HAVE DONE LITTLE BUT ESCALATE THE CHAOS.
JUNKIONS KNOW OF SUCH THINGS AS ENDINGS.
YOU AND I STOOD BY WHILE OUR HOMEWORLD DIED, MY LOVE. I REFUSE TO DO SO AGAIN.
I CAN'T HELP BUT FEEL LIKE MAYBE—JUST MAYBE—I ENCOURAGED SLIDE AND THOSE CRAZY KIDS.
BUT I GUESS IT'S OUTTA MY HANDS. HECK, I DON'T EVEN HAVE HANDS FOR IT TO BE INTA.
SO YOU WANNA SAVE THE WORLD. WELL—ANY LIGHT BULBS OVER YOUR BEAUTIFUL HEAD, DEAREST OF DEARS?

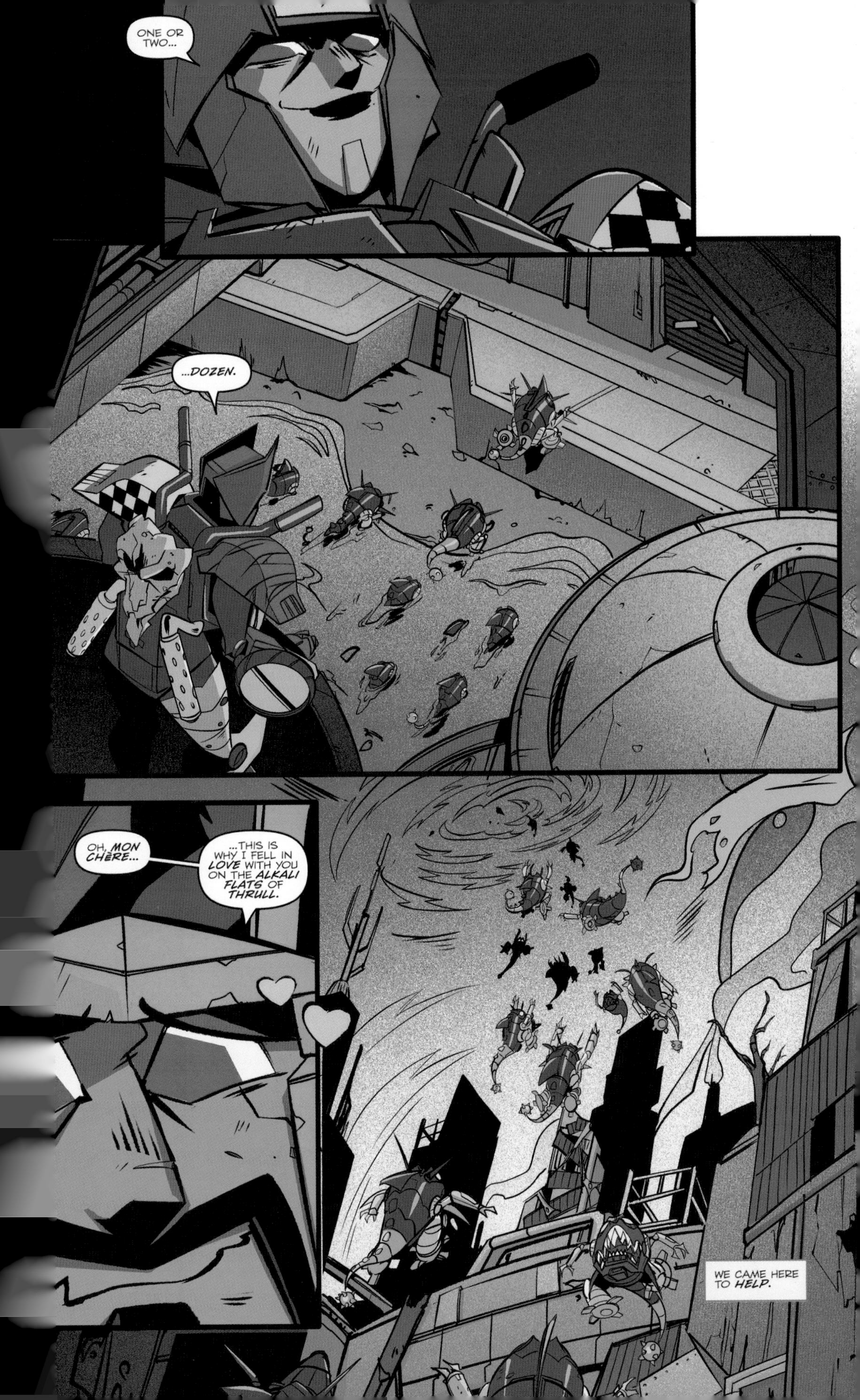
ONE OR TWO...
...DOZEN.
OH, MON CHÈRE...
...THIS IS WHY I FELL IN LOVE WITH YOU ON THE ALKALI FLATS OF THRULL.
WE CAME HERE TO HELP.

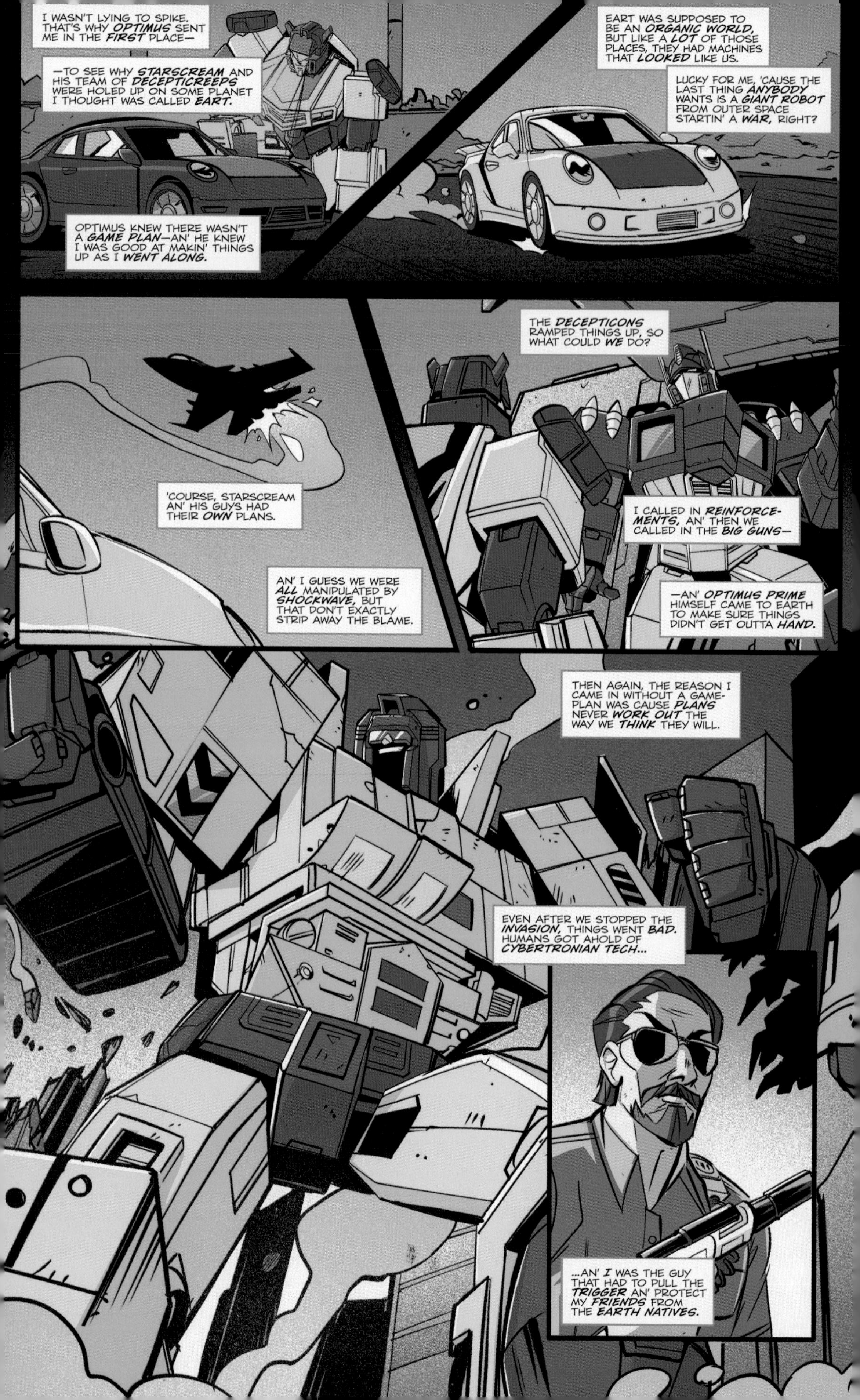
I WASN'T LYING TO SPIKE. THAT'S WHY OPTIMUS SENT ME IN THE FIRST PLACE—
—TO SEE WHY STARSCREAM AND HIS TEAM OF DECEPTICREEPS WERE HOLED UP ON SOME PLANET I THOUGHT WAS CALLED EART.
OPTIMUS KNEW THERE WASN'T A GAME PLAN—AN' HE KNEW I WAS GOOD AT MAKIN' THINGS UP AS I WENT ALONG.
EART WAS SUPPOSED TO BE AN ORGANIC WORLD, BUT LIKE A LOT OF THOSE PLACES, THEY HAD MACHINES THAT LOOKED LIKE US.
LUCKY FOR ME, 'CAUSE THE LAST THING ANYBODY WANTS IS A GIANT ROBOT FROM OUTER SPACE STARTIN' A WAR, RIGHT?
'COURSE, STARSCREAM AN' HIS GUYS HAD THEIR OWN PLANS.
AN' I GUESS WE WERE ALL MANIPULATED BY SHOCKWAVE, BUT THAT DON'T EXACTLY STRIP AWAY THE BLAME.
THE DECEPTICONS RAMPED THINGS UP, SO WHAT COULD WE DO?
I CALLED IN REINFORCE-MENTS, AN' THEN WE CALLED IN THE BIG GUNS—
—AN' OPTIMUS PRIME HIMSELF CAME TO EARTH TO MAKE SURE THINGS DIDN'T GET OUTTA HAND.
THEN AGAIN, THE REASON I CAME IN WITHOUT A GAME-PLAN WAS CAUSE PLANS NEVER WORK OUT THE WAY WE THINK THEY WILL.
EVEN AFTER WE STOPPED THE INVASION, THINGS WENT BAD. HUMANS GOT AHOLD OF CYBERTRONIAN TECH...
...AN' I WAS THE GUY THAT HAD TO PULL THE TRIGGER AN' PROTECT MY FRIENDS FROM THE EARTH NATIVES.

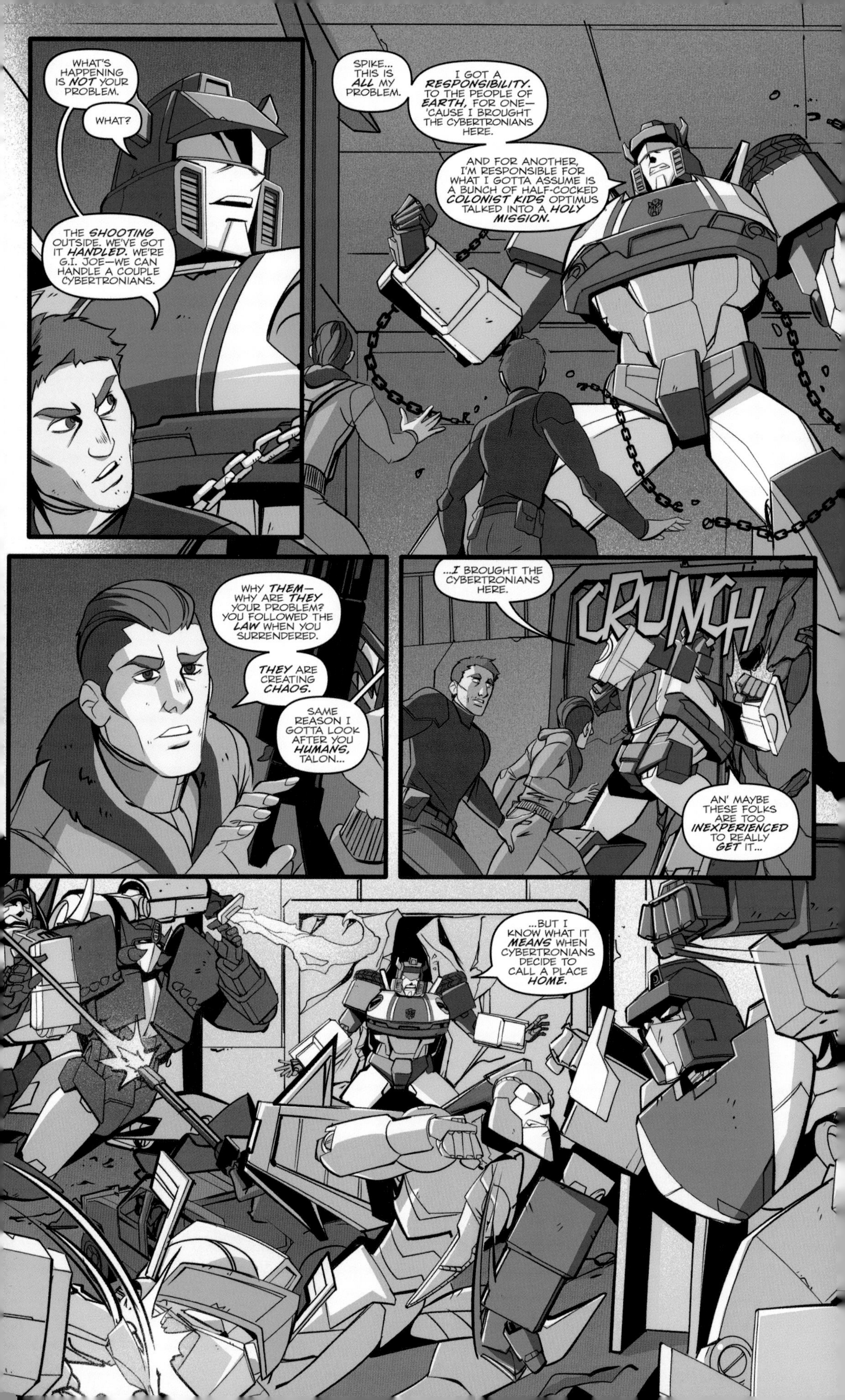
WHAT'S HAPPENING IS NOT YOUR PROBLEM.
WHAT?
THE SHOOTING OUTSIDE. WE'VE GOT IT HANDLED. WE'RE G.I. JOE—WE CAN HANDLE A COUPLE CYBERTRONIANS.
SPIKE... THIS IS ALL MY PROBLEM.
I GOT A RESPONSIBILITY. TO THE PEOPLE OF EARTH, FOR ONE— 'CAUSE I BROUGHT THE CYBERTRONIANS HERE.
AND FOR ANOTHER, I'M RESPONSIBLE FOR WHAT I GOTTA ASSUME IS A BUNCH OF HALF-COCKED COLONIST KIDS OPTIMUS TALKED INTO A HOLY MISSION.
WHY THEM— WHY ARE THEY YOUR PROBLEM? YOU FOLLOWED THE LAW WHEN YOU SURRENDERED.
THEY ARE CREATING CHAOS.
SAME REASON I GOTTA LOOK AFTER YOU HUMANS, TALON...
...I BROUGHT THE CYBERTRONIANS HERE.
CRUNCH
AN' MAYBE THESE FOLKS ARE TOO INEXPERIENCED TO REALLY GET IT...
...BUT I KNOW WHAT IT MEANS WHEN CYBERTRONIANS DECIDE TO CALL A PLACE HOME.

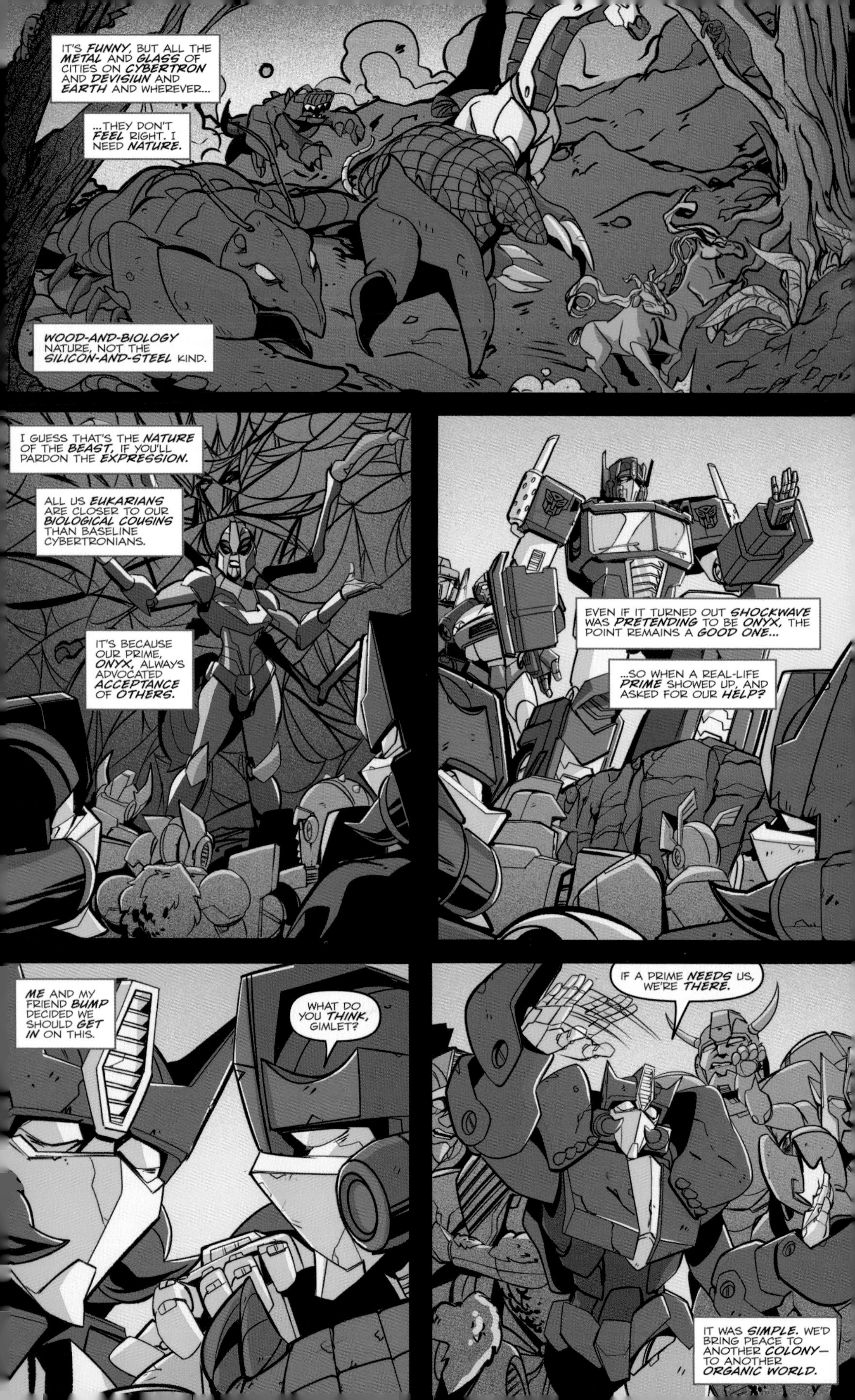
IT'S FUNNY, BUT ALL THE METAL AND GLASS OF CITIES ON CYBERTRON AND DEVISIUN AND EARTH AND WHEREVER...
...THEY DON'T FEEL RIGHT. I NEED NATURE.
WOOD-AND-BIOLOGY NATURE, NOT THE SILICON-AND-STEEL KIND.
I GUESS THAT'S THE NATURE OF THE BEAST, IF YOU'LL PARDON THE EXPRESSION.
ALL US EUKARIANS ARE CLOSER TO OUR BIOLOGICAL COUSINS THAN BASELINE CYBERTRONIANS.
IT'S BECAUSE OUR PRIME, ONYX, ALWAYS ADVOCATED ACCEPTANCE OF OTHERS.
EVEN IF IT TURNED OUT SHOCKWAVE WAS PRETENDING TO BE ONYX, THE POINT REMAINS A GOOD ONE...
...SO WHEN A REAL-LIFE PRIME SHOWED UP, AND ASKED FOR OUR HELP?
ME AND MY FRIEND BUMP DECIDED WE SHOULD GET IN ON THIS.
WHAT DO YOU THINK, GIMLET?
IF A PRIME NEEDS US, WE'RE THERE.
IT WAS SIMPLE. WE'D BRING PEACE TO ANOTHER COLONY— TO ANOTHER ORGANIC WORLD.

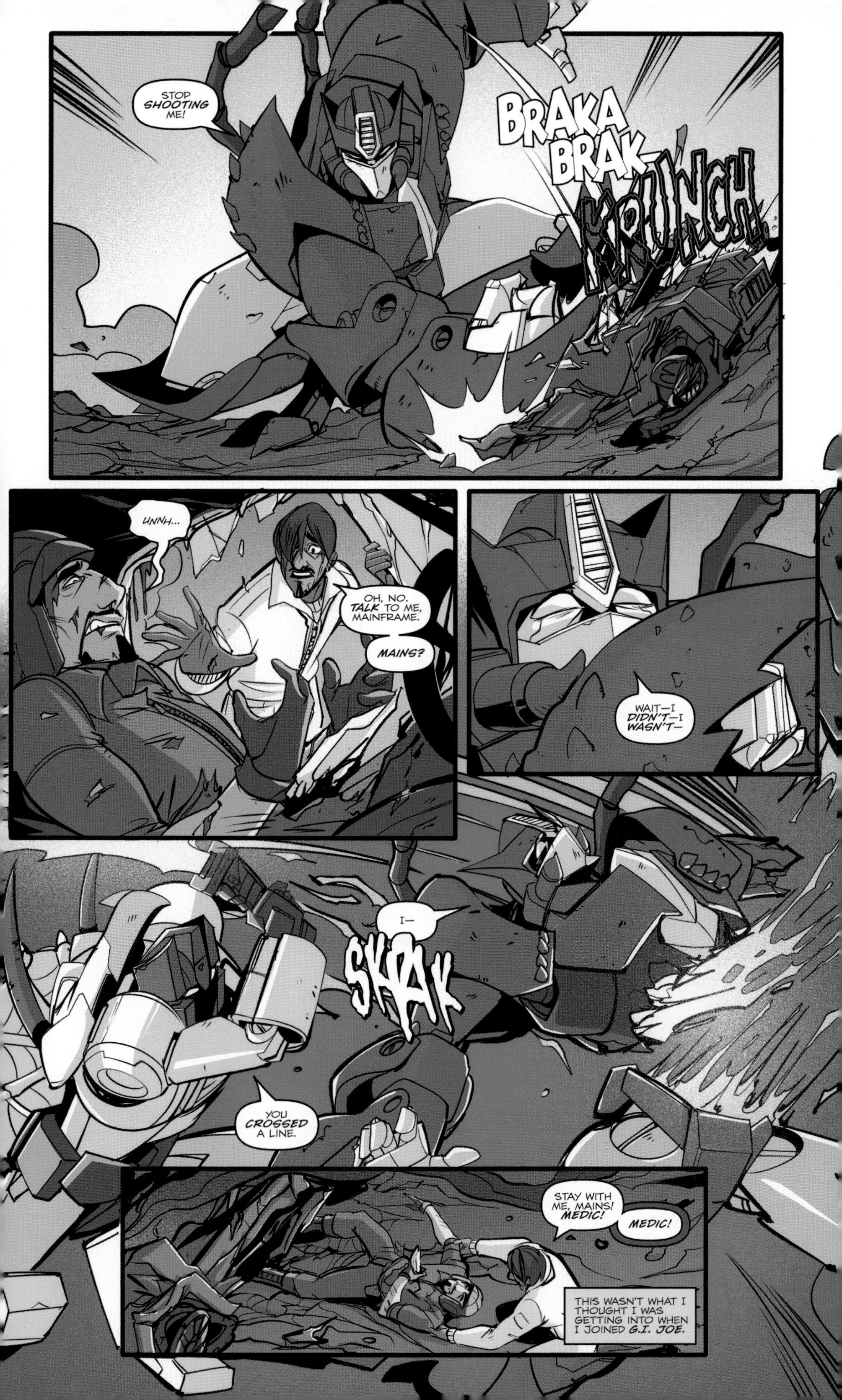
STOP SHOOTING ME!
BRAKA BRAK
KRUNCH
UNNH...
OH, NO. TALK TO ME, MAINFRAME.
MAINS?
WAIT—I DIDN'T—I WASN'T—
I—
SKAK
YOU CROSSED A LINE.
STAY WITH ME, MAINS! MEDIC!
MEDIC!
THIS WASN'T WHAT I THOUGHT I WAS GETTING INTO WHEN I JOINED G.I. JOE.

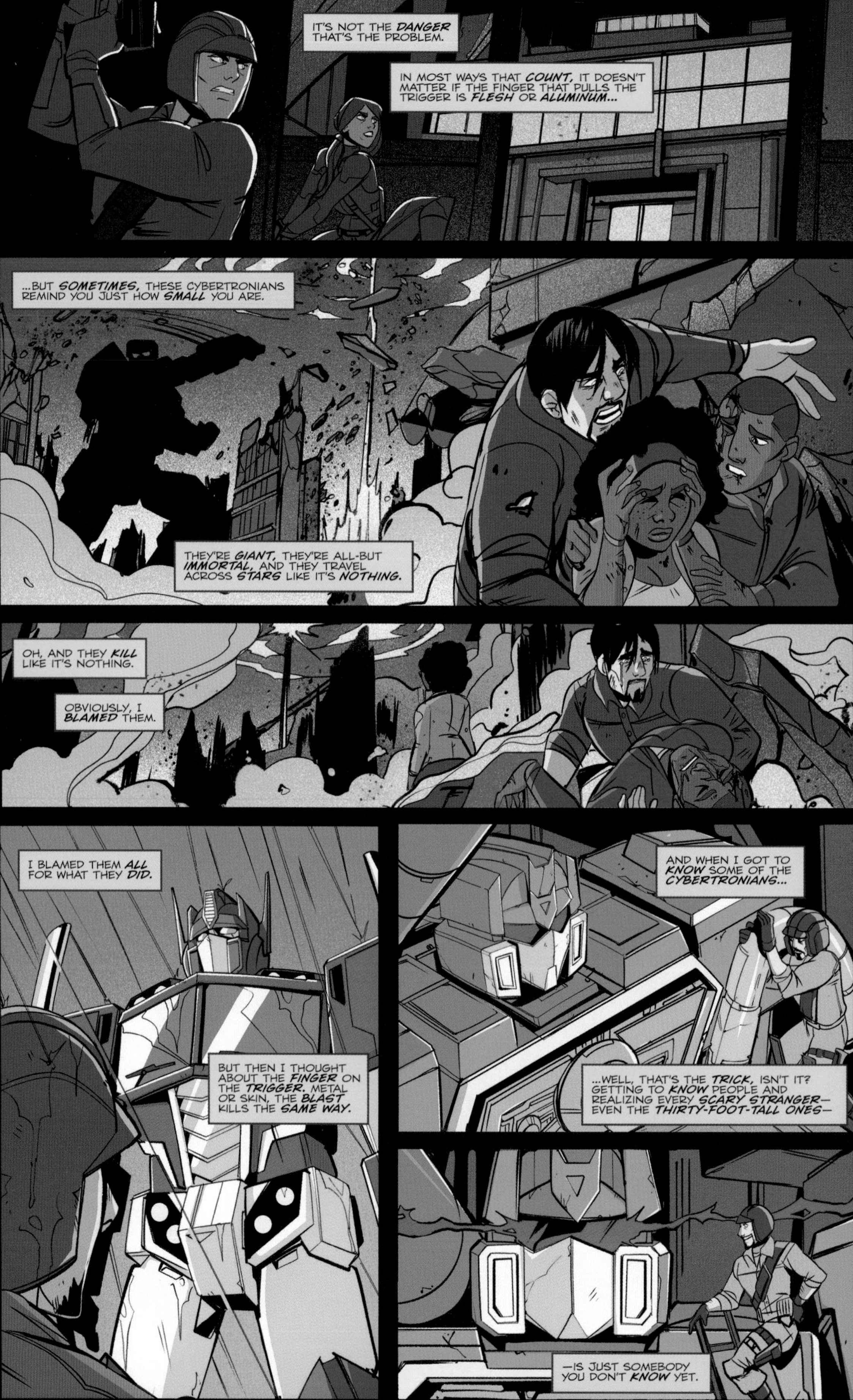
IT'S NOT THE DANGER THAT'S THE PROBLEM.
IN MOST WAYS THAT COUNT, IT DOESN'T MATTER IF THE FINGER THAT PULLS THE TRIGGER IS FLESH OR ALUMINUM...
...BUT SOMETIMES, THESE CYBERTRONIANS REMIND YOU JUST HOW SMALL YOU ARE.
THEY'RE GIANT, THEY'RE ALL-BUT IMMORTAL, AND THEY TRAVEL ACROSS STARS LIKE IT'S NOTHING.
OH, AND THEY KILL LIKE IT'S NOTHING.
OBVIOUSLY, I BLAMED THEM.
I BLAMED THEM ALL FOR WHAT THEY DID.
BUT THEN I THOUGHT ABOUT THE FINGER ON THE TRIGGER. METAL OR SKIN, THE BLAST KILLS THE SAME WAY.
AND WHEN I GOT TO KNOW SOME OF THE CYBERTRONIANS...
...WELL, THAT'S THE TRICK, ISN'T IT? GETTING TO KNOW PEOPLE AND REALIZING EVERY SCARY STRANGER— EVEN THE THIRTY-FOOT-TALL ONES—
—IS JUST SOMEBODY YOU DON'T KNOW YET.

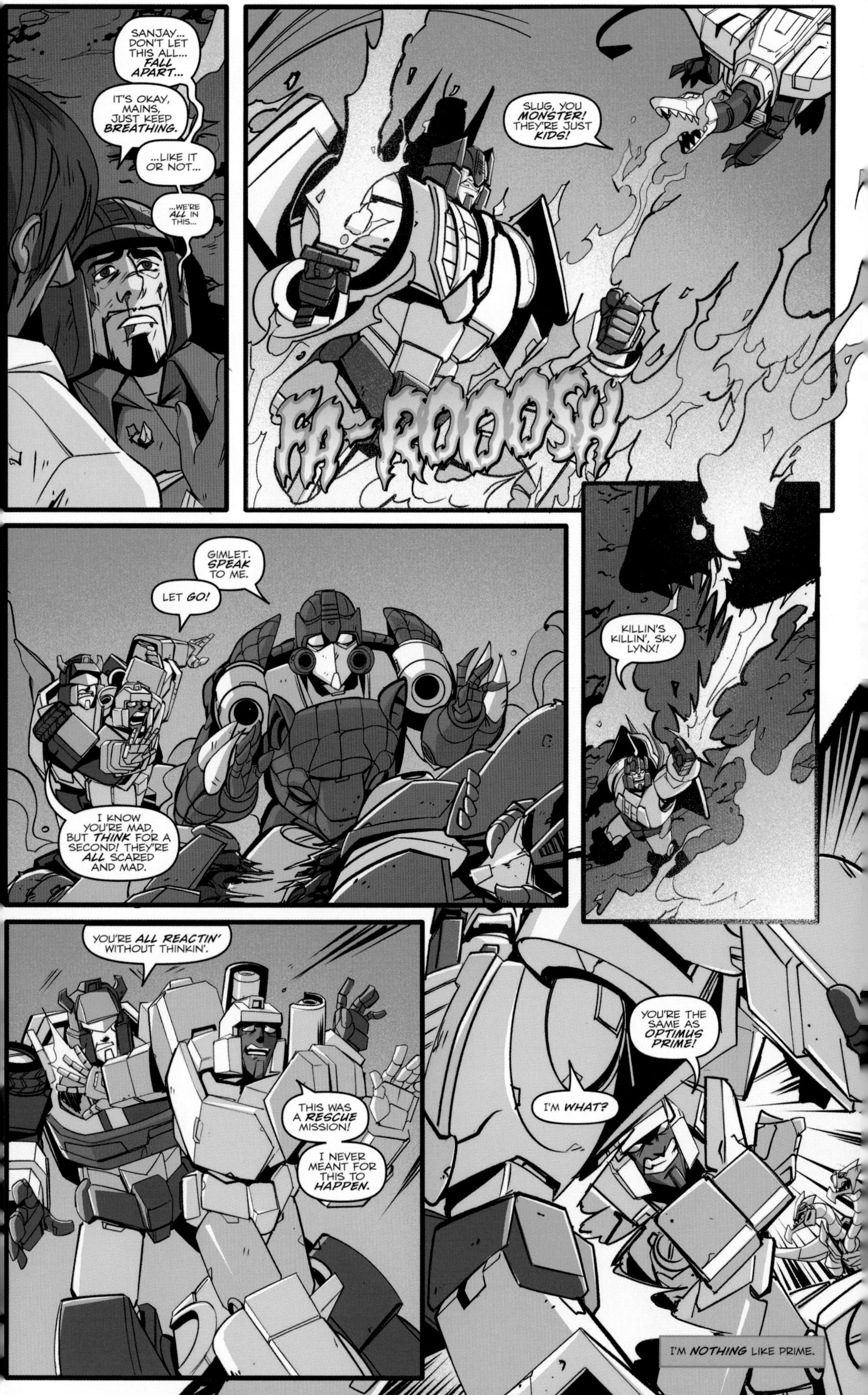

SANJAY... DON'T LET THIS ALL... FALL APART...
IT'S OKAY, MAINS, JUST KEEP BREATHING.
...LIKE IT OR NOT...
...WE'RE ALL IN THIS...
SLUG, YOU MONSTER! THEY'RE JUST KIDS!
FA-ROOOSH
KILLIN'S KILLIN', SKY LYNX!
GIMLET. SPEAK TO ME.
LET GO!
I KNOW YOU'RE MAD, BUT THINK FOR A SECOND! THEY'RE ALL SCARED AND MAD.
YOU'RE ALL REACTIN' WITHOUT THINKIN'.
THIS WAS A RESCUE MISSION!
I NEVER MEANT FOR THIS TO HAPPEN.
YOU'RE THE SAME AS OPTIMUS PRIME!
I'M WHAT?
I'M NOTHING LIKE PRIME.

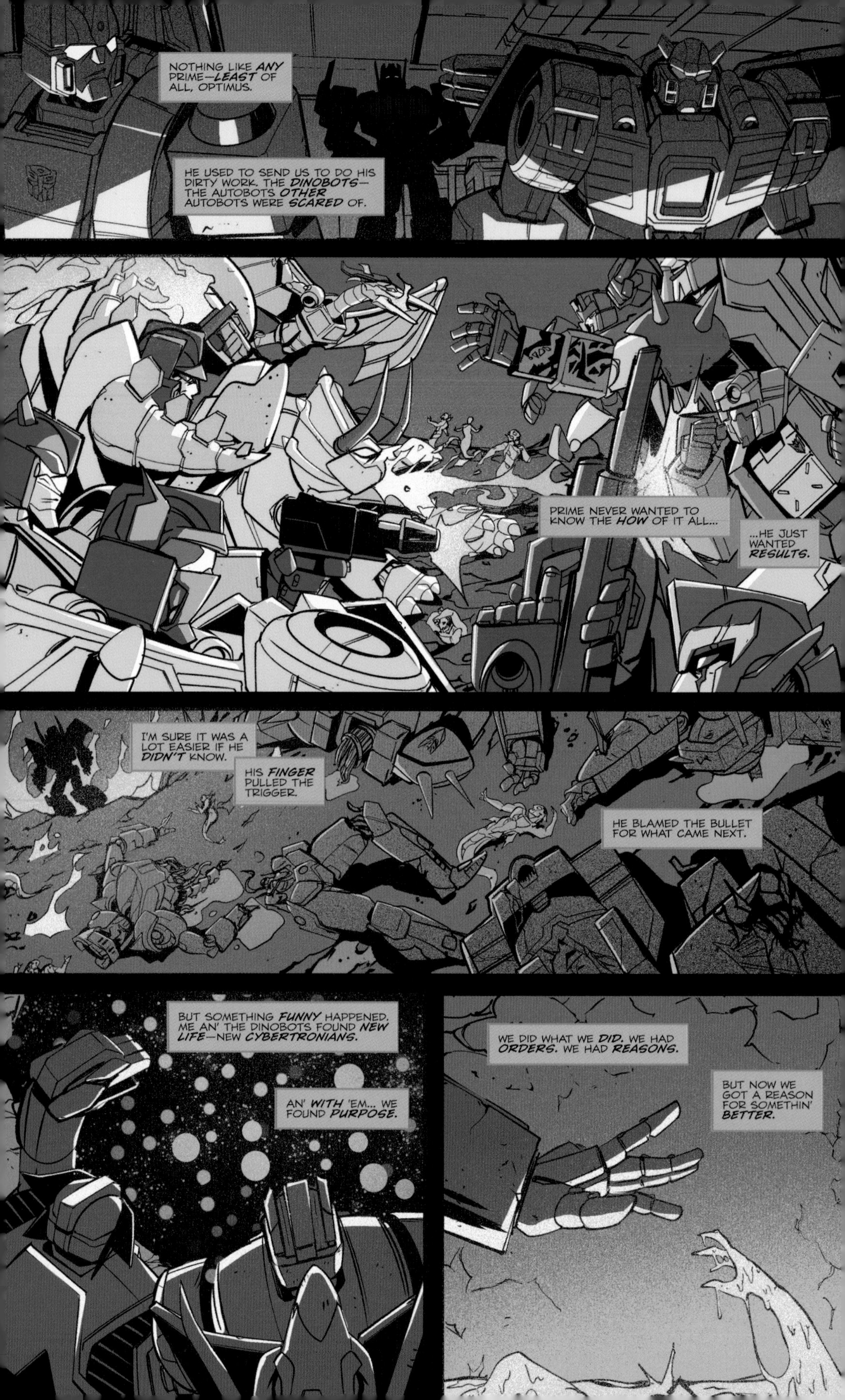
NOTHING LIKE ANY PRIME—LEAST OF ALL, OPTIMUS.
HE USED TO SEND US TO DO HIS DIRTY WORK. THE DINOBOTS—THE AUTOBOTS OTHER AUTOBOTS WERE SCARED OF.
PRIME NEVER WANTED TO KNOW THE HOW OF IT ALL...
...HE JUST WANTED RESULTS.
I'M SURE IT WAS A LOT EASIER IF HE DIDN'T KNOW.
HIS FINGER PULLED THE TRIGGER.
HE BLAMED THE BULLET FOR WHAT CAME NEXT.
BUT SOMETHING FUNNY HAPPENED. ME AN' THE DINOBOTS FOUND NEW LIFE—NEW CYBERTRONIANS.
AN' WITH 'EM... WE FOUND PURPOSE.
WE DID WHAT WE DID. WE HAD ORDERS. WE HAD REASONS.
BUT NOW WE GOT A REASON FOR SOMETHIN' BETTER.

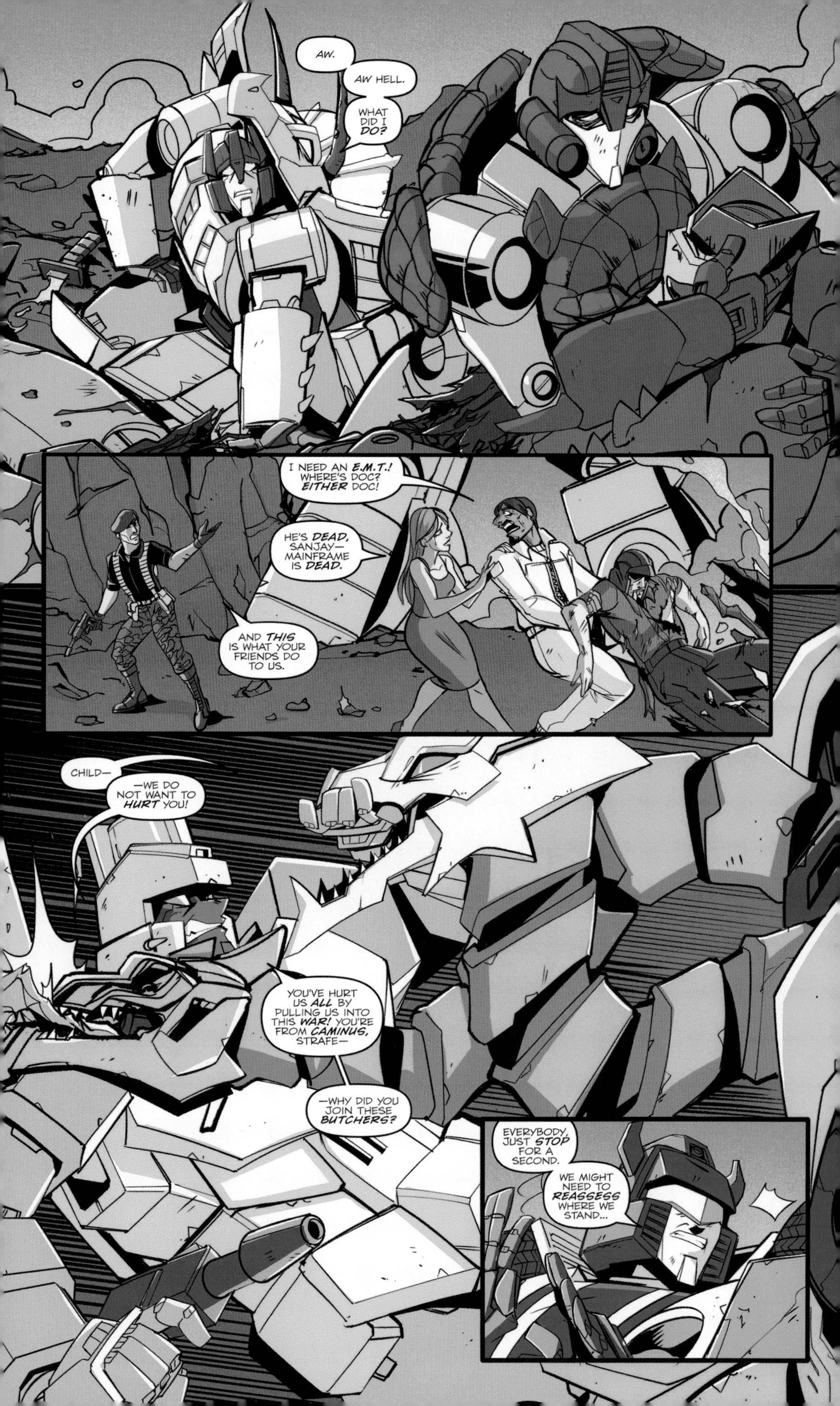
AW.
AW HELL.
WHAT DID I DO?
I NEED AN E.M.T.! WHERE'S DOC? EITHER DOC!
HE'S DEAD, SANJAY— MAINFRAME IS DEAD.
AND THIS IS WHAT YOUR FRIENDS DO TO US.
CHILD—
—WE DO NOT WANT TO HURT YOU!
YOU'VE HURT US ALL BY PULLING US INTO THIS WAR! YOU'RE FROM CAMINUS, STRAFE—
—WHY DID YOU JOIN THESE BUTCHERS?
EVERYBODY, JUST STOP FOR A SECOND.
WE MIGHT NEED TO REASSESS WHERE WE STAND...

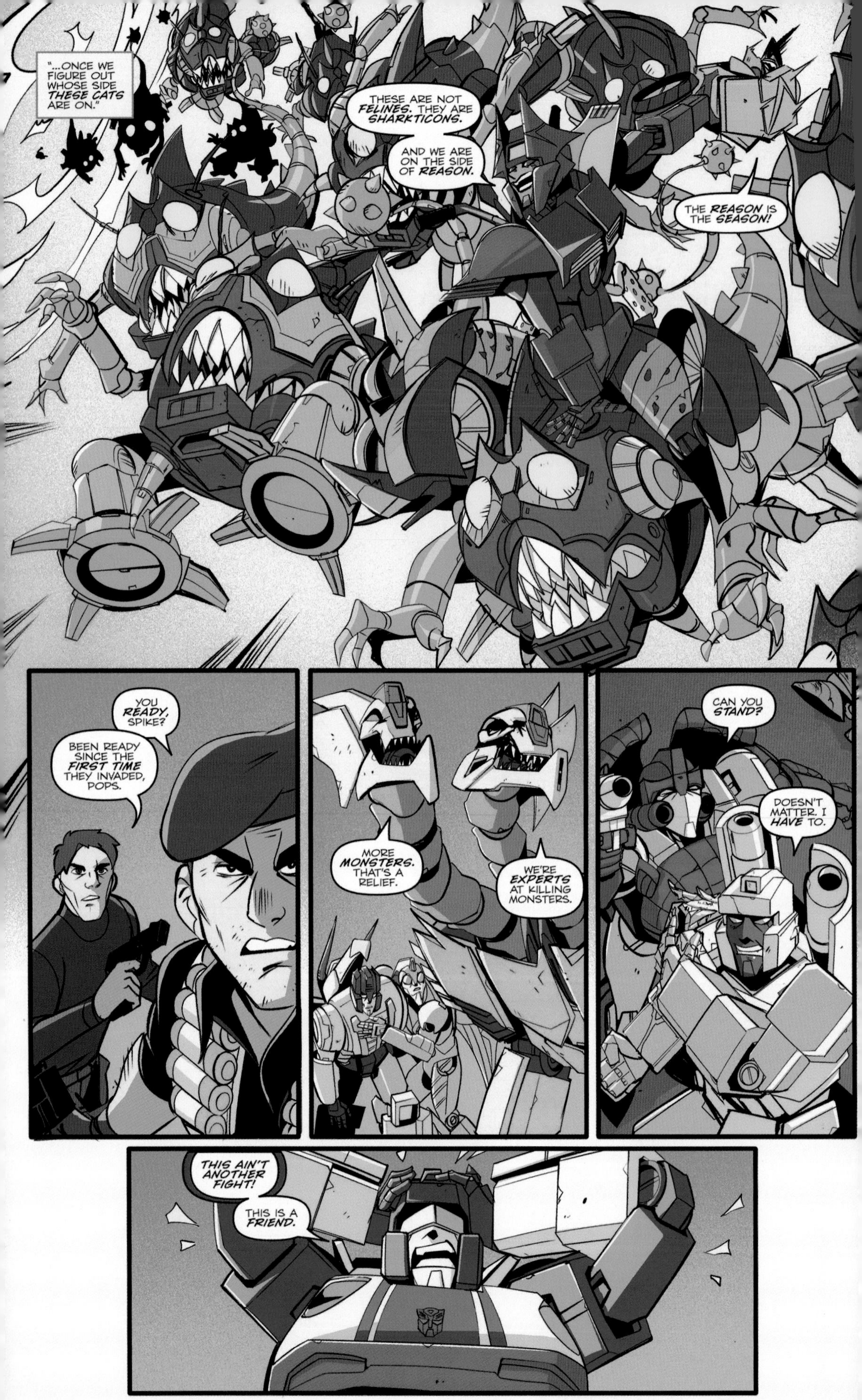
"...ONCE WE FIGURE OUT WHOSE SIDE THESE CATS ARE ON."
THESE ARE NOT FELINES. THEY ARE SHARKTICONS.
AND WE ARE ON THE SIDE OF REASON.
THE REASON IS THE SEASON!
YOU READY, SPIKE?
BEEN READY SINCE THE FIRST TIME THEY INVADED, POPS.
MORE MONSTERS. THAT'S A RELIEF.
WE'RE EXPERTS AT KILLING MONSTERS.
CAN YOU STAND?
DOESN'T MATTER. I HAVE TO.
THIS AIN'T ANOTHER FIGHT!
THIS IS A FRIEND.

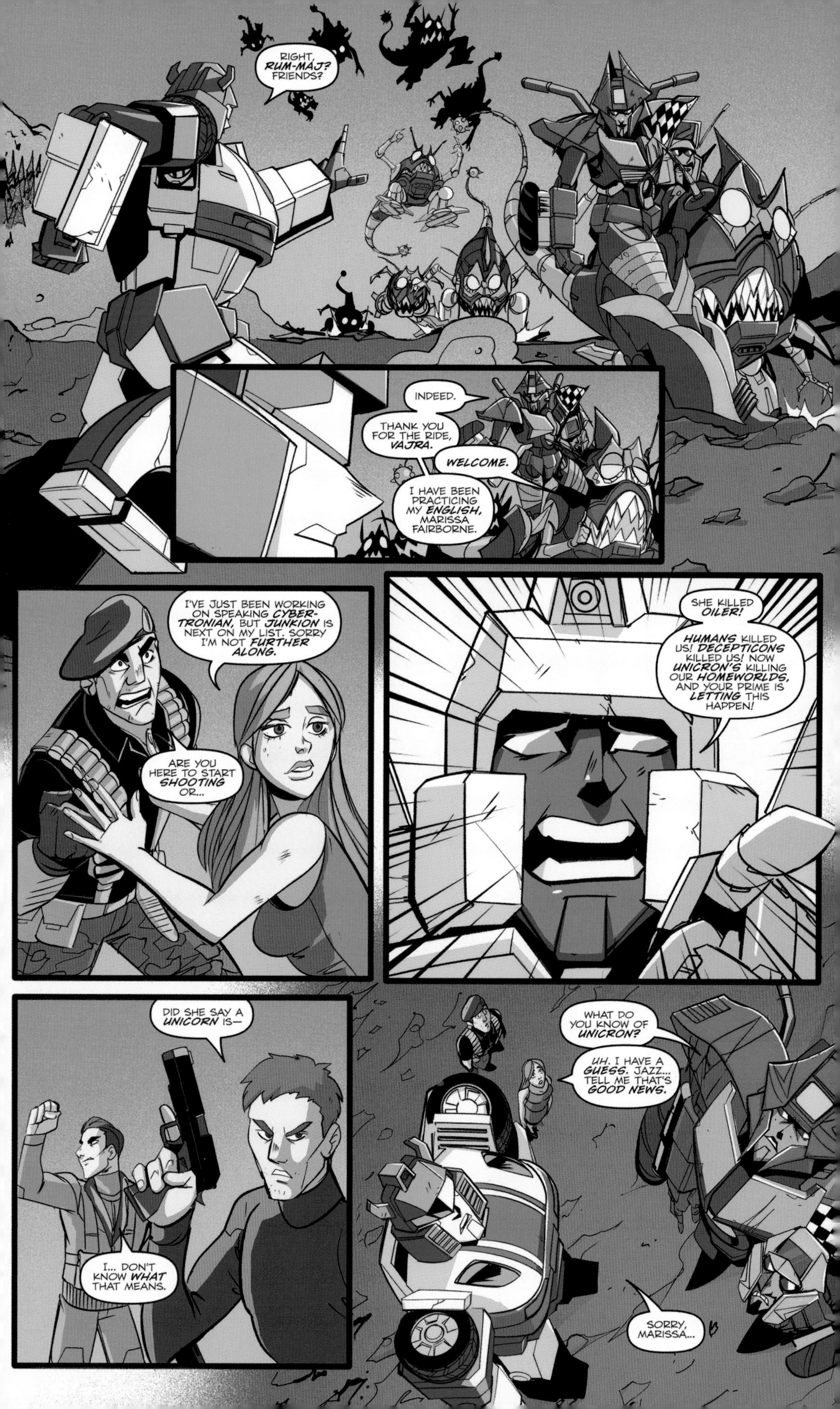
RIGHT, RUM-MAJ? FRIENDS?
INDEED.
THANK YOU FOR THE RIDE, VAJRA.
WELCOME.
I HAVE BEEN PRACTICING MY ENGLISH, MARISSA FAIRBORNE.
I'VE JUST BEEN WORKING ON SPEAKING CYBER-TRONIAN, BUT JUNKION IS NEXT ON MY LIST. SORRY I'M NOT FURTHER ALONG.
ARE YOU HERE TO START SHOOTING OR...
SHE KILLED OILER!
HUMANS KILLED US! DECEPTICONS KILLED US! NOW UNICRON'S KILLING OUR HOMEWORLDS, AND YOUR PRIME IS LETTING THIS HAPPEN!
DID SHE SAY A UNICORN IS—
I... DON'T KNOW WHAT THAT MEANS.
WHAT DO YOU KNOW OF UNICRON?
UH. I HAVE A GUESS. JAZZ... TELL ME THAT'S GOOD NEWS.
SORRY, MARISSA...

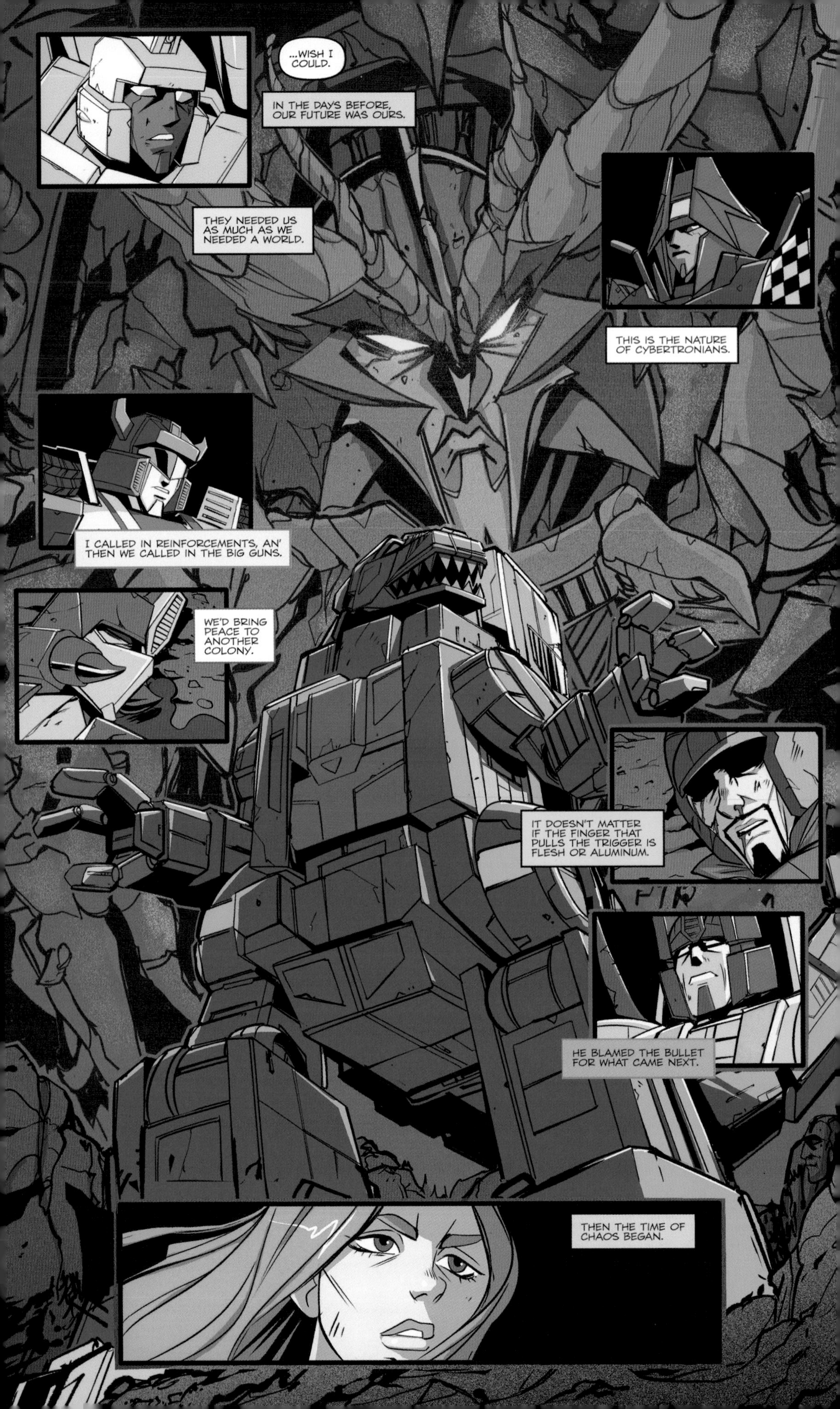
...WISH I COULD.
IN THE DAYS BEFORE, OUR FUTURE WAS OURS.
THEY NEEDED US AS MUCH AS WE NEEDED A WORLD.
THIS IS THE NATURE OF CYBERTRONIANS.
I CALLED IN REINFORCEMENTS, AN' THEN WE CALLED IN THE BIG GUNS.
WE'D BRING PEACE TO ANOTHER COLONY.
IT DOESN'T MATTER IF THE FINGER THAT PULLS THE TRIGGER IS FLESH OR ALUMINUM.
HE BLAMED THE BULLET FOR WHAT CAME NEXT.
THEN THE TIME OF CHAOS BEGAN.

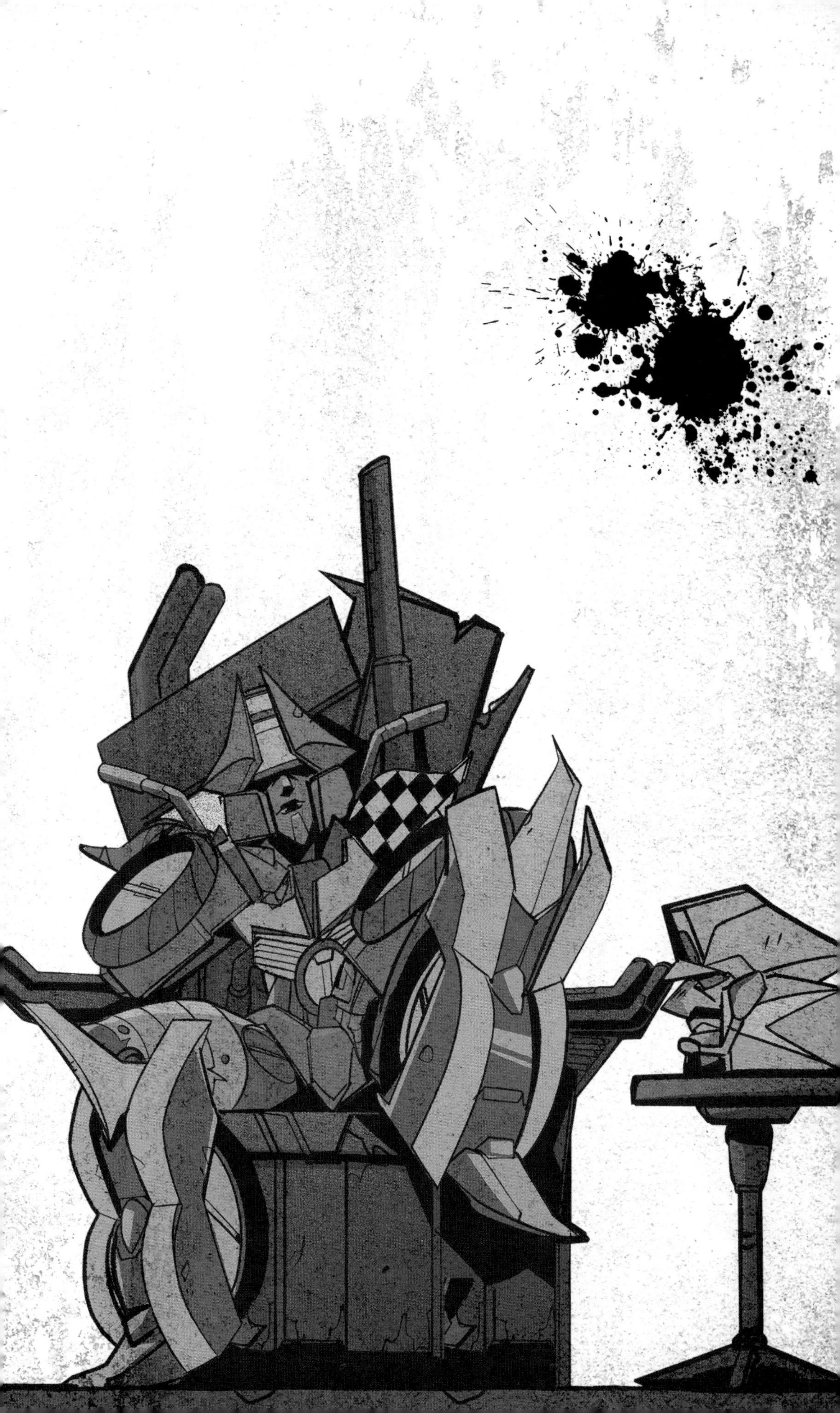

ART BY KEI ZAMA COLORS BY JOSH BURCHAM

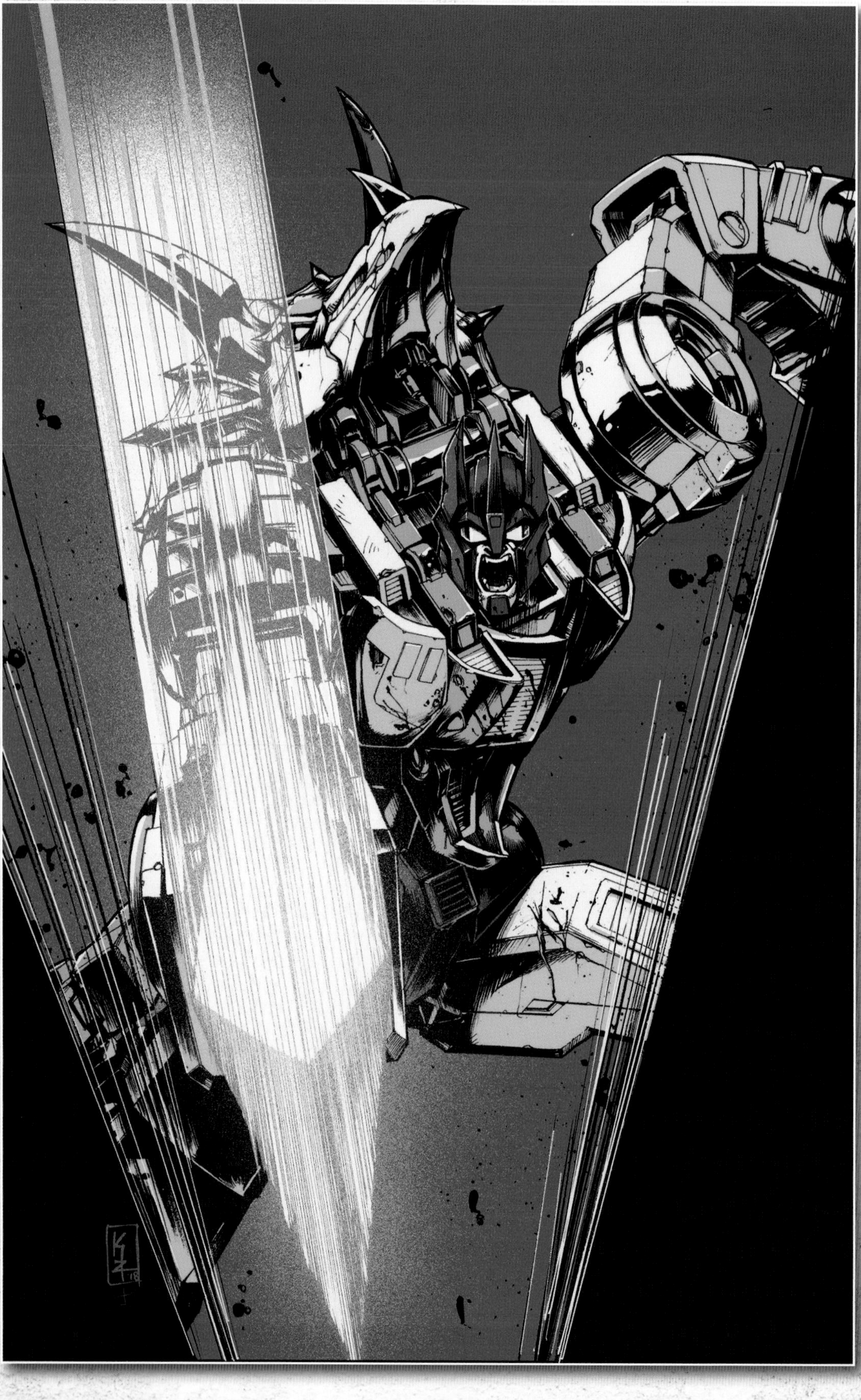

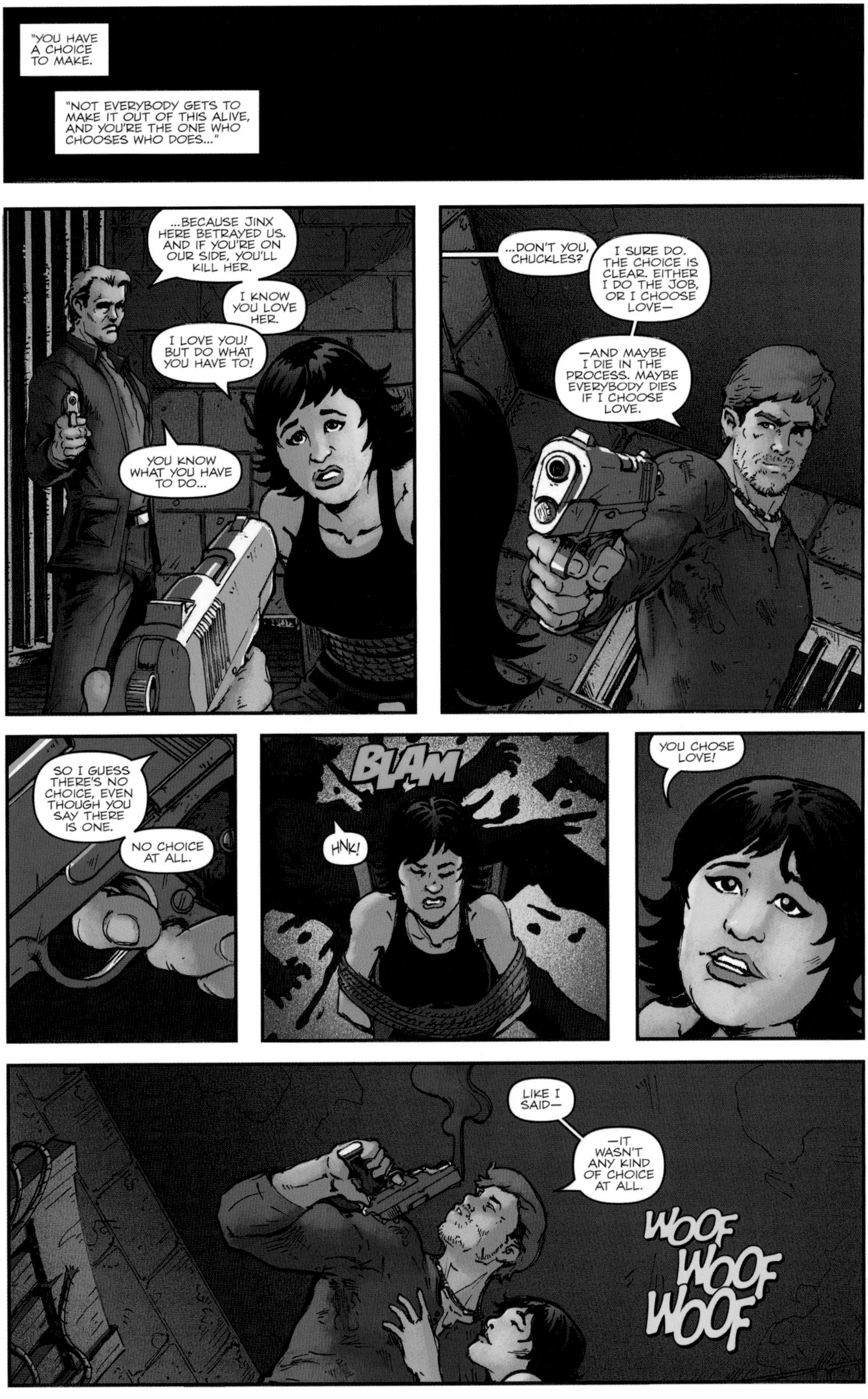
"YOU HAVE A CHOICE TO MAKE.
"NOT EVERYBODY GETS TO MAKE IT OUT OF THIS ALIVE, AND YOU'RE THE ONE WHO CHOOSES WHO DOES..."
...BECAUSE JINX HERE BETRAYED US. AND IF YOU'RE ON OUR SIDE, YOU'LL KILL HER.
I KNOW YOU LOVE HER.
I LOVE YOU! BUT DO WHAT YOU HAVE TO!
YOU KNOW WHAT YOU HAVE TO DO...
...DON'T YOU, CHUCKLES?
I SURE DO. THE CHOICE IS CLEAR. EITHER I DO THE JOB, OR I CHOOSE LOVE—
—AND MAYBE I DIE IN THE PROCESS. MAYBE EVERYBODY DIES IF I CHOOSE LOVE.
SO I GUESS THERE'S NO CHOICE, EVEN THOUGH YOU SAY THERE IS ONE.
NO CHOICE AT ALL.
BLAM
HNK!
YOU CHOSE LOVE!
LIKE I SAID—
—IT WASN'T ANY KIND OF CHOICE AT ALL.
WOOF WOOF WOOF

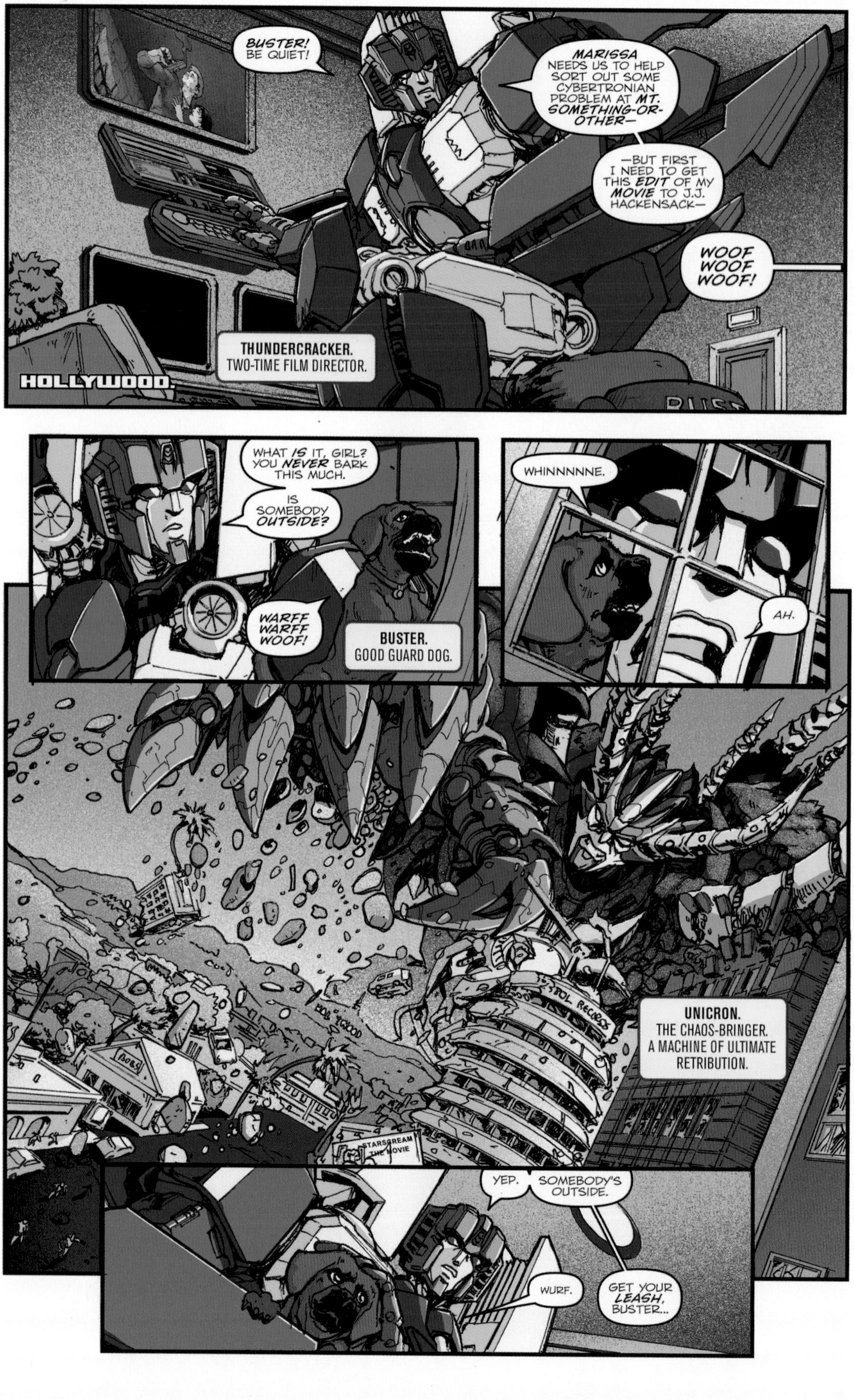
BUSTER! BE QUIET!
MARISSA NEEDS US TO HELP SORT OUT SOME CYBERTRONIAN PROBLEM AT MT. SOMETHING-OR-OTHER—
—BUT FIRST I NEED TO GET THIS EDIT OF MY MOVIE TO J.J. HACKENSACK—
WOOF WOOF WOOF!
THUNDERCRACKER. TWO-TIME FILM DIRECTOR.
HOLLYWOOD.
WHAT IS IT, GIRL? YOU NEVER BARK THIS MUCH.
IS SOMEBODY OUTSIDE?
WARFF WARFF WOOF!
BUSTER. GOOD GUARD DOG.
WHINNNNNE.
AH.
UNICRON. THE CHAOS-BRINGER. A MACHINE OF ULTIMATE RETRIBUTION.
STARSCREAM THE MOVIE
YEP.
SOMEBODY'S OUTSIDE.
WURF.
GET YOUR LEASH, BUSTER...

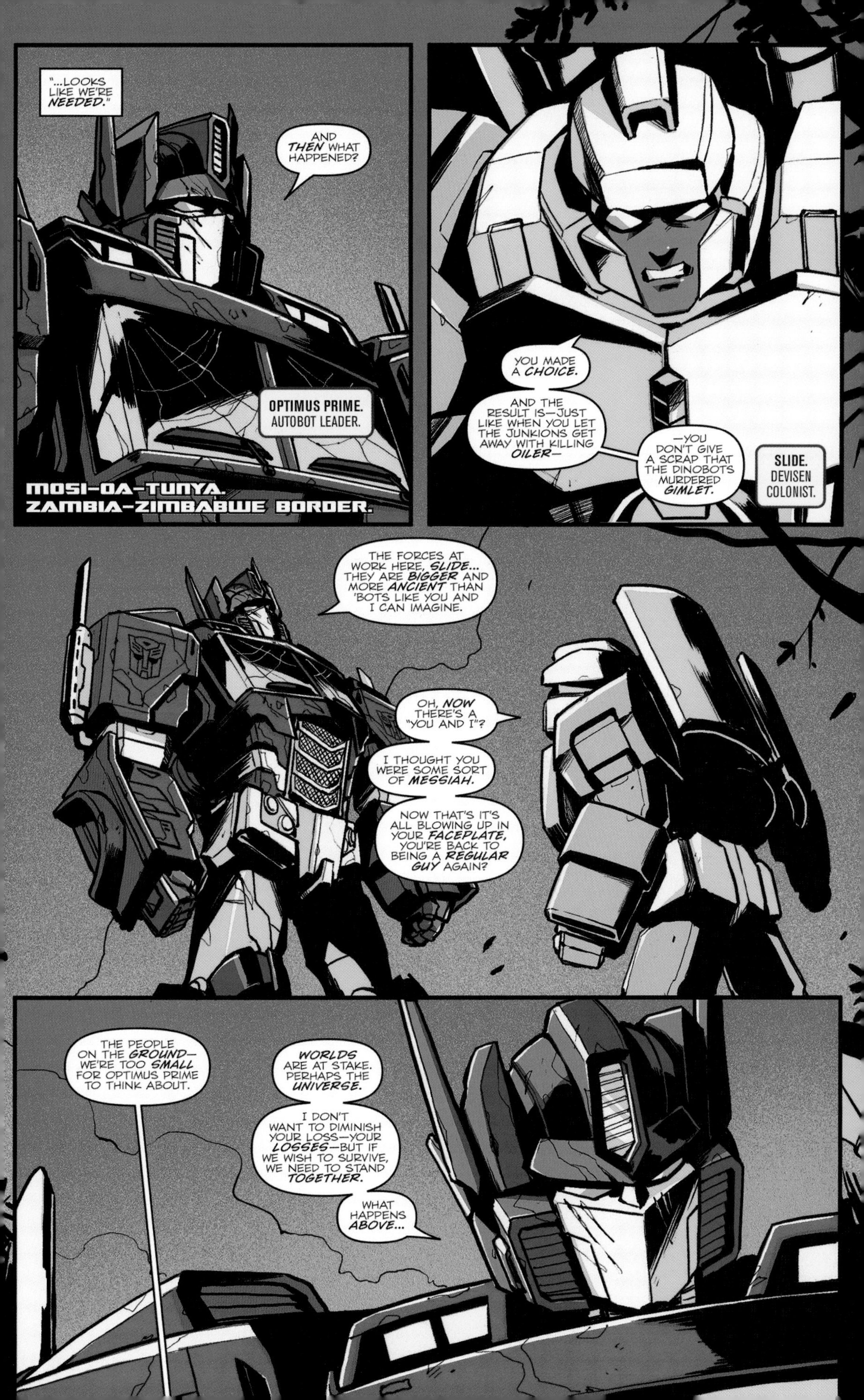
"...LOOKS LIKE WE'RE NEEDED."
AND THEN WHAT HAPPENED?
OPTIMUS PRIME. AUTOBOT LEADER.
MOSI-OA-TUNYA. ZAMBIA-ZIMBABWE BORDER.
YOU MADE A CHOICE.
AND THE RESULT IS—JUST LIKE WHEN YOU LET THE JUNKIONS GET AWAY WITH KILLING OILER—
—YOU DON'T GIVE A SCRAP THAT THE DINOBOTS MURDERED GIMLET.
SLIDE. DEVISEN COLONIST.
THE FORCES AT WORK HERE, SLIDE... THEY ARE BIGGER AND MORE ANCIENT THAN 'BOTS LIKE YOU AND I CAN IMAGINE.
OH, NOW THERE'S A "YOU AND I"?
I THOUGHT YOU WERE SOME SORT OF MESSIAH.
NOW THAT'S IT'S ALL BLOWING UP IN YOUR FACEPLATE, YOU'RE BACK TO BEING A REGULAR GUY AGAIN?
THE PEOPLE ON THE GROUND— WE'RE TOO SMALL FOR OPTIMUS PRIME TO THINK ABOUT.
WORLDS ARE AT STAKE. PERHAPS THE UNIVERSE.
I DON'T WANT TO DIMINISH YOUR LOSS—YOUR LOSSES—BUT IF WE WISH TO SURVIVE, WE NEED TO STAND TOGETHER.
WHAT HAPPENS ABOVE...

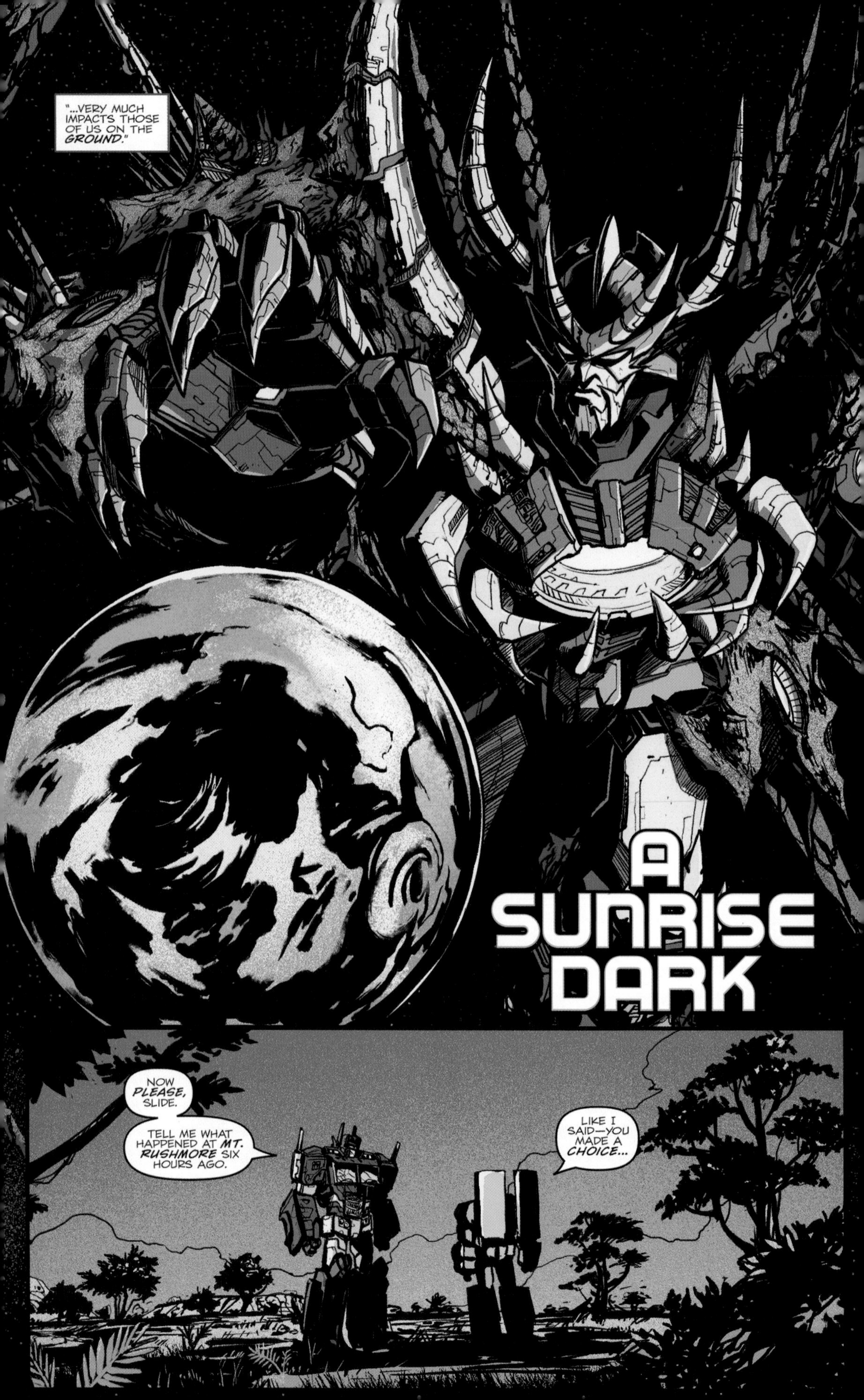
"...VERY MUCH IMPACTS THOSE OF US ON THE GROUND."
A SUNRISE DARK
NOW PLEASE, SLIDE.
TELL ME WHAT HAPPENED AT MT. RUSHMORE SIX HOURS AGO.
LIKE I SAID—YOU MADE A CHOICE...

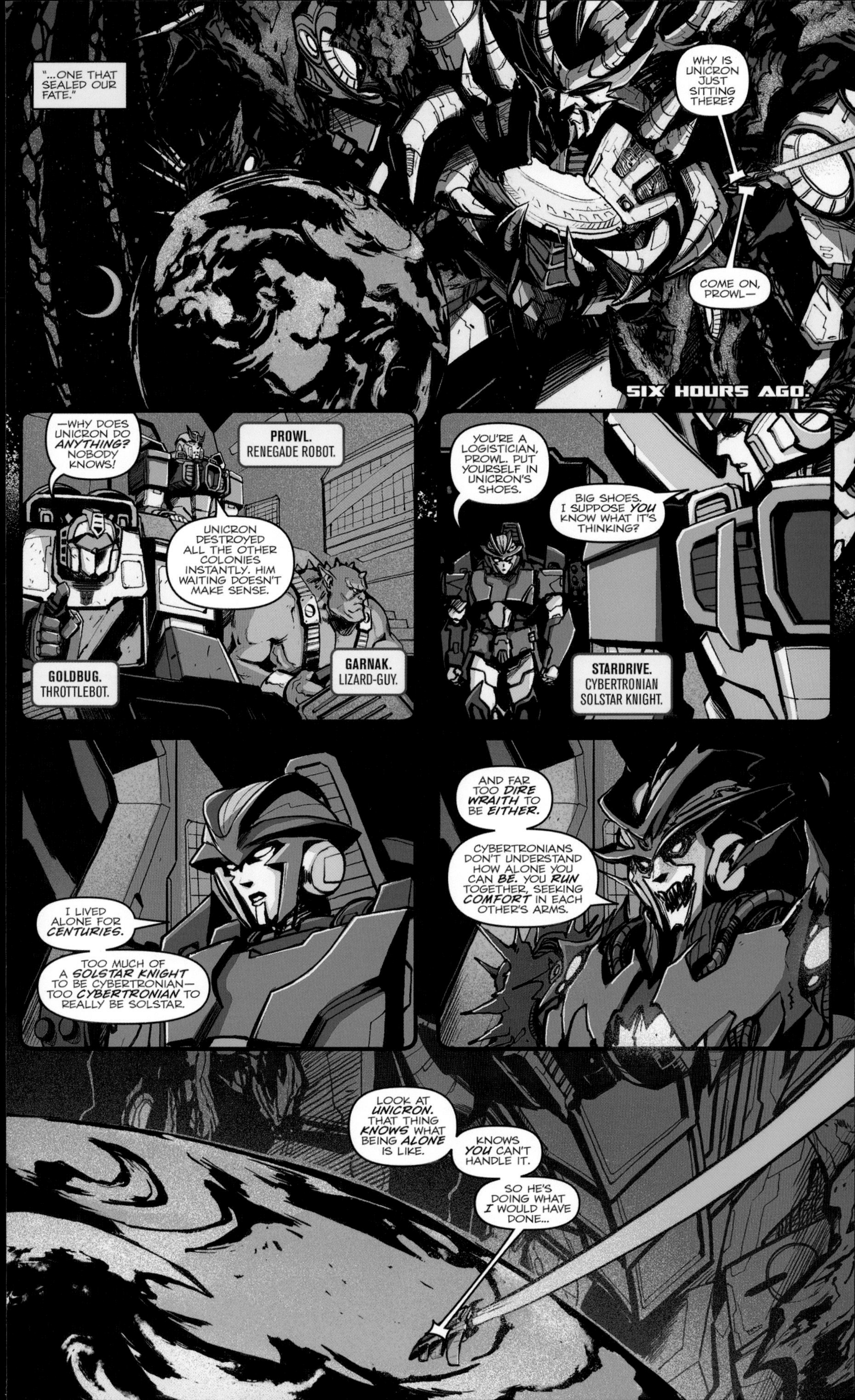

"...ONE THAT SEALED OUR FATE."
WHY IS UNICRON JUST SITTING THERE?
COME ON, PROWL—
SIX HOURS AGO.
—WHY DOES UNICRON DO *ANYTHING?* NOBODY KNOWS!
PROWL. RENEGADE ROBOT.
UNICRON DESTROYED ALL THE OTHER COLONIES INSTANTLY. HIM WAITING DOESN'T MAKE SENSE.
GOLDBUG. THROTTLEBOT.
GARNAK. LIZARD-GUY.
YOU'RE A LOGISTICIAN, PROWL. PUT YOURSELF IN UNICRON'S SHOES.
BIG SHOES. I SUPPOSE *YOU* KNOW WHAT IT'S THINKING?
STARDRIVE. CYBERTRONIAN SOLSTAR KNIGHT.
I LIVED ALONE FOR *CENTURIES.*
TOO MUCH OF A *SOLSTAR KNIGHT* TO BE CYBERTRONIAN— TOO *CYBERTRONIAN* TO REALLY BE SOLSTAR.
AND FAR TOO *DIRE WRAITH* TO BE *EITHER.*
CYBERTRONIANS DON'T UNDERSTAND HOW ALONE YOU CAN *BE.* YOU *RUN* TOGETHER, SEEKING *COMFORT* IN EACH OTHER'S ARMS.
LOOK AT *UNICRON.* THAT THING *KNOWS* WHAT BEING *ALONE* IS LIKE.
KNOWS *YOU* CAN'T HANDLE IT.
SO HE'S DOING WHAT *I* WOULD HAVE DONE...

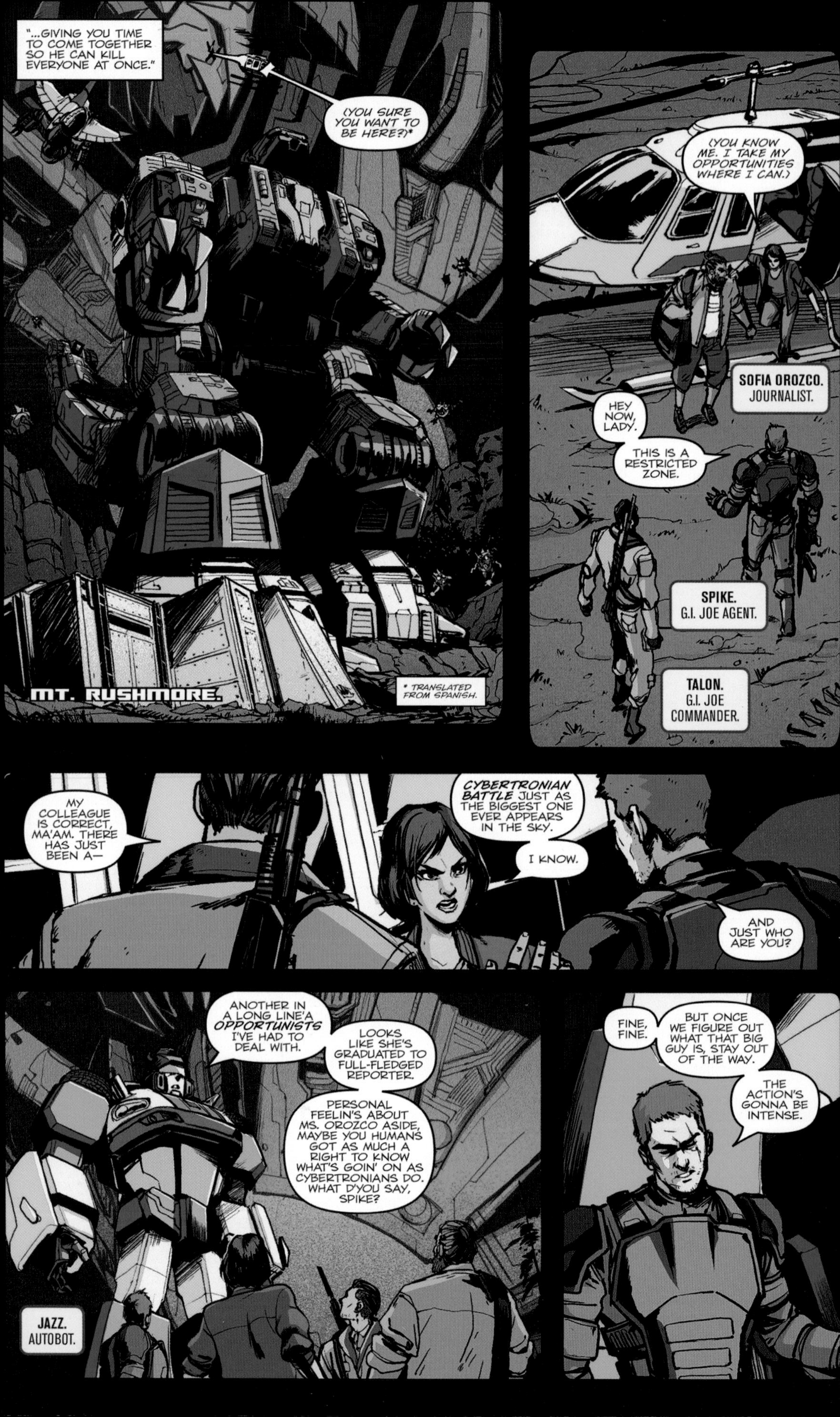
"...GIVING YOU TIME TO COME TOGETHER SO HE CAN KILL EVERYONE AT ONCE."
(YOU SURE YOU WANT TO BE HERE?)*
MT. RUSHMORE.
* TRANSLATED FROM SPANISH.
(YOU KNOW ME. I TAKE MY OPPORTUNITIES WHERE I CAN.)
SOFIA OROZCO. JOURNALIST.
HEY NOW, LADY.
THIS IS A RESTRICTED ZONE.
SPIKE. G.I. JOE AGENT.
TALON. G.I. JOE COMMANDER.
MY COLLEAGUE IS CORRECT, MA'AM. THERE HAS JUST BEEN A—
CYBERTRONIAN BATTLE JUST AS THE BIGGEST ONE EVER APPEARS IN THE SKY.
I KNOW.
AND JUST WHO ARE YOU?
ANOTHER IN A LONG LINE'A OPPORTUNISTS I'VE HAD TO DEAL WITH.
LOOKS LIKE SHE'S GRADUATED TO FULL-FLEDGED REPORTER.
PERSONAL FEELIN'S ABOUT MS. OROZCO ASIDE, MAYBE YOU HUMANS GOT AS MUCH A RIGHT TO KNOW WHAT'S GOIN' ON AS CYBERTRONIANS DO. WHAT D'YOU SAY, SPIKE?
JAZZ. AUTOBOT.
FINE, FINE.
BUT ONCE WE FIGURE OUT WHAT THAT BIG GUY IS, STAY OUT OF THE WAY.
THE ACTION'S GONNA BE INTENSE.

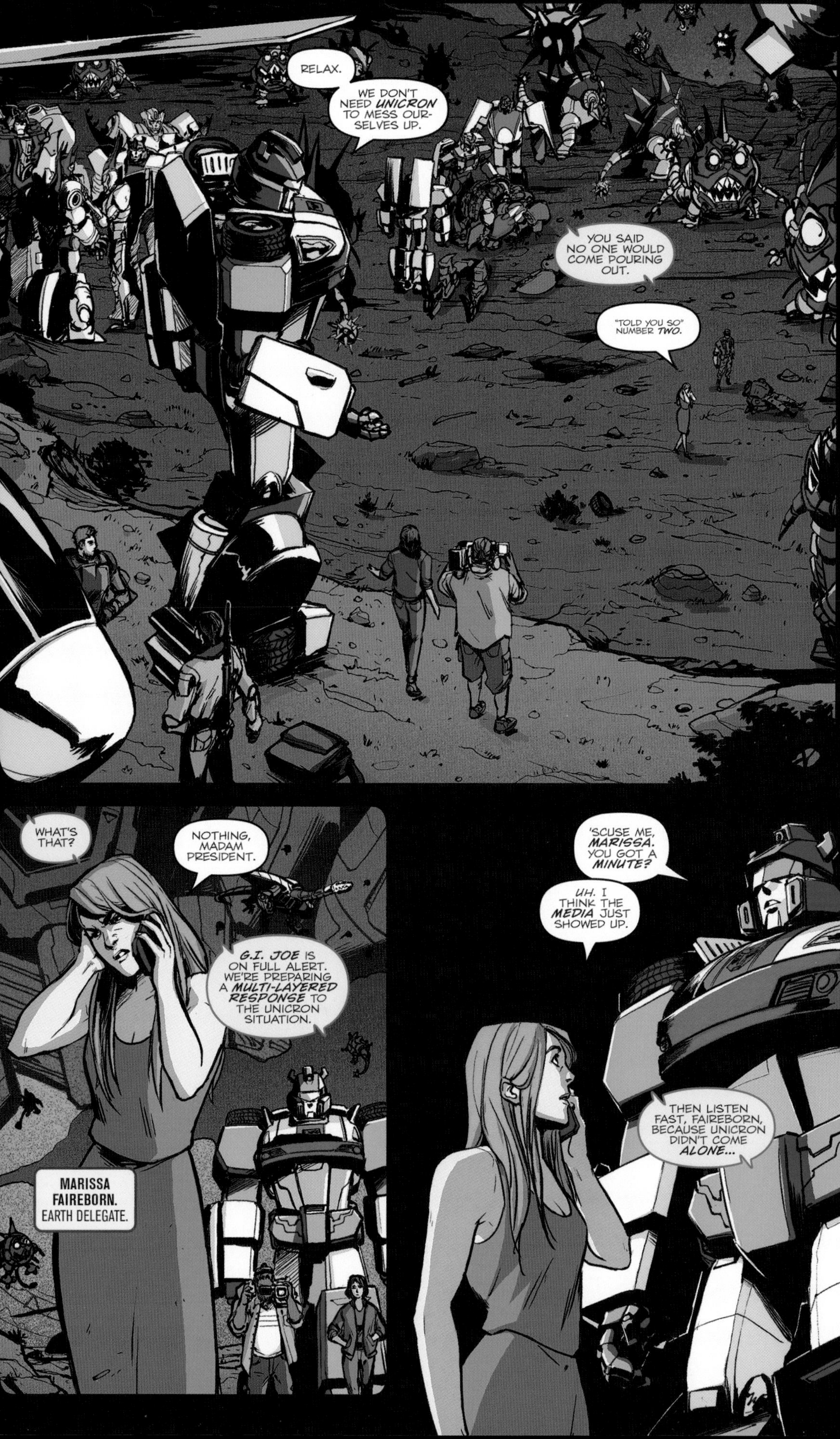
RELAX.
WE DON'T NEED UNICRON TO MESS OUR-SELVES UP.
YOU SAID NO ONE WOULD COME POURING OUT.
"TOLD YOU SO" NUMBER TWO.
WHAT'S THAT?
NOTHING, MADAM PRESIDENT.
G.I. JOE IS ON FULL ALERT. WE'RE PREPARING A MULTI-LAYERED RESPONSE TO THE UNICRON SITUATION.
MARISSA FAIREBORN. EARTH DELEGATE.
'SCUSE ME, MARISSA. YOU GOT A MINUTE?
UH. I THINK THE MEDIA JUST SHOWED UP.
THEN LISTEN FAST, FAIREBORN, BECAUSE UNICRON DIDN'T COME ALONE...

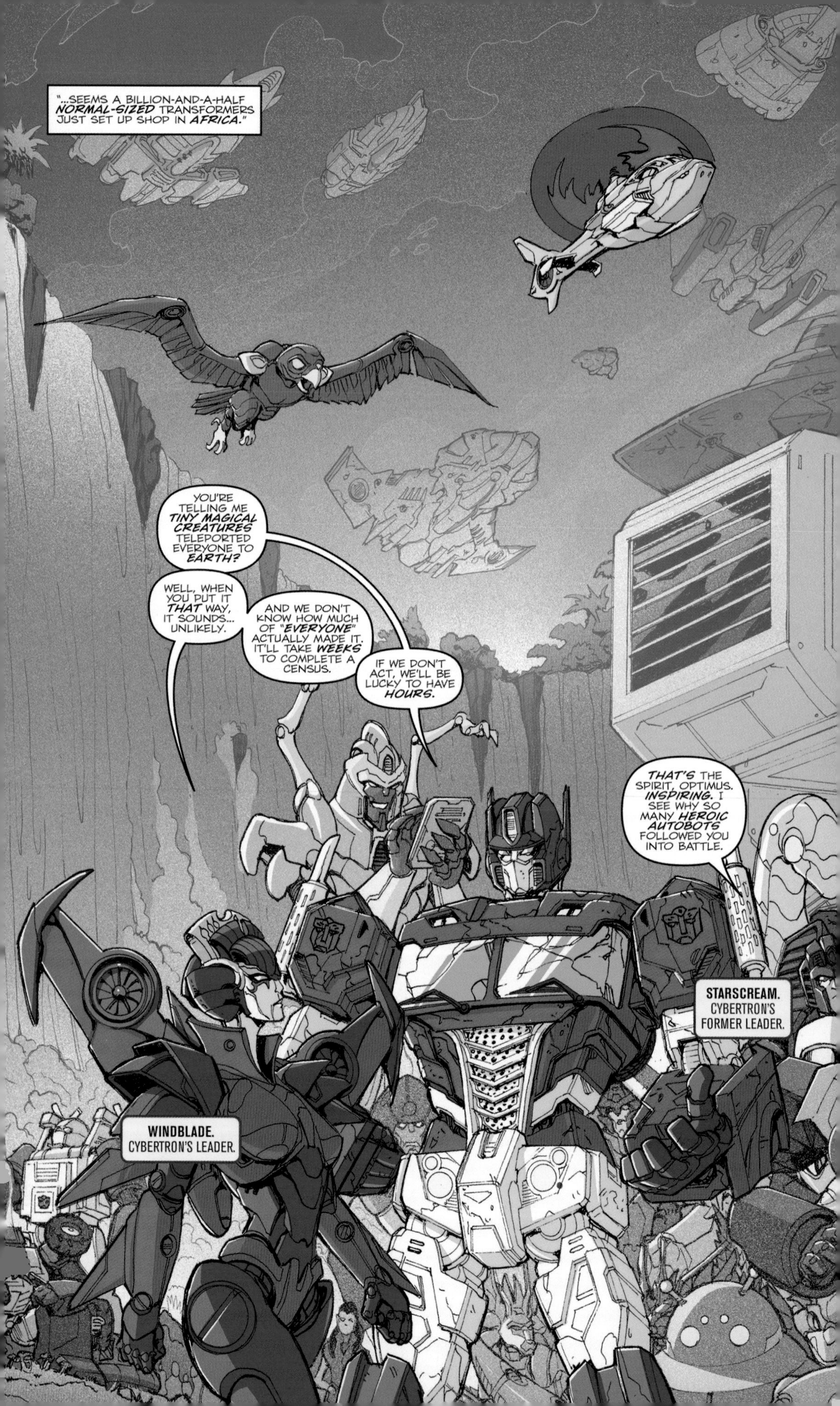
"...SEEMS A BILLION-AND-A-HALF NORMAL-SIZED TRANSFORMERS JUST SET UP SHOP IN AFRICA."
YOU'RE TELLING ME TINY MAGICAL CREATURES TELEPORTED EVERYONE TO EARTH?
WELL, WHEN YOU PUT IT THAT WAY, IT SOUNDS... UNLIKELY.
AND WE DON'T KNOW HOW MUCH OF "EVERYONE" ACTUALLY MADE IT. IT'LL TAKE WEEKS TO COMPLETE A CENSUS.
IF WE DON'T ACT, WE'LL BE LUCKY TO HAVE HOURS.
THAT'S THE SPIRIT, OPTIMUS. INSPIRING. I SEE WHY SO MANY HEROIC AUTOBOTS FOLLOWED YOU INTO BATTLE.
STARSCREAM. CYBERTRON'S FORMER LEADER.
WINDBLADE. CYBERTRON'S LEADER.

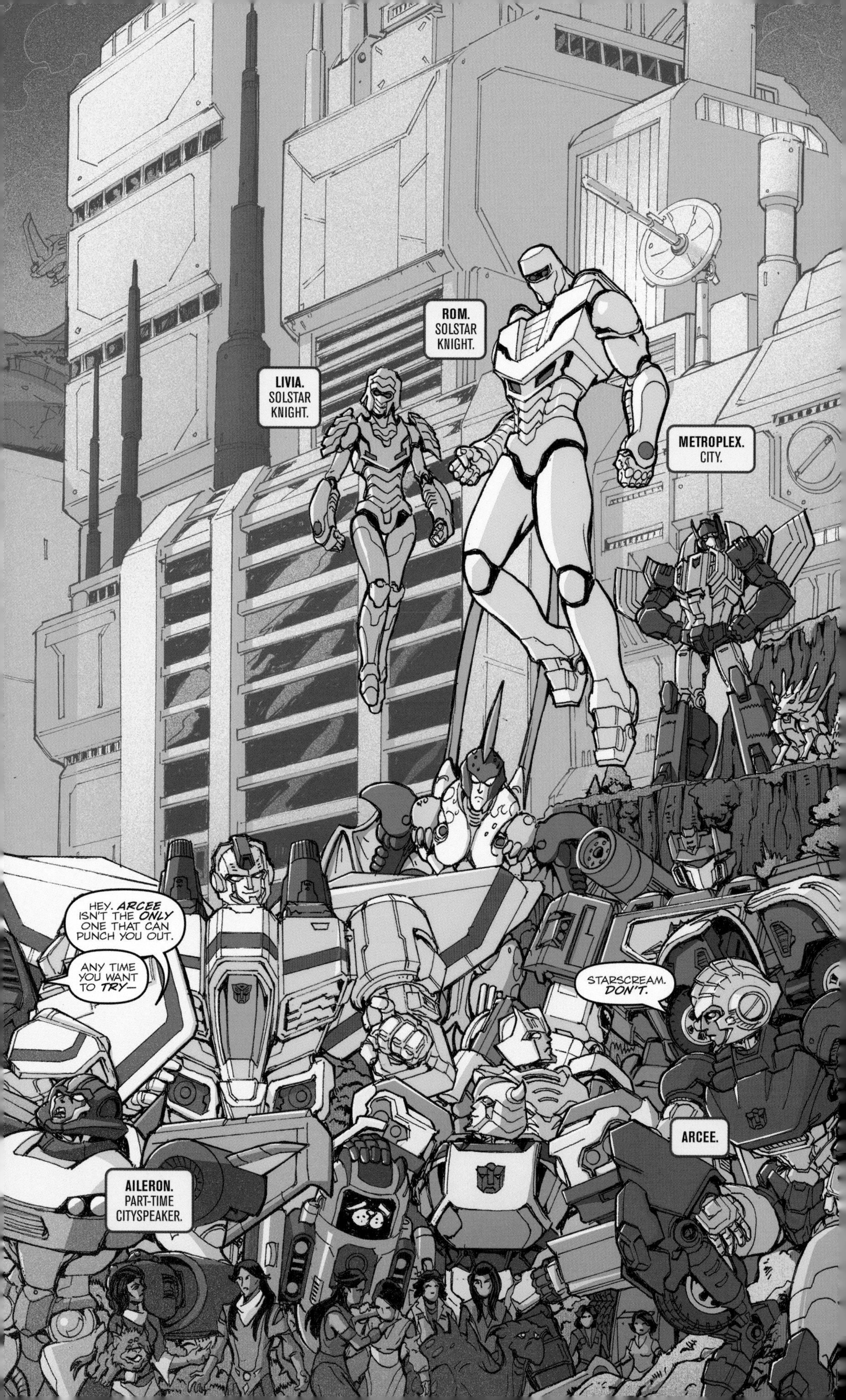
ROM. SOLSTAR KNIGHT.
LIVIA. SOLSTAR KNIGHT.
METROPLEX. CITY.
HEY. ARCEE ISN'T THE ONLY ONE THAT CAN PUNCH YOU OUT.
ANY TIME YOU WANT TO TRY—
STARSCREAM. DON'T.
ARCEE.
AILERON. PART-TIME CITYSPEAKER.

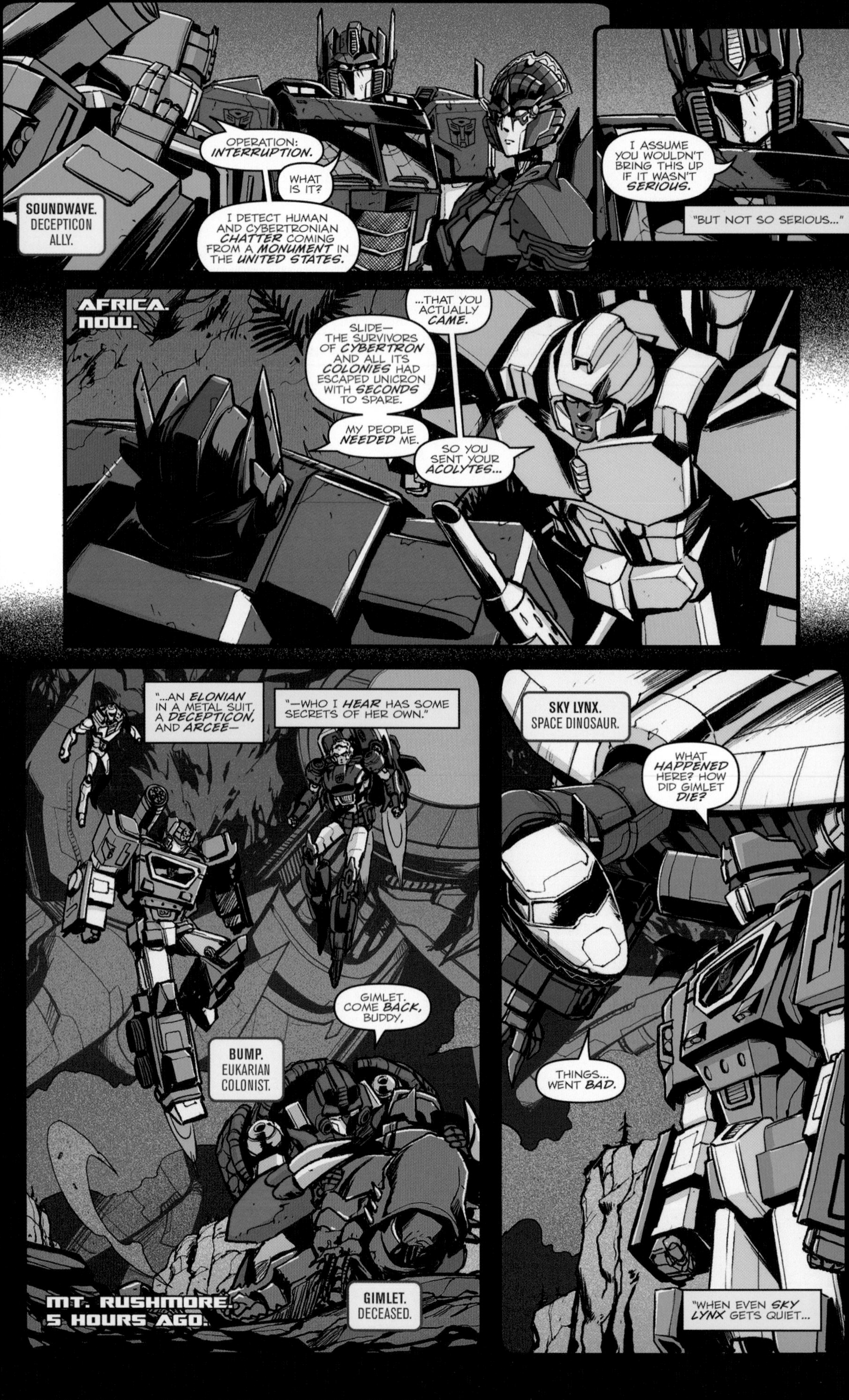
SOUNDWAVE. DECEPTICON ALLY.
OPERATION: INTERRUPTION.
WHAT IS IT?
I DETECT HUMAN AND CYBERTRONIAN CHATTER COMING FROM A MONUMENT IN THE UNITED STATES.
I ASSUME YOU WOULDN'T BRING THIS UP IF IT WASN'T SERIOUS.
"BUT NOT SO SERIOUS..."
AFRICA. NOW.
...THAT YOU ACTUALLY CAME.
SLIDE— THE SURVIVORS OF CYBERTRON AND ALL ITS COLONIES HAD ESCAPED UNICRON WITH SECONDS TO SPARE.
MY PEOPLE NEEDED ME.
SO YOU SENT YOUR ACOLYTES...
"...AN ELONIAN IN A METAL SUIT, A DECEPTICON, AND ARCEE—
"—WHO I HEAR HAS SOME SECRETS OF HER OWN."
GIMLET. COME BACK, BUDDY,
BUMP. EUKARIAN COLONIST.
MT. RUSHMORE. 5 HOURS AGO.
GIMLET. DECEASED.
SKY LYNX. SPACE DINOSAUR.
WHAT HAPPENED HERE? HOW DID GIMLET DIE?
THINGS... WENT BAD.
"WHEN EVEN SKY LYNX GETS QUIET...

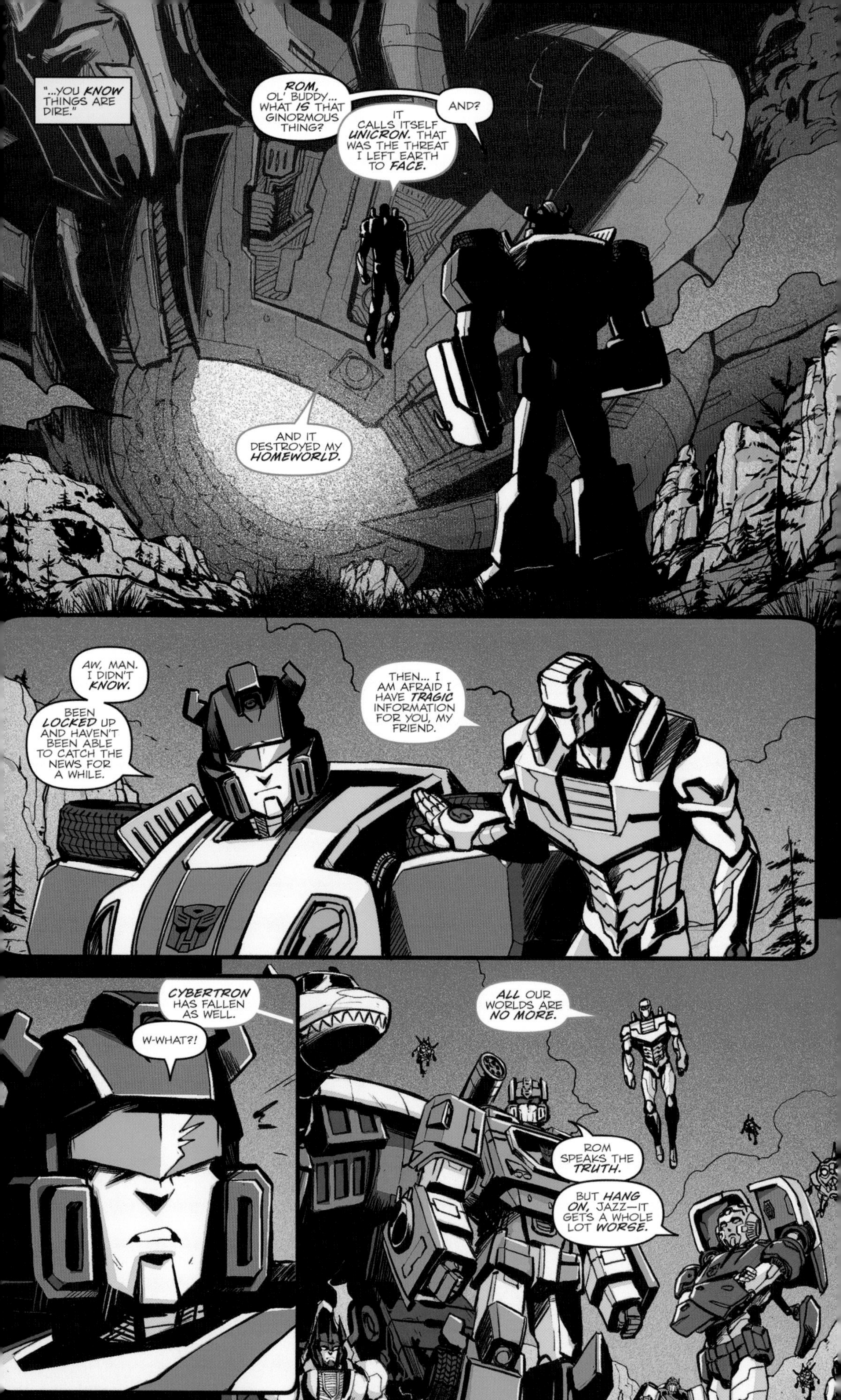
"...YOU KNOW THINGS ARE DIRE."
ROM, OL' BUDDY... WHAT IS THAT GINORMOUS THING?
AND?
IT CALLS ITSELF UNICRON. THAT WAS THE THREAT I LEFT EARTH TO FACE.
AND IT DESTROYED MY HOMEWORLD.
AW, MAN. I DIDN'T KNOW.
BEEN LOCKED UP AND HAVEN'T BEEN ABLE TO CATCH THE NEWS FOR A WHILE.
THEN... I AM AFRAID I HAVE TRAGIC INFORMATION FOR YOU, MY FRIEND.
CYBERTRON HAS FALLEN AS WELL.
W-WHAT?!
ALL OUR WORLDS ARE NO MORE.
ROM SPEAKS THE TRUTH.
BUT HANG ON, JAZZ—IT GETS A WHOLE LOT WORSE.

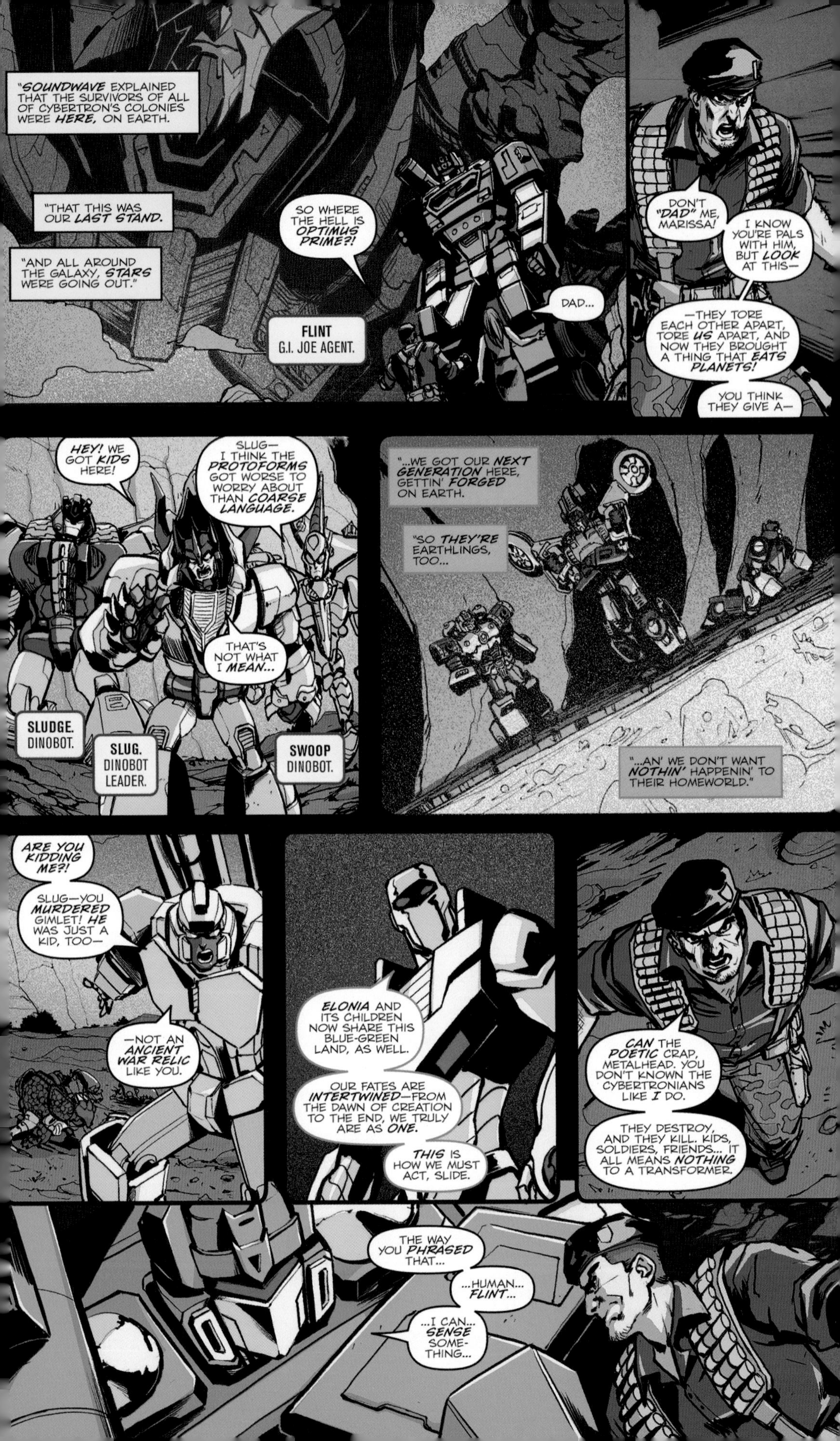
"SOUNDWAVE EXPLAINED THAT THE SURVIVORS OF ALL OF CYBERTRON'S COLONIES WERE HERE, ON EARTH.
"THAT THIS WAS OUR LAST STAND.
"AND ALL AROUND THE GALAXY, STARS WERE GOING OUT."
SO WHERE THE HELL IS OPTIMUS PRIME?!
FLINT
G.I. JOE AGENT.
DAD...
DON'T "DAD" ME, MARISSA!
I KNOW YOU'RE PALS WITH HIM, BUT LOOK AT THIS—
—THEY TORE EACH OTHER APART, TORE US APART, AND NOW THEY BROUGHT A THING THAT EATS PLANETS!
YOU THINK THEY GIVE A—
HEY! WE GOT KIDS HERE!
SLUG— I THINK THE PROTOFORMS GOT WORSE TO WORRY ABOUT THAN COARSE LANGUAGE.
THAT'S NOT WHAT I MEAN...
SLUDGE. DINOBOT.
SLUG. DINOBOT LEADER.
SWOOP DINOBOT.
"...WE GOT OUR NEXT GENERATION HERE, GETTIN' FORGED ON EARTH.
"SO THEY'RE EARTHLINGS, TOO...
"...AN' WE DON'T WANT NOTHIN' HAPPENIN' TO THEIR HOMEWORLD."
ARE YOU KIDDING ME?!
SLUG—YOU MURDERED GIMLET! HE WAS JUST A KID, TOO—
—NOT AN ANCIENT WAR RELIC LIKE YOU.
ELONIA AND ITS CHILDREN NOW SHARE THIS BLUE-GREEN LAND, AS WELL.
OUR FATES ARE INTERTWINED—FROM THE DAWN OF CREATION TO THE END, WE TRULY ARE AS ONE.
THIS IS HOW WE MUST ACT, SLIDE.
CAN THE POETIC CRAP, METALHEAD. YOU DON'T KNOWN THE CYBERTRONIANS LIKE I DO.
THEY DESTROY, AND THEY KILL. KIDS, SOLDIERS, FRIENDS... IT ALL MEANS NOTHING TO A TRANSFORMER.
THE WAY YOU PHRASED THAT...
...HUMAN... FLINT...
...I CAN... SENSE SOME-THING...

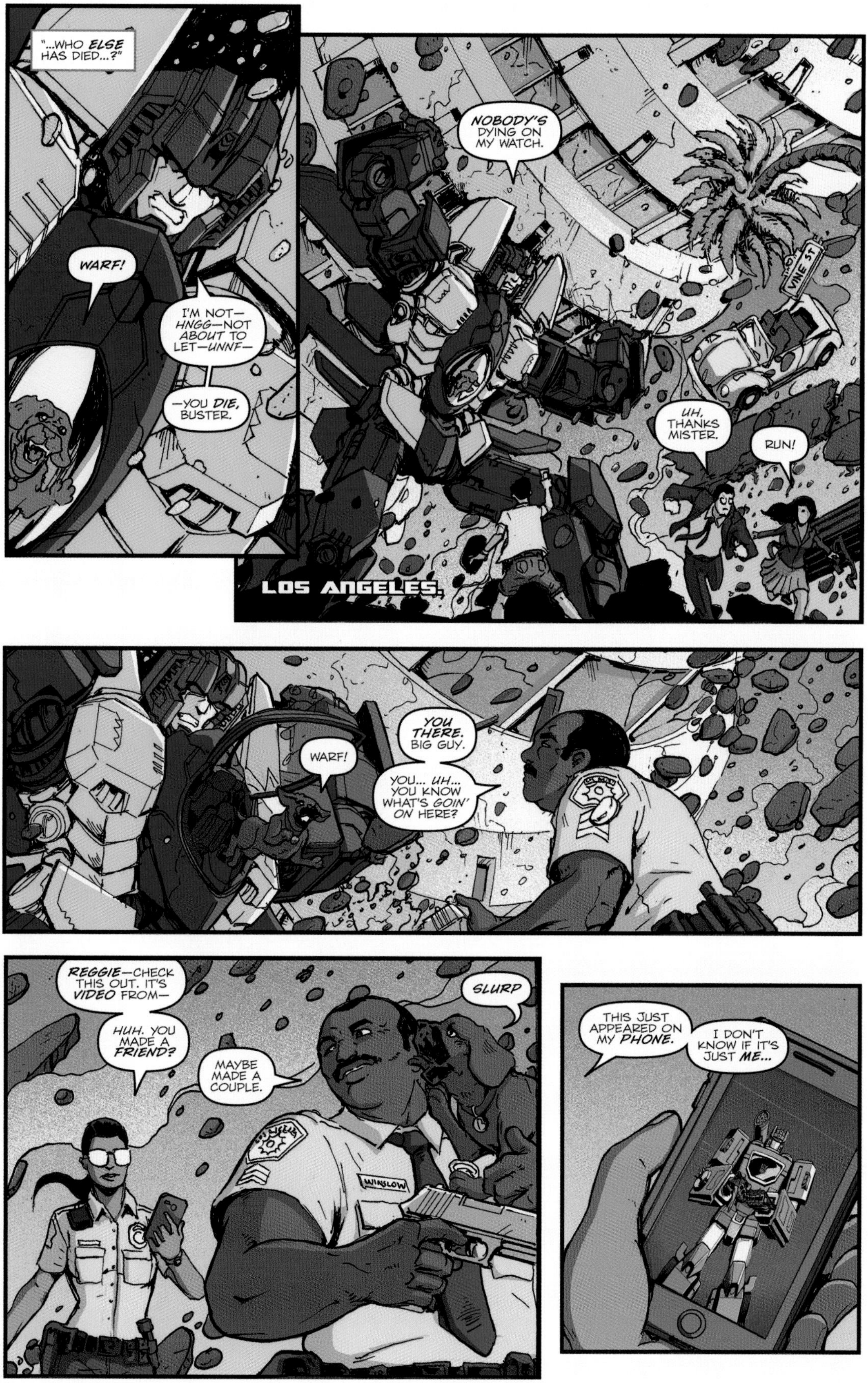
"...WHO ELSE HAS DIED...?"
WARF!
I'M NOT—HNGG—NOT ABOUT TO LET—UNNF—
—YOU DIE, BUSTER.
NOBODY'S DYING ON MY WATCH.
VINE ST
UH, THANKS MISTER.
RUN!
LOS ANGELES.
WARF!
YOU THERE. BIG GUY.
YOU... UH... YOU KNOW WHAT'S GOIN' ON HERE?
REGGIE—CHECK THIS OUT. IT'S VIDEO FROM—
SLURP
HUH. YOU MADE A FRIEND?
MAYBE MADE A COUPLE.
WINSLOW
THIS JUST APPEARED ON MY PHONE.
I DON'T KNOW IF IT'S JUST ME...

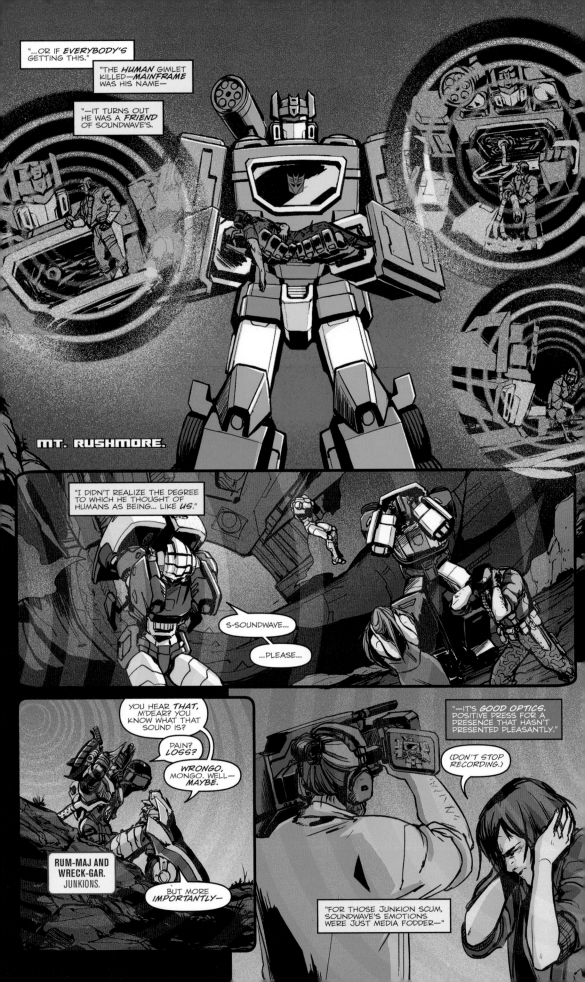

"...OR IF *EVERYBODY'S* GETTING THIS."

"THE *HUMAN* GIMLET KILLED—*MAINFRAME* WAS HIS NAME—

"—IT TURNS OUT HE WAS A *FRIEND* OF SOUNDWAVE'S."

MT. RUSHMORE.

"I DIDN'T REALIZE THE DEGREE TO WHICH HE THOUGHT OF HUMANS AS BEING... LIKE *US*."

S-SOUNDWAVE...

...PLEASE...

YOU HEAR *THAT*, M'DEAR? YOU KNOW WHAT THAT SOUND IS?

PAIN? *LOSS*?

WRONGO, MONGO. WELL— *MAYBE*.

RUM-MAJ AND WRECK-GAR. JUNKIONS.

BUT MORE *IMPORTANTLY*—

"—IT'S *GOOD OPTICS*. POSITIVE PRESS FOR A PRESENCE THAT HASN'T PRESENTED PLEASANTLY."

(DON'T STOP RECORDING.)

"FOR THOSE JUNKION SCUM, SOUNDWAVE'S EMOTIONS WERE JUST MEDIA FODDER—"

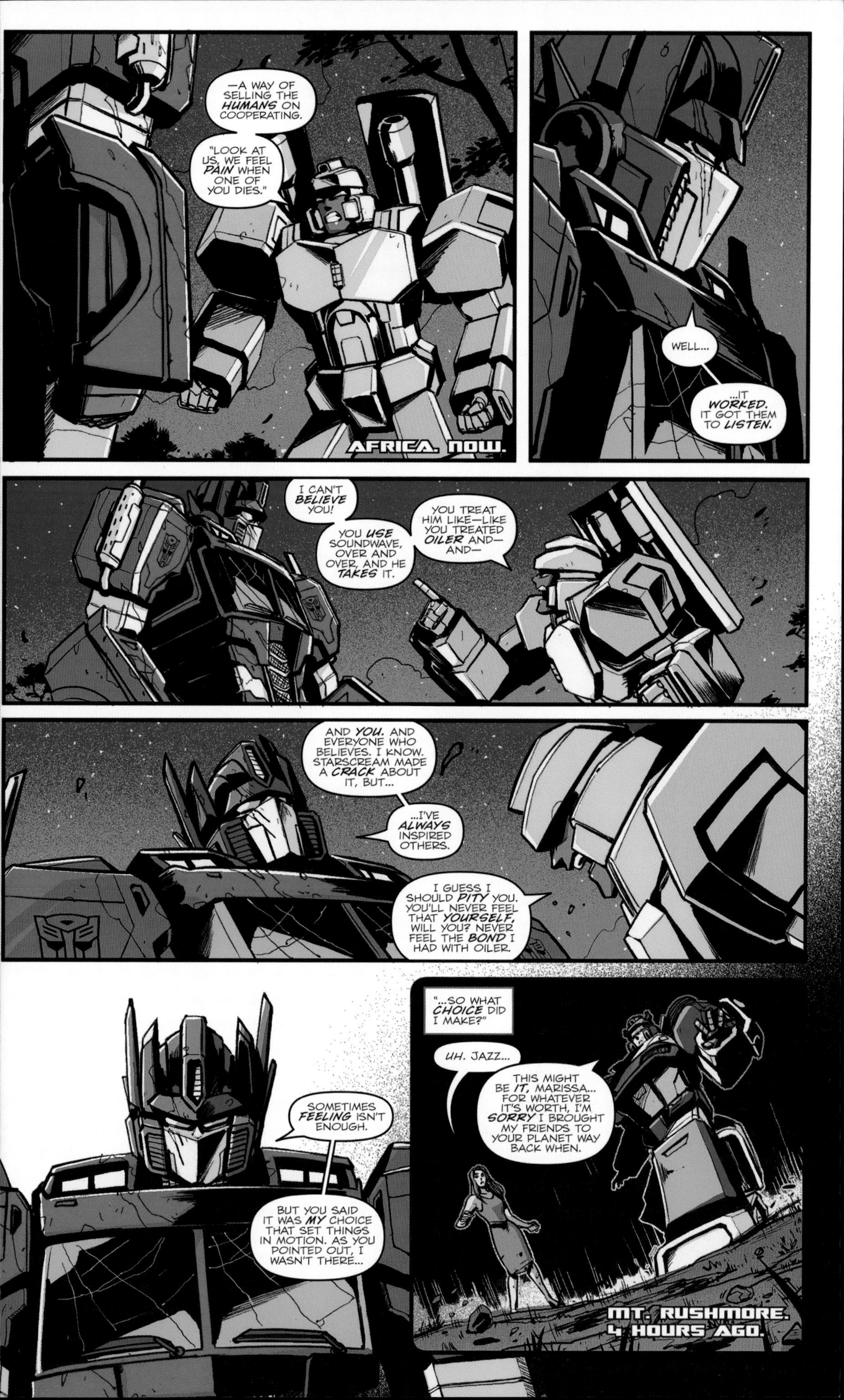
—A WAY OF SELLING THE HUMANS ON COOPERATING.
"LOOK AT US, WE FEEL PAIN WHEN ONE OF YOU DIES."
AFRICA. NOW.
WELL...
...IT WORKED. IT GOT THEM TO LISTEN.
I CAN'T BELIEVE YOU!
YOU USE SOUNDWAVE, OVER AND OVER, AND HE TAKES IT.
YOU TREAT HIM LIKE—LIKE YOU TREATED OILER AND—AND—
AND YOU. AND EVERYONE WHO BELIEVES. I KNOW. STARSCREAM MADE A CRACK ABOUT IT, BUT...
...I'VE ALWAYS INSPIRED OTHERS.
I GUESS I SHOULD PITY YOU. YOU'LL NEVER FEEL THAT YOURSELF, WILL YOU? NEVER FEEL THE BOND I HAD WITH OILER.
SOMETIMES FEELING ISN'T ENOUGH.
BUT YOU SAID IT WAS MY CHOICE THAT SET THINGS IN MOTION. AS YOU POINTED OUT, I WASN'T THERE...
"...SO WHAT CHOICE DID I MAKE?"
UH. JAZZ...
THIS MIGHT BE IT, MARISSA... FOR WHATEVER IT'S WORTH, I'M SORRY I BROUGHT MY FRIENDS TO YOUR PLANET WAY BACK WHEN.
MT. RUSHMORE. 4 HOURS AGO.

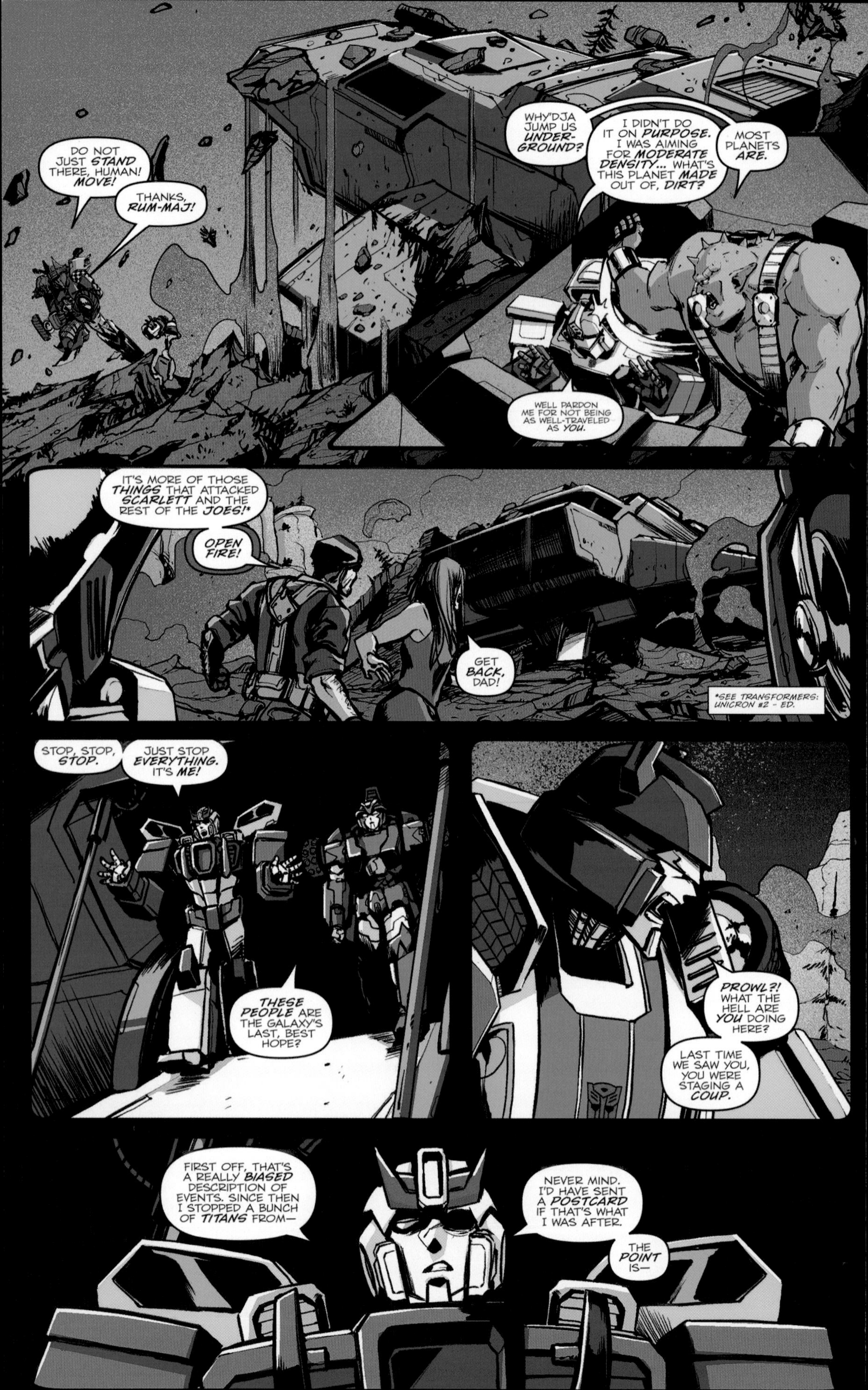
DO NOT JUST STAND THERE, HUMAN! MOVE!
THANKS, RUM-MAJ!
WHY'DJA JUMP US UNDER-GROUND?
I DIDN'T DO IT ON PURPOSE. I WAS AIMING FOR MODERATE DENSITY... WHAT'S THIS PLANET MADE OUT OF, DIRT?
MOST PLANETS ARE.
WELL PARDON ME FOR NOT BEING AS WELL-TRAVELED AS YOU.
IT'S MORE OF THOSE THINGS THAT ATTACKED SCARLETT AND THE REST OF THE JOES!*
OPEN FIRE!
GET BACK, DAD!
*SEE TRANSFORMERS: UNICRON #2 - ED.
STOP, STOP, STOP.
JUST STOP EVERYTHING. IT'S ME!
THESE PEOPLE ARE THE GALAXY'S LAST, BEST HOPE?
PROWL?! WHAT THE HELL ARE YOU DOING HERE?
LAST TIME WE SAW YOU, YOU WERE STAGING A COUP.
FIRST OFF, THAT'S A REALLY BIASED DESCRIPTION OF EVENTS. SINCE THEN I STOPPED A BUNCH OF TITANS FROM—
NEVER MIND. I'D HAVE SENT A POSTCARD IF THAT'S WHAT I WAS AFTER.
THE POINT IS—

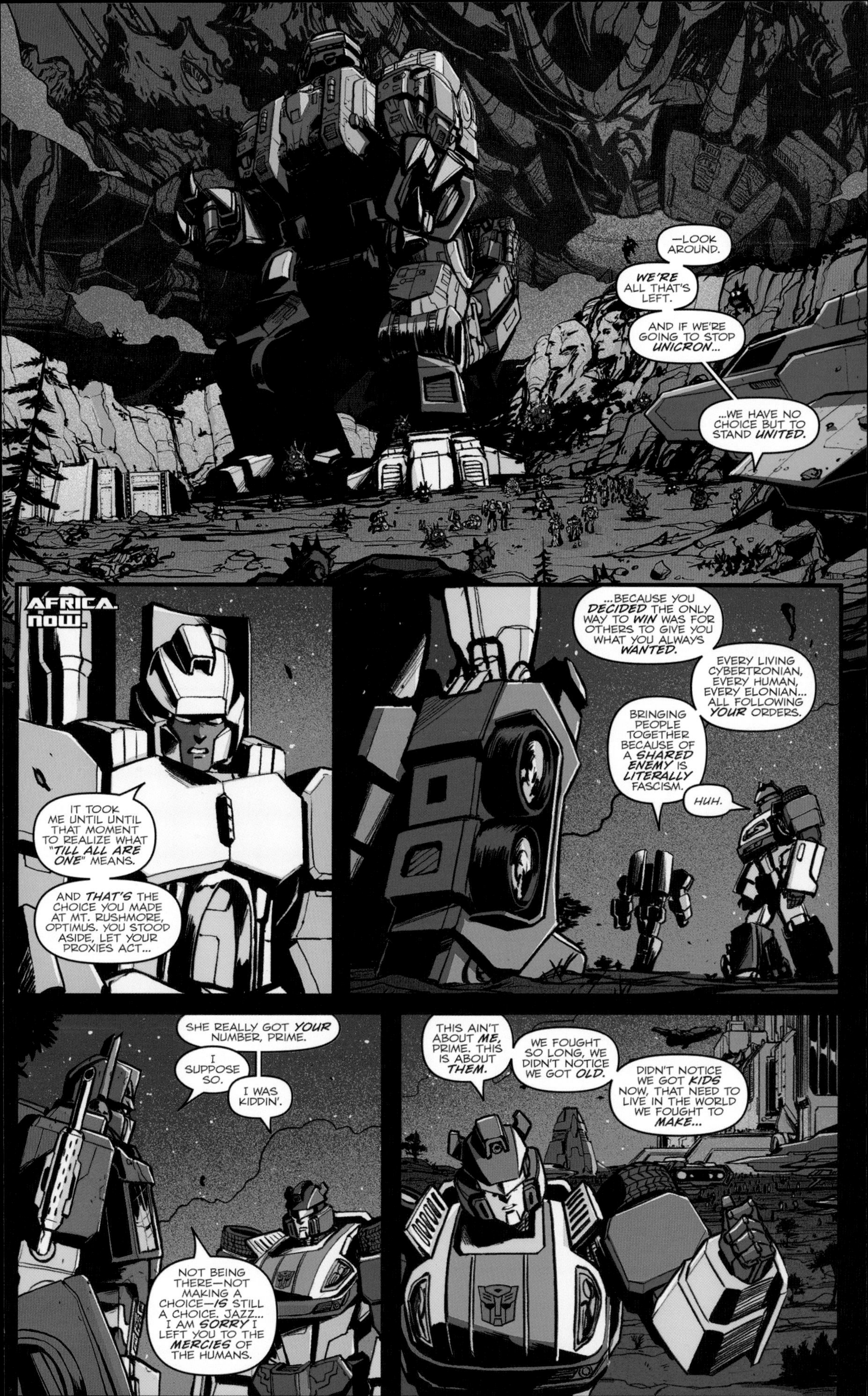
—LOOK AROUND.
WE'RE ALL THAT'S LEFT.
AND IF WE'RE GOING TO STOP UNICRON...
...WE HAVE NO CHOICE BUT TO STAND UNITED.
AFRICA. NOW.
IT TOOK ME UNTIL UNTIL THAT MOMENT TO REALIZE WHAT "TILL ALL ARE ONE" MEANS.
AND THAT'S THE CHOICE YOU MADE AT MT. RUSHMORE, OPTIMUS. YOU STOOD ASIDE, LET YOUR PROXIES ACT...
...BECAUSE YOU DECIDED THE ONLY WAY TO WIN WAS FOR OTHERS TO GIVE YOU WHAT YOU ALWAYS WANTED.
EVERY LIVING CYBERTRONIAN, EVERY HUMAN, EVERY ELONIAN... ALL FOLLOWING YOUR ORDERS.
BRINGING PEOPLE TOGETHER BECAUSE OF A SHARED ENEMY IS LITERALLY FASCISM.
HUH.
SHE REALLY GOT YOUR NUMBER, PRIME.
I SUPPOSE SO.
I WAS KIDDIN'.
NOT BEING THERE—NOT MAKING A CHOICE—IS STILL A CHOICE. JAZZ... I AM SORRY I LEFT YOU TO THE MERCIES OF THE HUMANS.
THIS AIN'T ABOUT ME, PRIME. THIS IS ABOUT THEM.
WE FOUGHT SO LONG, WE DIDN'T NOTICE WE GOT OLD.
DIDN'T NOTICE WE GOT KIDS NOW, THAT NEED TO LIVE IN THE WORLD WE FOUGHT TO MAKE...

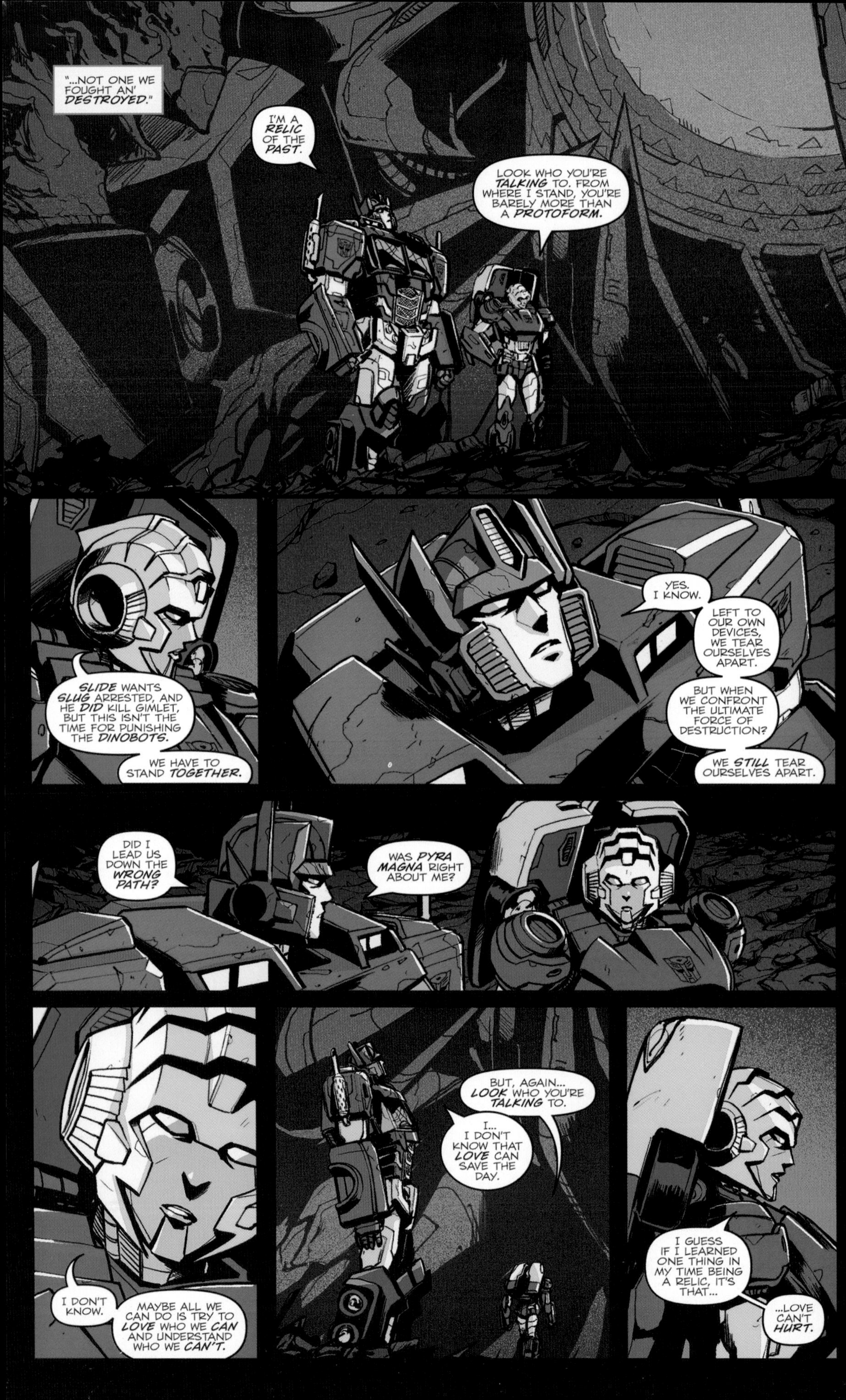
"...NOT ONE WE FOUGHT AN' DESTROYED."
I'M A RELIC OF THE PAST.
LOOK WHO YOU'RE TALKING TO. FROM WHERE I STAND, YOU'RE BARELY MORE THAN A PROTOFORM.
SLIDE WANTS SLUG ARRESTED, AND HE DID KILL GIMLET, BUT THIS ISN'T THE TIME FOR PUNISHING THE DINOBOTS.
WE HAVE TO STAND TOGETHER.
YES. I KNOW.
LEFT TO OUR OWN DEVICES, WE TEAR OURSELVES APART.
BUT WHEN WE CONFRONT THE ULTIMATE FORCE OF DESTRUCTION?
WE STILL TEAR OURSELVES APART.
DID I LEAD US DOWN THE WRONG PATH?
WAS PYRA MAGNA RIGHT ABOUT ME?
I DON'T KNOW.
MAYBE ALL WE CAN DO IS TRY TO LOVE WHO WE CAN AND UNDERSTAND WHO WE CAN'T.
BUT, AGAIN... LOOK WHO YOU'RE TALKING TO.
I... I DON'T KNOW THAT LOVE CAN SAVE THE DAY.
I GUESS IF I LEARNED ONE THING IN MY TIME BEING A RELIC, IT'S THAT...
...LOVE CAN'T HURT.

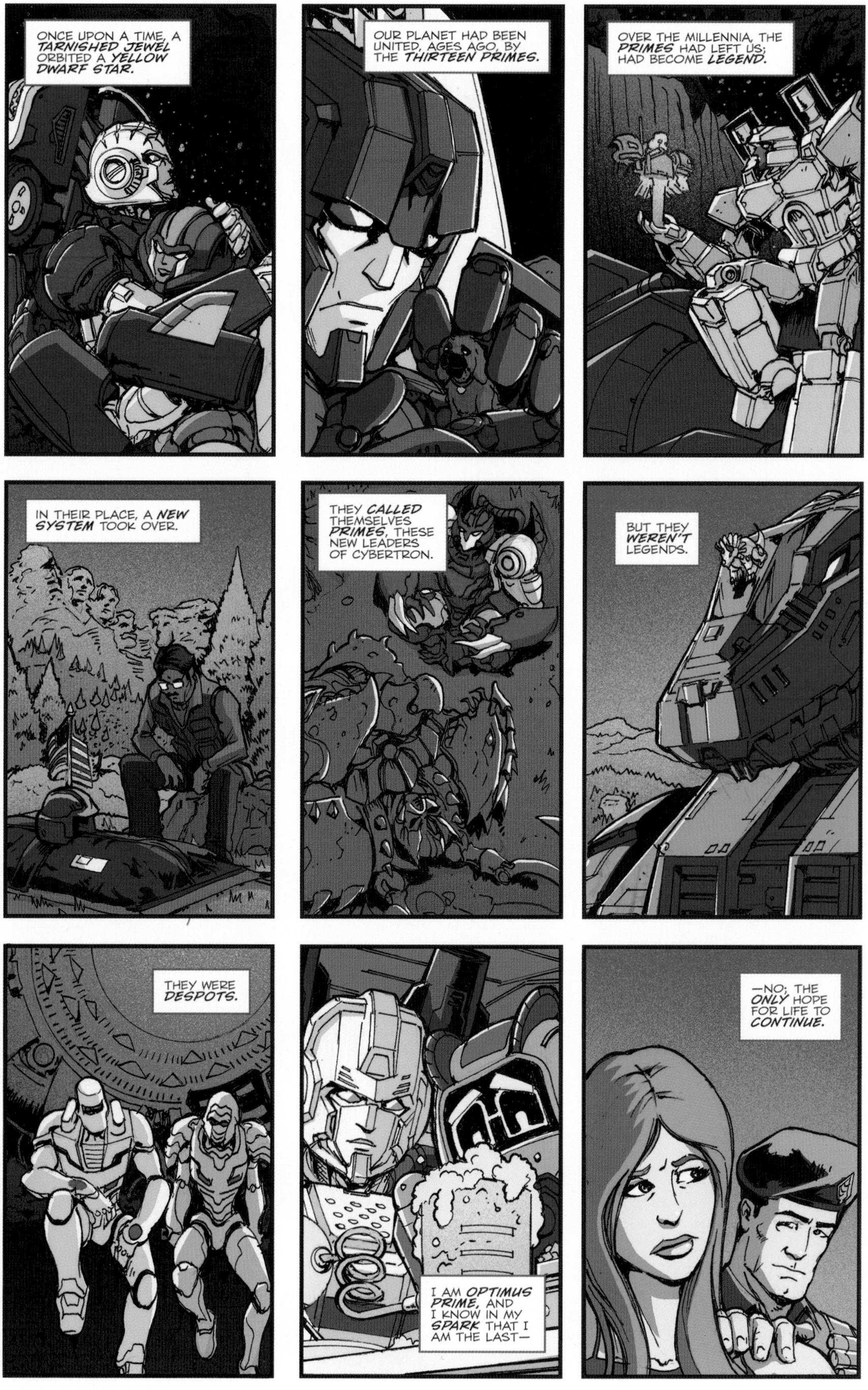
ONCE UPON A TIME, A TARNISHED JEWEL ORBITED A YELLOW DWARF STAR.
OUR PLANET HAD BEEN UNITED, AGES AGO, BY THE THIRTEEN PRIMES.
OVER THE MILLENNIA, THE PRIMES HAD LEFT US; HAD BECOME LEGEND.
IN THEIR PLACE, A NEW SYSTEM TOOK OVER.
THEY CALLED THEMSELVES PRIMES, THESE NEW LEADERS OF CYBERTRON.
BUT THEY WEREN'T LEGENDS.
THEY WERE DESPOTS.
I AM OPTIMUS PRIME, AND I KNOW IN MY SPARK THAT I AM THE LAST—
—NO; THE ONLY HOPE FOR LIFE TO CONTINUE.

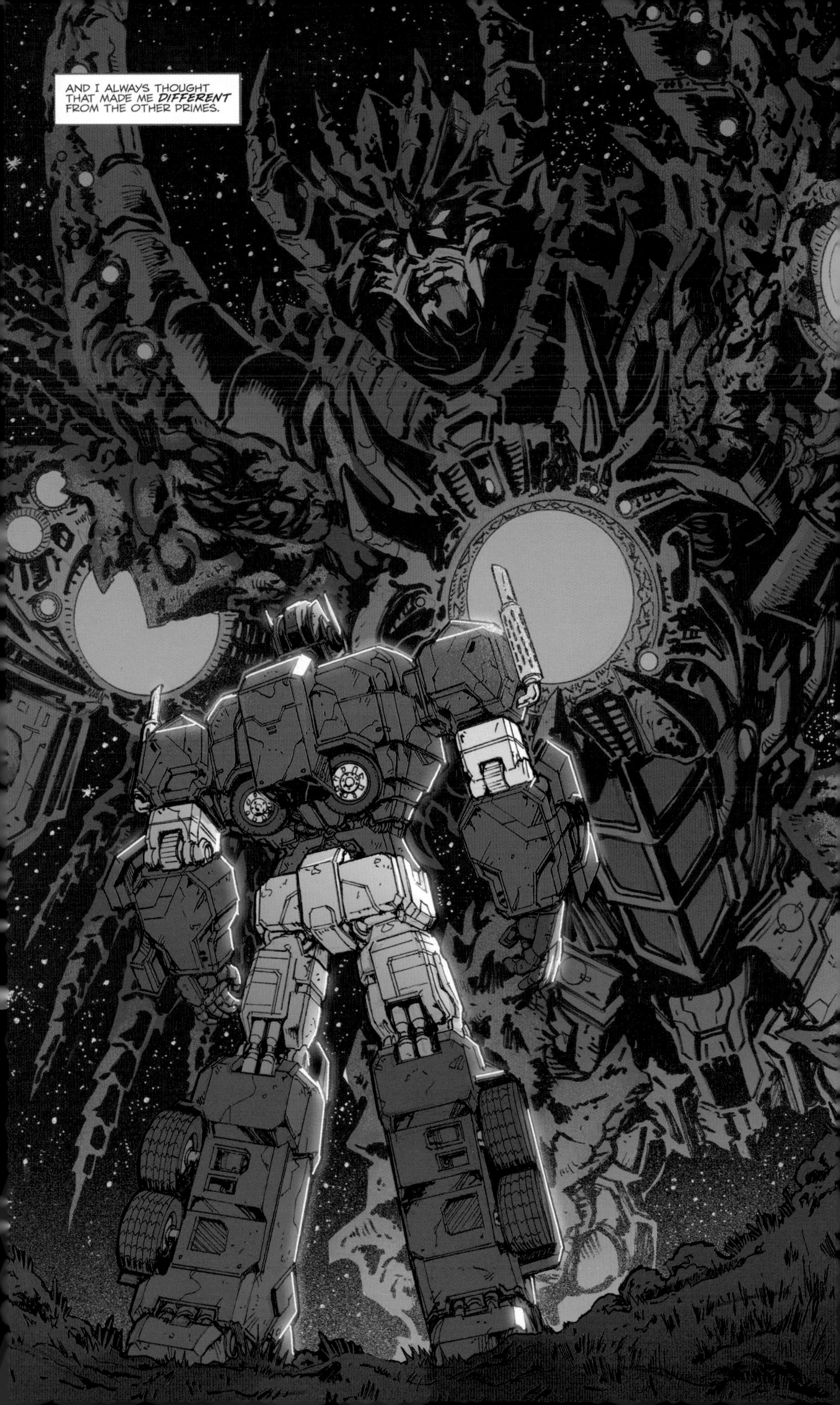
AND I ALWAYS THOUGHT THAT MADE ME *DIFFERENT* FROM THE OTHER PRIMES.

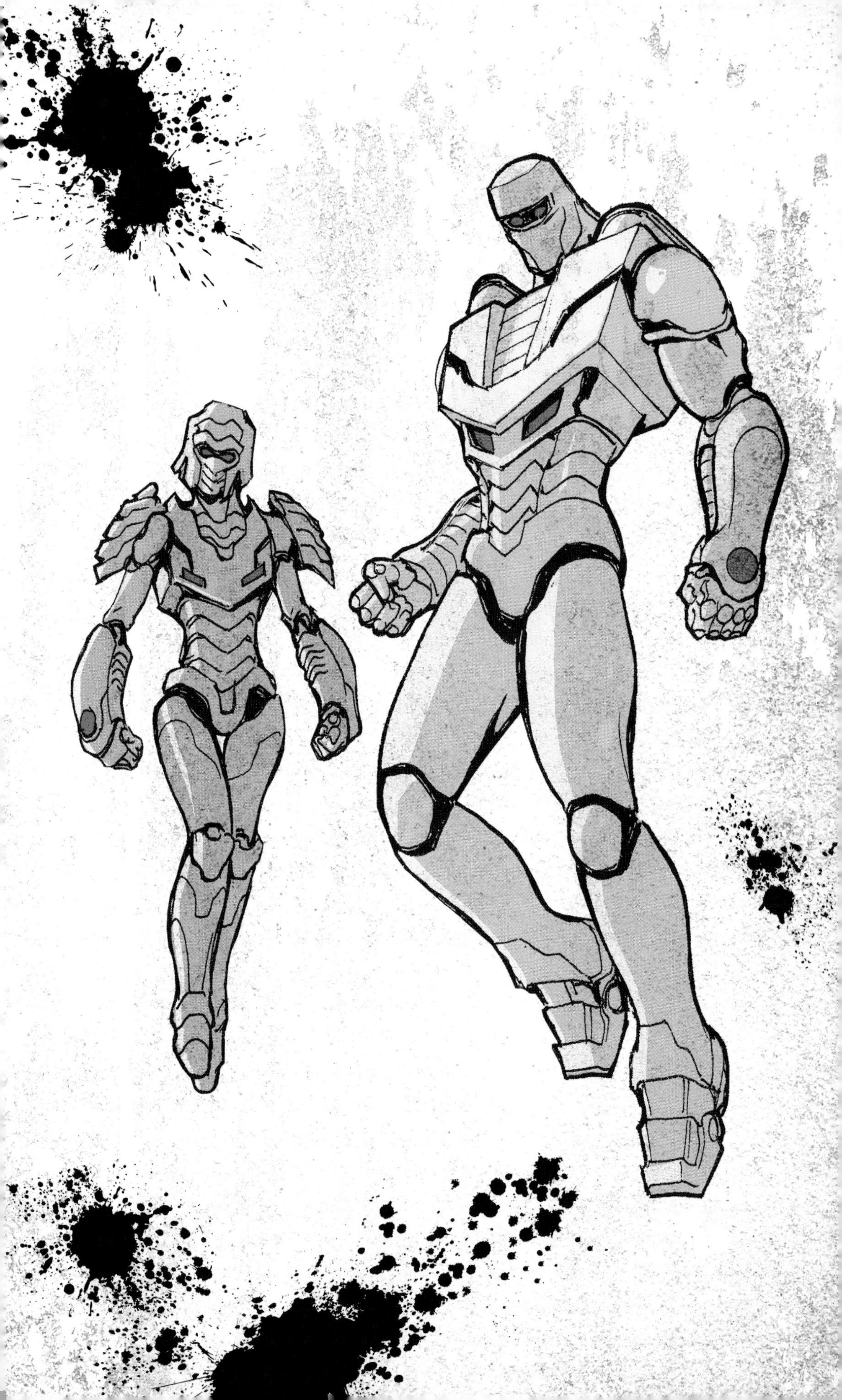

ART BY **KEI ZAMA** COLORS BY **JOSH BURCHAM**

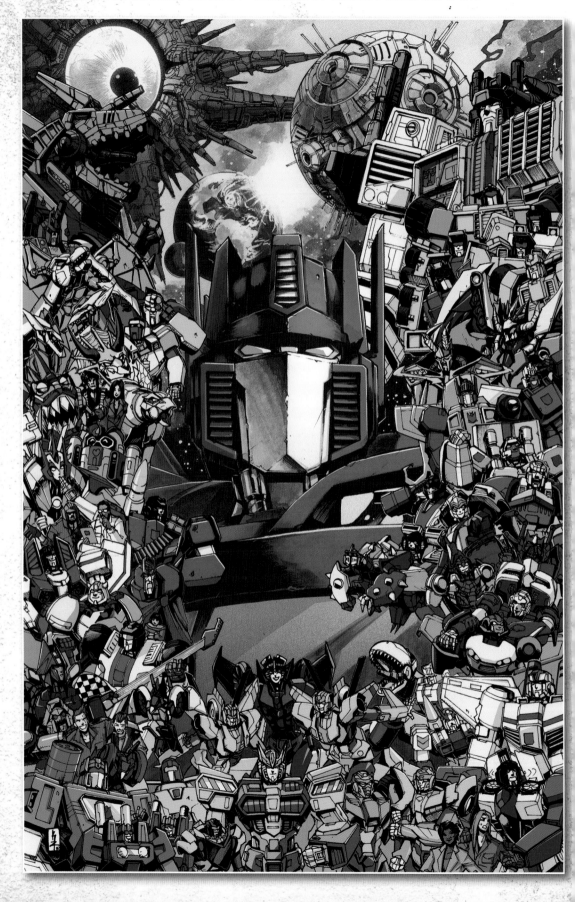

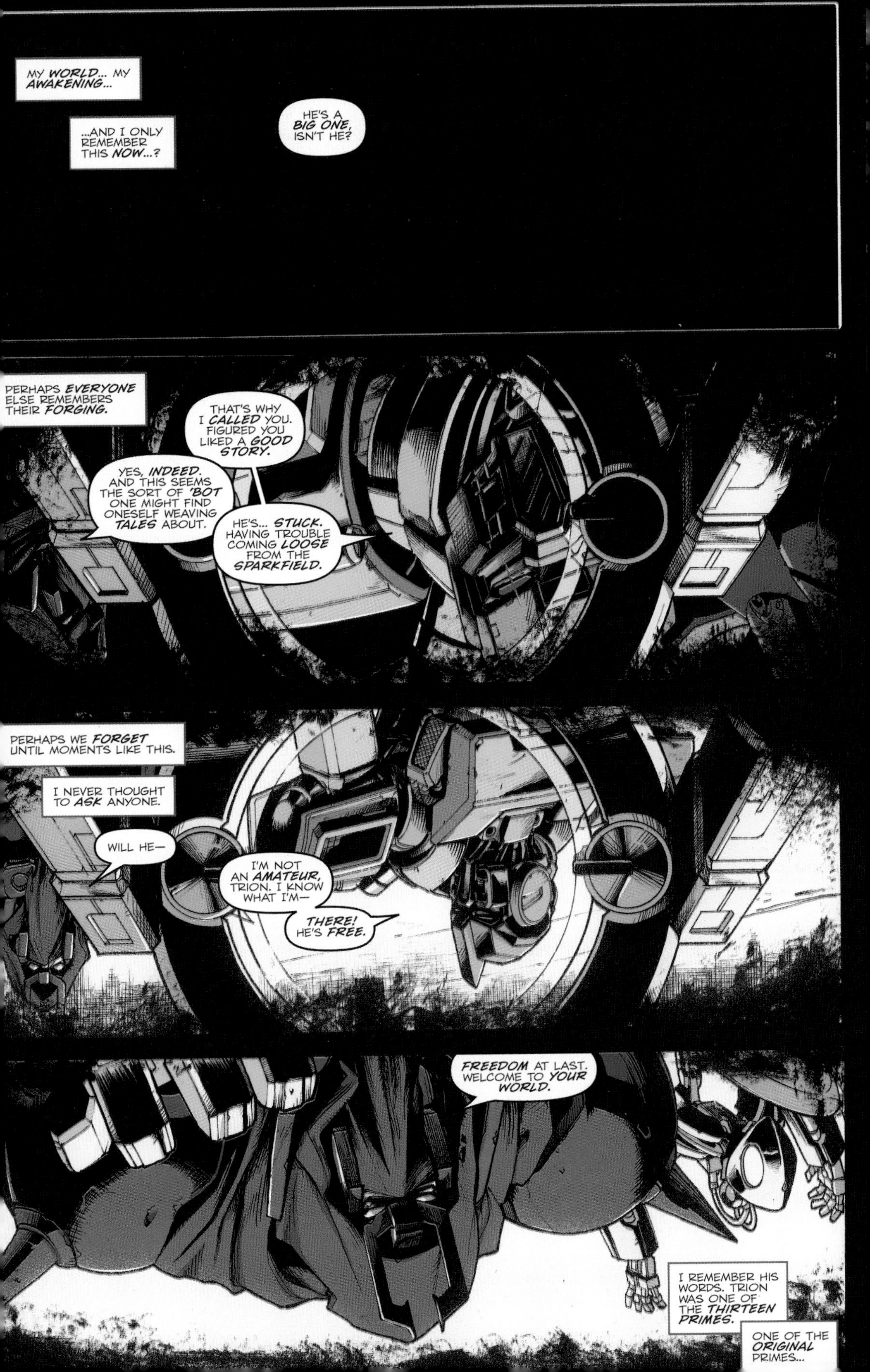

MY WORLD... MY AWAKENING...
...AND I ONLY REMEMBER THIS NOW...?
HE'S A BIG ONE, ISN'T HE?
PERHAPS EVERYONE ELSE REMEMBERS THEIR FORGING.
THAT'S WHY I CALLED YOU. FIGURED YOU LIKED A GOOD STORY.
YES, INDEED. AND THIS SEEMS THE SORT OF 'BOT ONE MIGHT FIND ONESELF WEAVING TALES ABOUT.
HE'S... STUCK. HAVING TROUBLE COMING LOOSE FROM THE SPARKFIELD.
PERHAPS WE FORGET UNTIL MOMENTS LIKE THIS.
I NEVER THOUGHT TO ASK ANYONE.
WILL HE—
I'M NOT AN AMATEUR, TRION. I KNOW WHAT I'M—
THERE! HE'S FREE.
FREEDOM AT LAST. WELCOME TO YOUR WORLD.
I REMEMBER HIS WORDS. TRION WAS ONE OF THE THIRTEEN PRIMES.
ONE OF THE ORIGINAL PRIMES...

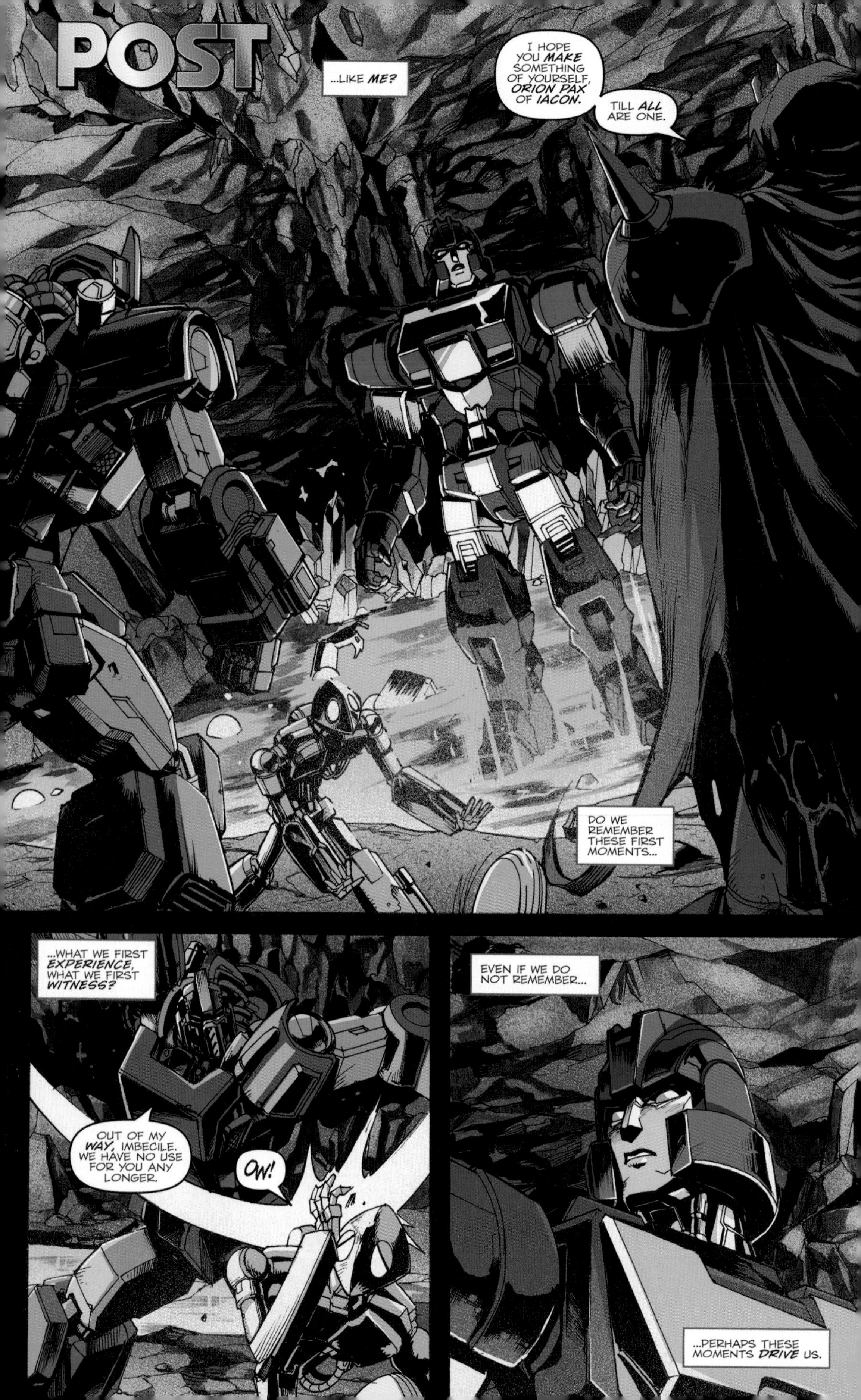
POST
...LIKE ME?
I HOPE YOU MAKE SOMETHING OF YOURSELF, ORION PAX OF IACON.
TILL ALL ARE ONE.
DO WE REMEMBER THESE FIRST MOMENTS...
...WHAT WE FIRST EXPERIENCE, WHAT WE FIRST WITNESS?
OUT OF MY WAY, IMBECILE. WE HAVE NO USE FOR YOU ANY LONGER.
OW!
EVEN IF WE DO NOT REMEMBER...
...PERHAPS THESE MOMENTS DRIVE US.

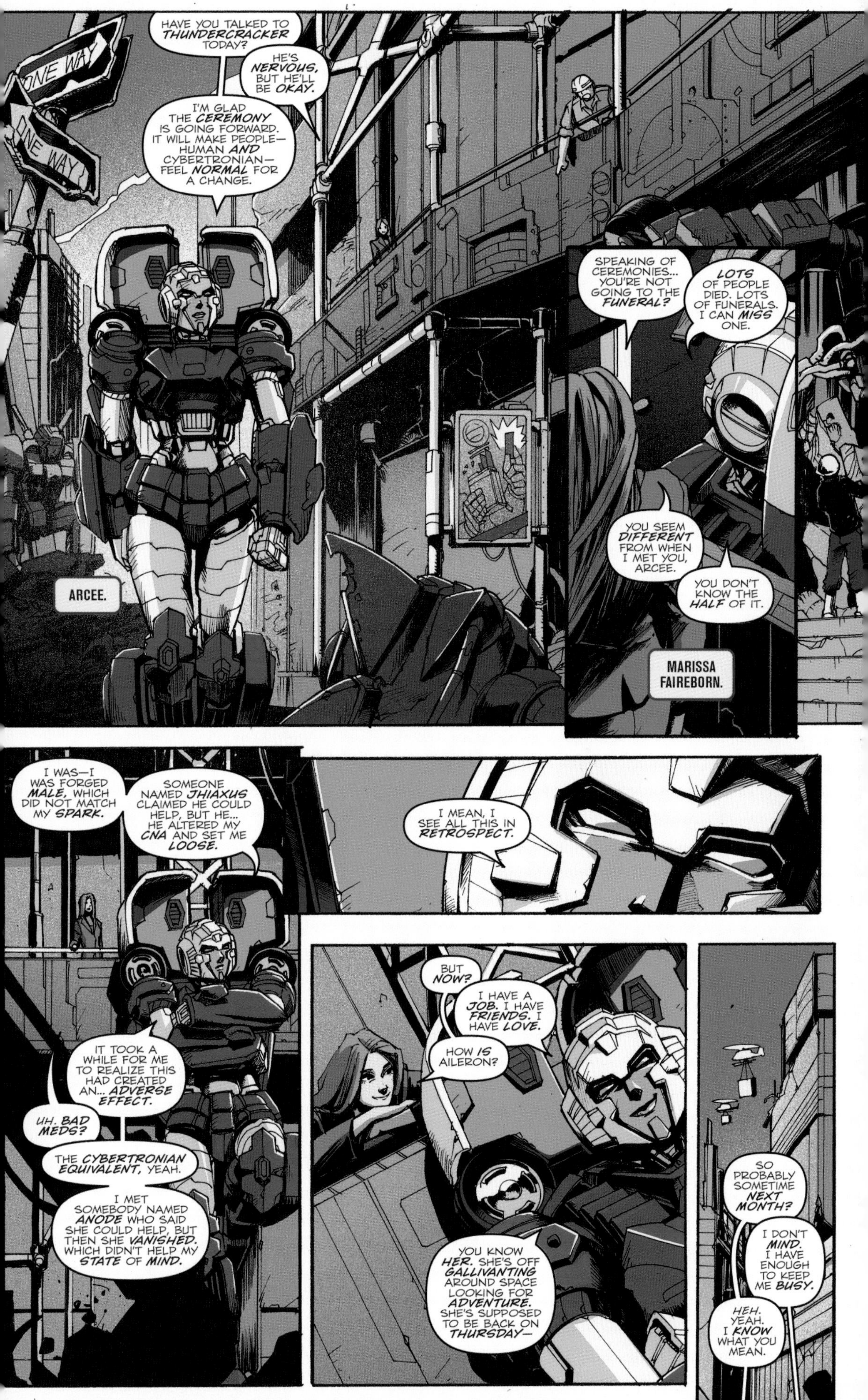

ONE WAY
ONE WAY
HAVE YOU TALKED TO THUNDERCRACKER TODAY?
HE'S NERVOUS, BUT HE'LL BE OKAY.
I'M GLAD THE CEREMONY IS GOING FORWARD. IT WILL MAKE PEOPLE— HUMAN AND CYBERTRONIAN— FEEL NORMAL FOR A CHANGE.
ARCEE.
SPEAKING OF CEREMONIES... YOU'RE NOT GOING TO THE FUNERAL?
LOTS OF PEOPLE DIED. LOTS OF FUNERALS. I CAN MISS ONE.
YOU SEEM DIFFERENT FROM WHEN I MET YOU, ARCEE.
YOU DON'T KNOW THE HALF OF IT.
MARISSA FAIREBORN.
I WAS—I WAS FORGED MALE, WHICH DID NOT MATCH MY SPARK.
SOMEONE NAMED JHIAXUS CLAIMED HE COULD HELP, BUT HE... HE ALTERED MY CNA AND SET ME LOOSE.
I MEAN, I SEE ALL THIS IN RETROSPECT.
IT TOOK A WHILE FOR ME TO REALIZE THIS HAD CREATED AN... ADVERSE EFFECT.
UH. BAD MEDS?
THE CYBERTRONIAN EQUIVALENT, YEAH.
I MET SOMEBODY NAMED ANODE WHO SAID SHE COULD HELP, BUT THEN SHE VANISHED. WHICH DIDN'T HELP MY STATE OF MIND.
BUT NOW?
I HAVE A JOB. I HAVE FRIENDS. I HAVE LOVE.
HOW IS AILERON?
YOU KNOW HER. SHE'S OFF GALLIVANTING AROUND SPACE LOOKING FOR ADVENTURE. SHE'S SUPPOSED TO BE BACK ON THURSDAY—
SO PROBABLY SOMETIME NEXT MONTH?
I DON'T MIND. I HAVE ENOUGH TO KEEP ME BUSY.
HEH. YEAH. I KNOW WHAT YOU MEAN.

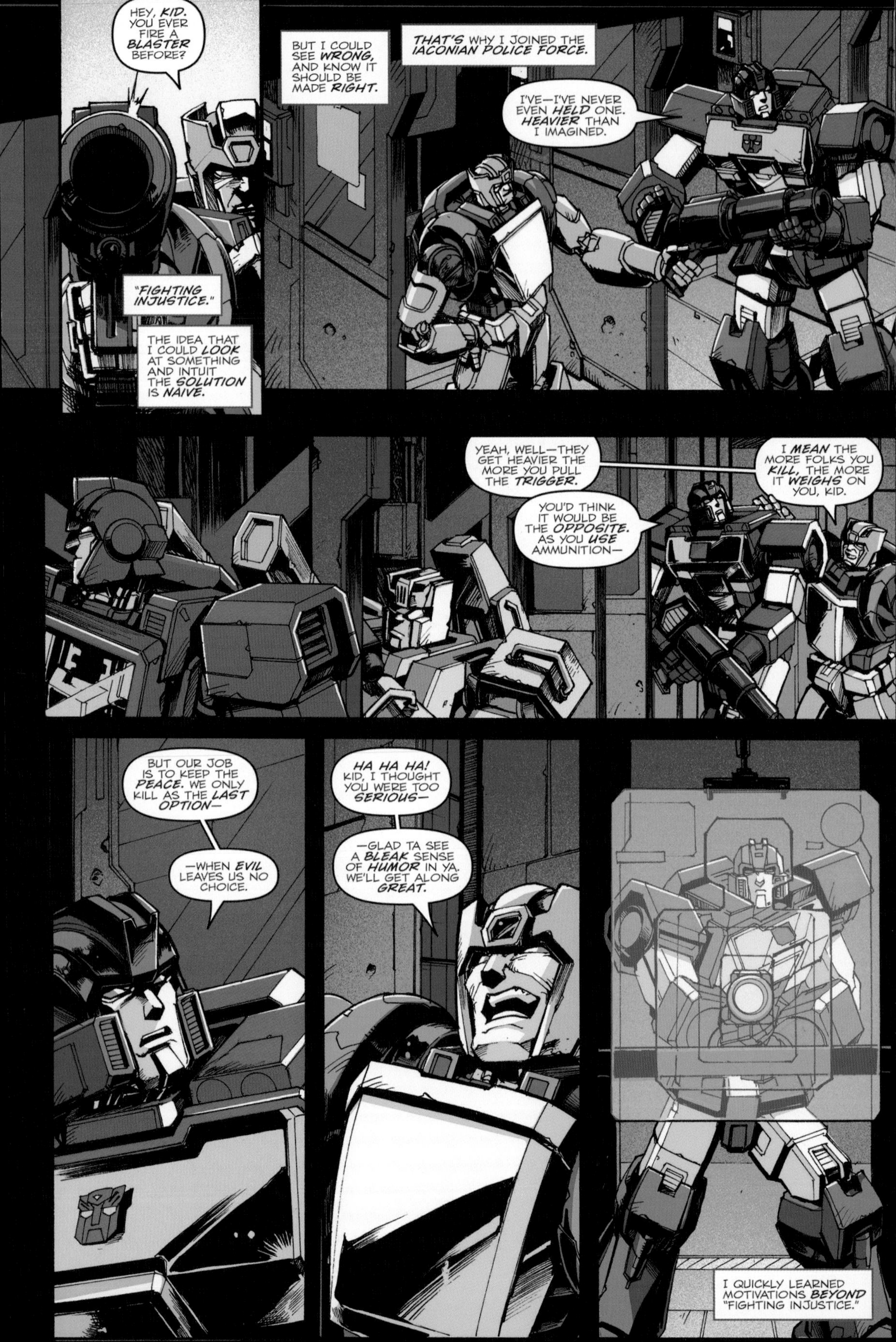
HEY, KID. YOU EVER FIRE A BLASTER BEFORE?
BUT I COULD SEE WRONG, AND KNOW IT SHOULD BE MADE RIGHT.
THAT'S WHY I JOINED THE IACONIAN POLICE FORCE.
I'VE—I'VE NEVER EVEN HELD ONE. HEAVIER THAN I IMAGINED.
"FIGHTING INJUSTICE."
THE IDEA THAT I COULD LOOK AT SOMETHING AND INTUIT THE SOLUTION IS NAIVE.
YEAH, WELL—THEY GET HEAVIER THE MORE YOU PULL THE TRIGGER.
I MEAN THE MORE FOLKS YOU KILL, THE MORE IT WEIGHS ON YOU, KID.
YOU'D THINK IT WOULD BE THE OPPOSITE. AS YOU USE AMMUNITION—
BUT OUR JOB IS TO KEEP THE PEACE. WE ONLY KILL AS THE LAST OPTION—
—WHEN EVIL LEAVES US NO CHOICE.
HA HA HA! KID, I THOUGHT YOU WERE TOO SERIOUS—
—GLAD TA SEE A BLEAK SENSE OF HUMOR IN YA. WE'LL GET ALONG GREAT.
I QUICKLY LEARNED MOTIVATIONS BEYOND "FIGHTING INJUSTICE."

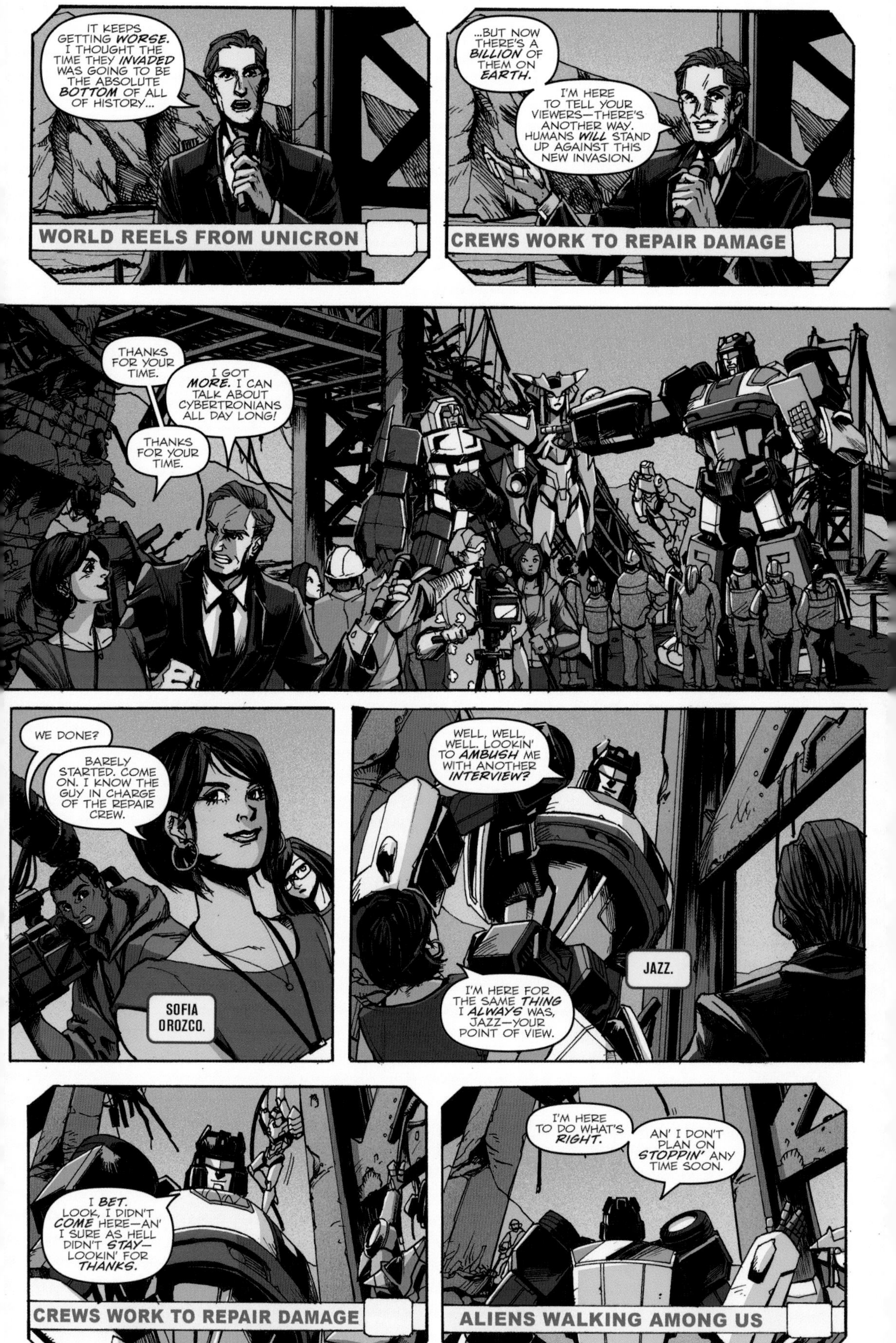
IT KEEPS GETTING WORSE. I THOUGHT THE TIME THEY INVADED WAS GOING TO BE THE ABSOLUTE BOTTOM OF ALL OF HISTORY...
WORLD REELS FROM UNICRON
...BUT NOW THERE'S A BILLION OF THEM ON EARTH.
I'M HERE TO TELL YOUR VIEWERS—THERE'S ANOTHER WAY. HUMANS WILL STAND UP AGAINST THIS NEW INVASION.
CREWS WORK TO REPAIR DAMAGE
THANKS FOR YOUR TIME.
I GOT MORE. I CAN TALK ABOUT CYBERTRONIANS ALL DAY LONG!
THANKS FOR YOUR TIME.
WE DONE?
BARELY STARTED. COME ON. I KNOW THE GUY IN CHARGE OF THE REPAIR CREW.
SOFIA OROZCO.
WELL, WELL, WELL. LOOKIN' TO AMBUSH ME WITH ANOTHER INTERVIEW?
JAZZ.
I'M HERE FOR THE SAME THING I ALWAYS WAS, JAZZ—YOUR POINT OF VIEW.
I BET. LOOK, I DIDN'T COME HERE—AN' I SURE AS HELL DIDN'T STAY—LOOKIN' FOR THANKS.
CREWS WORK TO REPAIR DAMAGE
I'M HERE TO DO WHAT'S RIGHT.
AN' I DON'T PLAN ON STOPPIN' ANY TIME SOON.
ALIENS WALKING AMONG US

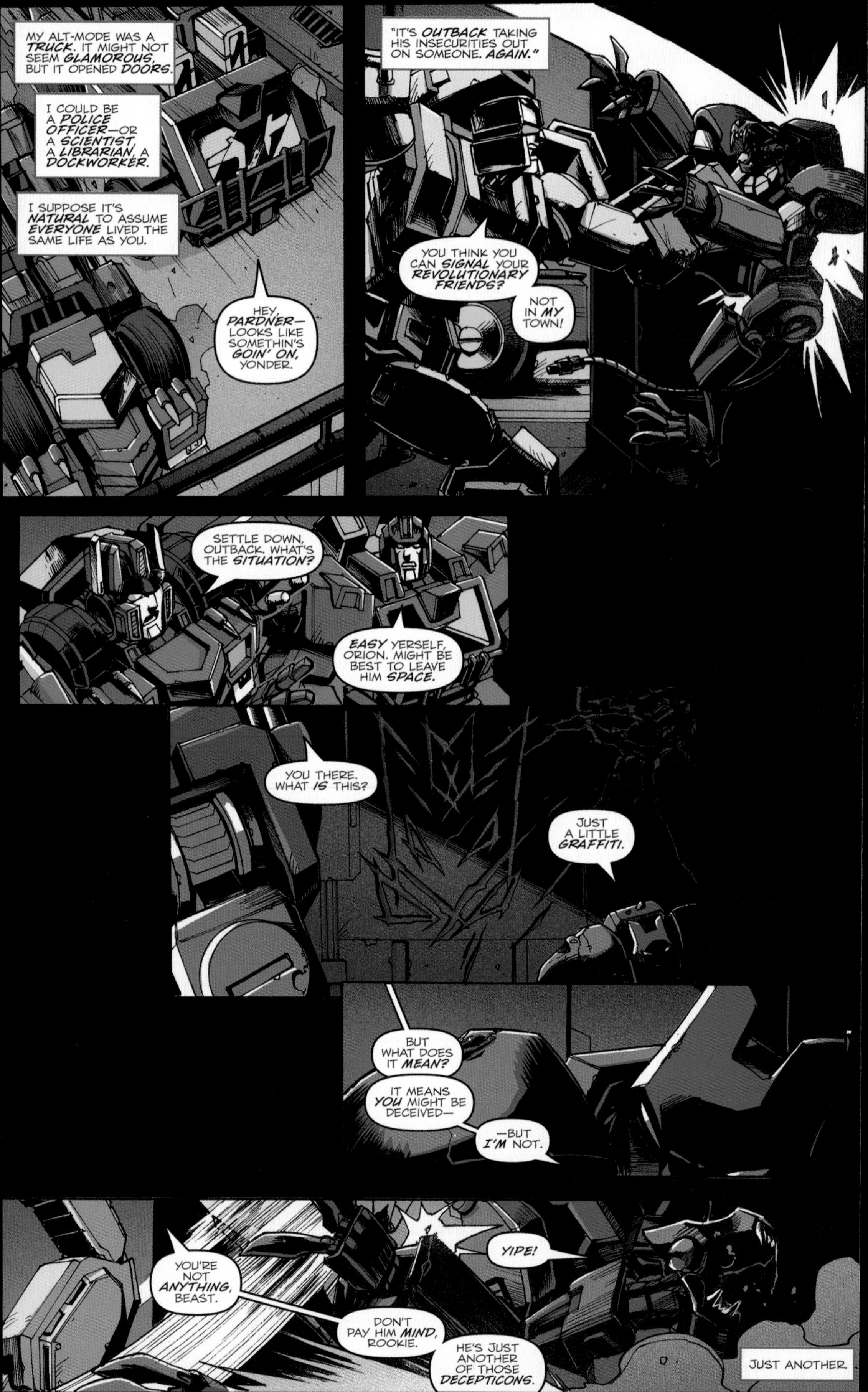

MY ALT-MODE WAS A TRUCK. IT MIGHT NOT SEEM GLAMOROUS, BUT IT OPENED DOORS.
I COULD BE A POLICE OFFICER—OR A SCIENTIST, A LIBRARIAN, A DOCKWORKER.
I SUPPOSE IT'S NATURAL TO ASSUME EVERYONE LIVED THE SAME LIFE AS YOU.
HEY, PARDNER—LOOKS LIKE SOMETHIN'S GOIN' ON, YONDER.
"IT'S OUTBACK TAKING HIS INSECURITIES OUT ON SOMEONE. AGAIN."
YOU THINK YOU CAN SIGNAL YOUR REVOLUTIONARY FRIENDS?
NOT IN MY TOWN!
SETTLE DOWN, OUTBACK. WHAT'S THE SITUATION?
EASY YERSELF, ORION. MIGHT BE BEST TO LEAVE HIM SPACE.
YOU THERE. WHAT IS THIS?
JUST A LITTLE GRAFFITI.
BUT WHAT DOES IT MEAN?
IT MEANS YOU MIGHT BE DECEIVED—
—BUT I'M NOT.
YOU'RE NOT ANYTHING, BEAST.
YIPE!
DON'T PAY HIM MIND, ROOKIE.
HE'S JUST ANOTHER OF THOSE DECEPTICONS.
JUST ANOTHER.

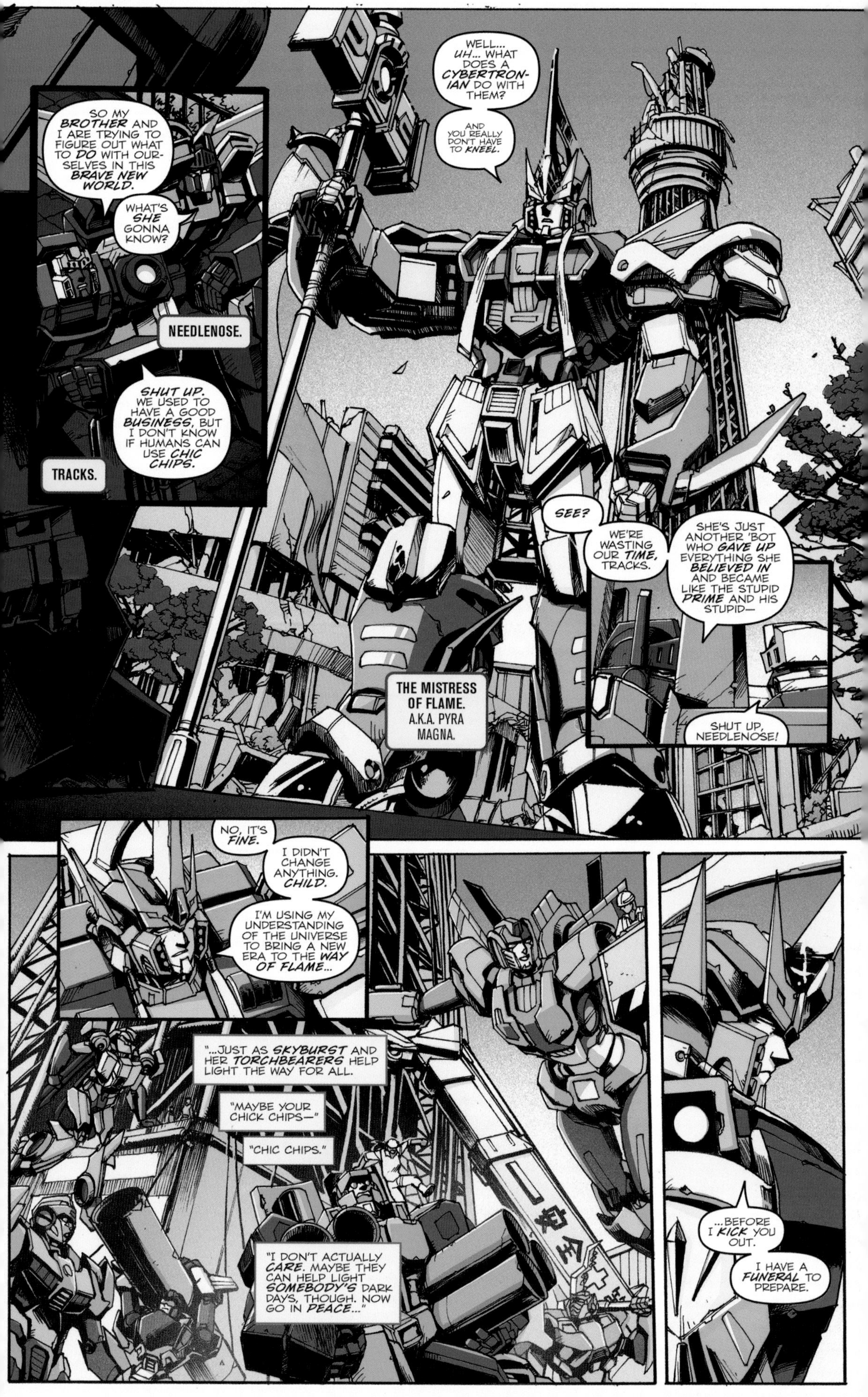
SO MY BROTHER AND I ARE TRYING TO FIGURE OUT WHAT TO DO WITH OURSELVES IN THIS BRAVE NEW WORLD.
WHAT'S SHE GONNA KNOW?
NEEDLENOSE.
SHUT UP. WE USED TO HAVE A GOOD BUSINESS, BUT I DON'T KNOW IF HUMANS CAN USE CHIC CHIPS.
TRACKS.
WELL... UH... WHAT DOES A CYBERTRONIAN DO WITH THEM?
AND YOU REALLY DON'T HAVE TO KNEEL.
THE MISTRESS OF FLAME. A.K.A. PYRA MAGNA.
SEE?
WE'RE WASTING OUR TIME, TRACKS.
SHE'S JUST ANOTHER 'BOT WHO GAVE UP EVERYTHING SHE BELIEVED IN AND BECAME LIKE THE STUPID PRIME AND HIS STUPID—
SHUT UP, NEEDLENOSE!
NO, IT'S FINE.
I DIDN'T CHANGE ANYTHING. CHILD.
I'M USING MY UNDERSTANDING OF THE UNIVERSE TO BRING A NEW ERA TO THE WAY OF FLAME...
"...JUST AS SKYBURST AND HER TORCHBEARERS HELP LIGHT THE WAY FOR ALL.
"MAYBE YOUR CHICK CHIPS—"
"CHIC CHIPS."
"I DON'T ACTUALLY CARE. MAYBE THEY CAN HELP LIGHT SOMEBODY'S DARK DAYS, THOUGH. NOW GO IN PEACE..."
...BEFORE I KICK YOU OUT.
I HAVE A FUNERAL TO PREPARE.

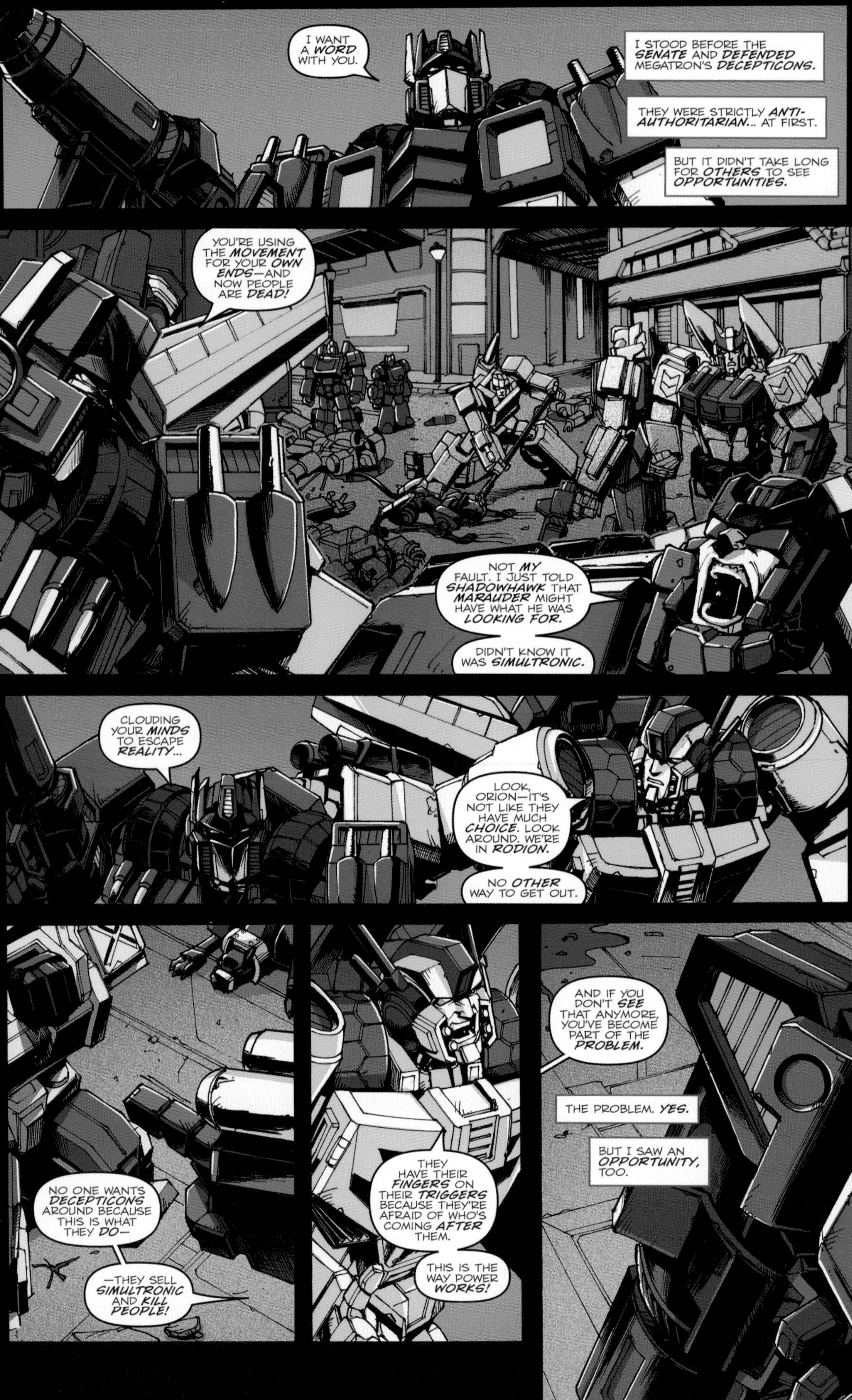
I WANT A WORD WITH YOU.
I STOOD BEFORE THE SENATE AND DEFENDED MEGATRON'S DECEPTICONS.
THEY WERE STRICTLY ANTI-AUTHORITARIAN... AT FIRST.
BUT IT DIDN'T TAKE LONG FOR OTHERS TO SEE OPPORTUNITIES.
YOU'RE USING THE MOVEMENT FOR YOUR OWN ENDS—AND NOW PEOPLE ARE DEAD!
NOT MY FAULT. I JUST TOLD SHADOWHAWK THAT MARAUDER MIGHT HAVE WHAT HE WAS LOOKING FOR.
DIDN'T KNOW IT WAS SIMULTRONIC.
CLOUDING YOUR MINDS TO ESCAPE REALITY...
LOOK, ORION—IT'S NOT LIKE THEY HAVE MUCH CHOICE. LOOK AROUND. WE'RE IN RODION.
NO OTHER WAY TO GET OUT.
NO ONE WANTS DECEPTICONS AROUND BECAUSE THIS IS WHAT THEY DO—
—THEY SELL SIMULTRONIC AND KILL PEOPLE!
THEY HAVE THEIR FINGERS ON THEIR TRIGGERS BECAUSE THEY'RE AFRAID OF WHO'S COMING AFTER THEM.
THIS IS THE WAY POWER WORKS!
AND IF YOU DON'T SEE THAT ANYMORE, YOU'VE BECOME PART OF THE PROBLEM.
THE PROBLEM. YES.
BUT I SAW AN OPPORTUNITY, TOO.

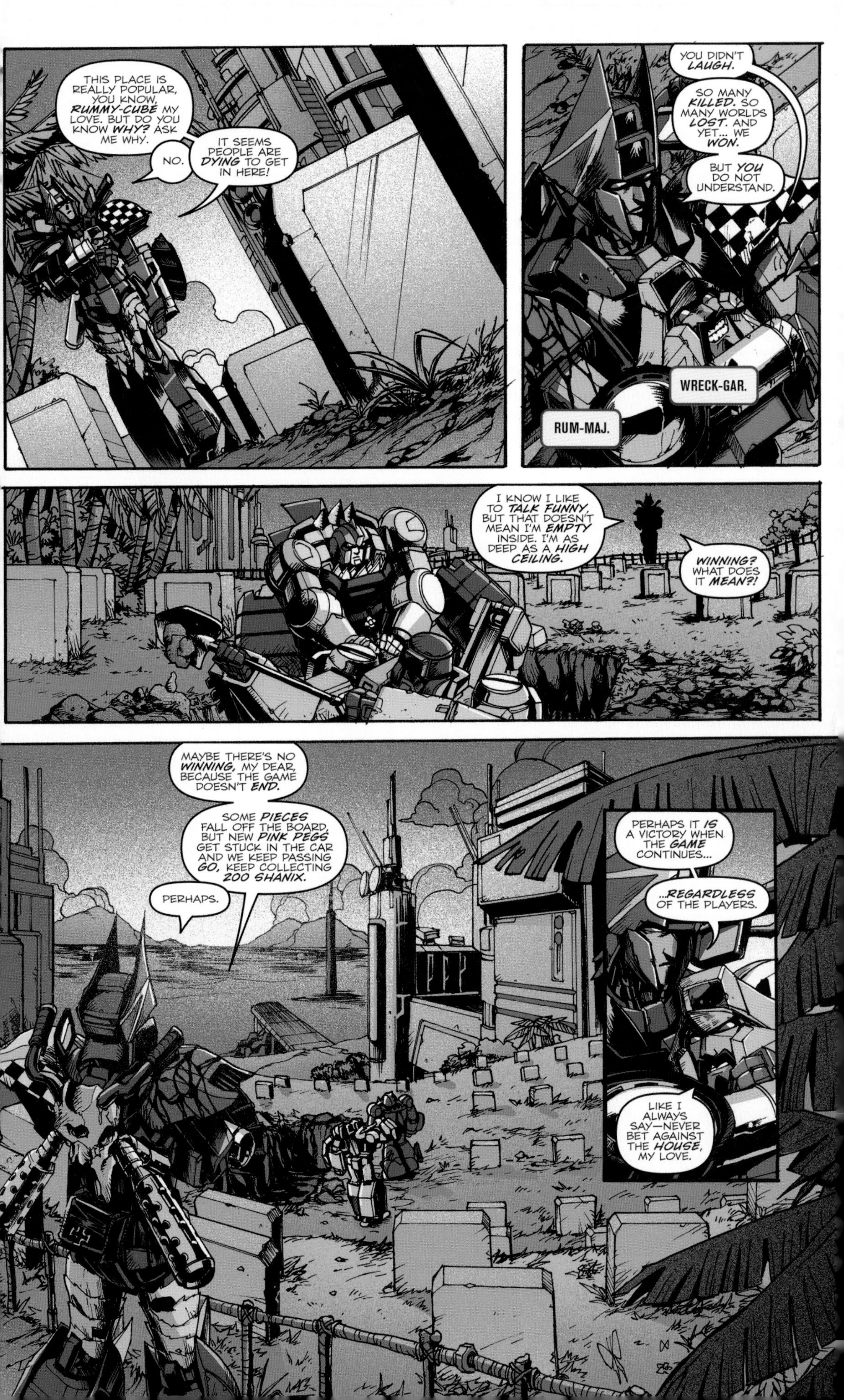
THIS PLACE IS REALLY POPULAR, YOU KNOW, RUMMY-CUBE MY LOVE. BUT DO YOU KNOW WHY? ASK ME WHY.
NO.
IT SEEMS PEOPLE ARE DYING TO GET IN HERE!
YOU DIDN'T LAUGH.
SO MANY KILLED. SO MANY WORLDS LOST. AND YET... WE WON.
BUT YOU DO NOT UNDERSTAND.
WRECK-GAR.
RUM-MAJ.
I KNOW I LIKE TO TALK FUNNY, BUT THAT DOESN'T MEAN I'M EMPTY INSIDE. I'M AS DEEP AS A HIGH CEILING.
WINNING? WHAT DOES IT MEAN?!
MAYBE THERE'S NO WINNING, MY DEAR, BECAUSE THE GAME DOESN'T END.
SOME PIECES FALL OFF THE BOARD, BUT NEW PINK PEGS GET STUCK IN THE CAR AND WE KEEP PASSING GO, KEEP COLLECTING 200 SHANIX.
PERHAPS.
PERHAPS IT IS A VICTORY WHEN THE GAME CONTINUES...
...REGARDLESS OF THE PLAYERS.
LIKE I ALWAYS SAY—NEVER BET AGAINST THE HOUSE, MY LOVE.

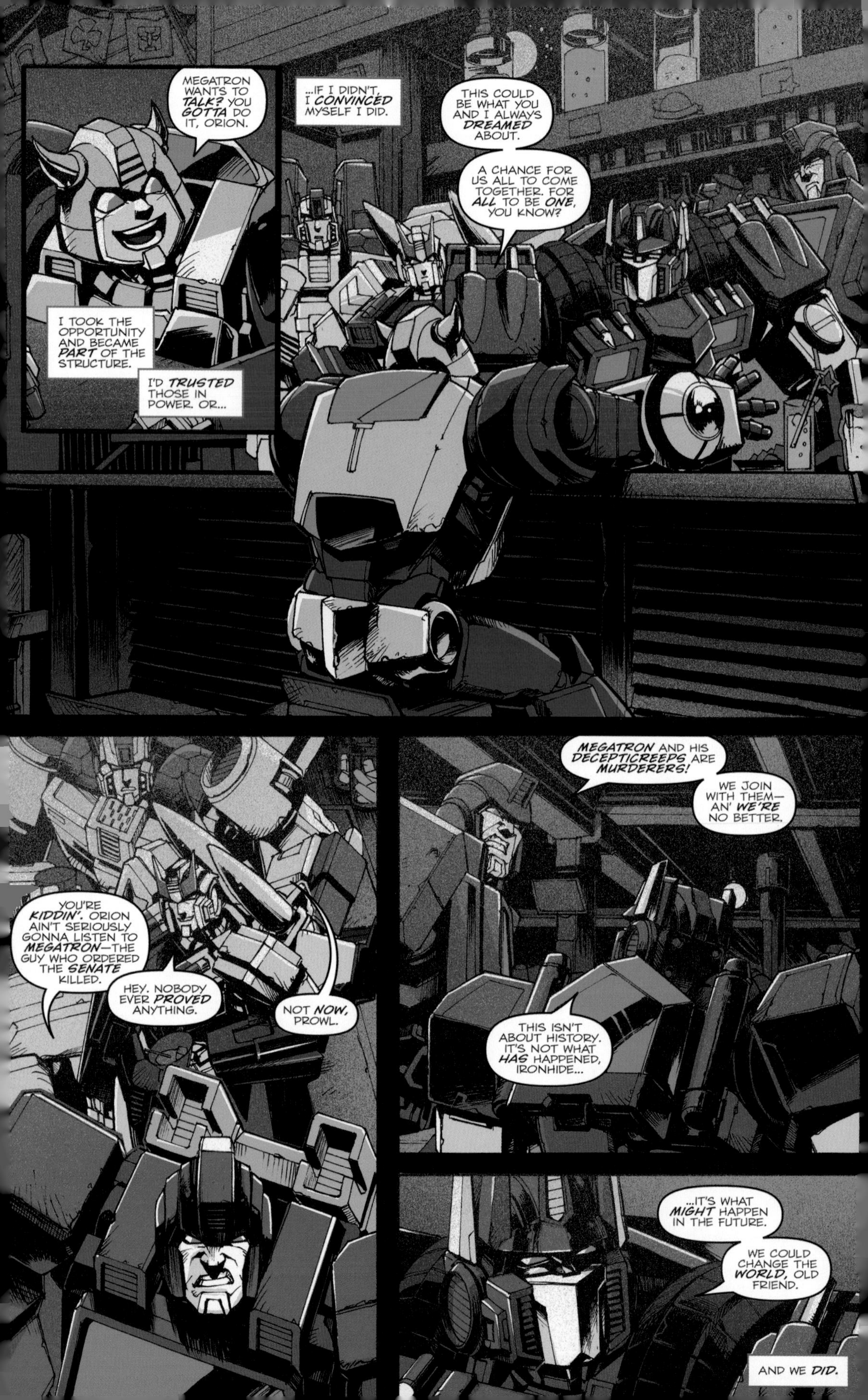
MEGATRON WANTS TO TALK? YOU GOTTA DO IT, ORION.
...IF I DIDN'T, I CONVINCED MYSELF I DID.
THIS COULD BE WHAT YOU AND I ALWAYS DREAMED ABOUT.
A CHANCE FOR US ALL TO COME TOGETHER. FOR ALL TO BE ONE, YOU KNOW?
I TOOK THE OPPORTUNITY AND BECAME PART OF THE STRUCTURE.
I'D TRUSTED THOSE IN POWER. OR...
YOU'RE KIDDIN'. ORION AIN'T SERIOUSLY GONNA LISTEN TO MEGATRON—THE GUY WHO ORDERED THE SENATE KILLED.
HEY. NOBODY EVER PROVED ANYTHING.
NOT NOW, PROWL.
MEGATRON AND HIS DECEPTICREEPS ARE MURDERERS!
WE JOIN WITH THEM— AN' WE'RE NO BETTER.
THIS ISN'T ABOUT HISTORY. IT'S NOT WHAT HAS HAPPENED, IRONHIDE...
...IT'S WHAT MIGHT HAPPEN IN THE FUTURE.
WE COULD CHANGE THE WORLD, OLD FRIEND.
AND WE DID.

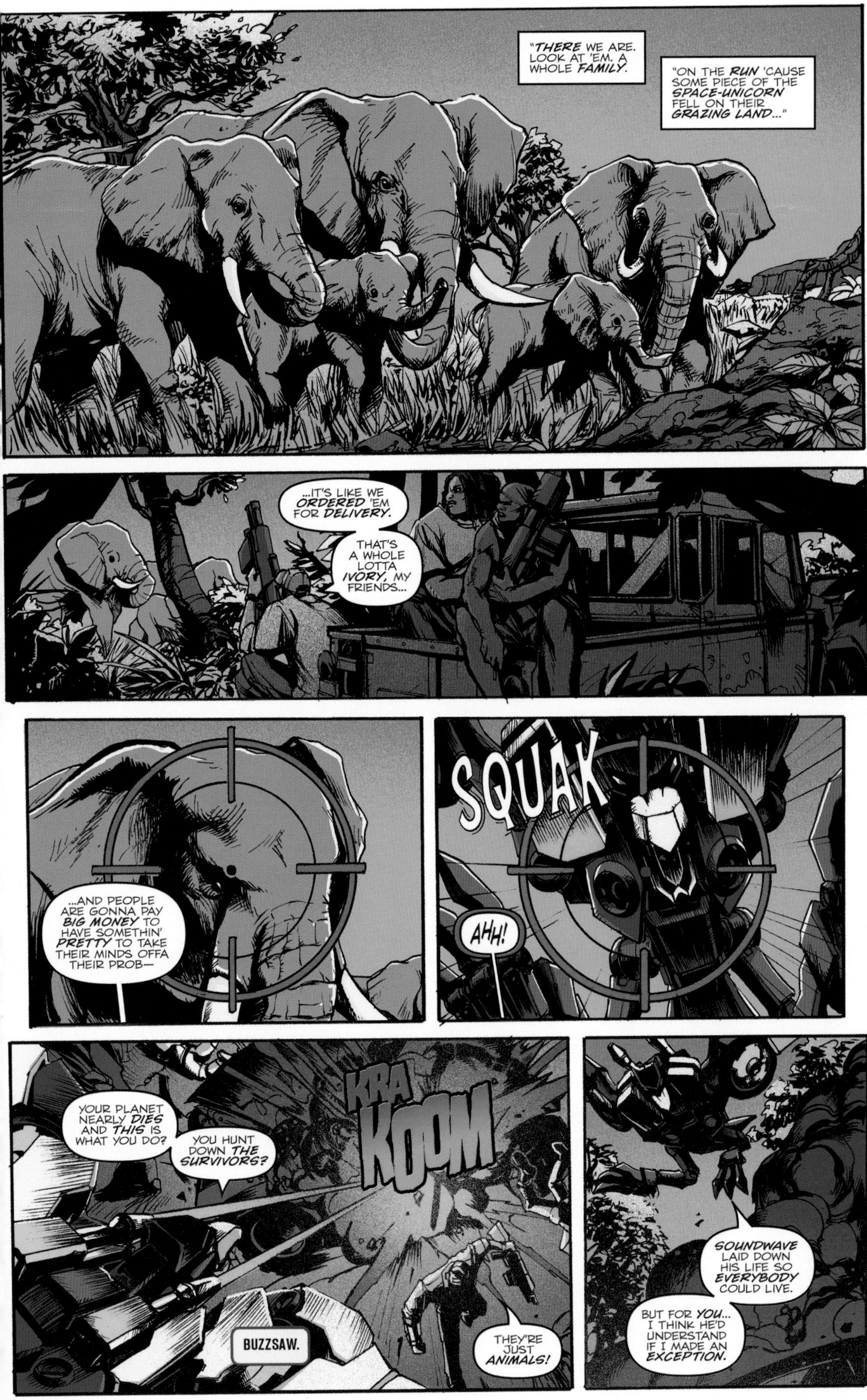
"THERE WE ARE. LOOK AT 'EM. A WHOLE FAMILY.
"ON THE RUN 'CAUSE SOME PIECE OF THE SPACE-UNICORN FELL ON THEIR GRAZING LAND..."
...IT'S LIKE WE ORDERED 'EM FOR DELIVERY.
THAT'S A WHOLE LOTTA IVORY, MY FRIENDS...
...AND PEOPLE ARE GONNA PAY BIG MONEY TO HAVE SOMETHIN' PRETTY TO TAKE THEIR MINDS OFFA THEIR PROB—
SQUAK
AHH!
YOUR PLANET NEARLY DIES AND THIS IS WHAT YOU DO?
YOU HUNT DOWN THE SURVIVORS?
KRA KOOM
BUZZSAW.
THEY'RE JUST ANIMALS!
SOUNDWAVE LAID DOWN HIS LIFE SO EVERYBODY COULD LIVE.
BUT FOR YOU... I THINK HE'D UNDERSTAND IF I MADE AN EXCEPTION.

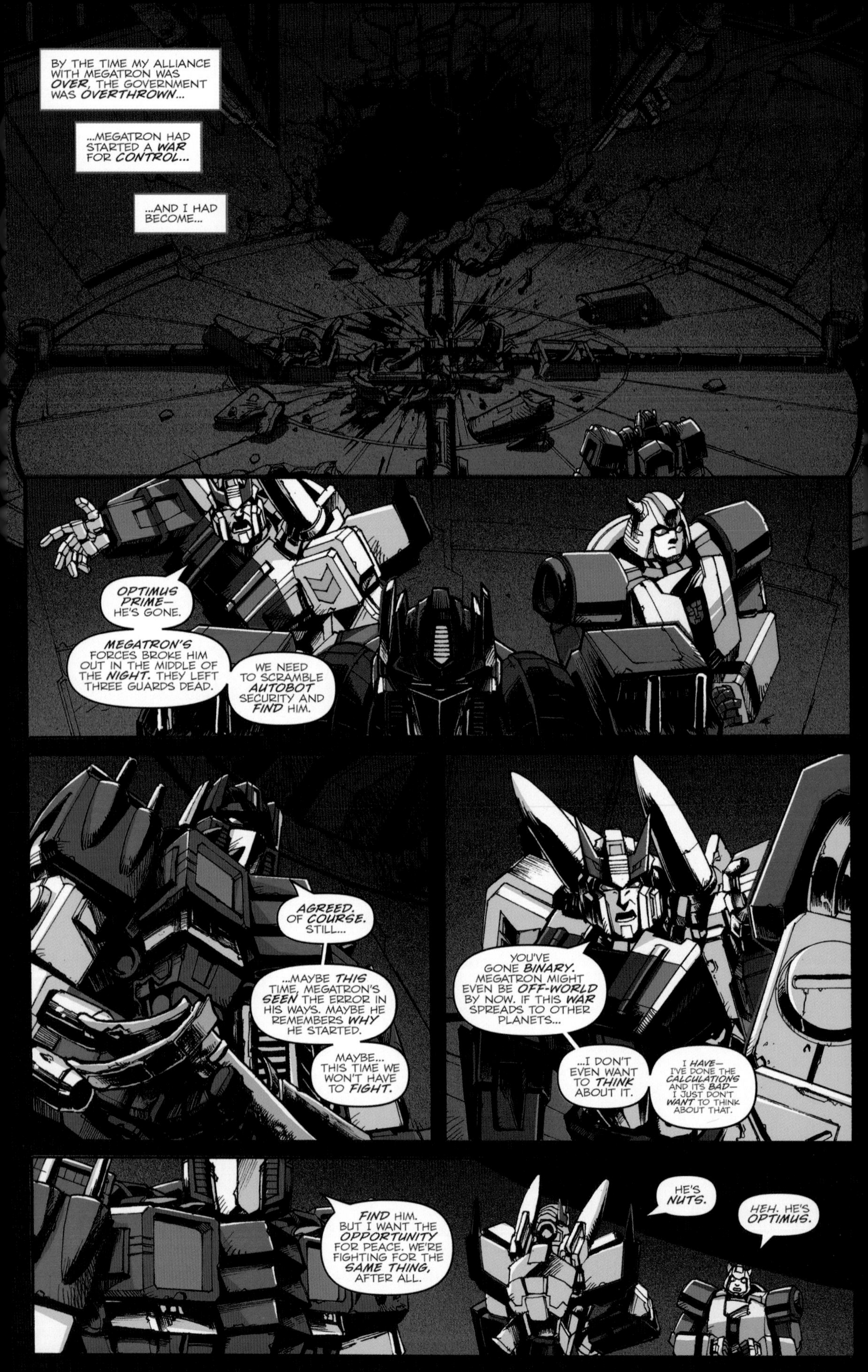

BY THE TIME MY ALLIANCE WITH MEGATRON WAS OVER, THE GOVERNMENT WAS OVERTHROWN...
...MEGATRON HAD STARTED A WAR FOR CONTROL...
...AND I HAD BECOME...
OPTIMUS PRIME— HE'S GONE.
MEGATRON'S FORCES BROKE HIM OUT IN THE MIDDLE OF THE NIGHT. THEY LEFT THREE GUARDS DEAD.
WE NEED TO SCRAMBLE AUTOBOT SECURITY AND FIND HIM.
AGREED. OF COURSE. STILL...
...MAYBE THIS TIME, MEGATRON'S SEEN THE ERROR IN HIS WAYS. MAYBE HE REMEMBERS WHY HE STARTED.
MAYBE... THIS TIME WE WON'T HAVE TO FIGHT.
YOU'VE GONE BINARY. MEGATRON MIGHT EVEN BE OFF-WORLD BY NOW. IF THIS WAR SPREADS TO OTHER PLANETS...
...I DON'T EVEN WANT TO THINK ABOUT IT.
I HAVE— I'VE DONE THE CALCULATIONS AND ITS BAD— I JUST DON'T WANT TO THINK ABOUT THAT.
FIND HIM. BUT I WANT THE OPPORTUNITY FOR PEACE. WE'RE FIGHTING FOR THE SAME THING, AFTER ALL.
HE'S NUTS.
HEH. HE'S OPTIMUS.

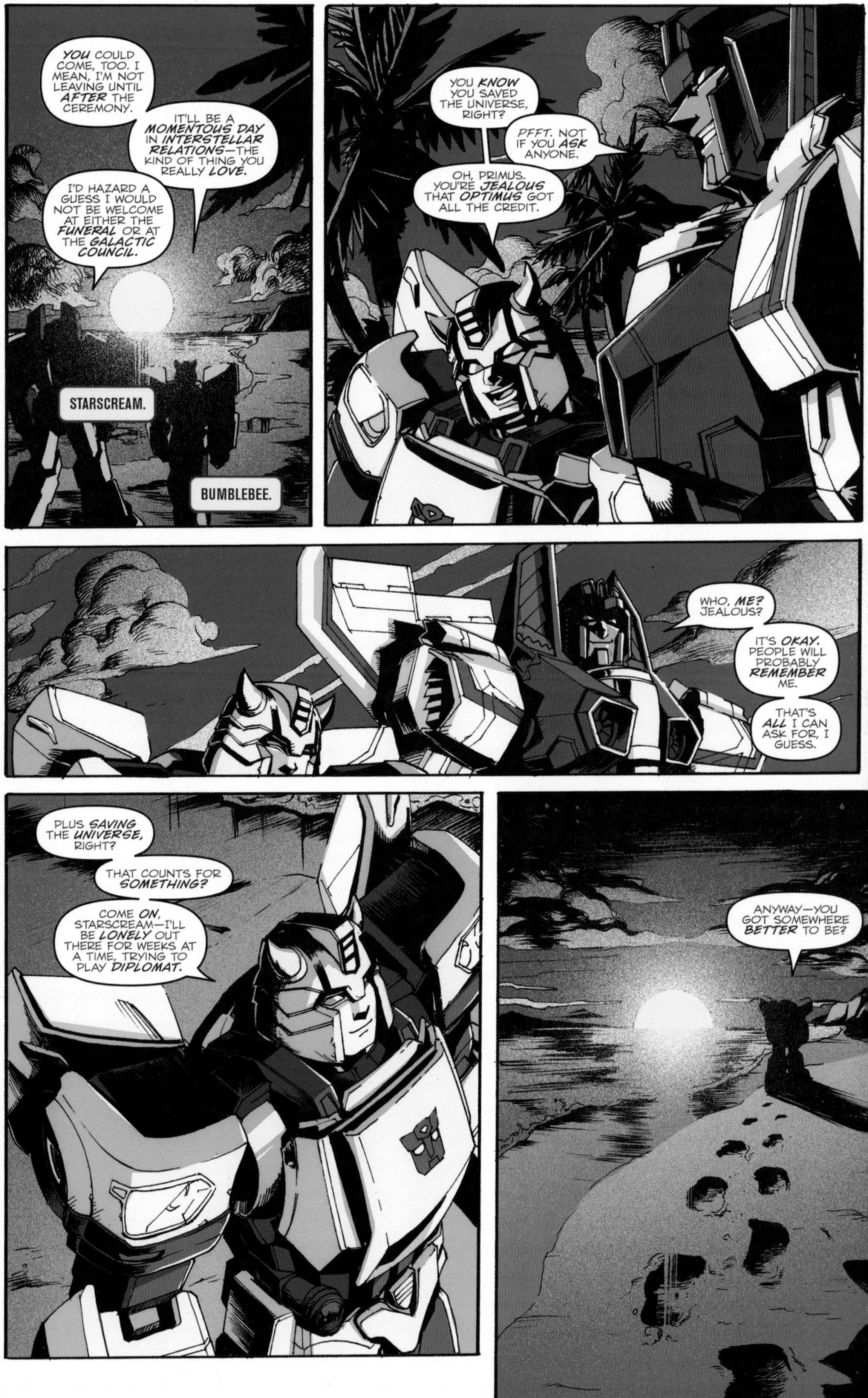
YOU COULD COME, TOO. I MEAN, I'M NOT LEAVING UNTIL AFTER THE CEREMONY.
IT'LL BE A MOMENTOUS DAY IN INTERSTELLAR RELATIONS—THE KIND OF THING YOU REALLY LOVE.
I'D HAZARD A GUESS I WOULD NOT BE WELCOME AT EITHER THE FUNERAL OR AT THE GALACTIC COUNCIL.
STARSCREAM.
BUMBLEBEE.
YOU KNOW YOU SAVED THE UNIVERSE, RIGHT?
PFFT. NOT IF YOU ASK ANYONE.
OH, PRIMUS. YOU'RE JEALOUS THAT OPTIMUS GOT ALL THE CREDIT.
WHO, ME? JEALOUS?
IT'S OKAY. PEOPLE WILL PROBABLY REMEMBER ME.
THAT'S ALL I CAN ASK FOR, I GUESS.
PLUS SAVING THE UNIVERSE, RIGHT?
THAT COUNTS FOR SOMETHING?
COME ON, STARSCREAM—I'LL BE LONELY OUT THERE FOR WEEKS AT A TIME, TRYING TO PLAY DIPLOMAT.
ANYWAY—YOU GOT SOMEWHERE BETTER TO BE?

PROWL WAS *CORRECT*, AS USUAL. MEGATRON DID *NOT* RENOUNCE HIS WAYS.

THE WAR *DID* MOVE OFF-PLANET.

YOU DON'T CARE ABOUT *ANY* OF THIS!

A THOUSAND AUTOBOTS—*DEAD*. AND WHATEVER THIS CIVILIZATION WAS— THEY'RE ALL *GONE*, PRIME!

WE MURDERED THEM!

I AM SURE YOU AND YOUR FELLOW *DYNOBOTS* DID ALL YOU COULD TO—

YOU DON'T CARE *WHAT* WE DID!

YOU JUST WANT *RESULTS!*

COME *ON*—HE ISN'T *WORTH* IT, SLAG.

WE GOT A *JOB* TO DO.

THAT IS *CORRECT*, GRIMLOCK—

—WE *ALL* HAVE JOBS TO DO.

AND *YOURS* IS TO KEEP YOUR MEN IN *LINE*.

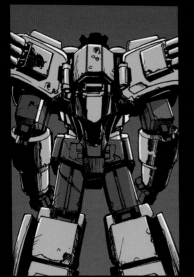

YOU DON'T *WANT* THAT, PRIME. YOU DON'T WANT "IN LINE."

YOU WANT *RESULTS.*

I NEVER DESIRED *WAR*. BUT I *THRIVED* IN IT.

AS IF I HAD BEEN *BORN* TO IT... AS IF I BELONGED IN ANOTHER *AGE*... AND CHANGED THE WORLD TO *FIT ME*.

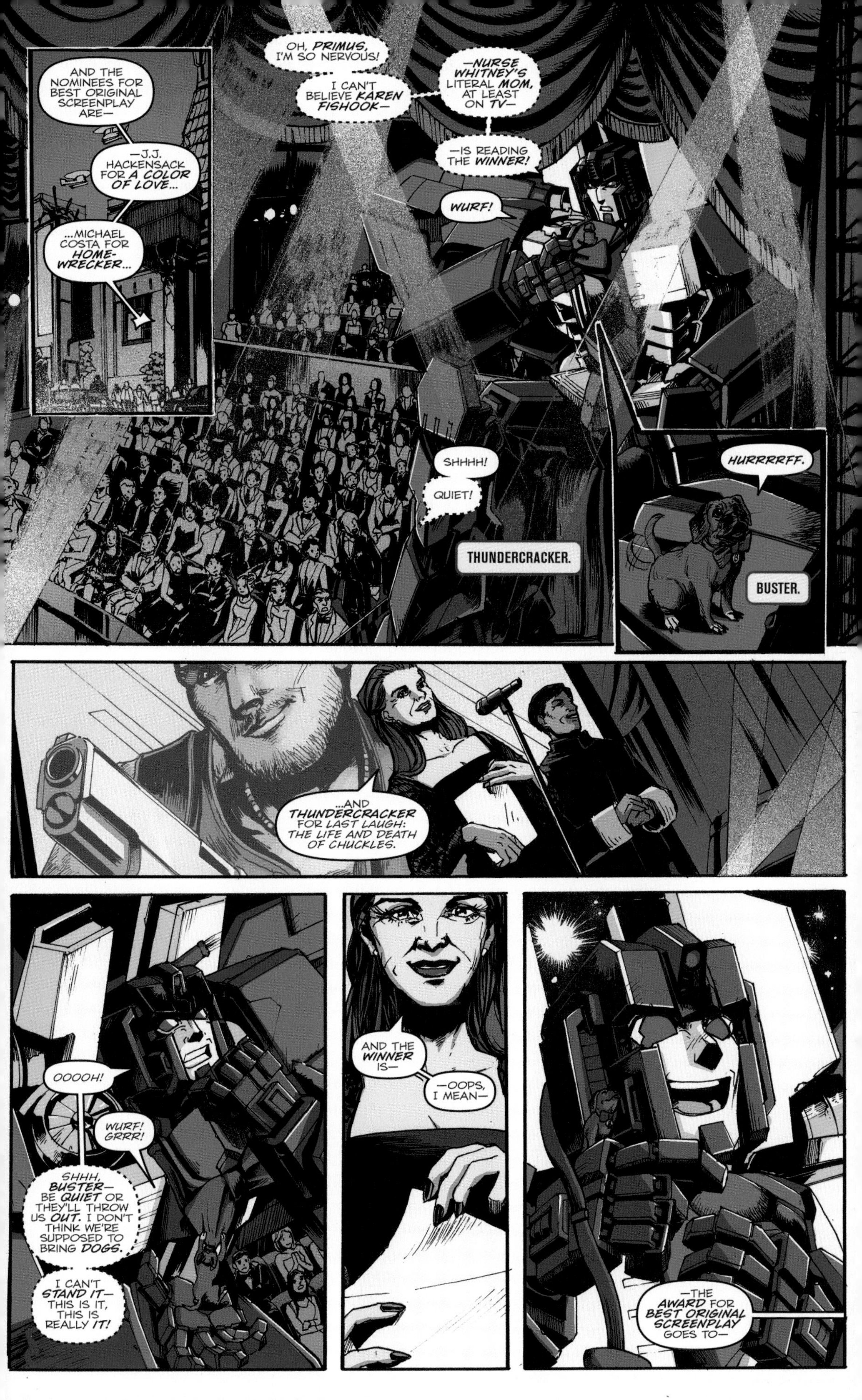

AND THE NOMINEES FOR BEST ORIGINAL SCREENPLAY ARE—
—J.J. HACKENSACK FOR A COLOR OF LOVE...
...MICHAEL COSTA FOR HOME-WRECKER...
OH, PRIMUS, I'M SO NERVOUS!
I CAN'T BELIEVE KAREN FISHOOK—
—NURSE WHITNEY'S LITERAL MOM, AT LEAST ON TV—
—IS READING THE WINNER!
WURF!
SHHHH!
QUIET!
THUNDERCRACKER.
HURRRRFF.
BUSTER.
...AND THUNDERCRACKER FOR LAST LAUGH: THE LIFE AND DEATH OF CHUCKLES.
OOOOH!
WURF! GRRR!
SHHH, BUSTER— BE QUIET OR THEY'LL THROW US OUT. I DON'T THINK WE'RE SUPPOSED TO BRING DOGS.
I CAN'T STAND IT— THIS IS IT, THIS IS REALLY IT!
AND THE WINNER IS—
—OOPS, I MEAN—
—THE AWARD FOR BEST ORIGINAL SCREENPLAY GOES TO—

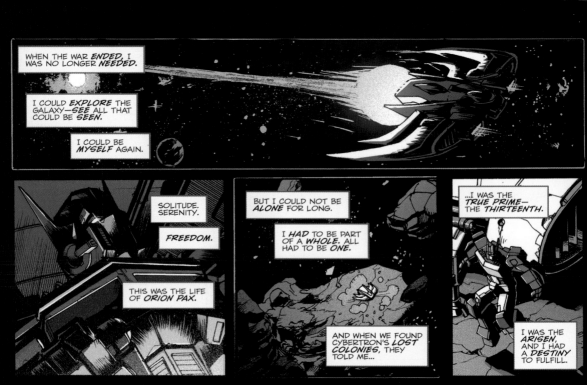

WHEN THE WAR *ENDED,* I WAS NO LONGER *NEEDED.*

I COULD *EXPLORE* THE GALAXY—*SEE* ALL THAT COULD BE *SEEN.*

I COULD BE *MYSELF* AGAIN.

SOLITUDE. SERENITY.

FREEDOM.

THIS WAS THE LIFE OF *ORION PAX.*

BUT I COULD NOT BE *ALONE* FOR LONG.

I *HAD* TO BE PART OF A *WHOLE.* ALL HAD TO BE *ONE.*

AND WHEN WE FOUND CYBERTRON'S *LOST COLONIES,* THEY TOLD ME...

...I WAS THE *TRUE PRIME*— THE *THIRTEENTH.*

I WAS THE *ARIGEN,* AND I HAD A *DESTINY* TO FULFILL.

MY WORLDS—*EARTH AND CYBERTRON*—NEEDED ME.

I *USED* THE COLONISTS' FAITH. BUT WERE THEY *RIGHT?*

WAS I SOMETHING *MORE*... IS *THAT* WHY *TRION* WAS THERE AT MY *FORGING*...?

I AGAIN BECAME *OPTIMUS PRIME.* LEADER. WARRIOR. *HERO.*

BUT FOR ONE MOMENT...

...I HAD BEEN *MYSELF.*

WELL?

ANYTHING?

A WHOLE LOTTA *ICE* AND *COLD* AND *NOTHING*, MA'AM.

I LIKE *IT.*

MIDNIGHT EXPRESS.

ROULETTE.

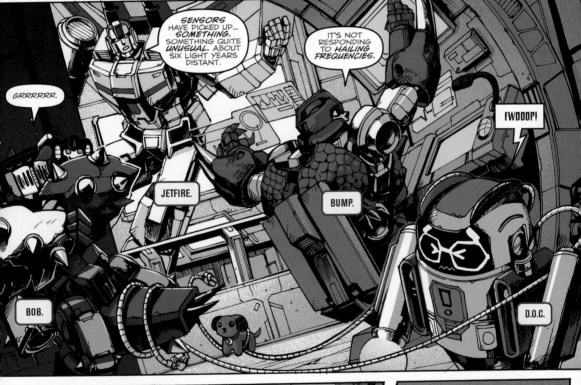

SENSORS HAVE PICKED UP... *SOMETHING.* SOMETHING QUITE *UNUSUAL.* ABOUT SIX LIGHT YEARS DISTANT.

IT'S NOT RESPONDING TO *HAILING FREQUENCIES.*

GRRRRRR.

FWODDP!

JETFIRE.

BUMP.

BOB.

D.O.C.

WELL, WHAT CHOICE DO WE *HAVE?*

HELM—SET A COURSE. LET'S SEE WHAT THAT ANOMALY IS...

...AND WE'LL TRY TO MAKE *FRIENDS* WITH IT BEFORE ANYTHING GOES *WRONG.*

AILERON.

OH, AND *BUMP*—CAN YOU CALL *ARCEE?*

I'M GONNA HAVE TO APOLOGIZE FOR BEING *LATE* AGAIN.

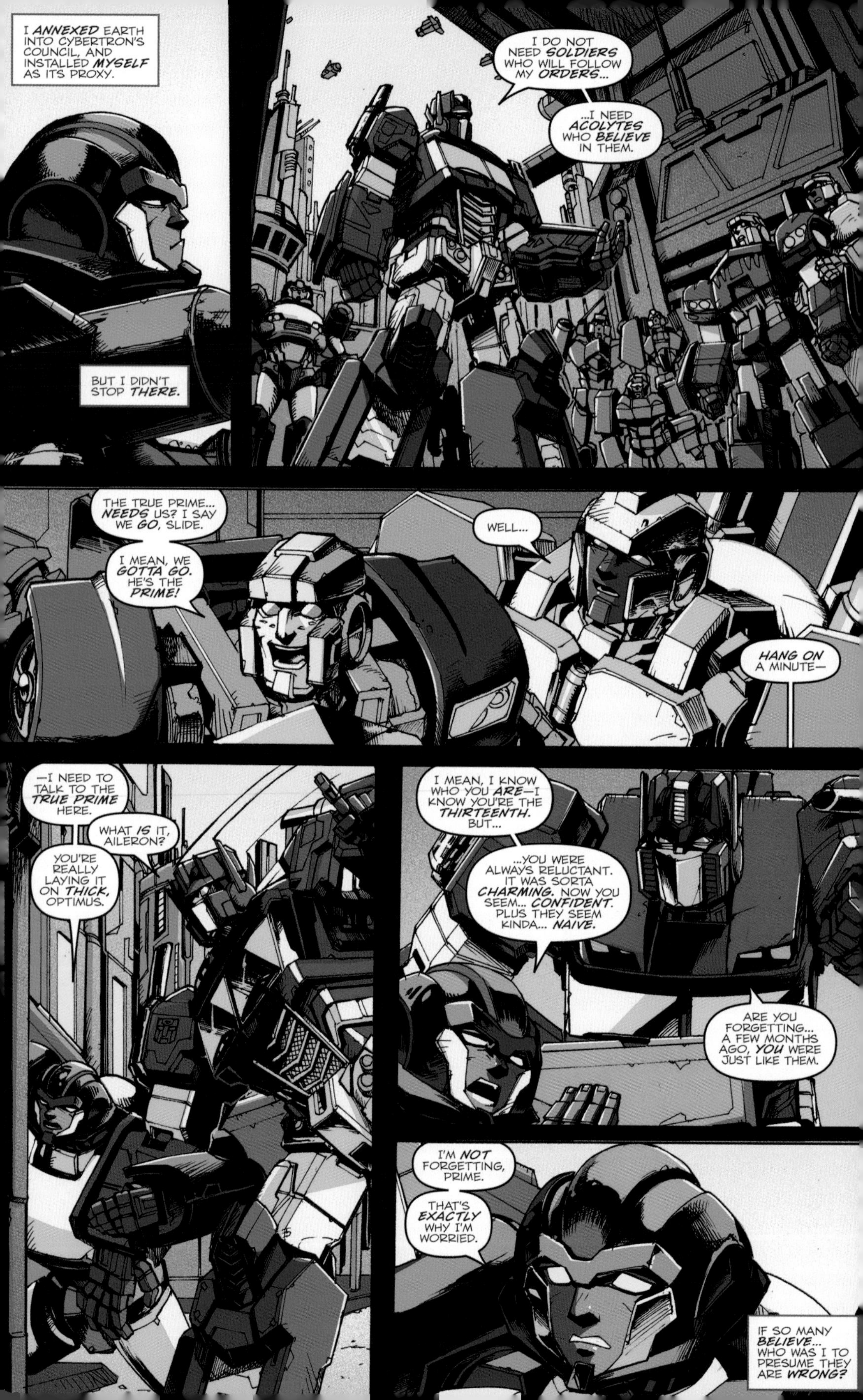
I ANNEXED EARTH INTO CYBERTRON'S COUNCIL, AND INSTALLED MYSELF AS ITS PROXY.
BUT I DIDN'T STOP THERE.
I DO NOT NEED SOLDIERS WHO WILL FOLLOW MY ORDERS...
...I NEED ACOLYTES WHO BELIEVE IN THEM.
THE TRUE PRIME... NEEDS US? I SAY WE GO, SLIDE.
I MEAN, WE GOTTA GO. HE'S THE PRIME!
WELL...
HANG ON A MINUTE—
—I NEED TO TALK TO THE TRUE PRIME HERE.
WHAT IS IT, AILERON?
YOU'RE REALLY LAYING IT ON THICK, OPTIMUS.
I MEAN, I KNOW WHO YOU ARE—I KNOW YOU'RE THE THIRTEENTH. BUT...
...YOU WERE ALWAYS RELUCTANT. IT WAS SORTA CHARMING. NOW YOU SEEM... CONFIDENT. PLUS THEY SEEM KINDA... NAIVE.
ARE YOU FORGETTING... A FEW MONTHS AGO, YOU WERE JUST LIKE THEM.
I'M NOT FORGETTING, PRIME.
THAT'S EXACTLY WHY I'M WORRIED.
IF SO MANY BELIEVE... WHO WAS I TO PRESUME THEY ARE WRONG?

I AM SURPRISED YOU ARE NOT IN *LITTLE CYBERTRON.* THERE CAN'T BE MUCH TIME BEFORE THE *FUNERAL.*

THERE *ISN'T.* IF I MISS IT, I MISS IT.

I'M ACTUALLY SURPRISED *YOU* REMEMBERED.

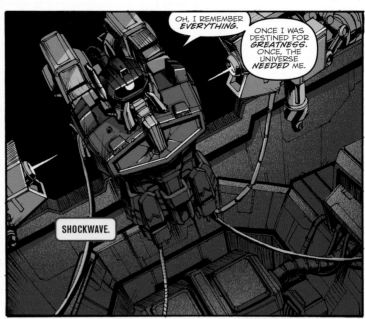

OH, I REMEMBER *EVERYTHING.*

ONCE I WAS DESTINED FOR *GREATNESS.* ONCE, THE UNIVERSE *NEEDED* ME.

SHOCKWAVE.

I HAVE WORN *MANY* GUISES... I ALWAYS DID HAVE A *FLAIR* FOR THE *DRAMATIC.*

I WAS *RIGHT,* YOU KNOW. WHEN IT ALL COMES DOWN TO IT, EVERY-THING IS ABOUT *RESOURCES...*

...THERE'S IS A *FINITE* AMOUNT OF *EVERYTHING.*

EVEN *IDENTITIES.*

AND I AM NO LONGER SURE WHICH VERSION OF *MYSELF* WAS THE *REAL* ONE.

THEY *ALL* WERE, SHOCKWAVE.

ALL THAT WAS DONE TO YOU, ALL THAT YOU DID TO YOURSELF...

...ALL THAT YOU DID TO *OTHERS.*

PROWL.

WE ARE OUR *ACTIONS...*

...NOT OUR *HOPES.*

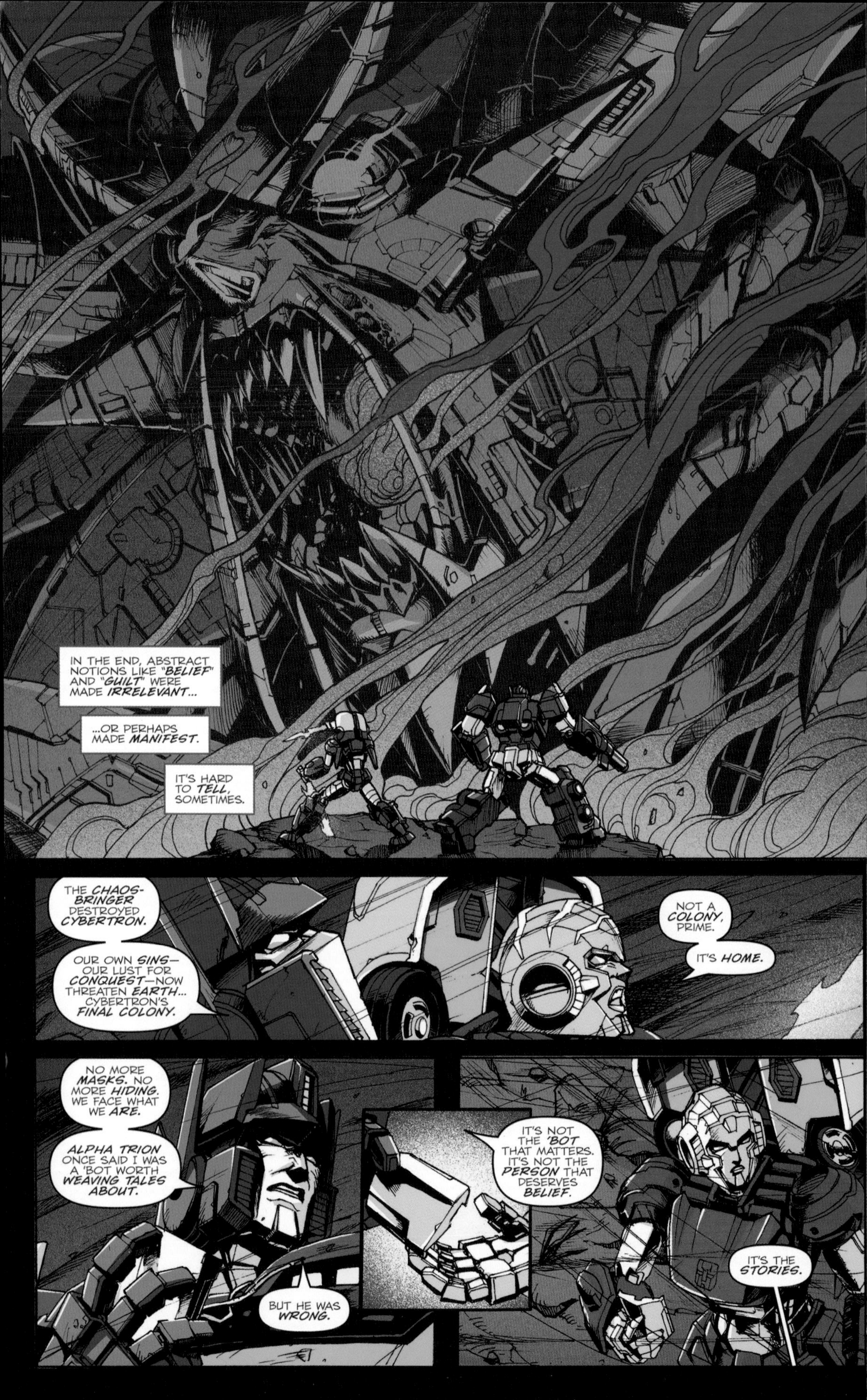
IN THE END, ABSTRACT NOTIONS LIKE "BELIEF" AND "GUILT" WERE MADE IRRELEVANT...
...OR PERHAPS MADE MANIFEST.
IT'S HARD TO TELL, SOMETIMES.
THE CHAOS-BRINGER DESTROYED CYBERTRON.
OUR OWN SINS—OUR LUST FOR CONQUEST—NOW THREATEN EARTH... CYBERTRON'S FINAL COLONY.
NOT A COLONY, PRIME.
IT'S HOME.
NO MORE MASKS. NO MORE HIDING. WE FACE WHAT WE ARE.
ALPHA TRION ONCE SAID I WAS A 'BOT WORTH WEAVING TALES ABOUT.
BUT HE WAS WRONG.
IT'S NOT THE 'BOT THAT MATTERS. IT'S NOT THE PERSON THAT DESERVES BELIEF.
IT'S THE STORIES.

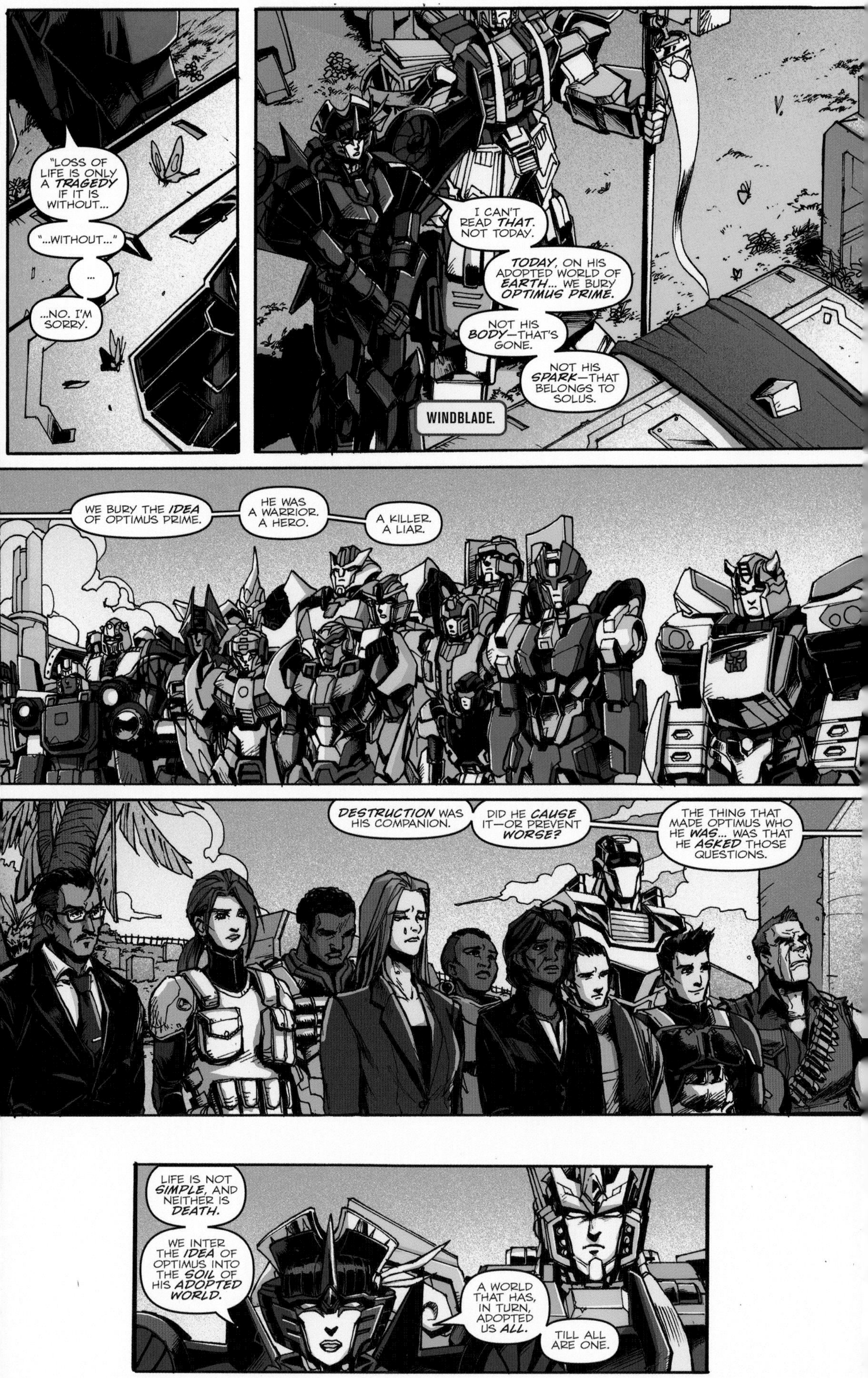

"LOSS OF LIFE IS ONLY A TRAGEDY IF IT IS WITHOUT...
"...WITHOUT..."
...
...NO. I'M SORRY.
I CAN'T READ THAT. NOT TODAY.
TODAY, ON HIS ADOPTED WORLD OF EARTH... WE BURY OPTIMUS PRIME.
NOT HIS BODY—THAT'S GONE.
NOT HIS SPARK—THAT BELONGS TO SOLUS.
WINDBLADE.
WE BURY THE IDEA OF OPTIMUS PRIME.
HE WAS A WARRIOR. A HERO.
A KILLER. A LIAR.
DESTRUCTION WAS HIS COMPANION.
DID HE CAUSE IT—OR PREVENT WORSE?
THE THING THAT MADE OPTIMUS WHO HE WAS... WAS THAT HE ASKED THOSE QUESTIONS.
LIFE IS NOT SIMPLE, AND NEITHER IS DEATH.
WE INTER THE IDEA OF OPTIMUS INTO THE SOIL OF HIS ADOPTED WORLD.
A WORLD THAT HAS, IN TURN, ADOPTED US ALL.
TILL ALL ARE ONE.

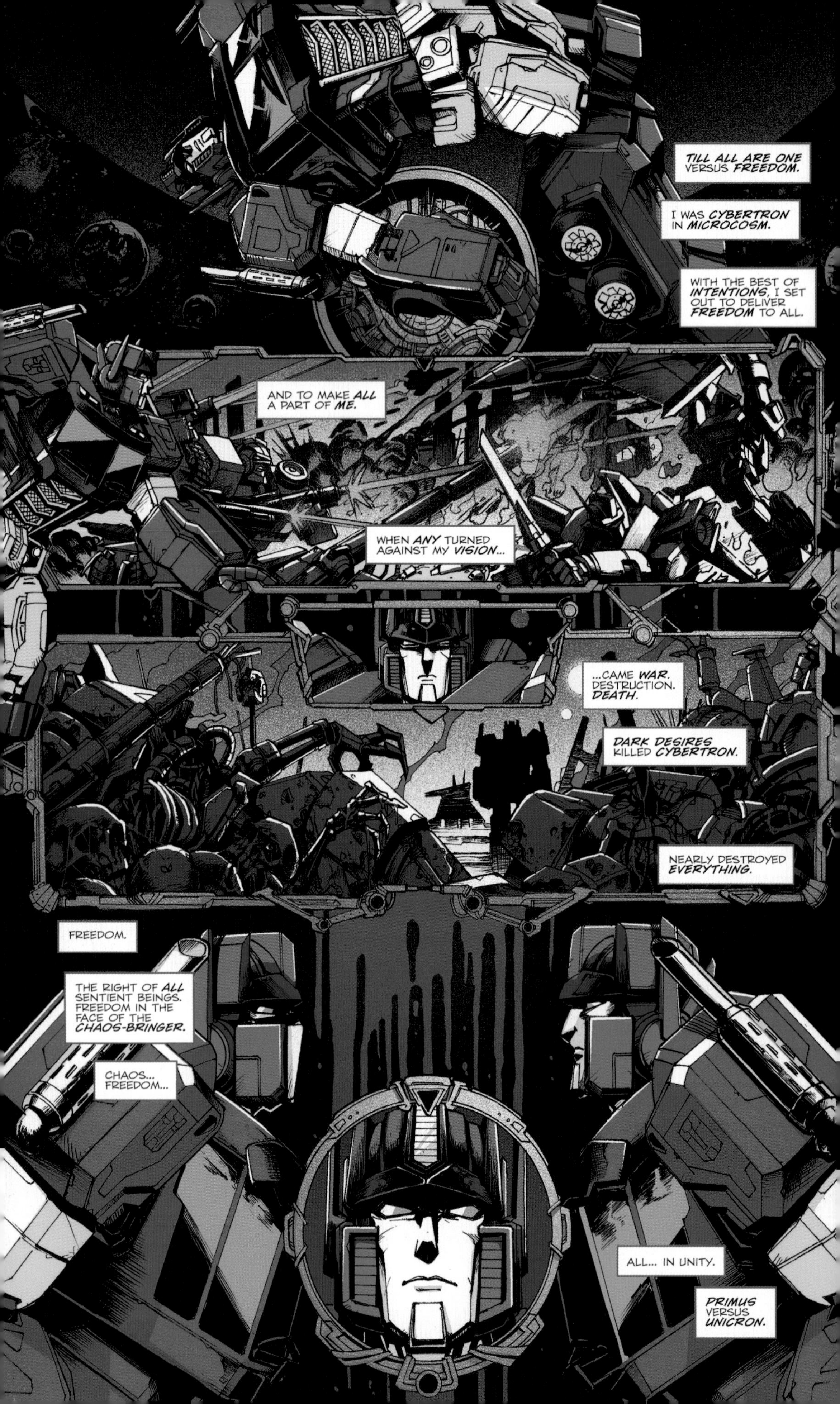
TILL ALL ARE ONE VERSUS FREEDOM.
I WAS CYBERTRON IN MICROCOSM.
WITH THE BEST OF INTENTIONS, I SET OUT TO DELIVER FREEDOM TO ALL.
AND TO MAKE ALL A PART OF ME.
WHEN ANY TURNED AGAINST MY VISION...
...CAME WAR. DESTRUCTION. DEATH.
DARK DESIRES KILLED CYBERTRON.
NEARLY DESTROYED EVERYTHING.
FREEDOM.
THE RIGHT OF ALL SENTIENT BEINGS. FREEDOM IN THE FACE OF THE CHAOS-BRINGER.
CHAOS... FREEDOM...
ALL... IN UNITY.
PRIMUS VERSUS UNICRON.

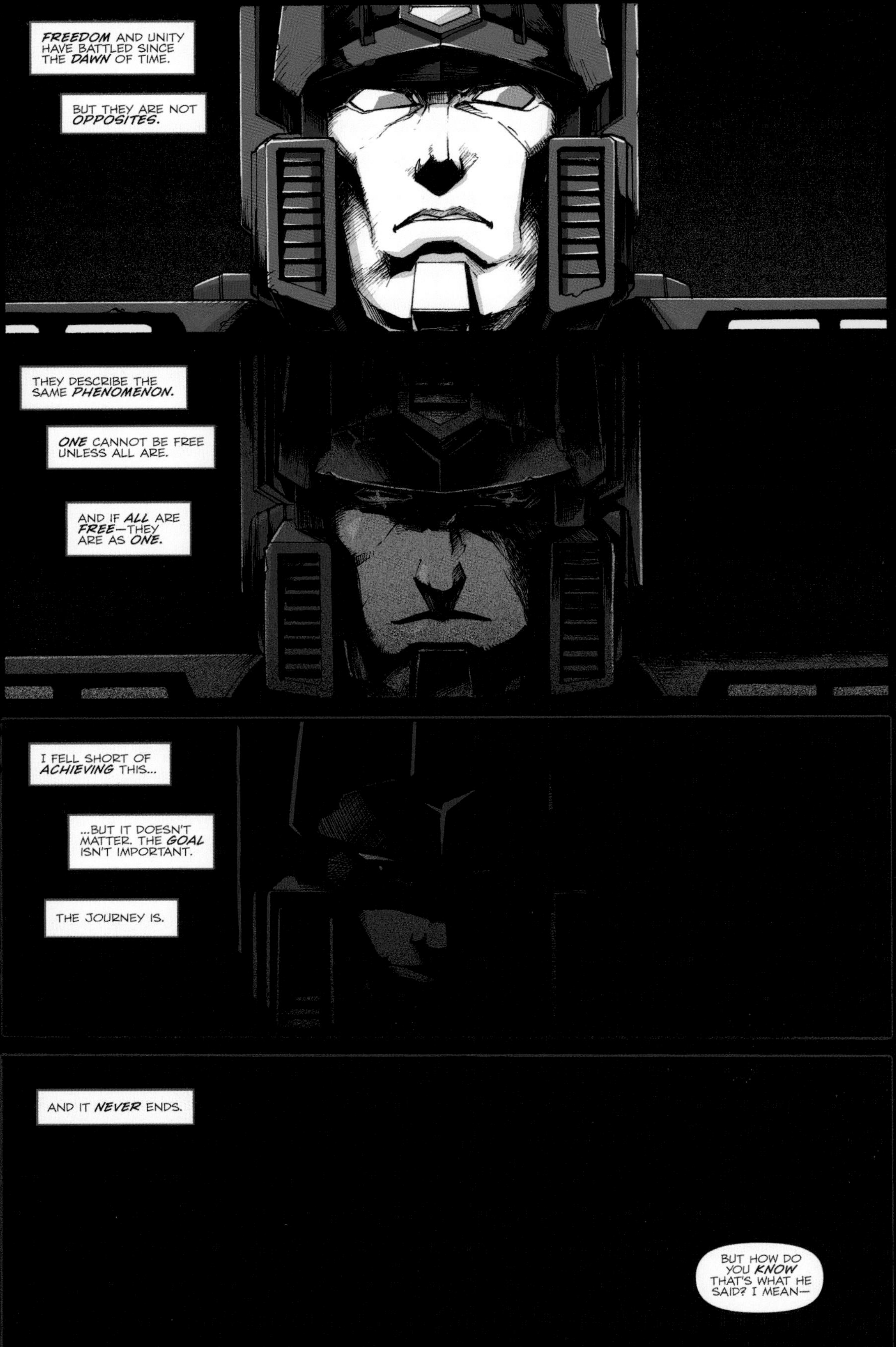
FREEDOM AND UNITY HAVE BATTLED SINCE THE DAWN OF TIME.
BUT THEY ARE NOT OPPOSITES.
THEY DESCRIBE THE SAME PHENOMENON.
ONE CANNOT BE FREE UNLESS ALL ARE.
AND IF ALL ARE FREE—THEY ARE AS ONE.
I FELL SHORT OF ACHIEVING THIS...
...BUT IT DOESN'T MATTER. THE GOAL ISN'T IMPORTANT.
THE JOURNEY IS.
AND IT NEVER ENDS.
BUT HOW DO YOU KNOW THAT'S WHAT HE SAID? I MEAN—

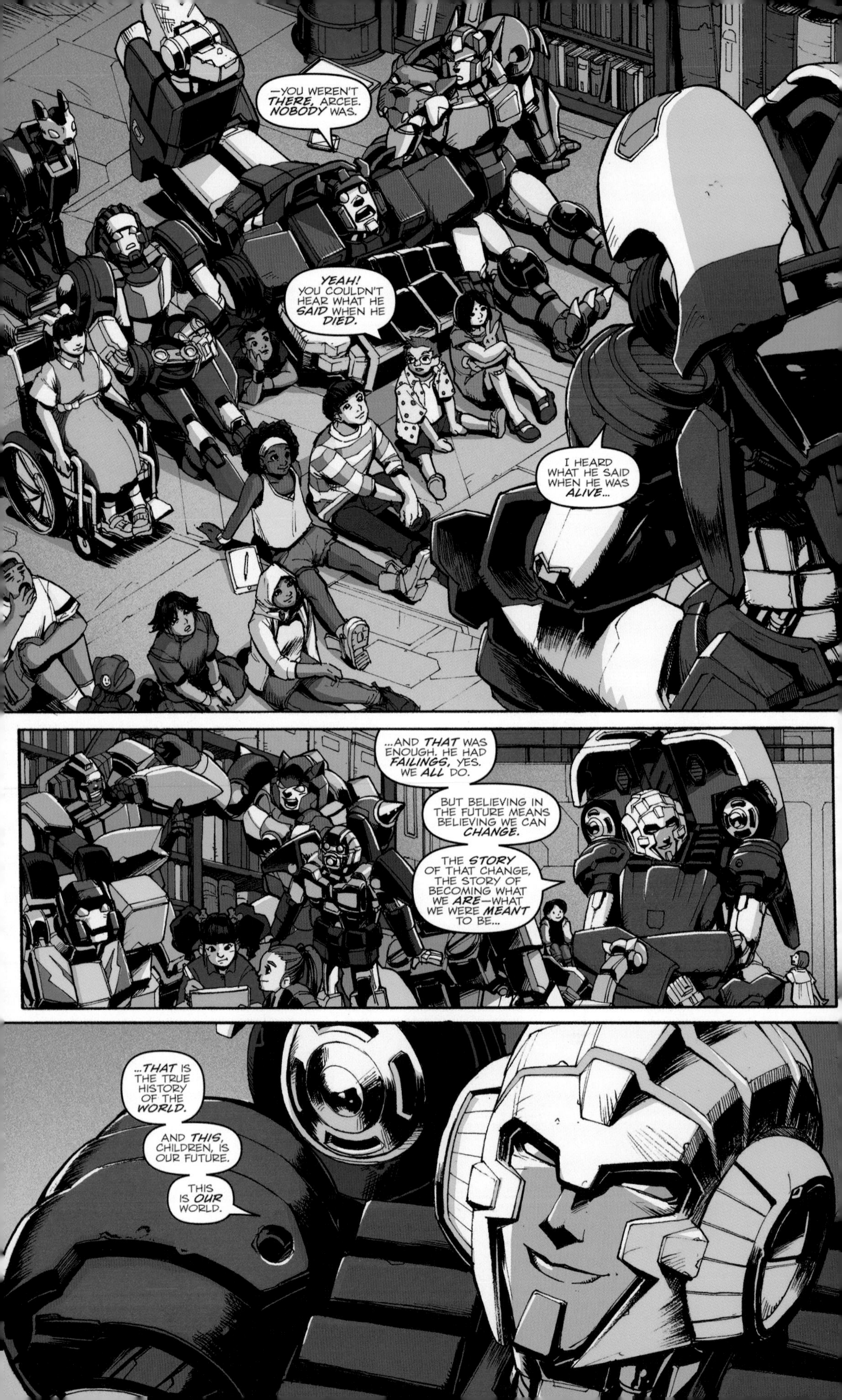

—YOU WEREN'T THERE, ARCEE. NOBODY WAS.
YEAH! YOU COULDN'T HEAR WHAT HE SAID WHEN HE DIED.
I HEARD WHAT HE SAID WHEN HE WAS ALIVE...
...AND THAT WAS ENOUGH. HE HAD FAILINGS, YES. WE ALL DO.
BUT BELIEVING IN THE FUTURE MEANS BELIEVING WE CAN CHANGE.
THE STORY OF THAT CHANGE, THE STORY OF BECOMING WHAT WE ARE—WHAT WE WERE MEANT TO BE...
...THAT IS THE TRUE HISTORY OF THE WORLD.
AND THIS, CHILDREN, IS OUR FUTURE.
THIS IS OUR WORLD.

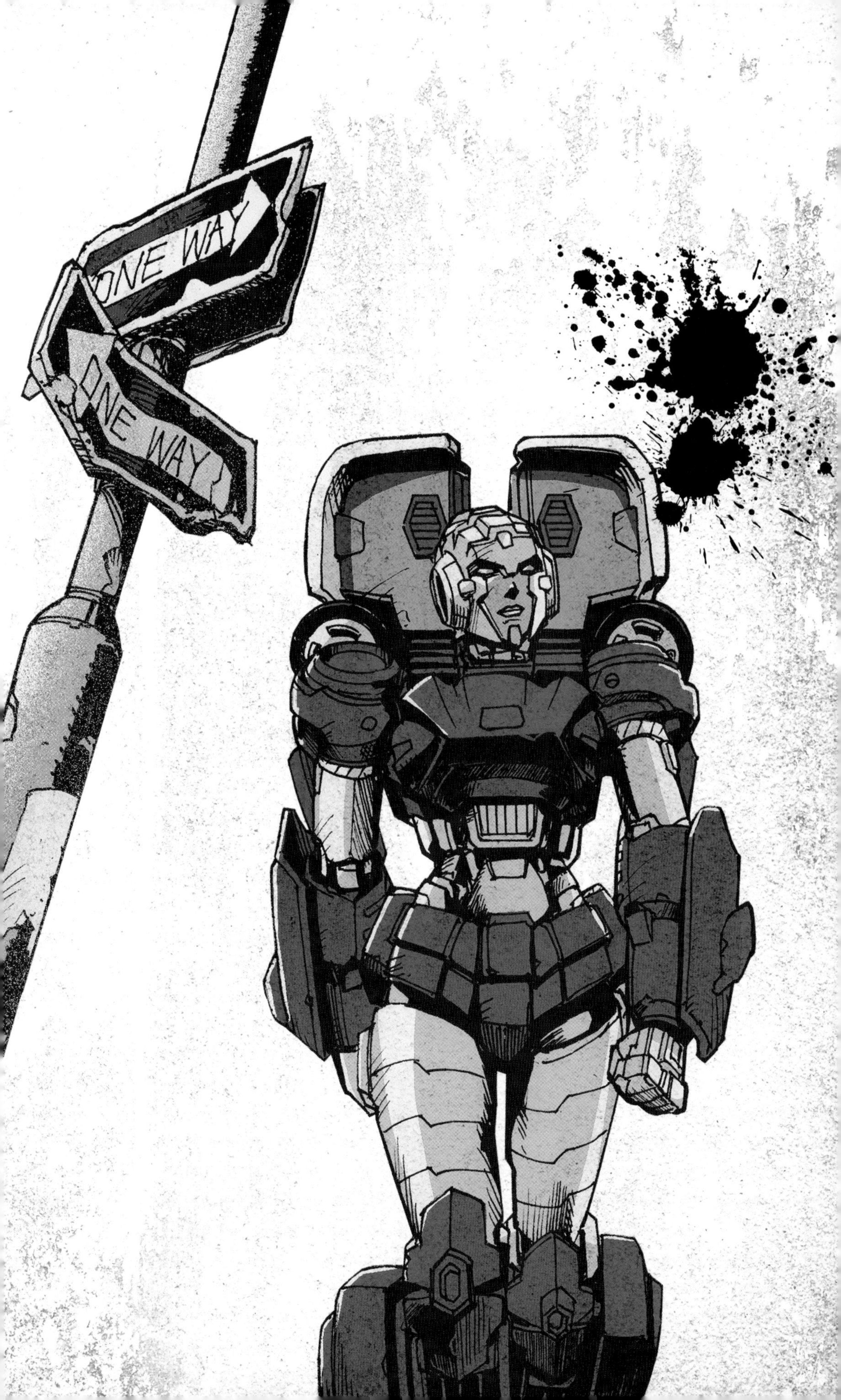
ONE WAY
ONE WAY

ART BY ANDREW GRIFFITH COLORS BY JOSH PEREZ

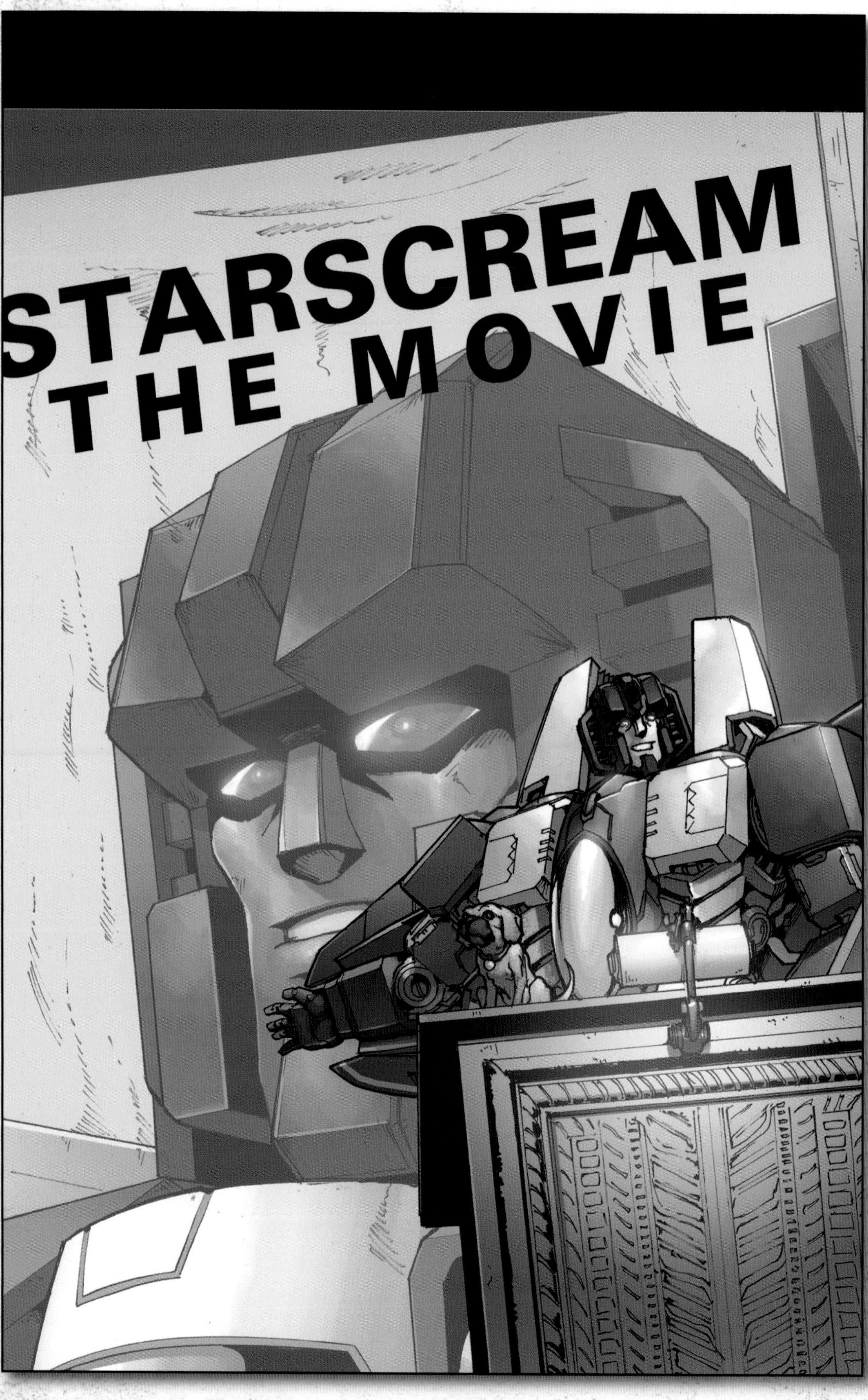
STARSCREAM
THE MOVIE

ART BY SARA PITRE-DUROCHER

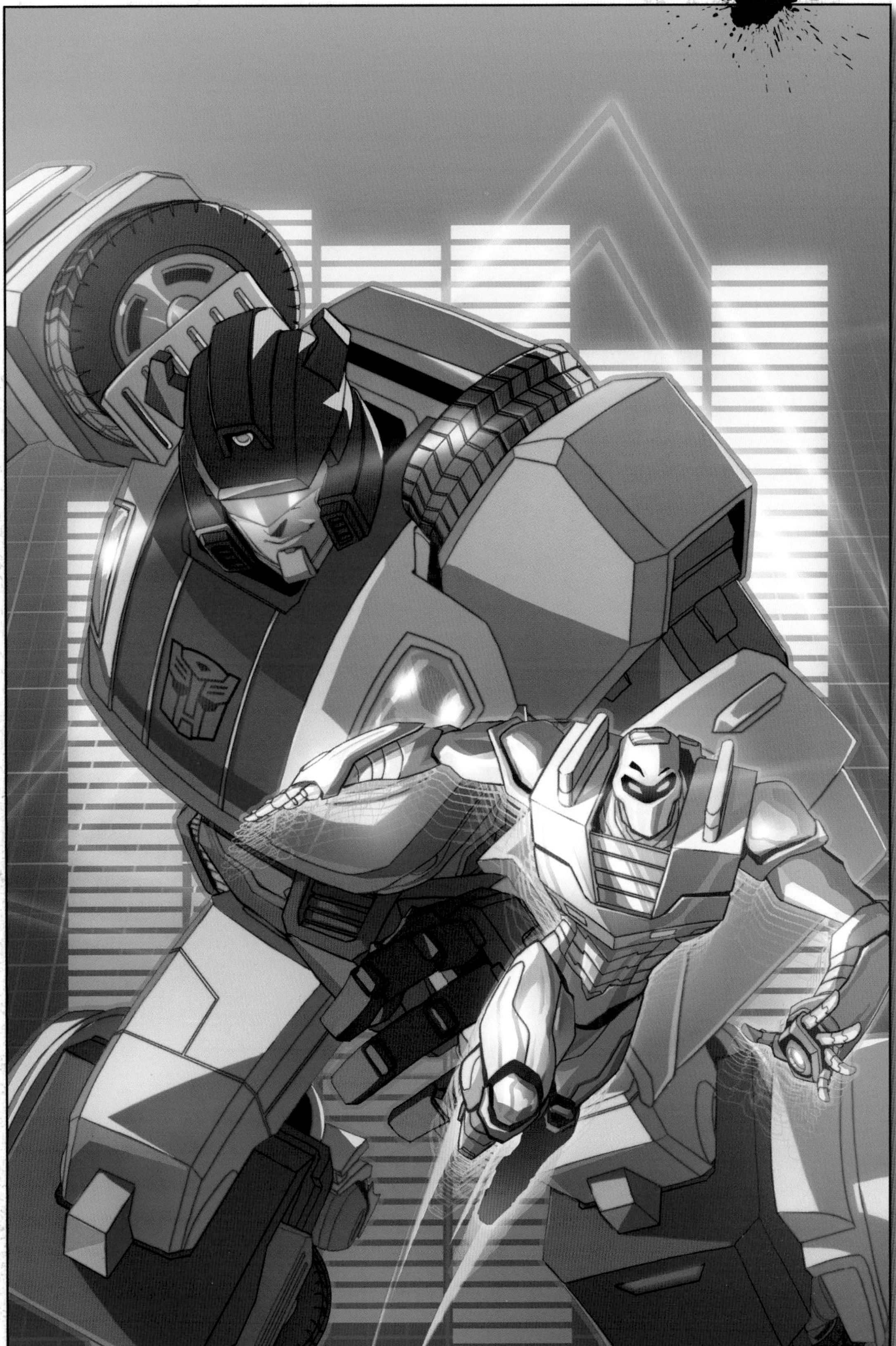

ART BY PRISCILLA TRAMONTANO

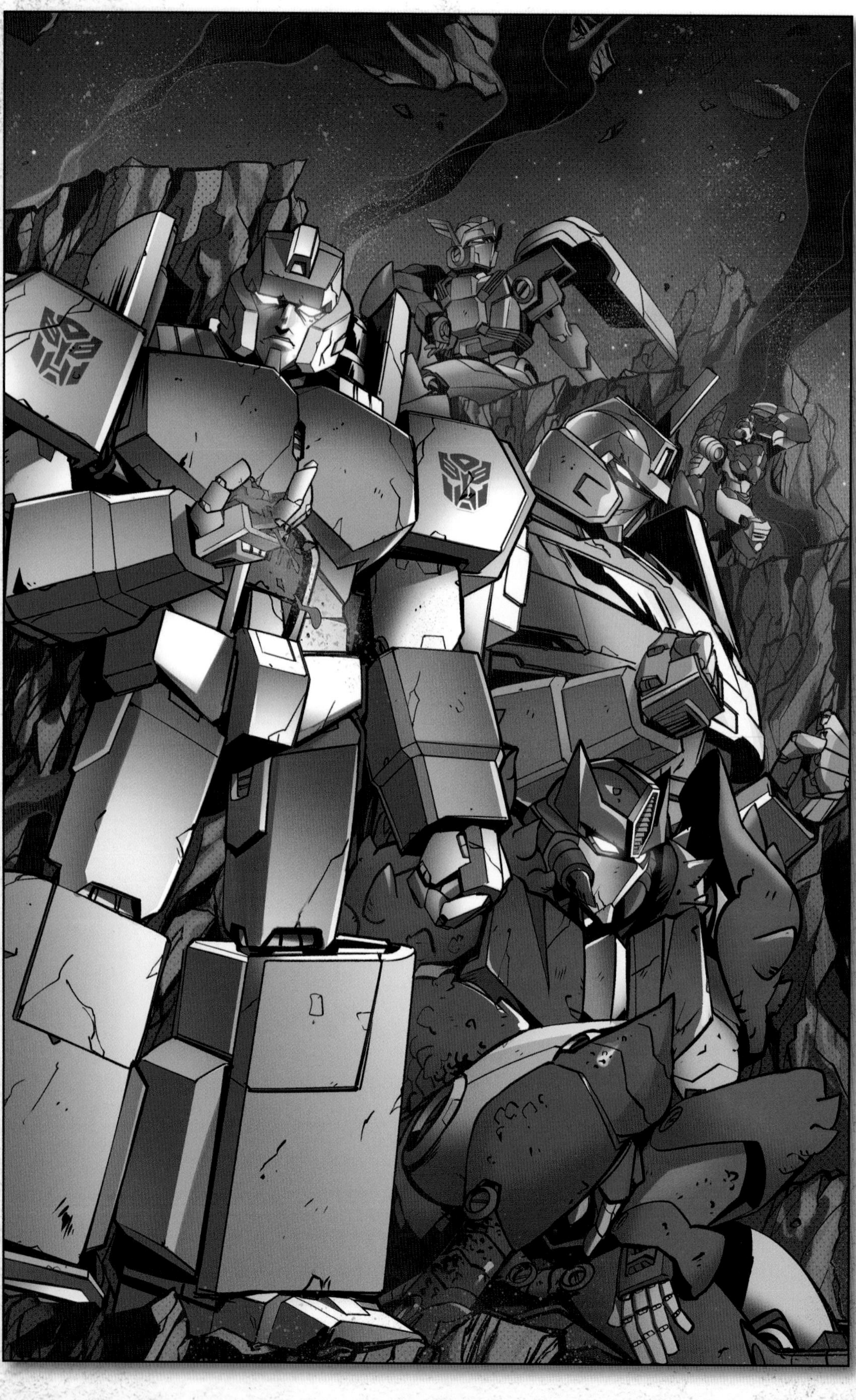

ART BY ANDREW GRIFFITH   COLORS BY JOANA LAFUENTE

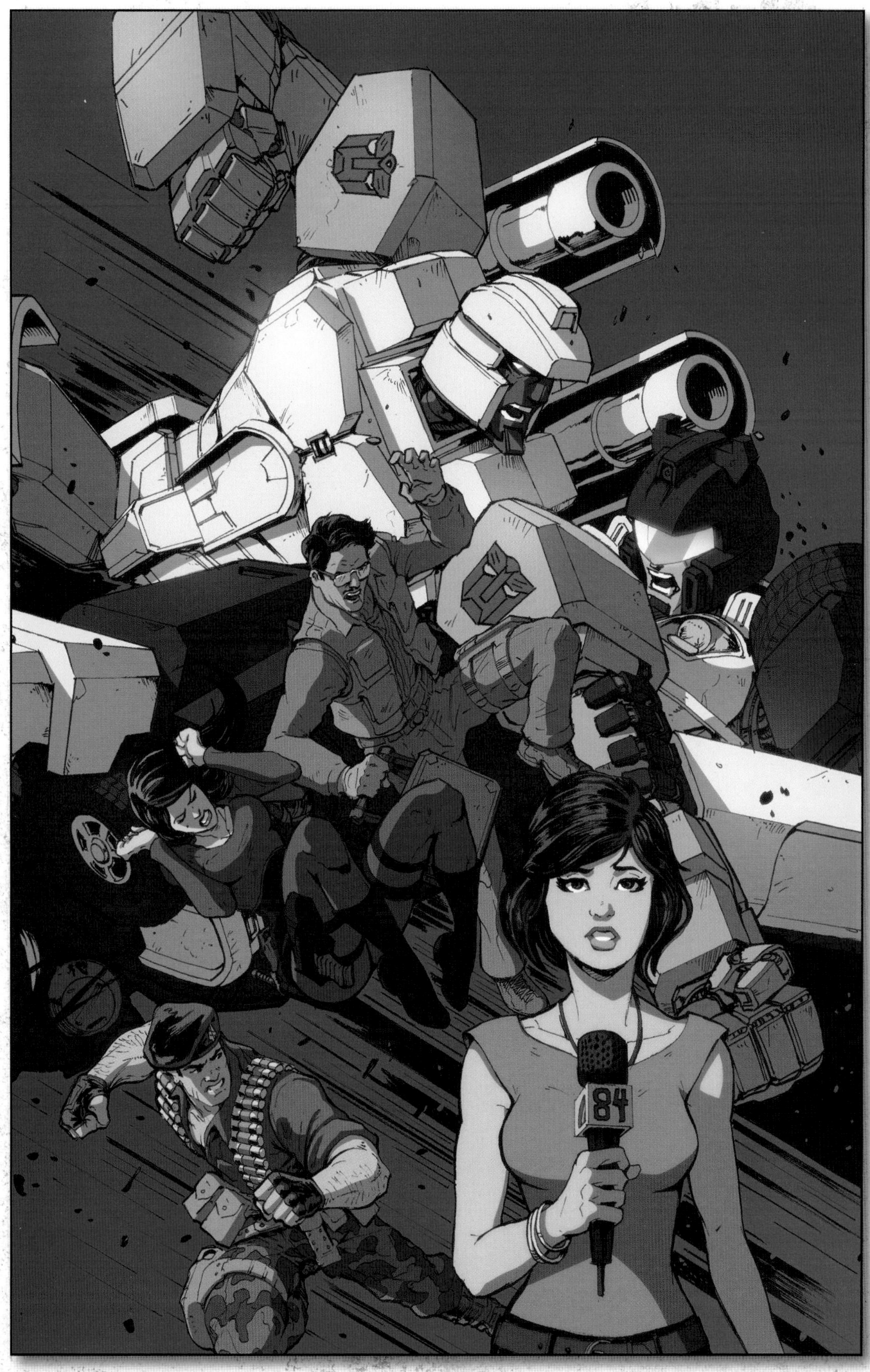

84

ART BY ANDREW GRIFFITH

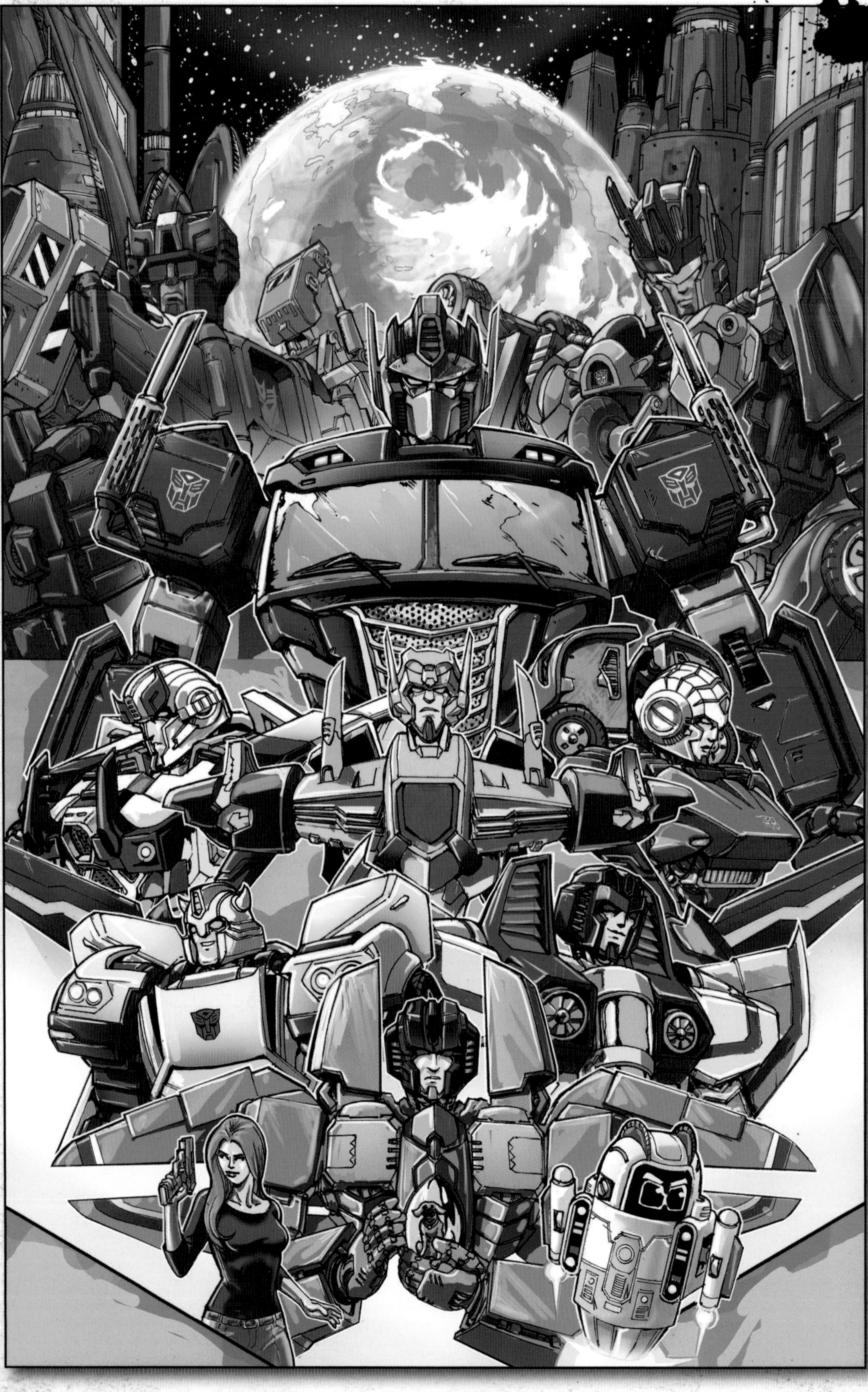

ART BY CASEY W. COLLER COLORS BY JOHN-PAUL BOVE

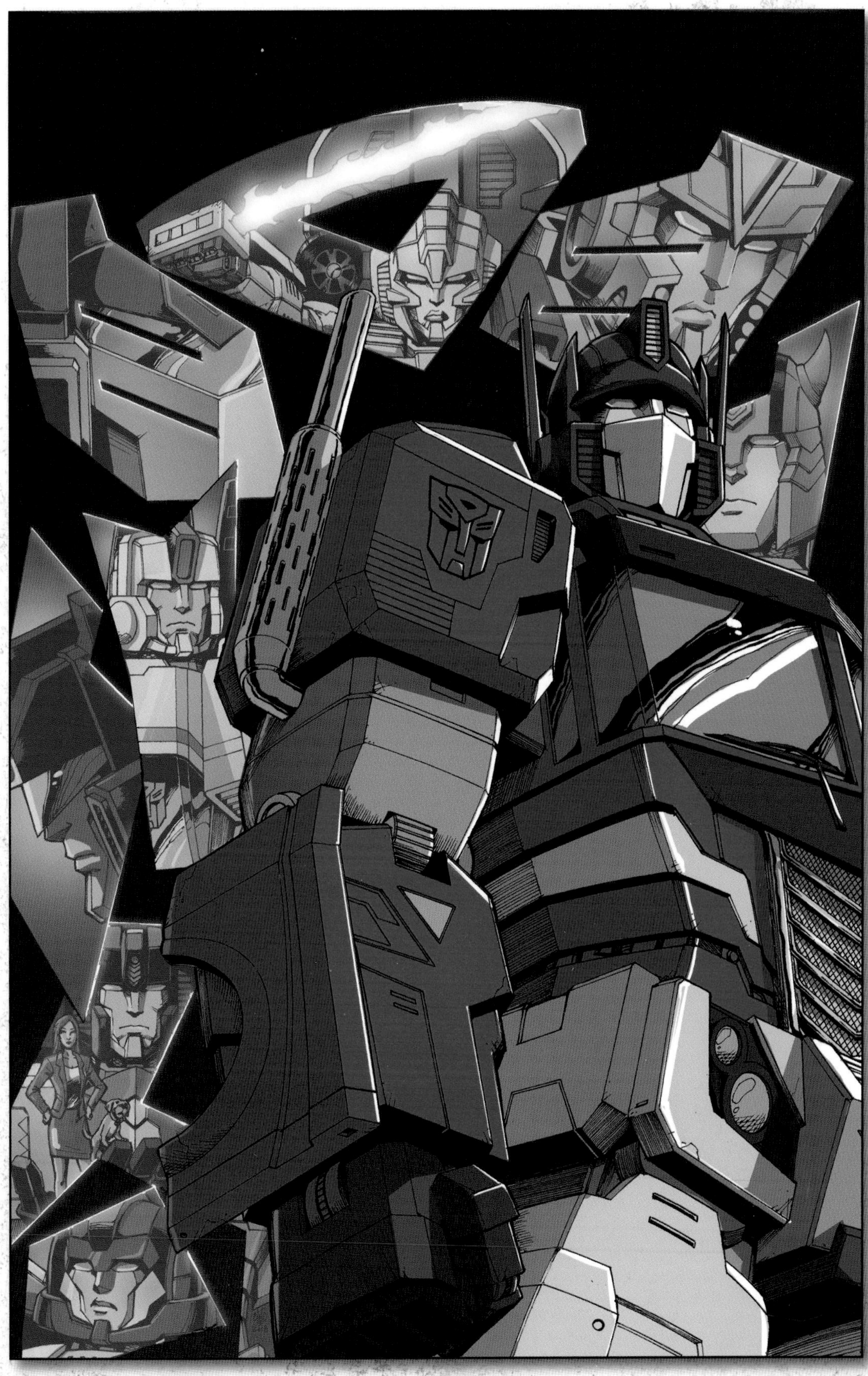

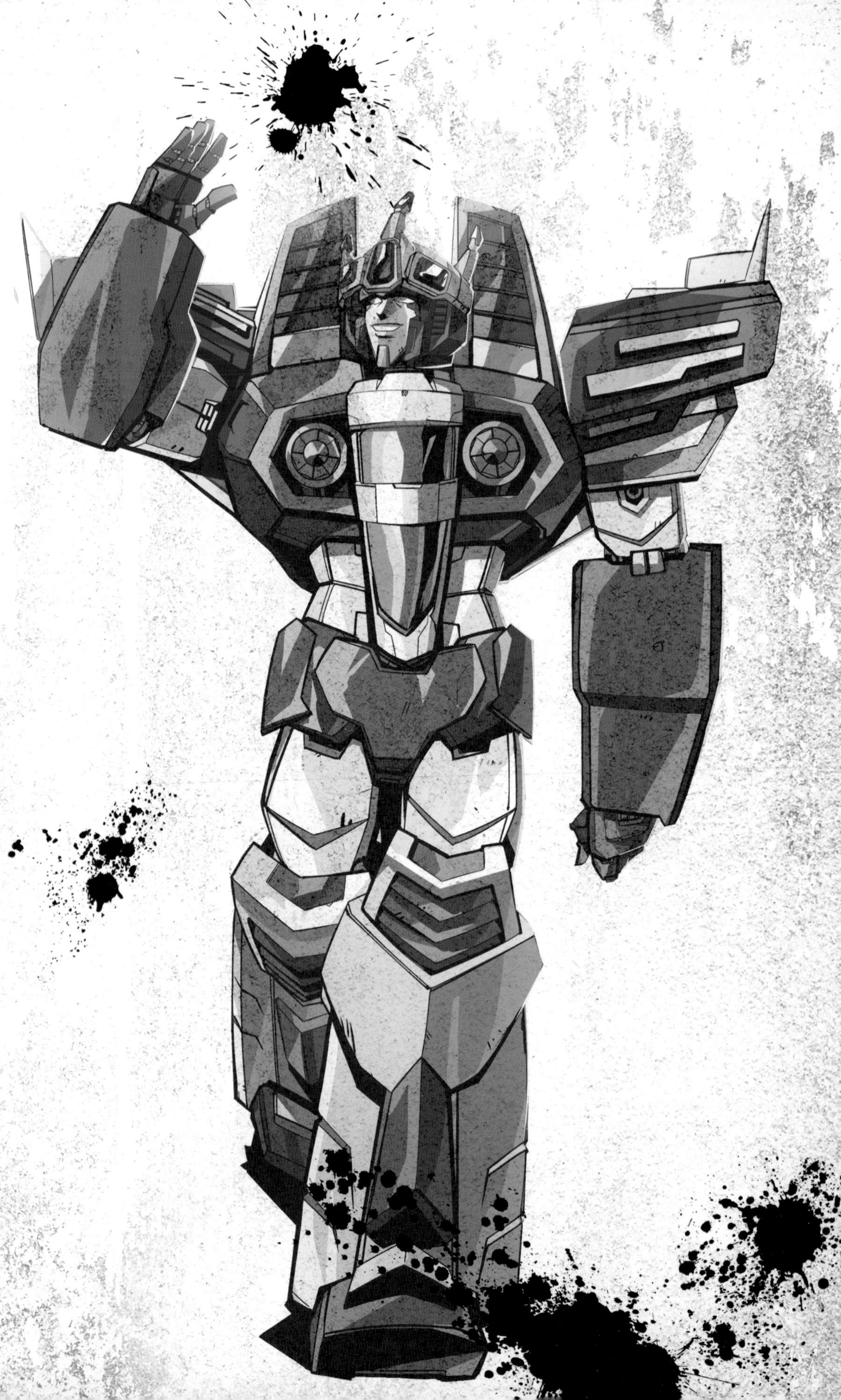